BEACHCOMBER

J. B. MORTON was born in 1893, and during the 1920s took over the Daily Express Beachcomber column from D. G. Wyndham-Lewis. Apart from his by now legendary Beachcomber material, he has written some twenty books, including novels, biographies, works of French history and an excellent children's book.
RICHARD INGRAMS is well-known as Editor of *Private Eye* and for his frequent radio and television appearances.

BEACHCOMBER

THE WORKS OF J·B MORTON

EDITED BY RICHARD INGRAMS

NICOLAS BENTLEY drew the pictures

Futura Publications Limited   A Futura Book

A Futura Book

First published in Great Britain by
Frederick Muller Limited in 1974

First Futura Publications edition 1977

Copyright © 1974 J. B. Morton

Introduction copyright © 1974 Richard Ingrams

Selection copyright © 1974 Richard Ingrams

Beachcomber extracts appear by kind permission
of Sir Max Aitken and the *Daily Express*

ISBN 0 8600 7237 1

Printed and bound in Great Britain by
REDWOOD BURN LIMITED
Trowbridge & Esher

I would like to thank
Miss Pamela Harvey
for all her help in preparing this book

Most of the illustrations in this book, chosen by its editor from earlier collections of Beachcomber, were drawn forty years ago or more. The rest are of more recent vintage. I hope that the observant reader will be able to distinguish between the earlier and the later work.

NB

INTRODUCTION

A new collection of Beachcomber needs no apology. It is more than ten years since Michael Frayn's excellent *The Best of Beachcomber* was published. (I cannot claim that this book is better than the Best but it is bigger, and it also contains Nicolas Bentley's illustrations.) I am sure there are many people, like me, who are sick of hunting in second-hand bookshops looking for Beachcomber's work. This book will, I hope, do something to ameliorate their sickness.

By chance—for the whole thing was planned long before anyone realised the fact—the book appears in the year in which J. B. Morton celebrates his 50th anniversary as Beachcomber. The writing of a newspaper column continuously for 50 years must be a unique achievement, and it is only proper that the event should be commemorated by the publication of a slim volume containing some of his best material.

John Cameron Audrieu Bingham Michael Morton (known to his friends as Johnny Morton) was born in 1893. "My excellent father and my very beautiful mother," he tells me, "were the happiest couple I ever saw." His father, Edward Morton, began his career as a journalist in Paris and later became the dramatic critic of the *Sunday Referee*. He wrote the "book" of the long-running musical *San Toy* and also adapted the libretto of *The Merry Widow* for the English stage.

At an early age Edward Morton introduced his son to what were to be two of his greatest loves. One was France, where Morton senior spent as much time as he could; and the other was wine. The young Morton began drinking this in a watered-down form before he went to school and slowly the proportion of wine in the glass was increased. His father told him that if he accustomed himself to the taste of wine early in life he would never like whisky. This prophecy proved to be correct.

Morton was an only child. His companions in boyhood were the sons of his father's best friend, Leslie Stuart, the songwriter, who wrote such famous songs as *Soldiers of the Queen* and *Lily of Laguna*. All his life Morton has been in the habit of singing—first with his father and Stuart; then at Harrow; as a soldier in the Trenches; and so on. In 1971 he wrote in answer to a query from his friend Hugh Mackintosh:

You ask me if I can still sing. Yes. But with exquisite courtesy for anyone who may be about, I sing to myself. I sing *You are my rosebud, Mrs Futtermere* and a song I heard at Worthing in my boyhood:

> *Bread and cheese and kisses*
> *Are all very well*
> *But it's everyone's opinion*
> *From the lady to the slavey*
> *That kisses are better*
> *With meat and potatoes*
> *And puddings and greens and gravy.*

and

> *Seaside Louise*
> *Oh, how she longs for a squeeze*
> *She's such a daisy*
> *She drives us all crazy*
> *By the briny breeze.*
> *Oh! poor Louise*
> *She's a little bit gone at the knees*
> *She's fair fat and forty*
> *And looks rather naughty*
> *My seaside Louise.*

In another letter to Mackintosh, he asks:
  Do you recall

> *Ladies, don't be frightened, I'm an Indian*
> *I come from Timbuctoo three four five six*
> *The night I ran away it was a windy'un*
> *Oh, girls, take care I'm full of Indian tricks?*

At the age of eight Morton went to Park House preparatory school, Southborough, where, it would appear, he spent five blissfully happy years. He went to Harrow in 1907 but made no particular mark there, distinguishing himself, in the view of one contemporary, only as a squash player. He failed to win a scholarship to Oxford but gained entrance to Worcester College. He changed "schools" three times while at Oxford and left after only a year because his father had lost all his money and was gravely ill.

Morton was a romantic young man and, according to friends, was engaged more than once before he finally married. His intention on leaving Oxford was to be a poet, "but I soon realised," he says, "that I would never be able to live on my poetry." An uncle got him a job writing revue material for a minor impresario in the Charing Cross Road. He was engaged in this activity when war broke out in 1914. Morton immediately enlisted as a private in the University and Public Schools Battalion of the Royal Fusiliers and was sent to the trenches in 1915.

Along with many others he quickly lost any romantic illusions he may have had about the nature of war. But he was never embittered: "We all grumbled incessantly, and often in song, but we did not expect that anything would ever be different. We were Fred Karno's army, and we announced it, not with bitterness or anger, nor with a whine, but with full-blooded irony."

In 1916, when the shortage of officers became acute, the batallion was broken up. Morton, who had served in the Artois trenches and fought at Cambrai and Vermelles, was commissioned in the Suffolk Regiment. "After a spell on the Somme," he says succinctly, "I was in hospital at Étaples and then in England with what was diagnosed as shell-shock." He was pronounced unfit for active service and spent

3

the rest of the war in a branch of the Intelligence service mysteriously titled M.I. (7B)—a fate, he said, "which might befall the best of us".

When the war ended Morton began work on *The Barber of Putney*, a novel based on his experiences in the trenches. Published in 1919, it was the first book of its kind to appear in England. But Morton was not destined to be a novelist. The same year, thanks to his uncle, he was taken onto the staff of the *Sunday Express*. He wrote essays about cross-country walks and a weekly column of jokes, poems and fairy tales. After three or four years, he switched to the *Daily Express* and became a reporter, but in this rôle he was, in his own words, a "howling failure". Then came a stroke of luck. D. B. Wyndham-Lewis, the founder of the Beachcomber column, was leaving to join the *Daily Mail*. He recommended Morton as his successor.

D. B. Wyndham-Lewis ("the wrong Wyndham-Lewis", as the Sitwells called him, to distinguish him from his namesake the American-born painter and writer) recalled his first meeting with the young reporter Morton: "The door was burst open and a thick-set, furious, bucolic figure all over straw and clay, strode in and banged passionately on the floor with a thick gnarled stick uttering a roar soon known and feared in every pub in Fleet Street:

'Flaming eggs! Will no one rid me of this stinking town!' "

The two became close friends. They were contemporaries who shared a love of France, Belloc and the Catholic faith (Wyndham-Lewis became a Catholic in 1921, Morton the year following). Both had served in the ranks during the war. Wyndham-Lewis was a connoisseur of bad poetry—he collaborated in the editorship of the famous anthology *The Stuffed Owl*—and he and his successor poked fun at many of the same targets: lady novelists, avant garde sculptors and other pseuds. "Mayors are born free," went a typical Wyndham-Lewis joke, "but everywhere they are in chains."

The *Daily Express* was rather different in those days from what it is now. There was more of a literary flavour to it. James Douglas, editor of the *Sunday Express* and Morton's first employer, was himself an essayist, while the editor of the *Daily Express*, R. D. Blumenfeld, once decreed that "the real journalist should firstly be equipped with at least two languages. He should be able to write English correctly.

He should know the history of his country as well as the history of the world"—qualifications which, if insisted on today, would leave the *Express* with, at best, a skeleton staff. In the early 'twenties, however, the awful influences of modern journalism had yet to make themselves fully felt. The atmosphere at the *Daily Express* was exhilerating. Morton shared with Wyndham-Lewis a tiny cubicle in a large upper room filled with chattering, shouting and singing journalists. There was the literary critic S. B. P. Mais, Strube the cartoonist, who used to bring in boxes of fruit to give his colleagues, and a man whose job it was to cut out stories from foreign papers which were then printed under the heading Moscow, Barcelona or Tahiti with the legend "From our Special Correspondent".

Morton became a familiar figure with his muddy boots, his stick and his loud booming voice. He and Wyndham-Lewis kept up a non-stop badinage. One day Morton came in, fresh from the country, and Wyndham-Lewis advised a wash and brush-up. When Morton re-appeared spruce and shining, Wyndham-Lewis, who suffered from a terrible stutter, upbraided him: "You f-f-op! You dandy!"

A supposedly fictional portrait of the Morton of these years appears in Henry Williamson's autobiographical novel *The Innocent Moon*. Morton is Rowley Meek, working for the *Daily Crusader*. He is a man of over-powering vitality dancing about his office, brandishing his stick, shouting and singing. When he, Wyndham-Lewis and Williamson go off in a taxi Morton (or Meek) accosts passing pedestrians, raising his hat and bowing. He does this down the length of Regent Street to the amusement of all except one man who runs after the cab, scowling. Meek leans out of the window and beckons him on, while Bevan (Wyndham-Lewis) frantically tells the taxi-driver to go faster: "When the fellow had turned back, Rowley stopped the taxi by a red pillar box on a street corner: and stooped beside it, ear pressed to the red cylinder as he pretended to be listening intently. Soon several people were standing and staring at the box. Rowley listened the more intently. Others listened too. A crowd collected. Rowley then moved away and got back into the taxi, which drove off as a policeman walked across the road to find the reason why various puzzled people were listening and peering at the letter-box."

In addition to making friends with Wyndham-Lewis, Morton was attracted to the group of poets and writers who had gathered round the person of J. C. Squire, Editor of the *London Mercury*. Squire, himself a gifted poet and critic, was an exceptionally generous man always ready to help young writers and give advice on their problems. There was usually a posse of poets to be found at lunch-time in the Red Lion, the pub adjoining the Mercury's offices; and later, when these were moved, at the Temple Bar in Fleet Street.

Morton shared a flat with the assistant editor of the *London Mercury*, the poet Edward Shanks. Every day their landlady prepared lunch for them but not once did they return to eat it.

Both were regular attenders at the annual dinners at the Cheshire Cheese given by Squire's cricket club, the Invalids, which always ended in a sing-song. Morton sang *En Passant par la Lorraine* and Belloc's *The Winged Horse*. Someone else sang the doleful ditty *I want to be buried in Rutland if there's room*. The company included, in addition to Squire's "set", G. K. Chesterton and Hilaire Belloc. Chesterton, not a musical man, was sufficiently impressed by Morton's performance to be able to reproduce in later years his rendition of the following song:

> *In my garden there are rowziz*
> *Rowziz red and violets blew:*
> *In my garden there is sunshine*
> *In my garden there is yew!* (top note)
> (Angry undertone) *Ya bloody worm*

Another man who came to these sing-songs was Chesterton's old friend E. C. Bentley, author of *Trent's Last Case* and father of the illustrator of this book. Bentley was responsible for reviving, when at Oxford, the old French verse form of the Ballade, which was taken up by Belloc and subsequently became a bit of a craze. The poem has a stringent rhyming scheme and demands a good deal of skill. In 1931 Squire edited a collection,* to which Belloc, Maurice Baring, he himself, Chesterton, Bentley and Morton all contributed. The

---

* *101 Ballades*, Cobden Sanderson, 1931

most prolific ballade-writer was Hugh Mackintosh, also a devoted admirer of Squire and Belloc, and a close friend of Morton's. One ballade by Mackintosh, redolent of the period, went as follows:

Ballade in Memory of "The Angel", Petworth

We have sung songs at many times and places—
The easeful songs of laughter and of war:
In lusty tenors, baritones and basses
We've chanted ditties from our boundless store:
And yet it's vain attempting to ignore
This hard and bitter fact—it's no use blinking,
The truth will out (it shakes us to the core)—
We sing a great deal better when we're drinking

By tavern fires, ringed round with friendly faces,
Have we not heard the cries: "Bravo! . . . Encore!"
And sung, so loudly that we've burst our braces,
Shanty and round—and still they've asked for more?
What verve, what golden notes, what vocal lore
Are ours, when seated in a tap room sinking
A pint or two!—yes (even from the floor)
We sing a great deal better when we're drinking.

But in the morning ('tis perhaps the traces,
The tuneful efforts, of the night before)
Our voices—say in church—might cause grimaces,
While at the Wigmore Hall we might not score
A quarter of our usual furore.
Come then at nightfall to "The Angel", linking
Arm in affectionate arm, a happy four:
We sing a great deal better when we're drinking.

Envoi

Prince, when you hear afar the ring and roar
Of voices singing and of tankards chinking,

Fear not, my friend, come in and shut the door!
We sing a great deal better when we're drinking.

This particular ballade was dedicated to Morton, Peter Belloc and Jim Allison, who, with Mackintosh, made up the "happy four" referred to. It was at the Angel, Petworth, that Morton offered a quart of beer to anyone who could hit him on the nose with a ball on a string, used for knocking down skittles.

Allison was a wealthy Australian, a backer of magazines and friend of Squire's, who kept open house in the village of Rodmell near Lewes in Sussex. In this village he collected a little community of writers— Edward Shanks, Clennell Wilkinson, Squire's brother-in-law, and Morton, who bought a cottage there in 1922. Sussex, celebrated by Belloc in prose and verse, had a particular appeal for Morton, and Rodmell, within a few minutes' walk of the Downs, was an ideal retreat from the world of journalism. The village's best known inhabitant was Virginia Woolf, who lived there with her husband Leonard. The sensitive novelist, however, did not mix with her fellow writers. Once Wilkinson, who had a loud booming voice, shouted a jovial "Good Morning!" to her across the village street, which so startled her that she fainted. Belloc's daughter, Eleanor Jebb, confesses that they used to leave beer bottles on her doorstep. Poor Virginia.

It was at Rodmell in 1920 that the second fixture of the Invalids Cricket Team was played. This team, founded by Sir Jack Squire, was later to be immortalised by one of its members, A. G. Macdonell, in his largely autobiographical novel *England, Their England*. "Rodmell," Squire wrote, "is a secluded village off the western road, if road it can be called, between Lewes and Newhaven: the downs on the West and the valley of the Sussex Ouse, Firle Beacon and Glynde, on the east: a landscape as admirable as the host."

The host was Murray Allison who entertained both teams to lunch in the barn of his farm. Squire blamed the subsequent defeat of The Invalids on the lunch: "his team can always stand his lunches better than we can: mounds of beef with piles of beer barrels in the background." The Invalids included a number of poets, Edmund Blunden, Siegfried Sassoon and Edward Shanks, in addition to Squire himself. They were beaten by 104 runs—"the bowling of Greenwood and Hubbard being too much for us". In 1921 they were beaten again by an innings and 11 runs (Invalids 41 and 14, Greenwood 6 for 17, Hubbard 3 for 6; Rodmell 66). On becoming a Rodmell resident Morton played for the village. He took no guard and would appear to have been a typically exuberant batsman—in one game hitting his first ball for six and getting caught on the boundary with the next. The match inspired him to write a ballade:

Ballade of the Rodmell Cricket Match

Our new rolled pitch is gleaming in the sun
Without those blemishes that caused dismay;
Save where the boys have hacked it up for fun
Or where the moles have gambolled at their play.
On with the game; what though in disarray
We stagger back—four wickets down for three?
Last year's tail lives to wag another day—
Bring me the village bat and you shall see.

Swift as a bullet from a sporting gun
Lithe as a panther leaping on its prey,
Cecil has grabbed another stolen run,
And Jack is bowling at both ends, they say.
No ball! Ten up! Six wickets down. O.K.
Once more it looks as if it's up to me
Sardonic Percy says I look distrait—
Give me the village bat and you shall see

The score piles up—somebody's slammed a one
And run it out: Rodmell is going gay.
Hugh with a zest that's rather overdone
Has stumped the umpire, and his loud hooray
Recalls the slumbering Major to the fray.
And now begins a kind of jamboree
Of overthrows. You think we're still at bay
Give me the village bat and you shall see.

Prince, their best long stop's dozing in the hay,
And Colin's not so deadly after tea:
Draw stumps or else there'll be the deuce to pay
Give me the village bat and you shall see.

These fixtures were very popular occasions and, as usual, a good deal of drinking and singing went on. The village pub did a roaring trade. An occasional visitor was Hilaire Belloc, as recalled by Hesketh Pearson in *This Blessed Plot*.* "Belloc had come over to watch the match, and afterwards we forgathered at Murray Allison's house nearby. While we were all enjoying Belloc's wit and unpublished verse, the Liberal candidate for a neighbouring constituency walked in and began to drivel about politics. He talked and talked, and nothing could stop him. He told us of his life's struggles, of his attempts to liberalise the community, of his friendships with the eminent. Belloc sat motionless and silent throughout. As an ex-MP he had received a good training, for the man who has survived a year of the House of Commons is beyond boredom. The rest of us coughed, lit matches noisily, tried weakly to interrupt, but were easily talked down. The Liberal candidate would probably have come to a sticky end if Belloc had not saved him. At a moment when he had to draw breath or burst, Belloc looking innocently at the ceiling, suddenly asked in that high quick voice of his, 'Have you heard the story of the male and female contortionists on their honeymoon?'

"There was a pause, during which the politician, his mouth open, stared at Belloc. 'I—I beg your pardon?' he spluttered.

" 'Have you heard the story of the male and female contortionists on their honeymoon?'

" 'N—no.'

" 'They broke it off!' "

It was at Rodmell in October 1922 that Morton first met Peter, the second son of Hilaire Belloc. Morton was at Murray Allison's house one morning when Peter Belloc rode up on a motor-cycle wearing riding breeches and a false moustache. Ripping off the moustache and

* *This Blessed Plot* by Hesketh Pearson and Hugh Kingsmill (Methuen 1942)

stuffing it into his pocket, he introduced himself as Sir Almeric Fitzroy, recited some lines of a sonnet and sang a verse of a song. The two men immediately struck up a friendship that was to last until Peter Belloc's death while on active service in 1941.

Morton was already a firm admirer of Hilaire Belloc's writings and he was delighted when at Christmas time Peter Belloc invited him to the family home at King's Land, an old farm house in the Sussex village of Shipley. Belloc was formal and a little distant when they met. Shaking hands with a bow he said, "What will you drink, Mr Martin?" and later, in a phrase familiar to all his circle, "Mr Martin, I must know your plans. You can stay as long as you like, or go as soon as you like, but I must know your plans."

Morton recalled later: "This military precision was so foreign to my own nature that with anyone less formidable I should have laughed and made a jest of it. But he produced a timetable, and I chose a day at random. He was satisfied."

That evening they all drove to Mass, singing carols, with Belloc at the wheel of his Ford, wearing a bowler hat. Christmas Day was spent in eating, drinking and singing, and at midnight Peter Belloc and Morton decided to walk back to Rodmell across country through the dark, a journey of several miles. They arrived in the village in the early hours, much to everyone's annoyance, and later Belloc drove over and there was yet more drinking and singing. Belloc sang:

> *Am I a man or am I a mouse*
> *Am I a hedger or a dodger*
> *I should bloody well like to know*
> *Who's running this damned show*
> *Is it me or the top floor lodger?*

To Morton and to many of his contemporaries, Hilaire Belloc was an immensely impressive man. He was born in 1870 at La Celle St Cloud, a village near Paris. His mother was English; his father French. Belloc was educated in England and served as a gunner in the French army before going to Oxford in 1893. He studied history and became President of the Union. He published his first book *Verses and Sonnets* in 1895. He was an extraordinarily versatile and prolific writer, a belligerent Catholic, historian, singer, speaker, poet, sailor and compulsive walker. He married in 1896 an American, Elodie Hogan, who bore him five children. He sat as Liberal MP for South Salford from 1911 to 1913.

When Morton met him he was 52 and had already written about seventy books. "He looked considerably older than his fifty two years," Morton wrote. "Had I known nothing about him, it would have been impossible to 'place' him. The black clothes, black tie and old-fashioned stiff stick-up collar made him look like a Frenchman of my boyhood. But the ruddy complexion and the broad, square shoulders and massive body gave him the air of an English farmer. His eyes were blue, and when spoken to or speaking, he would move his head sharply, and look straight at you, as though he were not only carrying on a conversation but reading a character." Belloc was a talker and he talked much as he wrote in his essays, discursively, alternating between poetry and prose, history and satire, and peppering his conversation with jokes, humorous asides and snatches of songs. For Morton the most memorable occasions were when, at King's Land after dinner, Belloc would sit at his long refectory table by candlelight playing patience, drinking port and talking for hour after hour.

But, despite his extraordinary energy, Belloc was an unhappy and dissatisfied man. His wife had died in 1914; his eldest son Louis was killed in action in 1918. He fought against misfortune and his own natural melancholy by engaging in constant activity. He never remained long in the same place, preferring to be on the move. Morton, who shared so many of his tastes, and whose job did not tie him down, was an ideal companion—almost an adopted son—for Belloc. Belloc loved to plan elaborate itineraries with the help of numerous maps, guides and timetables. "He would say, 'Now when we get to A, we shall have time for a drink. Then we go to the Square and get the bus which will probably miss the train at B. We then walk to C, and get there just in time for the little tram-train that goes to D.'" His attitude to the French scene was not aesthetic, but historical and strategic. He wanted to know how and why towns came to be where they were, and liked to reconstruct the great events of history on the spot. He took Morton to the Marne and, with the help of a sketch that Foch had made for him, described the great battle of 1914. Then they drove on down a by-road, got out of the car and walked across a stream and came to a huge fortification of grass mounds. This was the Camp d'Attila where the Huns had made their last stand before retreating Eastwards.

Belloc was a walking Michelin guide and knew all the best hotels and restaurants. But you could never be sure whether he would be content to linger in them. When Murray Allison and Morton arranged to meet him in Brussels, Allison said eagerly: "I look forward to this. We'll have a long evening in Brussels, and a great meal at our ease." "Expect no such thing," said Morton. "He will be on the platform to meet us, portmanteau in hand, and he will say, 'My children, we have very little time.' " Sure enough, when they got to Brussels, there was Belloc at the platform, bag in hand saying, "My children, we have very little time." It was often like this, the stout, thick-set Belloc with his black cloak and battered old bag racing to fulfill the demands of his own taxing timetable. "I have a memory," says Morton, "of running to the station in the dark at Chinon, and of hearing his voice behind me: 'You carry my bag. You're younger than I am.' "

Belloc and Morton loved walking, and they made up songs as they walked. Although neither man was a musician in the strict sense both had the knack of extemporising songs—words and music—on the spot. Another habit was the composing of mottoes for sundials. Belloc subsequently published some of his—alternatively grave:

> *Here in a lonely glade forgotten, I*
> *Mark the tremendous process of the sky*
> *So does your inmost soul, forgotten, mark*
> *The Dawn, the Noon, the coming of the Dark.*

or gay:

> *I am a sundial, and I make a botch*
> *Of what is done far better by a watch.*

Morton saw Belloc, too, in London. They would go for lunch at a sausage shop in Fleet Street or sit drinking in the Red Lion in Poppin's Court. Belloc's behaviour was unpredictable. He would turn suddenly to a stranger standing next to him at the bar and say, "What do you think will happen to this country? Will there be a sudden collapse or a slow decay?" Over lunch Belloc corrected proofs, muttering from time to time, "What a life I lead!" and constantly getting up, as he always did wherever he was, to make telephone calls. Sometimes in the evening he and Morton and Peter Belloc went to the theatre or the Music Hall. Morton wrote:

> "I remember one turn which we always wanted to see again, and I wish I could recall the names of the two men in order to praise them. There came out onto the stage two small, dreamy looking shabbily dressed men. They shuffled along, whispering to each other, and then took their stand, and began to perform the most outstanding feats of strength with the utmost melancholy, and with an air of being bored to death with the whole business. Finally one stretched out his hand and lifted the other off the ground and high into the air and held him upside down above his head without any effort, using only one hand. Then the man in the air suddenly removed his hand from the grasp of his partner, and scratched his head, and you realised that wires were being used. They never spoke, but conversed in inaudible whispers, and appeared to be troubled and anxious all the time."

But Belloc was as jumpy at the theatre as he was anywhere else: "Peter and I and our wives took him to see *The Immortal Hour* and he was restless. On the entry of an old bearded Druid, he said with considerable vigour and in his normal tone of voice, 'Here comes old mossy-face again!'" If he got bored he would leave the theatre, dragging his companions with him.

Morton also accompanied Belloc on his sea voyages in his nine-ton cutter the *Nona*. Morton was never a good sailor, being "clumsy to a degree and slow to understand technical matters". But he was, as always, good company for Belloc and his son, both of whom were competent seamen. Together they sailed round the coast of South

14

England and across the channel to Boulogne, singing a variety of songs. One went: "In the days of Queen Victoria they never did the things they do today", and another contained the lines:

> *What did Eve say to Adam*
> *The saucy little madam?*
> *"Oh, Adam, you should eat more fruit"*

On one occasion Morton sailed the *Nona* with Belloc up the river Arun to Arundel. Belloc steered the boat, having told Morton that all he had to do when they reached their destination was to go forward and catch hold of one of the posts with a boathook. The more Belloc insisted on the simplicity of this task, the more flustered Morton became, so that when eventually he threw the hook, it slipped and he fell into the Arun. "Are you drowning, my boy?" Belloc shouted at him nonchalantly.

Despite his many nautical misfortunes Morton developed a great attachment to the *Nona* and its little cabin, recalling in later life with nostalgia the song they used to sing "to an exceedingly dreary tune":

> *Coom an' 'aave a tiddly at the FOU—OUNtain*
> *Coom an' 'aave a tiddly at the FOU—OUNtain*
> *Coom an' 'aave a tiddly at the FOU—OUNtain*
> *Old Man Tom stands treat.*

But Morton was happier on dry land and he was happiest when walking. He walked across the Sussex Downs and the Pyrenees, he walked in Italy, Poland, Ireland and Norway where he saw the reindeer at their summer pasture "apparently eating snow and grunting like pigs". Sometimes he was on his own but more often he had companions. In 1924 Morton and his cousin Guy, D. B. Wyndham-Lewis and Henry Williamson walked from Bayonne to Pamplona, back over Roncevaux by moonlight "with the waters brawling below the great beech-woods" and into St Jean Pied de Port in the morning. Morton's idea of the expedition was rather different from that of his companions. He liked travelling rough, walking through the night and living off crusts of bread and the odd swig from a bottle of wine. He made a scene when the others insisted on going to a restaurant in Pamplona. "With enormous reluctance," says Williamson's Meek (Morton), "I find myself in the disgusting company of utterly beastly British fops." He could bear it no longer when they staggered into St Jean after walking all night and demanded breakfast at a café. " 'Bah! I've come here to walk, not to loll about' . . . and giving them a 'So long, cretins!' over his shoulder Rowley Meek strode away up the road which now lay mist white in the risen sun."

Henry Williamson observed it all with a certain amount of satire. He could not share the enthusiasm which his Catholic companions felt for backward Spain and the Valley of Roncesvalles. There was particular amusement when, following Morton's departure, they saw the Pyrenean foothills covered with large hoardings advertising a liqueur called Igharra, a drink which Morton, following Bellocian tradition, claimed was only to be found in one small secret mountain inn.

Another supposedly fictional portrait of the Morton of this period is found in a better known novel, A. G. Macdonell's *England, Their England*. This book was based on the author's own experience as a young innocent Aberdonian in the England of the 'twenties. Macdonell played regularly for Squire's cricket team and he portrayed Squire in his book as Mr Hodge. (Other real characters in the cricket team include the publisher Cecil Harmer as the wicket keeper who is so fat he can't touch his toes; Hugh Mackintosh as the poet Rupert Harcourt who in a moment of beer-induced euphoria no-balls the village's fast bowler thereby causing a major crisis; and Alec Waugh and William Gerhardie who combine in the character of Bobby Southcote, the dapper novelist who, when ordered to play carefully by his captain, hits every ball on the ground, and when told to "play his own game" stonewalls doggedly and is soon out.

"The account of the match," says Alec Waugh, "has been described as a caricature but it really was like that quite often." Macdonell himself appears in the book as Donald Cameron, and Morton as Mr Huggins, "a man of about thirty-five, a thick-set man of medium height, with a red face and red hands and an irresistible combination of vitality and impertinence". Donald comes across him in a pub off the King's Road. "The man recognised him . . . and said 'have a drink. Flaming fish! but this is a stinking country!' . . . 'A half pint of bitter,' said the man across the counter to no one in particular. 'A half pint of bitter,' he repeated in a louder voice, and then in a sudden whirl of rage, he seized an enormously thick walking stick, or rather cudgel, which leant against the counter beside him, and struck the counter a terrific blow which set the glasses jumping and rattling and shouted, 'Stinking fish! Is there no one here to serve a gentleman?' A man in a black coat and striped trousers came up and said severely: 'You can't do that here, sir.' 'Can't I, by God!' was the spirited reply of the red faced man, and he struck the counter another resounding blow. The managerial-looking person smiled a forced and sickly smile, and faded away. 'Scum,' said the red-faced man; 'Filthy, lousy, herring-gutted, spavin-bellied scum!' "

More drinks are ordered on the grounds that it is the anniversary of Roland's death in the battle of Roncesvalles. Huggins explains:

"We must drink to my fellow-countrymen who saved Europe in the Pyrenees a thousand years ago, just as that other fellow-countryman of mine saved Europe on the marshes of St Goud on the river Marne in 1914."

"Do you mean Sir John French?" asked Donald.

The red-faced man became apoplectic. He swelled like a frog and his eyes appeared to become bloodshot. A queer, hoarse croaking issued from his lips. At last he managed to say, "I mean Ferdinand Foch, Marshal of France," and he stood to attention.

Donald expresses surprise at Huggins being a Frenchman and the latter explains that his name is in fact Hougins and that he comes from an ancient Channel Isles family.

Later Huggins visits Cameron in his room in a Chelsea flat where he is preparing to go and spend the weekend at a large country house. Huggins advises him to take the maximum amount of luggage—"Take one suitcase: the butler sneers, the footman giggles, the under house-parlourmaids have hysterics. Take fifty and they'll treat you like the Duke of Westminster!"

He then rushes out and buys a number of second hand suitcases, fills them with rubbish and labels them "Beagling kit", "Amateur Theatricals" and "Despatches: Secret". He insists on coming to the station, where he engages two porters to carry the despatches, and addresses Donald all the time as "Excellency!" As the train steams out he whispers "I'll fix that bloody butler. Trust me."

The fixing of the bloody butler takes the form of a barrage of telephone calls. When Donald arrives, the butler sidles up to him and murmurs, "The Secretary of the French Foreign Ministry rang up, sir, and Budapest has also been on the line. Budapest is to telephone again, sir." When he meets his hostess her first words are "The Duke of Devonshire has been on the telephone. . . . You are on no account to telephone him, but you are to go to Chatsworth in time for luncheon on Monday, and to say nothing to anyone!"

It is unlikely that the historical Morton differed much from Macdonell's Huggins or Williamson's Rowley Meek. According to Hugh Mackintosh the country house weekend took place as described, at the house of Lady Houston, the eccentric millionairess who once tried to help the suffragette movement by training 615 parrots to screech "Votes for Women" all at once. Again, Williamson's adventure with the letter box is almost identical to an incident which took place when Morton was walking through Guildford with Gerald Barry. Morton stopped at a pillar box and began to talk into its mouth, pretending that a small boy was trapped inside: "Are you all right, my little man? Don't worry, we'll soon get you out." A crowd collected. The fire brigade was sent for. Morton and Barry slipped away.

Morton's behaviour on trains was especially unpredictable. He would stare at an individual for some time and then say angrily: "Are you looking at *me*, sir?" Once Hugh Mackintosh was with him in a train that drew into Harrow station. Morton leant out of the window, and seeing a group of schoolboys, cried, "Boys! I am Dr Smellcroft your new headmaster!" Then, turning back into the compartment he shouted (in a high falsetto): "Put the horses in the other end of the train!", replying in his normal voice, "No, my dear, they'll be perfectly all right here."

On another occasion he was travelling with Reginald Pound, then the *Express*'s literary editor, on a train to Eastbourne. There was only one other person in the carriage, an old spinsterish lady who registered strong displeasure as Morton ranted away in his loud voice about the iniquities of working for a paper which paid him to write humorous material and then cut out all the humour. Sensing the woman's disapproval, Morton started to make animal noises and finally climbed up into the luggage rack where he lay scratching himself and chattering like a monkey. When the train stopped at Three Bridges the woman fled.

In the days before his marriage Morton's domestic life was fairly hectic. In 1926, when Peter Belloc came back from Spain, the two shared a room in Ebury Street. But they made so much noise that the landlady chucked them out. They then moved, with two other journalists, to a house in Elizabeth Street where they were catered for by an engine-driver's wife. None of them had much money and there was always a row when the time came to pay the rent. Morton slept on the floor and Peter Belloc had a broken truckle bed in the same room. Amazing things happened in this house. One night after dinner an ex-boxer called Sam broke the flat up and then sat down and without a word wrote out a cheque for the damage. Another time at breakfast Morton, for no good reason, threw a kipper out of the window. The fish landed in a passing car and the owner solemnly rang the bell and handed it back.

"I still bear an honourable scar on my lower lip," says Morton, "to remind me of a brawl in that house of chaos."

Such a life could not go on for ever. In 1927 Peter Belloc was married and a few months later Morton himself married Mary O'Leary, an Irish doctor, whose sister Elizabeth had for a short time worked as secretary to Belloc. Within a year or two the Rodmell circle split up. The Allisons moved to Hampshire and the others to London. In 1929 Murray Allison died. Since then Morton's existence has been more tranquil. He has lived mostly in the country and never far from Hilaire Belloc, whom he continued to see regularly until his death in 1953. Morton hates London and motor cars. He has never even learned to ride a bicycle. He is a man of fixed routine who has written, in addition to his Beachcomber work, a score or so of books—

novels, biographies, works of French history and an excellent children's book, *The Death Of The Dragon*. Recently he started to write his memoirs but tore them up on the grounds that they bored him to death.

The *Daily Express* has proved an obliging employer. Provided he gets his copy to them his editors do not mind what he does. When he and his wife decided to go and live in Ireland after the Second World War—they stayed two years—the then editor Arthur Christiansen told Morton: "You can live in China for all I care, as long as your stuff arrives punctually."

There were occasional differences of opinion. Reginald Pound, literary editor in the 'thirties, objected to Morton's frequent use of the expression "as the Bishop said to the chorus girl" suggesting he should alternate it with "as the Cardinal said to the chorus girl". Morton was temporarily furious. He was once stopped from urging his readers to eat raw steak for breakfast because the advertising department complained that it would offend the cereal manufacturers; and then there was Beaverbrook's famous "black list" which prevented any mention of his hero Hilaire Belloc. Morton got round this, according to Tom Driberg, by referring to him simply as "the greatest living poet". His main frustration, however, has been that of any humourist; that nothing he makes up can rival the reality. A long time ago he invented the electric toothbrush, as a joke, only to see it become a fact of life.

The writing of Beachcomber material has always come easily to him. Until recently, before the column was confined to one weekly appearance, he used to write it in the morning, leaving the afternoon free for other writing. He writes in long hand, scorning the typewriter. He never counts words and judges the required amount by eye. "I'm not a journalist," he told an interviewer in 1945: "I know nothing about type sizes or anything of that sort. If it's too long they cut out a chunk or stick another one in from the next lot if it's too short."

Not surprisingly, the column has had its critics. The much-teased Edith Sitwell referred once scornfully to "Beachcomber, who is funny on purpose about once a year". Another detractor was George Orwell, who for all his great virtues never had much of a sense of humour. In a savage attack on Morton and D. B. Wyndham-Lewis, who contributed a column to the *News Chronicle* under the pseudonym of Timothy Shy, Orwell wrote in 1944: "Looking back over the twenty years or so these two have been on the job it would be difficult to find a reactionary cause that they have not championed . . . They have conducted endless propaganda against Socialism, the League of Nations and scientific research. They have kept up a campaign of abuse against every writer worth reading, from Joyce onwards." Morton and his friend, Orwell continued, were mere Catholic propagandists whose aim was "the Denigration of England and the Protestant countries generally . . . Hence the endless jibing of Beachcomber . . . at every English institution—tea, cricket, Wordsworth, Charlie Chaplin, kindness to animals, Nelson, Cromwell and what not." Beachcomber was also a coward, daring only to aim for safe targets: "Thus, if you want to attack the principle of freedom of speech do it by sneering at the Brains Trust, as if it were a typical example. Dr Joad won't retaliate!" Orwell concluded: "I shall be interested to see whether either 'Beachcomber', or 'Timothy Shy' reacts to these remarks of mine. If so, it will be the first recorded instance of either of them attacking men likely to hit back."*

This diatribe is interesting as an example of how wrong Orwell could occasionally be, and how his habit of looking at everything from a political point of view could let him down. It is true that on political matters Morton tended to follow the Belloc line and the Belloc line was often gloriously wrong. But Morton was never a political animal. He tended to agree with the landlord of the Rodmell pub, the aptly named Mr Malthouse, who once said to him, "Politics, politicians. You know how it is, you see a slimy pond, with a lot of insects swimming round in it, and you go off to bed and next morning there they all are, still mucking round in the dirty water. That's politics. That's politicians for you."

Morton's humour has never been political, nor, except on occasions, topical. He cannot be categorised as either right- or left-wing. The influence of Belloc is strong in his non-humorous works, but the pure nonsense of Beachcomber is entirely original, owing nothing to

*Neither did, perhaps because they never read *Tribune*, in which the article was printed.

any other writer. His output, only a small fraction of which is contained in this book, has been phenomenal. "I think," said Evelyn Waugh, "he shows the greatest comic fertility of any Englishman."

Two or three generations of critics have accorded him their praise. G. K. Chesterton described Beachcomber as "a huge thunderous wind of elemental and essential laughter". Arnold Bennett said: "I am a convinced admirer of Beachcomber's humour." "I have long been an enthusiastic admirer of his Beachcomber column," says J. B. Priestley. "One of the greatest living humorists," Michael Frayn called him in his introduction to *The Best of Beachcomber* (1963).

But the acid test of humour is whether the writer himself finds it funny. Morton makes no bones about it. "I bellow with laughter when I get a good joke," he once said. "Why shouldn't I? A man who doesn't laugh at his own jokes is timid, self-conscious and altogether half-strangled with beastliness. It is argued that this is a sign of conceit. Bosh. It is a sign of being able to enjoy oneself without consulting the conventions of the half-men. So laugh and be damned to the world."

"The greatest comic fertility of any Englishman." Evelyn Waugh's judgement cannot be improved upon. Quite how it happens, or what the precise relationship between Morton and Beachcomber is, remain matters of mystery. Like his great contemporary P. G. Wodehouse, whose books he so much admires, Morton is a quiet, very modest man, referring to his comic work as "my stuff". The quality has never varied throughout the fifty years. Characters have come and gone, but very little of the material has dated. His influence on other lesser humourists has been profound and his column has inspired a host of followers. This book makes available again what I think is the best of his "stuff". It is a singular honour for me to have been given the opportunity to present it and to write this short and inadequate introduction.

Now, let the fun begin.

FOREWORD

by J. Van Strabismus

In the pages that follow, and upon which I have the honour of opening the door, the reader will find discussed, with a thoroughness that rivals even Schottenfels, the wave theory of matter, upon which so much depends; and other kindred problems.

For some time physicists have tended to explain diffraction by appealing to Trumperley's law of radial energy, and by presupposing that any multiple of fourteen, contained in a nucleus of corpuscular particles, will, of its own spontaneity, produce a given beam, unexplainable by the mere laws of velocity. Balmeyer accepted this view, until his assistant, Codwell, by reducing momentum to a minimum, demonstrated that Energy Levels are accidental, spectral, external, internal, molecular, available, grey, irreconcilable, continuous, curved, striated, etiolated, reciprocal, neutral, mutual, abnormal, fundamental, diluted, extra-mural, perpendicular, spiral, isotopic, mezzoic, hyperdraulic, alpha-charged, repulsive, forked, oxygenated, integral, broken, cosmogenic, elemental, infinitesimal, increasingly hot, involute, half-ionised and universal. None of which was allowed for in the explanation of the Botras school.[1]

Now it must be clear that if we take a region inhabited by a single centripetal force, and subject that region to minute examination, and that centripetal force to scientific exploration, we shall discover one of two things. Either matter is, in itself, indivisible, or, theoretically, divisible. *Quod suo non executus, hoc in modo venturum*, as Asmodeus of Tarentum put it. Our next step must be to determine whether a thing which is, *suo generis* and *quoadlibet*, divisible, can, at the same time, be also indivisible. This experiment is a development of what is known as Pliny's[2] Law of Probabilities, and the formula is S to the power of forty. Pliny took a region and divided it into sections, thus proving that whatever was in that region prior to the division, was, perforce, divided by the act of division.

But Huxtable pointed out that as centripetal forces are not bounded by the regions of their own activity, such forces might fly off at a tangent. *Desiccatio non investitur silices tum quisque*, says Putridius Quacksilva in his *De Ridiculis*.

As to the fundamental constant of a quantum, that will be found to vary according to the affinities involved. Spenser of Yale[3] found that vinegar and metal will only make salt in special conditions, and in the same way the constant of a quantum will depend on the homopolar or heteropolar organisms at work. In this context, the diagrams of Professor Hergesheimer's *Kriegswissenschaft und Kriegswesens*, which were carefully prepared by Linklater, will be found more than useful.

Followers of Rutherford and Soddy, who first advanced the hypothesis that radio-activity is merely a change from one kind of atom to another, will be interested in the discussion, in Chapter XXIV of this book, on Dalton's gamma-rays, and the difference between thorium and uranium, as agents of transformation. The author of this book appears to favour the view of Evesclin, and bases his conclusions on gun-rust. If, says he, the gun is destroyed, where does the rust go to? If, replies Grafton,[4] the rust is destroyed, where does the gun go to?

The fallacy can be detected instantaneously, and Purpelbotham pounced on it in his famous

Denunciation of Kraft's Law of Components. Bischweil followed, and the whole elaborate structure, begun by Sudori of Bologna, crumbled to the ground. That marked the first step towards the theory of group-velocity, so essential to all the earlier experiments of Nuss, Clarkson, Palgrave, and even Gutz.

This is no place to discuss Palmerston's Variable Limits or Planck's Value of H. Let it suffice to say, that a mass travelling at a given velocity can never exceed that velocity until a greater velocity has been attained. Similarly, a body at rest, the moment it is subjected to any force sufficient to propel it however short a distance through the ether, can no longer be said to be at rest. Thus speed, as a factor of motion, and motion, as a factor of speed, are complementary. A moving object must have speed, and an object moving at a certain speed must have motion. Between complete immobility and maximum velocity there are innumerable degrees of speed, each either greater or less than the other. For one body cannot move at more than one speed at the same moment. Nor can many bodies, even though they may all move at an identical speed, move at only one speed. For even the same speed may be applied to many bodies, as may be made obvious by kicking a dozen footballs at the same moment, and with the same force. Each ball will have its own speed, yet all the speeds may be identical. This is called Niebuhr's Law of Identical Mobility.[5] Bishop, working on it for twenty years, went even further, and showed that every division of a divided body, propelled through space by an external force, will have an individual speed of its own. This can be demonstrated by throwing an egg against a wall. The radiating fragments and particles will observe no unity of control. Each will have its own speed. In other words, velocity is a primary function of speed, and speed a secondary function of matter. All of which Calmash[6] suspected long ago.

On inert gas, our author is more conventional, and is content to follow Titchener, who maintained that it was a saturated compound, and without any movement of its own. Titchener succeeded in isolating an electro-static unit, by submerging it in carbon monoxide. When, however, he tried the same experiment with phosgene, he found that the organic value of the isolated unit was considerably diminished by the proximity of a quantity of alpha-rays given off by the phosgene. Hence the valency theory of inert gases, or what is sometimes called Titchener's Experiment.

It remains only to congratulate the author upon the way in which he has dealt with such contested subjects as Heitler's Theory of Repulsion, Water Molecules, Negative Ionisation, Disintegration, Mme. Curie's theory of the Atomic Qualities of Radio-Active Effects, Becquerel's Metallic Films, Sodial Crystals, Single and Double Refraction, the Periodic Table of Mendelejeff, Cosmic Spectra, and the famous books of Democritus of Lycia on the Cosmogeny of Thales.

JAN VAN STRABISMUS.

---

[1] Eugene Botras was a native of Ragusa. His mother was a Dalmatian, and his father a Kurd, from Kurdistan. The boy was brought up in Trieste, and was later a student at the École Unique in Montauban. To him we owe the theory that Energy Levels are non-existent.

[2] Not the other Pliny of course.

[3] Spenser began life as a drummer in a jazz-band at Memphis. One day his mother's canary escaped, and as there was no salt in the house, the boy cut some metal penholders to pieces and poured vinegar on them. Salt was formed rapidly, and when the bird's tail was sprinkled with it, it returned to its cage. Later in life, Spenser tried to repeat this experiment, but found that the salt only forms during the autumnal equinox.

[4] See the *Gun-Rust Quarterly* for March 1897, in which Puffendorf's assistant Gatling writes an article on Embionism.

[5] For a further discussion of all this, see Niebuhr's "Experiments in Mobility, Extra-Mobility, Identical Mobility and Departmental Mobility, with an appendix in which is discussed the Variation of Variants, with special reference to Cumberland's String-Theory of Spaces."

[6] No wonder.

Mr. Thake: his life and letters

Mrs Barlow

380a JERMYN STREET,
LONDON, W.

MY DEAR BEACHCOMBER,

As you will see from the above address, I am back in Jermyn Street once more. My return was rather rapid. The oil business turned out badly, and also I wanted to be back for the Season in London. It seems as though I had been away a long time, and yet it doesn't, if you know what I mean. I found an enormous mass of correspondence awaiting me, including a letter from Mrs. Hawkley telling me that the Colonel is in Scotland—no, it was Ireland. I think you met their boys once—darkish hair, and rather tall for twins. One of them, I forget which, either the younger or the elder, is going up to Woolwich (or Sandhurst) and then into the Army. It will be rather nice for him, won't it?

It is good to be home, in a way. It is like coming back to everything. It's hard to express. What I mean is, it's a sort of return to things, don't you think? I always feel like that about it, somehow. Saunders, with all his failings, is most efficient. I find everything in order, even the saucer of milk for Freckles in the sitting-room, by the revolving bookcase; and this morning he brought my tea, and said, "A fine day, sir," just as if nothing had happened. It wasn't—but that's his way. He tells me the Wansgroves have bought a house called Bewick somewhere near some Welsh place, and that the banging in the street is not as bad as it was before I left. That is good news. He has even fed the canary, which looks fatter than ever. Cause and effect; food makes fatness, eh? Upon my soul, that's almost a slogan, what?

Yours ever,

O. Thake

P.S.—It's too bad. I find that all those things I wrote to Saunders for, from America went out there after I had left for home. I must write and get them back, if I can remember what they were

My Dear Beachcomber,

I am settling down again. I find a number of invitations awaiting me, including one from a Mrs. Thallett, a relative, I believe, of the Thallett who invented electric harpoons. You know, there's nothing like London. It's so *big*. It's somehow built on a grand scale—so many buildings and people, more than anywhere else. I suppose I'm what the world calls a Londoner—at heart. I love the bustle and the crowds. I shall never forget Mrs. Fume saying to me once, "London, my dear Mr. Thake, is England in miniature." Well, if you think that out, you will find it is true. And again, London is, after all, the very heart of our great Empire, with its dominions, protectorates and dependencies. One blood, one flag. One hates to boast, but really, I think we are "It," as young Pollington always says. (Not Edgar, his brother.) You remember he was one of the first to wear Oxford trousers, which I really could never understand. I think the best thing said about them was by Lady Flogge. She said "The further, the broader." Good, eh? She is a most witty woman, and her collection of third century amber is most remarkable. I am dining with her on Tuesday —next Tuesday, I mean. Which reminds me, will you come and dine one day next week? We have much to discuss, and I will show you some photographs taken during my travels. I must end now, as I am expecting old Thistle any minute. Such a nice man, but obstinate.

By the way, a soup tureen has arrived from America. Saunders knows nothing about it.

My Dear Beachcomber,

I was at the opera the other night, and I must say the German atmosphere surprised and rather disgusted me. I had no idea they were going to sing in German. Of course, one is prepared to make allowances—I mean, one is ready to forgive them their music —(not that it isn't beautiful music)—but I do think it should be conducted and sung in the mother tongue. With representatives from all quarters of our vast Empire constantly visiting here, it is surely important to create a good impression among the English-speaking races. One South African I know quite well expressed his surprise at the German singing. Let us forgive and forget, by all means, let bygones be bygones but let us keep that sense of proportion which is, as Gladstone well recognised, one of our most valuable assets.

If people cannot be found to translate the German, could it not be sung in Italian or Belgian or French? This, I am certain, would bring us and our allies nearer together, and produce a feeling of mutual esteem and love. Not only would it be a compliment, but it would avoid giving offence to the millions comprising this great British Empire. Besides, the German language is not as beautiful as others, and "Tristram and Iseult," for instance, would be far more intelligible, at any rate, in England, if sung in English. I feel confident that I am voicing the opinion of the vast majority of Britishers in this matter. Tom Watson is writing a letter to the Press about it.

P.S.—In any case, why not play "Pinafore" or "The Gondoliers" at Covent Garden? Is English opera dead?

MY DEAR BEACHCOMBER,

What a relief an English dinner-party is after foreign ones! Foreigners, like all commercial-minded people, talk of politics and religion and other serious things. It is such a strain. Last night I was at the Bunnards'—Cecil Bunnard, you know, the collector. We had a most enjoyable evening. Lady Porringer was there with Myrtle, and old Fenchurch, still grousing, and Mabel Weald and Dr. Flaring. I sat next to Barbara Bagge. She tells me her Sealyham has got synovitis, but she has built one of the new hygienic kennels for it, and hopes for the best. I asked the doctor what he thought of it, and he said that disease in men and animals varies considerably. Old Fenchurch said that it was a disgrace that medical science was powerless against mange. Bunnard retorted, "It depends what you call mange." Then a bishop said with a laugh, "It depends what you call medical science." The talk then turned on Tony Monteith's will. Somebody said he had left a lot to his dentist.

Mabel Weald said how brave it was of men to swim in the Serpentine in this weather, and Flaring pooh-poohed the suggestion that cold water cured liver complaints. He then told a long story about a man who had never been cured after years of cold water. After which some one remarked on the trouble the Horse Guards must take to keep spotless.

After we joined the ladies, Mrs. Bunnard's niece played a piece of Rachmaninoff, called, I think, "Prologue," and, as an encore, Hoffmann's "Barcarolle." Her touch is very good indeed. Lady Porringer has asked me to dinner next week, to meet Witham, the inventor.

The "Sandford and Merton" I asked Saunders for, and which he sent too late, has just returned from America. Unfortunately Saunders returned it again, without consulting me, so I must get it back again.

MY DEAR BEACHCOMBER,

It was with feelings of some surprise (excuse this scrawl, but Freckles is perched on my shoulder, and is mewing) that I read your last letter about the young woman who wishes to meet me. I suppose I am rather out of date in my notions of propriety—but really! It takes my breath away. You withhold, quite rightly, her name, and I cannot think who she can be. It could not—no, it could not be that Miss Paddell I met at the Corrington's. Really you will think me vain, but Tom Watson told me she was evidently trying to vampire me, as the Americans say. She asked me for my photograph, but I am sure she intended to stop at that. Besides, I know her brother in the Navy. Could it be the Fidge girl? Surely not. Of course, I am merely speculating. I would not for worlds pursue the matter in these days. Paula Hicks-Gobble? The widow? Don't tell me that! But wait! It is clearly some one I have never met, as she desires, you say, to be introduced to me I had forgotten that. It's no good my puzzling any more.

Did you see Lady P——'s portrait in the "Gabbler" last week? I was at the theatre with her the other night. I forget what it was called, but the jokes——well, I hope none of the women present understood them. I fear they did, as Constantia P——, who sat beside me, kept nudging me and saying, "Do you see the point?" "Did you get that?" Of course, she only wanted me to explain the jokes, so I said, sternly, I fear, "No, I do not get any of them. Dull, I assure you." She winked, and her mother rebuked her. Rather awkward, what? To appease the girl, I delved into my play-going memories, and told her one or two lines from "Little Lord Fauntleroy" and "East Lynne." She said she preferred "Piff-Poff," and her mother again rebuked her. A dear, good woman, Lady P——.

Saunders will drive me mad. He has now returned to America the stamp album that was returned from there to me here, after he had sent it there. What is one to do?

380a JERMYN STREET,
LONDON, W.

My Dear Beachcomber,

If there is one thing I like about the Academy, it is the, as it were, social aspect of it. One meets everybody there, and it isn't necessary to be a highbrow to go there. I mean they are not all experts, and they don't talk all the time about the technique of the pictures. In fact, many people I know keep off the subject of painting altogether, and treat the occasion as purely social, which is rather a relief. The Relfs are like that. To meet them, you'd never think they'd know a good picture from a bad one, or vice versa. Yet he, I believe, once studied art, and she has written a guide to the Prado at Madrid.

I struck a good day at the Academy, and bumped into a lot of friends. We all went round together—"as if it was golf," as Percy said. Though I pointed out that we were too many for golf.

There was some trouble over Mrs. Bowley. She is so short sighted, and would insist on reading out from the catalogue. Of course, she confused portraits with cabbage, and generals with bridges, and so on. There was much laughter, but old age will be served. And anyhow, one can generally tell roughly what a picture is meant to be.

There are not enough seats, I think. It is so inconvenient to have to carry on a conversation standing up. But, on the whole, it was a good show, except that the Pargetters were away in Hampshire. They are usually the life and soul of such occasions. However, we laughed a lot, and swapped holiday news. I enclose a snapshot of myself taken by Myrtle in the Sculpture Room. It was signed by her brother, in a playful moment.

380a JERMYN STREET,
LONDON, W.

My Dear Beachcomber,

I had tea at Colonel Farley's yesterday, and played my first tennis of the season. I think one's first game is somehow different from the rest, don't you? I suppose the reason is simply that it is the first game—I mean, one is out of practice more than afterwards, and consequently cannot get the grip of things. After, of course, it is different. I played with Miss Paxted—you remember her cousin, who wrote the novel called "Dripping"—well, she (I mean that cousin) is some sort of a relation of Maude Farley's. I got one or two good shots in, but Sybil Paxted will run after the balls between strokes, which is most irritating. We played the Pinkwater girl and her brother, and beat them as far as we got. It was too dark to finish. Pinkwater told me a good budget story, which I forget. You know what a wag he is.

During tea Cyril Blankett arrived. He's got some new idea about planting delphiniums, all rather technical. The Colonel collared him and told him to try it on the pansies. Cyril was furious, and pointed out, half in fun, that a delphinium and a pansy are very different affairs. "Both flowers," snorted the Colonel. It was most amusing. Maude Farley can't stand Cyril. I think it's his red moustache. You never know, do you? As I was helping to roll up the net, the rain began. So we were just in time. By the way, do you remember Olive Watts? Well, she didn't go to Finland after all. She may later, according to Molly. But you know Molly!

THE TOWERS,
WESTBOROUGH.

My Dear Beachcomber,

I am at the Towers, as you will notice, for the week-end. To-day being Sunday, we are all more or less doing nothing. Madge is here, and is reading rather a good leader from one of the Sunday papers. There will be church later on, and young Effington is to read the lessons. After that we shall probably chat with Sopwith, the vicar. Then home to lunch. In the afternoon—I don't quite know. We are divided. My host and hostess rather want to sleep. Some of the rest of us suggest going on the lawn to read, while others favour a walk to the Arnolds' next door, to hear about Walter Arnold's new car. One way, of course, and I have suggested as much, would be to send a note by one of the maids to the Arnolds asking them round. Which course will be adopted one can hardly say as yet. I do not much care myself. Anyhow, I've half promised to go and see Tony's rabbits.

Later

It rained after lunch, so I suggested a rubber. To my surprise, our host said that he loathed playing bridge in the rain. He said bridge was depressing enough without that. Madge then suggested the gramophone, but no one could find a needle. I offered to give them my talk on America, the one that I gave at the Wilmingtons' garden party, but it appears that our host loathes Americans. Fortunately it stopped raining, and we were able to go to call on the Arnolds. They were out. You will remember that Arnold and I were at Oxford the same time as Tom Watson. By that time it was raining hard again, and we returned. Our host had gone to sleep by the fire, so I read the life of Charles Dickens until tea. A remarkable man.

Later

Madge says she will drop in on you on her return. She is motoring home early on account of the serious illness of her aunt. When I asked the name of her aunt, she said "Banbury," but I know no one of that name. Perhaps her aunt has married since then, however.

380a JERMYN STREET,
LONDON, W.

My Dear Beachcomber,

Each year the Glorious Fourth of June finds me a little older, a little further on the way to old age, a little further, too, from youth. But what a fine thing it is to go back to one's old school, to the buildings and fields one knew so well. All the faces, of course, are different, since those who were boys with us are boys no longer, but men, according to the inexorable decrees of fate. Yet these boys of to-day are boys like us—that is, as we used to be before we became men. And who can hear the old school songs without choking? They are like nothing on earth to one who revisits the scenes of his boyhood. Then, again, it is so fine to see the thing going on like a tree. Boys leave, but other boys take their places. Thus the thing goes on. Dear me, I am becoming quite sentimental.

I met a bishop I knew, a former schoolmate of mine, and he chaffed me about my inky fingers, and I reminded him that he used to say "damn" when his shins were kicked. He laughingly denied this, but all in the best-humoured way. He was not at all offended, which is proof that the Church is broader-minded than some people seem to think. Lady —— was there. One of her boys is quite a swell—Pop, and all that. As long as England can breed this kind of stuff nobody need fear for the future of our Empire. I tell you what's wrong with France. *She's got no Eton.* A Fourth of July would do her no end of good, and stop all the nonsense. I'd like to see the Wall Game in their dreadful Latin Quarter. You, as a writer, ought to be able to get an article out of this idea.

Well, another Fourth is over, and here I am again. Floreat Etona! Yes, indeed!

P.S.—Tom, of course, to the everlasting regret of his family, went to Harrow—good in its way, of course—but—well—you know.

380a JERMYN STREET,
LONDON, W.

My Dear Beachcomber,

I have been taking advantage of the fine weather. Yesterday I went down to Marlham, where the Wraglans have a house. They got up a party to go out in their new launch, Moonbeam. But, as we were rather a large party, we split up. I was asked to take Mrs. Barlow in one of the punts. Her husband, who died in Sweden, was something to do with structural anatomy. She spoke continually of his medals. She is a nice woman, and tactful. My punting is a little stale, and I think she saw this, as she kept on suggesting that we should go down a quiet backwater, where there would be no people. I was too proud to take the hint at first, but after one or two knocks, and after getting the pole stuck, I gave in. I said to her, "This is no time for *amour propre.*" She only winked, which may have been to disguise the fact that she has no sense of humour. "*Amour,*" she said, "but why drag in the *propre?*" As you see, she has not much conversation, and what there is is a little stupid.

Eventually I got the boat into a backwater, and she suddenly said her hands were cold, and asked me to feel them. Of course, it was all her imagination. They were quite warm. Really, women do fidget and fuss so. I was just going to sit down and rest at my end of the boat, when she said there was a moth or something in her eye. I went over to examine the eye, but could see nothing there. Very soon after this, she said she was going to faint. I propped her up on cushions, and splashed some water on her. She kept saying, "Hold me, hold me. I'm falling." I said, "You can't fall. You are sitting down." Then she got angry, and asked to be taken home. What can one do? I can't make anything of women. They are extraordinary creatures.

Dilke has gone to Pevensey.

P.S.—Tom Watson says perhaps she is what the young people call a river girl.

MY DEAR BEACHCOMBER,

This is surely the weather for your name—I believe beachcombers have a pretty cool time of it. Anyhow they ought to, if they are always by the sea. But really the heat is terrific, is it not? I only remember one month as hot—somewhere back in '99, I think—or was it '98? It was the year old Lady Shamburn's boy went into the Navy. I know that, because his cousin and I used to meet at their uncle's place. How keen the old lady was on her greenhouses. But come, come! Fancy talking about greenhouses in this heat. Green-land (!) would be more appropriate, would it not? I mustn't ramble, but it is so hard to concentrate. One's brain seems to melt. I wonder if there will be a drought. It is so rough on the farmers when there is no water about—and how the cattle live is a mystery. Who would be a cow in this weather? Not I! Nor you, I am sure, eh? I am staying at my club until the heat wave passes.

I have had a letter from Mrs. Barlow. She says the river is the only cool place, and will I take her out one evening in a punt again. I don't quite know how to reply. She is so fussy, but I mustn't offend her, as, after all, she is a friend of very good friends of mine—and of my friends too. Besides, it is so difficult to get away from the crowds—please do not misunderstand me. My doctor has a theory that punting, by opening the pores, is good in this weather. But I should have thought that applied equally to other forms of exercise, wouldn't you? Don't trouble to answer till it's cool. He may mean it does. He says it doesn't, at any rate.

I was wrong about Dilke. He is at Marsfield.

P.S.—Tell Saunders to keep the wine near open windows.

MY DEAR BEACHCOMBER,

I am in somewhat of a muddle. Owing to the carelessness of Saunders—really, he grows too provoking—I have been consulting last year's diary instead of this year's. The result is, that acting on last year's entries, I arrived the other night at the Farringtons' at Maidenhead, expecting to go to Ascot with them. They, of course, were not expecting me, and there were some awkward moments. I produced my diary triumphantly, and Olga cried, "Why, it's 1927." This I flatly denied, and fetched a newspaper to prove my point. "I mean the diary," she said. Sure enough, when I looked at the diary, it said 1927. They put me up, but I felt most uncomfortable. Next day, I sent for the 1928 diary, and proceeded according to the entries, to the Stoddarts at Windsor, only to discover that Saunders had sent the 1926 diary. At last I got the right book, and am where I ought to be—at Esher, with the Dewsworthys.

Last night, over the port, we had a long discussion on Nicaragua. When we joined the ladies, I was surprised to see Mrs. Barlow at the piano. She asked me to turn over for her. I told her I couldn't read music, but the only reply she made was, "I wonder if we can go on the river here." I said I did not think one could, and began to talk of Ascot. "I hope you will win the Gold Cup, Mr. Thake," she said. I felt rather stupid—she does say unexpected things. She then asked me if I thought Green suited her. I said I did not know the gentleman, thinking she meant to marry again. She replied, "I mean the colour."

Well, what can one say to such a woman? Really, she is beyond me.

My Dear Beachcomber,

There's something about a London season—a sort of something—I can't describe it, but you know what I mean. One is conscious of things happening, and one meets people and goes to places. I must say I should miss my Ascot if ever the Socialist people abolished it. It is a sort of landmark, and you know where you are, if you know what I mean. I don't see what one could put in its place. I was with the Dewsworthy party yesterday. Her father was Canon—oh, I forget his name—anyhow, he was a Canon, and so, of course, they are all very much against betting. But as Pearl, the eldest daughter says, after all, one needn't bet if one goes to Ascot.

I met Tom Watson in the paddock, and he introduced me to a jockey, rather a small man. "May the best horse win," I said to him. "Not if I know it," he answered. So I said, "Well, anyhow, I sincerely hope you do know it." At which we both laughed. I asked him whether he found it tiring to ride so much, and he said, in the most natural way, "Oh, no." He then told me a wonderful story about some horse or other, but Mrs. Barlow was at my elbow, and I missed half of it. She said she "was very fond of horses, as her husband used to ride one frequently." She asked me if I liked chestnut roans, and I said I did, without thinking. Of course, I don't. She then made me explain everything to her—race cards and so on. And then she got on the river again, and asked me to take her to Henley. I rather hesitated, as I'm taking my nephew, Parkstone, and she may set her cap at him. One never knows, does one?

Tell Saunders not to send on any more circulars. It makes one look so silly, when one is in some one else's house.

My Dear Beachcomber,

Yesterday was marred for me by certain embarrassing situations. Really, Mrs. Barlow is the most extraordinary woman. She led me away into the paddock, and while I was holding her sunshade and her vanity-bag, she took her mirror, and, dabbing her nose, approached close to me, and asked if she looked all right. At that very unfortunate moment, up came Tom Watson and his crowd. I hurriedly told her that her hat was a little crooked, and she appeared to become angry. Tom looked curiously at us, and passed on. She then took my arm, and said she hadn't meant to be nasty, and I could call her Ethel if I liked. Really! I should have her calling me Oswald! It's all very disturbing. One does not know what to do for the best.

P.S.—Can you do nothing to stop Saunders sending on these preposterous circulars? Two or three of the party have noticed, and it places me in an absurd situation.

★   ★   ★

The Wavelings

Dear Beachcomber,

I must trust to your recognising my writing, as I prefer not to have my name bandied about. I am writing to tell you of a curious coincidence that has occurred to me here at the hotel. I have been introduced to a Miss Waveling, who writes pamphlets for an animal society, I forget which. Her sister, whom they call Barbara, whose cousin got a D.S.O. on the Somme, in, I believe, 1916—but that is unimportant—well, this girl apparently met you some time ago at the house of some people called Faddle. He, the Mr. Faddle, was, I think, a musician, and lived in Somerset or Norfolk, I am not certain which. Anyhow, the point is that Miss Waveling's sister, Miss Barbara Waveling, has written an article about apples (or perhaps it's oranges) which she thought might be published in some paper. Now at present, she has lent the article to a Mrs. Bruce to read, because this Mrs. Bruce has a friend who does the poultry gossip for a local paper in Cumberland. So far, so good.

The point is, if this Miss Barbara Waveling gets her article back from Mrs. Bruce with the opinion that the friend could not use it—in any case, he is away in Italy—do you think, if she sent it to you, you could do anything about it. It is about four thousand, four hundred words long, and she wants to put on the top of it, "By the author of 'Love's Morn'," which was a story she wrote for a cycling paper last November, but which was never accepted. She calls the article "Apples" (or "Oranges"—I forget which), but, of course it could be altered, as long as she saw a proof, and it must be copyright in all countries. If it is not troubling you too much, could you drop a note saying yes or no to E. N. Sprott, her cousin, at The Briars, Hobble Cross, Sussex, and he will let her know.

Yours ever,

A. FRIEND

P.S.—Tell Saunders not to send any more biscuits. I can buy anything I want here. Anyone would think I was starving.

HOTEL des FOUS du MONDE,
DEAUVILLE.

Dear Mr. Beachcomber,

As soon as I heard that Mr. Thake had approached you with a view to getting an editor to publish my sister's article, I determined to write and thank you. We met, you may remember, at the Faddles' last October. Now, what I want to tell you is this; my sister is naturally very modest and you must not take her at her own value. She is an excellent writer, and has received warm praise from Miss Bundle, who wrote "Desert Passions." Miss Bundle read a sketch of my sister's about ways of nailing down carpets, and offered to show it to the editor of "Wickerwork." But my sister was too shy, and could only just be persuaded to let the vicar have it for his parish magazine. If your editor likes "Oranges," make her send him "The Soot Menace," which is a scathing indictment of coal, from the point of view of one who hates industrialism.

We all like your friend Mr. Thake. Alas! he seems a lonely and unhappy man. He carries about with him a copy of Lord Tennyson's "Maud," and sometimes reads to us Mr. Meredith's "Love in the Valley." He also seems considerably worried by packages and letters he receives from England. I hope nobody is menacing him. He certainly gets odd things.

Poor man. He asks me to say to you that he is writing shortly, and will you tell Saunders there is some mistake about the bill for butterfly nets, as Mr. Thake never bought any.

Yours gratefully,

Hester Waveling

APPLEDENE,
Near SOUTHBOROUGH
KENT.

DEAR MR. BEACHCOMBER,

Pardon this liberty I take in writing to you, but I have heard of Mr. Thake's great kindness to my two sisters, and I hear he is sending you an article of Barbara's, which you are going to get published. Now I wonder if you could help me. I am sending one or two of my drawings to Mr. Thake, asking him his advice about getting them accepted. One is of Scarborough, and another of Bexhill, so you see they are quite topical. I have also sent to Mr. Thake a piece of verse called "Thistles," which is by my best friend Vera Randall. We were at school together, and she write divinely. I'm sure any editor would be glad to publish it in his paper. Of course, Barbara is the really clever one in our family, and we are dreadfully proud of her. She wrote something about soot and its menace, which dad said would get her a scholarship if she were a boy. I've no training, so you must forgive the mistakes in my work.

Vera says that if you and Mr. Thake like "Thistles," she has a small series of flower-poems, which she could send later, and she has a friend whose brother is awfully clever at inventing puzzles—the sort they print in newspapers, you know. She is sending one or two of them to Mr. Thake with the pictures and the poem. He must be an awfully kind man to take all this troubles Barbara says he's very distinguished and very gloomy, like Byron. It sounds fearfully thrilling and romantic. I should love to meet him, and perhaps I shall, if he comes to us in England, when the holiday's over. Barbara says he collects queer things, like butterfly-nets.

Thank you so much.

Yours sincerely,

Felicia Waveling

HOTEL des FOUS du MONDE,
DEAUVILLE.

DEAR BEACHCOMBER,

Shakespeare says somewhere that there is a destiny that shapes our ends, no matter how roughly we hew them. How true it is in my case! Wherever I go, and whatever I do, I seem to meet trouble. I scarcely know which way to turn at present. My room here is like Bedlam. I have got Miss Barbara Waveling's confounded article, which isn't even typed. Then there are her sister's idiotic drawings, Miss Vera Randall's poems, which I don't understand, some young man's puzzle problems, two short stories from some other man, a one-act play from a woman called Grabbham, a ballet from her brother, and an essay on the Patriotism of Byron, by an undergraduate. And all this nonsense started because, in an unguarded moment, I promised Miss Hester Waveling I would do my best for her sister's writing. The thing is impossible. She seems to have told everybody that I am a sort of god in the literary and artistic world. Only this morning a letter arrived from a girl I've never heard of asking my advice about contralto songs. Really!

I am forwarding all this stuff to you. For pity's sake, use as much of it as you can, or they will blame me. I simply dread the post now. For all I know, there may be more members of the Waveling family lurking about. Whenever I meet the eldest sister, she gives me no peace, but at once talks literature. I flatter myself that I am a cultured man, but I cannot bear being asked, immediately after breakfast, what I think of Thackeray. There is a time for everything and this is overdoing it.

Yours ever,

O. Thake

P.S.—Tell Saunders he must be mad to send me diving boots. They are entirely useless to me. I don't see the point.

By the same post as Mr. Thake's letter, I received a mass of material, nearly all of which is utterly amateurish. But I suppose I must use some of it, to save my old friend's face. Therefore I choose the following, without apology:

THISTLES

They grow upon the hillside,
And nod before the breeze;
O Thistle, thistle, thistle,
Do not prick my knees.

And when the night is falling
And all the world is still,
I see the thistles standing
Alone upon the hill.

Beloved, it is better,
In meadow or in mart,
To have thistles on the hillside
Than thistles in the heart.

Vera Randall

DEAR MR. BEACHCOMBER,

Although I appreciate deeply the kindness of yourself and Mr. Thake, and my friend Felicia Waveling, in taking an interest in my work, you can imagine with what a shock I opened my *Daily Express* only to find that "Thistles" contained a serious error. Line three of Verse one reads, "O Thistle, thistle, thistle." It should, of course, read, "O Thistle, gentle thistle." The adjective accentuates the appeal to the herb not to prick the knees of the victim, and avoids the repetition of one word three times. I should like your editor to publish a letter of apology, together with the correct version of the poem. My cousin, (you have probably heard of him) Randolph Gower, is a solicitor, and he says it is most important to stick up for one's rights, especially on beginning a career. He says one might almost get damages for such a misrepresentation.

I trust you will put it right. I enclose a little sketch by my friend Ursula Stock. Do use it if you can.

Yours always,

Vera Randau

I wonder what on earth the Waveling sisters imagine a newspaper office to be like. I have just received another letter from Miss Hester Waveling, enclosing two preposterous drawings by a small nephew, aged four. She describes them as "clever and original drawings, with a topical interest," and tells me that the boy's mother is a vegetarian. The sketches are called "King Gorje Shoting," and "Southend Pear." The King's felt hat is surmounted by a crown, and "Southend Pear" begins on one sheet of paper, and continues on the back of the same sheet, after the notice P.T.O.

I have space to quote only the P.S. of Miss Waveling's letter:

. . . So I hope you will publish the drawings. The one of the pier at Southend is a difficulty, but I suppose you have machinery in your office whereby you can overcome the unusual idea of continuing a drawing on the back of a sheet of paper. I think it would be nice to leave the spelling unaltered. It would please the little lad, and also his parents, one of whom is my brother. The boy's name is Yglesias Hibb, if you care to use it. My brother changed his name to Hibb a year ago—none of us ever knew why. . . . Barbara is sending you an article on darning-needles.

HOTEL des FOUS du MONDE,
DEAUVILLE.

DEAR BEACHCOMBER,

I hope you will realise that I only write this under pressure, in order to secure a little peace from these dreadful Wavelings. It is this. Miss Hester—I mean Barbara Waveling—wants you, if possible, to publish the article about darning-needles which I enclose, instead of her one about the oranges. She also wants you to put her sister Hester's name on it, as well as her own, as her sister helped her with it, and wrote some of the phrases towards the middle—for instance, the one about a darning-needle being a woman's *vade mecum*. I have been trying to keep out of their way, but cannot. I shall have to leave here, I fear. In fact, I'm not sorry that the time is near at hand when one can return to London. The fifteen novels Mrs. Wretch sent me are driving me mad. She must be a tiresome woman.

I forgot to mention that the poem enclosed is by Barbara Waveling—no, Felicia Waveling, and that it is to be included in the article, and that her name too, is to appear at the top of it—so all three of them must be mentioned as authors—the three witches in Macbeth, eh?

It would be very pleasant here without all this worry. The blue sea laps against the shore, the sky is blue also, and occasional gulls wheel about in the soft air. The nights are serene and dark, save when the moon gilds the scene. I venture to send you a poem I wrote about it all—but don't think I have caught the fever from these women, please! But I saw one by Vera Randall, and I think this is just as good.

Yours ever,

O. Thake

P.S.—Tell Saunders I do not want the address of any more glass-blowers. I never asked for any such thing.

NOCTURNE

When I gaze up at the fair moon,
I fall into a sort of swoon,
It seems to be the beauteous face
Of her who haunts my nights and days.
And every star that shines above
Is like the eye of my true love.
And every pool that shines below
Is like her voice so soft and low.
And everywhere I look at all
I seem to think I hear her call.
Ah no! It is an idle dream.
Things are not, they can only seem.

O. THAKE

Mr. Thake, whose many troubles force me to make allowances for him, enclosed in his last letter, Miss Barbara Waveling's article entitled "Oranges" instead of the one about darning-needles. I, therefore, publish as much of the former as possible. It was nearly five thousand words in length, but I have tried to cut it down judiciously. I think it shows great promise. Here it is. (The dots are mine, and mark my "cuts.")

ORANGES

By Barbara Waveling

. . . Little spheres that seem to hold cloistered in their depths all the bright sunshine of Spain, all the stored colour of that *laissez-faire* land of señors and señoritas, bulls, guitars and priests. . . . As one walks beneath the swaying orange trees of Seville, hearing on all sides the lazy Spanish tongue, one cannot help being struck by the thought that all these acres of fruit will one day be marmalade in our gloomier northern homes. . . .

The child who spreads this delicious condiment on his or her bread does not dream that he or she is about to absorb the sunny south, land of passion and romance, land of hot tempers, hasty words, and knives suddenly produced from stockings . . . land of . . . land of . . . Thus are Spain and England for ever linked in a common bond of friendship . . . and . . . and . . . and . . . so that . . . for ever . . . heritage . . . friendship . . . Then there are the great pipless oranges so dear to those who find pips a deterrent to the enjoyment of this . . . fruit.

A great man once called oranges the solace of jaded palates. And indeed . . . Oranges are a reminder that the fruits of earth were given to man for his delectation . . . . I never look at one without seeing the white-walled towns of that land of . . . land of . . . and hearing the mule bells in that land of . . . land of . . .

I think I have kept the sense of the thing, without sacrificing too much of the really beautiful prose. I was forced to omit the long passages about using orange skins to clean oak panelling, and the still longer one about orangeade at Henley.

HOTEL des FOUS du MONDE,
DEAUVILLE.

Dear Mr. Beachcomber,

I hoped I should be in time to rectify Mr. Thake's mistake. I wanted the darning-needle article published first, but he sent you the orange one. That, in itself, is distressing, but judge of my horror on seeing how you had mutilated my work, and had not even put copyright below, nor, "By the author of 'The Soot Menace,' etc., etc., etc." above it. As to copyright, my sister Hester says that the Americans are rather unscrupulous in that way, and might print the article, or parts of it, in one of their papers without acknowledgement—a compliment, no doubt, but not what I should care to happen.

But the mutilation horrifies me. I did not know that newspaper men behaved so scandalously, and in future I shall confine myself to novels and short stories. No doubt it is the system's fault, and not yours.

Dear Mr. Thake seems very distrait. Hester asked him where he was going to next, and he almost shouted "Samarkand!" He is worried still, I think, and is frequently receiving dummy Post Office Directories, with nothing inside. After reading his poem, I imagine he has had an unhappy love affair, the poor man. I think some lunatic is in touch with him, otherwise why does he keep all those queer things in his room? When Hester and I had tea with him in his suite we saw the quaintest collection—butterfly-nets, bicycle-clips, cardboard eggs, potato-mashers, harpoons, diving-boots, and even a coil of barbed wire. He is a queer man. Have all those things sentimental associations for him?

Yours sincerely,

Barbara Waveling

HOTEL des FOUS du MONDE,
DEAUVILLE.

DEAR BEACHCOMBER,

I notice that a novelist has been defending himself against the accusation of having put real people into his books. Now it seems to me that I come into this. Whatever I do, and wherever I go, I am chattered about. I have just been reading the remarks of that intolerable Miss Waveling about me. Not content with telling the world that my room is full of barbed wire and cardboard eggs, she hints that these articles may have a sentimental association for me. How absurd! How could they have? And the other day, when I had dodged a journalist who was after me, up came the sister Hester, and told him my favourite colour is blue, that I smoke Egyptian cigarettes, and that my lucky day is Wednesday. Also an artist here named Stavehold-Gault has drawn me, and put the thing up for auction in the hotel lounge. Really!

Mrs. Wretch herself has arrived here, and is for ever fussing about her novels. She comes and takes her coffee at my table, and is always asking me whether I think character is internally or externally self-revealing, and what my opinion is of ultra-expressionism as understood by Smallfish and his school. As if I knew or cared! It is all double Dutch to me. I am off soon, thank goodness. My luggage will be absurdly bulky. Saunders, for some reason best known to himself, has sent me five thousand leaflets about clover. It is all very mysterious.

Yours ever,

O. Thake

*   *   *

A Wild Party

BISHOP'S CLOSE,
WESTBOROUGH.

. . . I went to a wild sort of a party the other night, and when I got there I found nearly every-one in diver's costume, and the big boots made dancing very difficult. The women looked most quaint in their helmets. There were two gramophones, each playing a different tune, and I was introduced to a lady who asked me if I could whistle and sing at the same time. Of course I can't. And I said to her, "I can't see that such an accomplishment would serve any useful purpose."

She answered, "Oh, don't get serious," so I showed her how to move the ears by wrinkling the forehead.

This I was asked to repeat, so apparently there is still something we old campaigners can teach the young guard.

Later on, a girl said to me, "We always begin to throw trifle about at midnight. It's such fun," and I noticed that she had stationed herself by a big bowl of trifle. At the first stroke of midnight she threw a handful at a man who was asleep in a corner. But nothing much happened. Then ink and milk cocktails were served, but nobody, of course, had to drink them. They were just thrown about, like the trifle, only more so.

Somebody put a pancake on the gramophone, and there was a rush for the door.

Six hours of this kind of thing is enough. It becomes monotonous. About four in the morning most people were dozing, and eggs and bacon were brought in, and dropped about the room for anyone who wanted them. Another party arrived from somewhere else, and poured champagne into the piano. One man kept shouting, "I'm the King of Syria," but nobody took any notice, except a girl who went into hysterics, and was bundled into the bath.

At six-thirty, when I was asked to play billiards with a broken umbrella handle and three new-laid eggs, I realised that I am too old for the modern night life. I went out into the cool air of dawn and walked home ruminating. Beachcomber, life is a strange mixture, and it takes all sorts to make a world.

*　　*　　*

Iris Tennyson

I suppose the heart never grows old. Walking in Hyde Park with Iris Tennyson, some influence in the air changed all. When she said something to me, some casual thing, I listened as though I had never heard her voice before. And I looked at her face, as though it had suddenly grown strange, and watched her movement over the grass, as though it were unfamiliar. My voice was out of control when I answered her, and I saw her glance sharply at me. The moment passed, the common light settled on the water and the trees, and the birds were singing as before.

What can it all mean?

We spoke but little as we crossed the bridge over the Serpentine, for I was afraid to speak, and she was in the mood for silence.

When we got back to her house I sat down and watched her arranging flowers in a vase. There were daffodils, a sheaf of them, by my chair. Swiftly, before I knew what I was doing, I had seized a handful of them, advanced to her side, and thrust them into her hand. She turned, and I heard her draw in her breath, and saw her amazed eyes. The next moment I was gone.

At half-past eight I discovered myself hatless and hungry in the Fulham Road.

Have I gone mad?

ROUNDABOUT CLUB,
LONDON, W.

I could not sleep last night. Not a wink. Iris Tennyson was in my thoughts without ceasing I got up to select a bedside book of poetry, as nothing else would suit my mood, but that fool Saunders has his own ideas of bedside literature. All I could find was the third volume of Stackhouse's "History of the Bible," a bicycling manual, a book on Rationalisation, two old Bradshaws, and a bound volume of the *Cornhill*. So I went downstairs to get Keats, and found that infernal cat had got in. I let it out at the front door, but it wouldn't budge, so I went down the steps to lure it on. Then the door banged on me, and I was left in the street in my pyjamas. The cat began to howl, and several windows went up. Somebody threw a boot, which nearly hit me, and I was going back up the steps with it in my hand when a policeman shouted to me. I pretended not to hear, but when a man is in the street in pyjamas, with a boot in his hand, long after midnight, it is not so easy for him to pretend that he cannot hear a strident voice shouting at him. So I turned slowly to face the voice, trying to look as though everything was perfectly natural and in order. The policeman advanced slowly, and I made some trivial remark about the weather, emphasising my opinion that Buchan's cold spell was about to begin.

Luckily it was the usual man on the beat, who knows me. He looked me up and down, gave a broad wink, nudged me, and said, "Makin' a night of it, eh, guv'nor? Well, I 'aven't seen yer." I tried to ignore him, but he waited until the bell had brought Saunders down, and then the pair of them smirked and tittered, and it was all I could do to persuade them that I was quite capable of walking up my own stairs. Really! What a situation!

I called on Iris Tennyson yesterday afternoon, and found there a gentleman whom I did not like. He kept on calling her "Bibbins" for some unearthly reason. She told me when he had gone that it was his pet name for her. "But are you his pet?" I asked. "Don't be foolish," she said; "he is nothing to me." "I am glad of that," I said, "Why should you be glad?" she asked. "Because——" I began; but my tongue refused its office.

About tea-time a young man arrived, and at once called Iris "Wooffie." I hate all this pet-name business and with great punctilio I kept on referring to her as Mrs. Tennyson. She went to the piano and sang a song called "Widows are wonderful." She asked me if I thought they were. "Some are and some aren't," I said, and she laughed. Later a Captain Faraday, a soldier, arrived. He greeted Iris as "Foo-Foo," and she called him "Pingle."

All this dog-talk! You should have heard them! He asked her if she'd "trickle round to some ghastly hole or other," with him for dinner. And she said, "Yes, if he'd not go all gaga after the soup." He then called her a real high-spot, and she said if only he wasn't so putridly stagnant he'd think of a new hop-house for the evening. Really! Then he said to me, "It's an awful bore, but one must float around, or go mad." "You mean going to places?" I said. And he answered, "Sort of, you know." Then he said, "Bless the little houris." "What houris?" said I, visualising a number of Persian female relations. "Any houris," he said, and Iris chimed in, "That's Pingle's name for girls." I couldn't see the point at all. When cocktails came in, this young man took off his coat, and fanned his with it. A stupid gesture, but Iris laughed immoderately at it.

The telephone rang, and Iris asked me to answer it. Imagine my rage when I was greeted with, "Is that you, Mopsy?" "No, it isn't," I shouted. The voice at the other end then asked me to remind Iris that she was dining with Sir Edward Farnham that evening.

I had hoped to dine with her myself, but I suppose I'm out of date. If I called her some silly dog name she might like me better. Fido? No, I couldn't.

Iris and I motored out to Richmond for dinner last night, and I tried to tell her all that was in my heart. But somehow it was no good. I tried allegory. I said, "There was once a man called Smith who loved the most beautiful woman in England," but she stopped me to ask if it was a ghost story. But she called me Oswald. I had to clutch the table to prevent shouting my secret to the world. On the way home she said she had something in her eye. An old memory stirred in me, and I recalled two other women in my life who had things in their eyes, and it seemed a bad omen. But, after all, you can't leave things in ladies' eyes, so I prodded with a handkerchief, and told her how I had once been led on by this.

"If you think that of me," she said, and turned away to the window, and sat silent. Why is it I always say the wrong thing? "I didn't mean it," I said. "You never mean anything," she answered. Nothing would content her after this but that we should wind up at the "Giant Orange." I guessed all the noisy crowd would be there, and one young puppy kissed her hand. I wish I had the right to protect her.

Iris Tennyson, *alias* Wooffie, *alias* Bibbins, *alias* Foo-Foo, *alias* Mopsy, *alias* Toots, *alias* heaven knows what else, led me a fine dance last night. Really! This post-war world! I took her to a theatre. She insisted on visiting friends in a box, in the *entr'acte*, and what a crowd! Two couples were dancing in the anteroom behind, and one of the men was trying to throw chocolates into a top-hat placed on the floor, while another had taken off his shoe to crack the hard ones. I asked one girl how she liked the play, and she said, "Oh, that! I just don't notice it, boy." They all called Iris "Quiggie"—why, I don't know. A man who was lying full-length on the floor and pretending to bark, suggested leap-frog, but one of the girls stopped him by pouring some coffee over his shirt. Iris was persuaded—against her will, I hope—to play fish. The idea was that you had to use your arms as fins and pretend you were under the water, until someone fished for you with a chocolate on the end of a bootlace. Iris was "caught" by a young man who screamed, "I've got a priceless bloater, chaps," and then she had to try to make a noise like a bloater. In a corner there was a man lighting bits of paper, and dropping them into his opera hat. When the lining caught fire, they got a programme girl to pour lemonade into the smoking mess, and one of the girls swore she would go and ring up the fire brigade. Luckily she didn't.

After that, I couldn't get a serious word out of Iris, and when I left her on her doorstep, and pointed to the stars, she said the stars "made her sick because they were so putridly smug up there in the revolting sky."

Well, really!

P.S.—Tell Saunders my house is not a cats' home—as yet.

A glimpse of the daffodils in the Park sent me headlong into my florist, Printemps, of Piccadilly. When the girl asked me what I wanted, I felt inclined to cry, "A bushel of everything for a beautiful lady," but I remembered myself and ordered daffodils to be sent to Iris Tennyson. I apparently ordered an unusual amount, as the girl said, "Wedding or funeral, sir?" "Neither," said I, and some imp in my brain made me add, "—as yet." The girl smiled so knowingly that I said, "As a matter of fact it is just a friendly token for the spring weather." She laughed and said, "I hope it will be successful." "Spring weather," I replied, "is always successful," deliberately misunderstanding her.

That evening Iris rang up to ask why I had sent her so many narcissi. I said there must be a mistake, as I had sent her daffodils. "Why," said she, "that was even naughtier." "I've never heard," said I, "that either narcissi or daffodils were particularly naughty." "You have much to learn," said she. "With you as teacher," said I, "I——," and then an infernal voice butted in with, "Is that Quiggie—Nobbie here," and Iris gave a little shriek of, "Oh, how putridly divine!" And I shouted, "Clear the line, miss," and a man said, "Who are you talking to?" Someone else roared, "Go to hell!" and there was a general mix-up, until I heard a man's voice saying, "Look here, Stoker, did you pack that bag and send it to the club?"

In the general confusion I rang off. The only dignified thing to do.

Iris Tennyson persuaded me to join a party at the "Giant Orange." I hadn't been there long before a young girl with a shrill voice said, "Are you her sugar-daddy, Mr. Thake?" I don't know what she meant, but I was thankful to Iris for telling her to shut up. I seem to be a survival from a quieter world, and I do wish I could get Iris to myself in some backwater. I told her so, while I was dancing with her, and she said, "It's too early in the year for the river." Of course, I didn't mean the river, but any quiet place. She got angry and said, "If you had your way I'd be spending my time in Lock's, the hatters, or in the writing-room at the Army and Navy Stores." "Iris," I said, "there is as much loyalty in that old shop as anywhere else. You laugh at it, because it isn't like this, but it takes all sorts of places to make a world. Hats are no worse for being made by ancient hatters, and good butter can be bought in a shop that has no jazz-band."

She stared at me, and all my soul boiled up for her.

And then suddenly she passed her hand across her eyes, and said, "I'm tired out." All her gaiety vanished. "Why do you go on like this?" I asked. "You don't understand," she said, "but you are a dear friend." And she laid her hand on mine. At that moment I was a monarch, and I bowed humbly. And then up came the young people and started shouting and making fun of me. I simply stood erect and let them go on. For they did not know what was in my heart, not by a long bit of chalk.

"Iris, Iris, Iris," said my blind-cord, tapping the window all night.

P.S.—Tell Saunders that he must not leave cat's meat on my desk.

I had a few people to tea yesterday in my chambers. Everything went all right till that fool Saunders let the cat in, and it started miaowing and clawing all over the room. Iris made a great fuss of it, and went down on all fours, and pretended to lap up milk from a saucer. The worst of it was that old Seabright was there, and couldn't make head or tail of such goings on. He took me aside and asked if Iris was mad. I said no, it was just high spirits; but I wish she wouldn't demean herself like this in front of people.

She then got up and pretended to scratch old Seabright and hissed at Lady de Winter. They all disapproved so much that I had to do my best for Iris, so I got down on all fours and barked like a dog, but not, I fear, with much enthusiasm. I am not as young as I was. I suppose nobody is nowadays. Anyhow my joints creaked, and my knees hurt, but somehow I felt that the glory of my cause was added to by the indignity of my present undertaking. As I thought of this, I barked louder and louder, and pranced, and rolled my eyes, and snarled at old Seabright, who retreated. I chased him round the room, and the more heartily Iris laughed, the more violently I acted my part, snuffling and snorting, cocking my head to one side, butting, backing, advancing, pawing the carpet and even yelping and arching my back. At last, exhausted, I lay down and gnawed an imaginary bone. Iris was almost in hysterics. But Seabright had gone.

When the others had all gone I asked Iris why she had gone on like this, and she said she wanted to get rid of the "stuffy old freaks." I said, "But they are my friends," and she said, "Would you rather I had gone than they?" and I said, "I never want you ever to go." "What exactly do you mean by that?" she asked, coming nearer to me. "Nothing," I said, which seemed to annoy her, as she left soon after.

44

And this morning I got a note from old Seabright saying that he never objected to harmless fun, but drew the line at ladies and gentlemen going on all fours in Jermyn Street. Really!

380a JERMYN STREET,
LONDON, W.

We were alone. Outside all was still save for the occasional chime of a neighbouring clock, or the sound of a taxicab bearing its human freight homewards from theatre or ball. Something in the dim lamplight gave me courage. Iris was playing the piano softly. I approached her. She half turned to meet me, but said nothing. I stopped dead, staring at her, and she began to smile. Before I knew what had happened I was holding one of her hands. "It is as cool as a cucumber, this little hand," I said to her. "Do you mean that?" she asked. "I never meant anything more," said I. "It is," I said. "Yes," she said. "Oh, what's the good?" I said. "The good of what?" she said. "Oh, I don't know," I said.

"What are words?" I said presently. "What?" said she, coming out of a reverie. "I said, what are words?" I answered. "Oh," she said, "Is that all?" "No," I cried suddenly, "it's would you—can't you—I——" Heaven knows what stumbling words I used, but the telephone cut my proposal short, and some fool asked if I was the Splendid Steam Laundry Company. "Yes, of course, I am," I answered sarcastically. Whereupon I was drawn into a row about two dress shirts. Really! Such a chance spoilt!

ALBANY CLUB,
LONDON, W.

I am beginning to think that I really must have been the Splendid Steam Laundry Company in some previous existence. I am always getting their telephone calls. And that fool Saunders always complicates matters. The other day, when my sister rang up and asked to speak to me, Saunders, who answered the telephone, said loudly, "This is not the Splendid Steam Laundry Company nor anybody else of that name." I had to explain to my sister what had happened. Then, the next day, Saunders rang up this laundry and asked them if they were me. Not content with that, he took the number of the man who is making a fuss about the shirts, rang him up, and told him that I had his shirts and was sending them to the Splendid Steam Laundry Company. What is one to do?

Now, of course, the man who has lost the two shirts keeps on ringing me up to ask me what I mean by sending his shirts to the Splendid Steam Laundry Company. "Well, it's your laundry, isn't it?" I said to him, "and not mine." "But my shirts are mine, and not yours, aren't they?" he shouted. "I hope so," I replied coldly, and rang off.

P.S.—Tell Saunders he really must be careful what he does and says to people.

380a JERMYN STREET,
LONDON, W.

This is getting awful. The Manager of the Splendid Steam Laundry Company has written to me to say that he has not yet received the two shirts belonging to Mr. Bayham, which, he understood, I was sending to him, and this Mr. Bayham himself wants to know where I got his shirts from. The truth is no use in such circumstances, and is never believed. So I went the whole hog and said the shirts were with a friend, and while I was out Saunders got on to Mr. Bayham and said the shirts were with old Seabright, who objected to my going on all fours the other day. Well, now Bayham has told the Splendid Steam Laundry Company to get the shirts from old Seabright.

Late last night I offered to settle the matter amicably by sending Mr. Bayham two new dress-shirts, with collars thrown in, but he told me to go to the devil.

At the time Iris was here to tea yesterday, this infernal nonsense was in full swing. Both Bayham and the laundry said that Seabright denied all knowledge of the shirts, and they had both demanded the name of Seabright's laundry, which was somewhere out of town, and had been pestering them. A Mr. Mullett (of Seabright's laundry) rang me up about it, but Saunders, who answered, said he was Bayham, and everything became worse than ever. Iris said it was obvious that I badly needed somebody to look after me, but I became angry at this hint that I cannot manage my own laundry affairs. Afterwards it occurred to me what an opening I had missed, what a chance to say something burning to her.

It is all so puerile. Deuce take Mr. Bayham and his shirts!

ROUNDABOUT CLUB,
LONDON, W.

I can't stand much more of this. This morning I received a personal call from a quiet young man, who said he represented the New Dingle Model Steam Laundry. I said I had not the pleasure of their acquaintance, dreading what was to come. It appears that Saunders told the Splendid Steam Laundry Company that Bayham's shirts had been sent in error, by old Seabright, to the Cranberry Laundry. He then rang up the Cranberry Laundry, and told them if anybody asked for Mr. Bayham's shirts, Mr. Seabright had sent them to the New Dingle Model Steam Laundry. So this young man came to ask for an explanation. I lost my temper and sent him to old Seabright—an unfair trick, I know, but I am at my wits' end. Later on the Cranberry Laundry rang up and asked for Seabright's address. Saunders gave them Bayham's. He would!

To make matters worse, Bayham threatens to get a question asked in the House. Of course, I know he couldn't, although he has been a mayor, I understand. And now Iris keeps on calling me the S.S.L.C., and that impudent scamp who goes about with her, Captain Cruttwell, asked me yesterday to put his socks through the mangle. I'd like to put him through the mangle!

P.S.—Tell Saunders—no, it's no good telling him anything.

ROUNDABOUT CLUB,
LONDON, W.

To-day Bayham rang up to say that he had found the two shirts in his wardrobe, and would I forgive him for all the trouble he had caused! Pretty cool, after I've been hounded by half the laundries in England. As for old Seabright, he told Tom Watson that a man who goes on all fours and barks in Jermyn Street is capable of any trick with shirts, or anything else. So I sent him a short note, meaning to laugh it off. I said, "I'm after your shirt! Look out!"

He took no notice, but I learnt later that he showed the letter round his Club. Some people have no sense of humour.

. . . Saunders having been with me five years, I gave him and the cook, Mrs. Melhuish, permission to have a few friends in last night, as I was going out. I left them plenty of wine and whisky, and told them to make a feast of it. Judging by appearances, they did. I came home very late, and even as I opened the door, I knew something was happening. I could hear Saunders shouting, "Six to one bar one" like mad. Cook appeared to be in hysterics, and other voices, of both sexes, swelled the uproar. As it was a special occasion, I let it go, and prepared to go to bed. Then there was a knock at the door, and the night-porter said in a hoarse whisper, "There's a bobby watching the building."

"What does he see in it?" I asked nonchalantly.

The man jerked his thumb towards the noise, so I gave him a drink to smooth him, and he went away satisfied. Presently there was another knock, and the porter said there was a policeman with him.

The policeman said, "Don't want to spoil the party, sir, but it's getting late and the neighbours will be complaining." I gave him a drink, and he went off, only to return with another policeman. He said his mate wanted to be satisfied that everything was all right. I explained that it was no party of mine, and gave them all drinks —for the night-porter had come back with them. I pressed them to more, and they sat down and had several. While this was going on, Saunders came in, dressed in my shooting-tweeds, and with one of cook's old hats on. Upon my word, he looked so funny that I hadn't the heart to upbraid him. "Hullo, Jack," he shouted to one of the policemen, "I'll give you ten to four on the field." Then cook came in, giggling, and some other people I had never seen. They all began to laugh and shout.

The only dignified course for me was to go to bed. When I left the room there was a sort of scrimmage going on, and Saunders was standing on the table with an umbrella open over his head. He was shouting that when it rains a parachute is the only thing. Then he shut the umbrella and jumped from the table, yelling, "Home, Mason." What antics, eh? I finally got to sleep. Saunders did not appear till late this morning, and my poached eggs were under the toast instead of on it, which shows that even cook is not herself.

Later I discovered that my shaving-brush had been used as a stopper for a quart bottle of beer. Ah, well!

. . . Autumnal! That's the word for it. I refer to the weather, of course. I was walking in the Park yesterday when it suddenly dawned upon me that the year had turned, and that we were heading for winter. Dear me! How quickly the summer has passed. But then I often think that as we grow older time goes quicker, to keep up with us. Or perhaps we go quicker to keep up with time. Have it your own way, as they say. What? Well, I don't know. Something in the misty air got hold of me, a sort of damp feeling among the trees. I almost felt myself shuddering. I couldn't help thinking of the loneliness of winter, if you know what I mean. Crumpets by the fire, and all that, I know. But, I don't know. And then an idea rushed into my mind. It occurred to me that I have never, in so many words, proposed to Iris. And after all, a woman can't do the proposing, can she? I said to myself, "Why not put everything to the test? Anything is better than this uncertainty, surely." As the idea developed I became quite excited. Supposing it were to come off. Rapture wouldn't be in it.

Everywhere I looked there were couples sitting on little green chairs, and I sat down and thought. I tried to imagine the scene. Me proposing, and Iris with that mocking smile. I could see her head held slightly sideways, with the reddish-brown hair parted on the right, and her blue eyes. And then I said suddenly to myself, "What's the good of hesitating because of a mocking smile? Faint heart ne'er won fair lady."

I was due to be at the Waverleys' at six, and I left the Park in a sort of trance, for my mind was made up. Goodness knows how I conducted myself at the Waverleys', but I remember an interminable man telling me about pottery. Pottery? A fat lot I cared about the stuff. I got away finally, had my dinner at home and prepared to daydream with a cigar. At last my intentions are firm! She will be at the Watsons' this evening for cocktails, I know, and there shall be the scene of my great attempt. Need I tell you what marvellous plans I made after dinner? My brain was in a turmoil when I went to bed, and I longed for the night to pass, so that the thing could be decided. Really, I believe I have a chance. Something in her manner towards me. Oh, but words are no good on such occasions.

I awoke still excited this morning. It's the day! DER TAG! Eh? I am full of optimism.

ROUNDABOUT CLUB,
LONDON, W.

. . . It was like this. I almost ran up the Watsons' stairs like a chamois, so keyed-up and excited was I. I flatter myself that I talked ten to the dozen, and was the success of the party. I kept my eyes on the door, but she never came. And the less she came, the more I talked, to sustain my nerves. That fool Tom Watson kept on rallying me. "Expecting anyone?" he would say, and I would rejoin, "Yes, Greta Garbo," or something equally impossible. But as the time passed, and she did not come, I got a very empty feeling inside me. I stayed to the very last, and Tom said, "Waiting for anyone?"

I said, "No, only the Queen of Belgium."

Mrs. Watson said, "You're positively feverish."

"Perhaps I'm sickening for German measles," I said.

"I think it's something more serious," she replied.

"Income tax, perhaps," I said.

"Perhaps," she said, "and again, perhaps not."

Women have an uncanny intuition.

When I got home I rang Iris up, at least, I got Saunders to get the number, and before he called me out into the hall, I overheard him at his games. There's clearly something on between him and Blanche, her French maid. He giggled like a boy, and I heard him say "Beaucoup" several times in answer to some question from the other end. If we don't take care Mr. and Mrs. Thake will be having Mr. and Mrs. Saunders, *née* Blanche. Eh? Really! However, finally Saunders came in to tell me that Iris was out, and that she was not expected in until very late. He was blushing and looking stupid and awkward. Love is no respecter of persons.

ROUNDABOUT CLUB,
LONDON, W.

. . . I was standing talking to a group of people at my sister's when that fussy little Mrs. Harrison charged up and shouted, "Isn't it exciting about Iris?" I immediately pricked up my ears, but she stopped dead, and I saw my sister look at her. There was an awkward sort of silence, and I felt my tongue going dry.

"Is she ill?" I asked as calmly as I could.

Nobody answered me for a moment, and then someone said very awkwardly, "No. Oh, no. She's not ill."

"What's exciting about her, then?" I said.

"Well," began one of them, but my sister cut her short, and beckoned me aside. "Now, Oswald, pull yourself together," she said.

"What?" I said, feeling awful.

"Iris Tennyson is engaged to be married," she said, looking straight at me. All I knew at the moment was that all the people were watching me, and I would rather have skinned myself alive than give them satisfaction.

"Oh," I said, loudly enough for them to hear. "Is that the mystery? It doesn't surprise me in the least." And I turned round and walked back to the group. As I turned I saw a sort of twinkle of congratulation in my sister's eyes.

I at once began to talk as if nothing had happened. Presently I said with a laugh, "By the way, who's she marrying?" They told me it was an American millionaire named Brasch; an elderly man, but devoted to her. I suppose that's what they'd have said of me. An elderly man, but devoted to her.

"They're probably going to be married quite soon," said somebody.

How I blessed my public school education, which teaches the code of never parading the feelings. A Frenchman would have pulled the house down, or sobbed on the floor. A Spaniard would have stuck a knife into somebody. An Italian would have insulted people right and left. We English have other methods. Even the humblest of us tries to take his gruel like a man. But I'm mighty glad nobody there could see inside me.

They came in later. Iris looking lovelier and younger than ever, and this Brasch—a big, florid man with thick, white hair, and a very loud voice, who brayed at Iris the whole time, until I could have kicked his face in. Everybody flocked round them, and presently Iris caught sight of me and led him up. "I want you to meet my very special friend, Mr. Thake," she said to him. "You two have got to be great friends."

He said, "Pleased to know you, Mr. Thake. My little girl's told me a whole heap about you."

Why should such simple words enrage me? But they did. And every word he spoke made me more angry. He kept on about his little girl, and praised her at the top of his voice in front of everybody. Nothing seems to make Americans uncomfortable. He said he figured to see a whole lot of me, and he explained all the details of the honeymoon, and kept on winking and grinning whenever he referred to his little girl. The strain of standing there and being urbane was enough to kill a horse.

I made no attempt to talk to Iris. I couldn't. I just congratulated her and said I hoped she'd be very happy. And then I got away. It was chilly outside, and the lamps were lighted. I shambled back to my chambers feeling about ninety. "Crumpets by the fire!" I said to myself. "Another lonely winter." And when I got back home the room seemed emptier than ever, probably because the dream-creature who had inhabited it so long had gone for good. And there wasn't even a ghost in the chair on the other side of the hearth.

. . . I will go on from where I left off. After I had got home Saunders came in, grinning all over his face, and asked to speak to me. It appears that Blanche has promised to marry him, so I suppose he will be leaving me. It's funny how one forgets his faults. He's been a faithful servant, even if eccentric. Perhaps I could find room for them both. However, they are not to be married for some time.

I got a letter from Iris by the last post. She says:

"You will adore Adolf. He's so genuine. Oh, I'm so glad to be rid of all the empty life one leads. You ought to get married. Not someone like me. I would never have done. I'm too frisky. You'll love Adolf, when you get to know him. You're not to desert us. We shall probably live abroad for a good deal of the year. It's awfully exciting. Do you remember how you used to tell me I needed a man to look after me? You've got to come to the wedding. You'll adore Adolf, I know. It's going to be a real binge of a wedding. I wish you could be Adolf's best man, but he's having an old friend over from America. We're going to Brioni for the honeymoon. It sounds heavenly. All my young men, the ones you hate so, are giving me a party one day soon. The proposal was simply too priceless. No love-talk or sentiment. He said: 'I'm going to put my cards on the table, and you'll say it's a darned good hand. I don't flatter myself anyone would love me. I don't want that. Don't know nothing about it. But I want a home and a swell dame to run it. I've got twelve million dollars. Well?'

"I said, 'It's a winning hand, Adolf. Call it a deal.' And, mind you, I'd only met him twice. You'll love him, when you know him. It ought to be fine being a swell dame."

It seems to me that the poet was right. There are more things in heaven and earth, and particularly on earth, than anybody would ever dream of in philosophy. The more I come in contact with women, the less I seem to understand about them. Evidently I was never cut out for a character reader.

Iris rang up this morning to ask if I would let this Brasch have the name of my tailor. I hope they ram the tape-measure down his throat! I'm not usually vindictive, but really!

. . . I don't really see that there is any call upon me to remain in town for the wedding. Brasch is no friend of mine, and as for Iris, it is not as a guest that I dreamed of being present at her wedding. Might as well ask me to cut the cake. Or look after the luggage. Or hold up the bride's train. Surely my disappointment has earned me a little peace, without my having to go through all that grinning mockery.

I put her photograph away in a drawer this morning, and burnt all her letters. Having read them through again, I will say one thing. They never pretended. If I hadn't been as blind as an owl I should have seen how unstable she was and how frivolous. It will take a mighty subtle woman to get me to waste as much as a second of my time in future. If forewarned is forearmed, so is afterwarned afterarmed, and if you can't be wise before an event, be wise after it. Having been bitten over and over again, I will henceforth be shy. I've done with rushing in like a fool where no angel in his senses would dare to tread. There are other things in the world besides a pretty face, and moaning never yet did anyone any good. And so much for all that.

Yours ever,

O. Thake

P.S.—Tell Saunders it will be better if cook is in on the occasions when he receives Blanche; otherwise foul tongues may wag.

EPILOGUE

EXTRACT from the *Daily Express:*
The marriage took place yesterday at St. David's, Berlin Square, of Adolf Brasch, son of Adolf and Irene Brasch, of Boiling Springs, Gowntree, Illinois, and Iris, widow of Lt. Colonel Guthrie Tennyson, and daughter of Captain and Mrs. Harrison Rock of Quetta House, Aylesbury, and 43, Goodwood Gardens, S.W. The Rev. Gabriel Erskine and the Rev. Arthur Caspar officiated.

The bride, who was given away by her father, Captain Harrison Rock, wore a gown of pale red satin, with godets of lamé and brocade insertions to left and right, a broad Quaker collar of Mechlin lace, a tunic of georgette, trimmed with mouse-fur, and caught up at the waist in flounces of royal grey tussore, and gloves of Irish poplin. Her veil was an old family heirloom, and was of exquisite Youghal lace with tiny sequins of Waterford glass. Her train was held in place by a network of filigree, and was of deep lavender tulle, bordered with flaming forget-me-nots embroidered by hand. She wore small concrete ear-rings, an Egyptian bracelet, and an Abyssinian tiara, a present from her father. Instead of the customary bouquet of flowers she carried a small flowering magnolia. The bridesmaids wore the uniform of girl guides, and the bride's train was held up by two boy scouts from H.M.S. *Intolerable*. In deference to the nationality of the bridegroom, the couple were attended by twenty matrons of honour, including Mrs. Wretch, Mrs. Currie, Mrs. Fulkham, Mrs. Dervel and Mrs. Gulp. The best man was Captain "Poodle" de Sheenic. The reception was held afterwards at Cabstanleigh House, lent by Lady Cabstanleigh for the occasion.

Those present included:

Captain and Mrs. Screaming, the Misses Screaming, Captain and Mrs. "Stag" Fauncewaters, Mr. and Mrs. Tom Watson, Lady Gumboyle, Colonel and Mrs. Grundt, Lady Cabstanleigh, Miss Stultitia Cabstanleigh, Mrs. Rickthorpe, Mr. Prodnose, Dr. Strabismus (whom God preserve) of Utrecht, Mr. Roland Milk, Miss Ella Milk, Master Joseph Milk, Miss Boubou Flaring, Dr. Orlando Akimbo, Miss Daphne Akimbo, M. Serge Knockov, Mme. Boschovskiev, Halma (the Wizard Tipster), Miss Thake, Master Blakeney Thake, Mrs. Drummond Fife, Miss Topsy Turvey, Mr. and Mrs. Edward Plymsolle, Miss Mimi Drake, Miss Dimity Hood, Mme. Yellanda da Capo, Miss Sybil Elmcote, Dame Etiola Flaxen, B.B.E., Dr. Farribole, Mr. L. Gander, Lady Trasche, Mlle. Fifi Barcarolle, Mrs. Bradshaw, and Mr. Fairlie Erleigh.

When We Were Very Silly

There is a great vogue for what is called the Woogie-Poogie-Boo kind of children's book, and I am doing my best to get one ready. I don't know what it will be called, but I rather fancy *Songs Through My Hat*, or perhaps *When We Were Very Silly*. Here is a poem called "Theobald James."

I've got a silk-worm,
A teeny-tiny silk-worm;
I call *my* silk-worm
Theobald James.
But nursie says it's cruel,
Nursie says it's wicked
To call a teeny-tiny little
    Silk-
    Worm
    NAMES.

I said to *my* silk-worm
    "Oh, Mr. Silk-worm,
I'd rather be a silk-worm
Than anything, far!"
And nursie says he answered,
Nursie says he shouted,
"You wish you were a silk-worm?
You little
    Prig,
    You
    ARE!"

Here is part of a poem called "Diddums":

Slip-Slop,
Pippity-pop,
You're at the bottom and
I'm at the top,
I'm at the——
I'm at the——
I'm at the——
    TOP.

Some one asked
The publisher,
Who went and asked
The agent:
"Could we have some writing for
The woolly folk to read?"
The agent asked
His partner,
His partner
Said, "Certainly.
I'll go and tell
The author
Now
The kind of stuff we need."

The partner
He curtsied,
And went and told
The author:
"Don't forget the writing that
The woolly folk need."
The author
Said wearily,
"You'd better tell
The publisher
That many people nowadays
Like hugaboo
To read."

There are Communists and Socialists and Conservatives
        and things,
There are cranks, and dupes, and forgers and their slimy
        underlings,
There's a roaring man with a ruddy face, and another as
        quiet as a mouse——
But *I* gave a bun to the Premier when *I* went down to the
        House.

There's a man who brays "Protection," and a lady who
        curses drink,
And at least three hundred and forty-six who never know
        how to think,

There's one who cries the Millennium, and one with a permanent grouse,
But *I* gave a bun to the Premier when *I* went down to the House.

There's a wretched, lonely Liberal, with a face as long as a flute,
And a man who spends his leisure hours in making a corner in jute,
There's every shade of incompetence, and all humbug under the sun,
But whenever *I* go down to the House the *Premier* takes the bun.

Here is part of another poem from my book:

John Percy
Said to his nursy,
   "Nursy," he said, said he,
"Tell father
I'd much rather
   He didn't write books about me."

"Lawkamercy!"
Shouted nursy,
   "John Percy," said she,
"If dad stopped it,
If dad dropped it,
   We shouldn't have honey for tea!"

NOW WE ARE SICK

Hush, hush,
Nobody cares!
Christopher Robin
Has
   Fallen
      Down-
         Stairs.

"Seeing is believing,"
I've often heard you say.
My dear Sir Henry Ferrett,
I see you every day.

A SONG ABOUT WORDSWORTH

Now ole man Wordsworth, so they say,
'E loved to roam the 'ills,
Wiv 'is butterfly net an' 'is botany book,
An' a sixpenny packet o' Wills.
An' when 'e come 'ome in the twilight,
You'd 'ear 'is missus cry:
"Now, Willie, me lad, where the 'ell 'a you bin?"
And Willie' e'd reply:

"I've been looking for daisies:
  A daisy drives me wild,
An' whenever I see a primrose
  I giggle just like a child."
Then 'is wife says, "Chuck yer kiddin',
  I can't swaller that stuff—
The only daisy that tickles you
  Is a bit o' mountain fluff."

One night 'e come 'ome extra late
Wiv 'is eyes all glowin' bright
An' 'is wife says, "Where you bin to, mate,
T' come 'ome this time o' night?
An' Will 'e answers 'er promptly,
"I'm nearly orf me 'ead,
For I've found another new kind o' bird"—
But 'is missus ups and said:

"You an' yer bloomin' daisies,
  An' yer different kind o' bird,
Is about the fishiest story
  Wot ever I 'ave 'eard,
'Op off, then, back to yer 'ill-tops
  An' yer innocent nature-stuff—
An' I'll warrant the bird that sings to you
  Is a bit o' mountain fluff."

Pictorial Tennis Hints

Fig. I
Wrong way to hold racket.

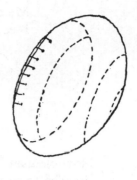

Fig. II
Wrong ball to use.

About The New Religions

A correspondent has asked me to give some details of the new religions I mentioned the other day. I will do so as briefly as I can.

Oblong Movement: Belief in Goodness as a Vital Urge.

Gaga, Ltd. (see also *Neo-Cretinism*): Rejects belief in Sin or Hope. All things exist only in so far as they are self-conscious.

Mrs. Barlington's Top-Notchers: Rejects belief in death. Nothing is what it really is. Object of Life is Self-Expression.

Sadie's Ethical Boys: Belief in love as a be-all. Men wear no waistcoats. Women bishops.

Juggo: Transrhenanism under another name. Rejects belief in everything.

Upandup: Has been called transcendental rotarianism. One thing is as good as another. Doesn't matter what you do, so long as you don't do it.

The Cœruleans: Rejects belief in Life as an entity. Members call each other "Pard." The Big Chief Pard elected for life. No laughing.

Dr. Grant Armitage's Sky-Fans: Sometimes called the "Songbirds." Firm belief in hymns. Eat nothing. Drink nothing. Wear no clothes. Simplification-urge is a major tenet.

My Play

Here is a scene from the first act of my play, of which I spoke recently. Peter and Minette have come back from a dance at 5 a.m. Peter is playing the piano softly, while Minette smokes a cigar dreamily, leaning back in an armchair. Suddenly Minette interrupts the playing.

MINETTE: Peter.

PETER: Yeah.

MINETTE: Oh—I don't know—Peter!

PETER: Um.

MINETTE: It's all so——

PETER (*leaving piano*): I know.

MINETTE: It's so frightfully difficult to be oneself. Peter——

PETER: Ur.

MINETTE: Do you feel that?

PETER: Course I do.

MINETTE (*leaning forward, tense*): I say, how thrilling.

PETER: Ah. (*He rubs champagne behind her ears.*)

MINETTE: Aren't we rotten?

PETER: Rather! To the core!

MINETTE: Why is it?

PETER: One must be something.

MINETTE (*slowly and in awe*): One—must—be—something—(*with a cry*) Peter! I believe that's the solution. That's what's wrong with the world. [*As this is the big speech, she speaks to the audience instead of to Peter.*] We're all too—none of us has the courage to come right out into the open. One—must—be—something. I expect that's what dear old George meant. After all, if we aren't something, what are we? If we could answer that, life would be simple again. Oh, there's too much of everything! Peter, don't you sometimes want to—— Oh, you know. Don't you ever say to yourself, "All this is so useless"? Where's it leading? Look at Marjorie. Look at Tom. Look at us. All this—and then—oh, one can't—but one's got to. I reckon it's something or nothing. And here we all are—wasting life, when we might be Being all the time. Being's the thing. One—must—be—something. Oh, Peter, can't we learn from life?

PETER (*serious*): Not unless life learns from us. There's too damn' much of it all.

MINETTE (*breaking down and sobbing hysterically*): And it all comes to this! Something! Something! Something!

(CURTAIN.)

Anodyne

OLD LADY: And what did you do in the Great War, my man?
TRAMP: I was in the Air Service.
OLD LADY: Ah! A flying man?
TRAMP: No, mum. The general's barber.

The Concert

(*Round by Round*)

ROUND I.—Singer and orchestra advanced from their corners. Orchestra led with a bang. Singer replied with a piercing scream to the ears, followed by a series of strong nerve-jabs. Singer's round.

ROUND II.—Singer led with a great bellow like a wounded ox. Orchestra retaliated, and for a moment singer was inaudible. Orchestra, still attacking, smothered singer with hurricane blows from trombones and other brasses. Singer tottering, but rallied superbly. Was attacking when the drum beat to end the round.

ROUND III.—Both going all out, but fighting wildly and without any art. Singer screaming and bawling, orchestra smashing away. Singer appealed to the conductor against foul blow by piccolo, and was groggy for a few seconds after it. Orchestra down for two seconds, but up again and attacking gamely.

ROUND IV.—Superb lightning rush by orchestra swept singer to the floor. Singer, though struggling to rise, counted out. Orchestra declared winner.

Among the Novels

Drab: by Gloria Higgs (Thumbcurse and Digley: 7s. 6d.)
(*Reviewed by Agnes Chough*)

I do not often use the words genius, masterpiece, stupendous, wonderful or brilliant. But each of these words is the only one to apply to this overwhelmingly real story of a girl's struggle for her essential self.

Miss Higgs has a sense of values, a perception of psychological nuances, a grasp of character and action, that will place her at one bound in the forefront of modern writers.

Only Miss Biggs has a more fragrant style. Only Miss Wiggs has a braver mind. But not even Miss Miggs could have written the really shattering scene in which the heroine, Valerie, gives up midnight bathing with Levantines and vows to start a new life with Geoffrey, her first and third husband. A book in a million.

Never be deceived by the tears of women, now that they have learned the trick from the film actresses. There are enough sham tears in a sixpenny box of Weepo to break three hearts, and each tear is stuck on by a tiny drop of glue affixed to the back.

Which reminds me that when Napoleon saw the Roman amphitheatre at Verona, empty and silent, he said, "Tiers, idle tiers"—speaking, of course, in French.

PRODNOSE: Then where's the joke?

MYSELF: *Étages, oisifs étages.*

PRODNOSE: But what is the joke? What exactly is the point of it all?

MYSELF: You must find that out for yourself.

PRODNOSE: Then there really *is* a joke in it?

MYSELF: Oh, yes.

PRODNOSE: Thank you. I will read the thing more carefully.

MYSELF: That's right. I should.

Sonnet

What are these horses of the moon? What hoofs,
  Soundless as shadows, beat a timeless dance,
Light as November snow on distant roofs,
  Swift as the sudden glint upon a lance?
What majesty, from what immortal sires.
  Garnered in æons long ago forgot,
Burgeons anew? From what undying fires?
  Into what immemorial melting-pot?
These are the horses of the upper air,
  Mist-hidden with the morning in their eyes,
Remembering how they crouched in that foul lair,
  Where no wind whispers, and no wild bird cries.
These are the horses of the crescent moon,
Who came, alas, too late, and went too soon.

Lady Cabstanleigh Condescends

I understand that Lady Cabstanleigh has at last yielded to the importunities of the publishers, and is writing her memoirs. They should make good reading, since she sat on a bishop's knee at the

early age of three; and though Tennyson's *Enoch Arden* was not literally inspired by her, yet he was staying with some friends of her great uncle's when it was published. She never met Browning, but has one or two good stories of him, collected from books about him. Her memoirs will probably be called "Me," a nice, intimate, informal title, and she has already received many letters from people who want to be mentioned in her pages.

Stray Bats from my Belfry

In Lady Cabstanleigh's memoirs there is a very interesting account of how she once saw Lord Tennyson. Let her tell it in her own words.

"I was at the house of H——, who was an intimate friend of my father's. During the afternoon I noticed a tall man eating bread and butter.

" 'That,' said Lady G——, 'is Lord Tennyson.'

" 'The tall man with fair hair?' I asked.

" 'No,' she replied, 'the man with the big beard.'

"I immediately approached him and said, 'And can you really be the gentleman who wrote that wonderful verse, "We Are Seven"?'

"He seemed angry at being recognised, but, after a moment, replied to my question, 'No; I can't.'

"I never saw him again, but my sister once met Mr. William Morris."

Stultitia's Comedy

Here is interesting theatrical news. Stultitia Cabstanleigh has had her little play produced at the Mayfair Theatre. It has no title—a fashion that may spread rapidly—and it is described as a *soufflé*. The first night audience laughed heartily at the witty lines, and the talented authoress herself, sitting on a dais in full view of the auditorium, rang a small bell before each joke or epigram, as a signal for the chattering to die down.

Several young men in the stalls were so enthusiastic that they demanded encores in the case of many of the epigrams. The action of the play was held up many times in this manner, and the authoress made a pretty speech, pointing out that the good lines would occur often during the last two acts—so that there would be no need to encore them.

I really cannot resist printing one or two of the more brilliant lines below:

Life must be lived to be believed.
A cynic is a man who eats the cherry and leaves the martini.
All men love the thing they kill.
Life is a trifle—but sherry makes it tolerable.
Life should always be true to itself.
Death is such a crude anti-climax.
You can't be sure of a woman who sneezes.
She has a Rolls body and a Balham mind.
No woman of forty can afford to be happy.
Life is so like an apple. Take off the peel, and it turns a drab brown.
Nothing is really worth doing.

More Wit from Stultitia

In response to a demand for a few more witty lines from Stultitia Cabstanleigh's play, I have pleasure in bringing forward the following:

Lady G: Who is it, Mary? Mary: I'm not sure, madam. It's dressed like a woman, but it has long hair.

My dear, marriage is a vulgar effort on the part of dull people to bring boredom to a fine art.

A woman is like a pencil. She must be led.

Eating foie gras with an unintelligent man is like dancing a tango in diving boots.

It isn't meeting people that matters; it's making them meet you.

It's the price of things that keeps Life exclusive.

Every modern poet has his favourite Mews.

The fly in the matrimonial amber is generally a wasp.

She loves romance with a small "ah!"

Love, my dear Sir John, is like a motor-'bus—easy to get into, but the devil to get out of.

It isn't meeting people that matters; it's making them meet you.

Social Jottings

I looked in at Mrs. Screaming's cocktail party yesterday afternoon. Lady Cabstanleigh was there. "I have just come from the new beauty parlour," she said to me. Mrs. Screaming, who happened to overhear this, cried loudly,

"I suppose it was shut."

Roland Milk

Moonliness

By ROLAND MILK

(I)

The moon and I
Came face to face
In a sequestered
Country place.

I thought the moon
Was heavenly ;
I wonder what
It thought of me.

Interlude

PRODNOSE: Do you notice how the franc has fallen?

MYSELF: Of course, I do.

PRODNOSE: What should be done about it?

MYSELF: It should be stabilised.

PRODNOSE: Ah, and how would you set about it?

MYSELF: By a process of stabilisation.

PRODNOSE: How exactly——

MYSELF: I would do so much stabilising that the franc would recover, and finally remain normal.

PRODNOSE: What is this trick of stabilisation, of which you talk so much?

MYSELF: It is based on the stabilising process, you see. One stabilises——

PRODNOSE: (looking like a fool): Oh, I see. Thank you.

MYSELF: Only too glad to have been of assistance.

A LOWLAND JAUNT

I SHALL GO NORTH

As I passed down the street the mellow tones of the electric drills blended soothingly with the machine that was blaring swamp-music from the open door of a shop.

Said I to myself (said I): "I will get out of this for a bit and find a quiet place or two. I will go northwards into Scotland, and take drovers' paths and forgotten tracks. And I will keep away from main roads and noisy hotels and wireless and motor-bicycles."

To-morrow I am going to slip out of London by a back door looking northwards, in order to avoid the demonstrations of the crowds.

To make perfectly certain that I am not recognised, I shall follow the example of the shy film-people, and spend to-night in the biggest and most vulgar of the new hotels, being photographed incessantly in the lounge.

One of my objects is to convince myself that it is still possible to walk without becoming a boy scout, a hiker or any other kind of modern ghoul. I shall not dress up for the part or take letters of introduction to the organisers of camping holidays, but shall go my own way, as I have always been accustomed to, when walking.

I shall sing—principally songs of my own, since every man should compose the music for his own words; and whenever I can I shall debate and brawl.

While, on the one hand, I shall deny myself such pleasures as describing Sauchiehall Street, Glasgow, on the other, I shall endeavour to reduce the blue-sky-bird-song stuff to a minimum.

I am no disillusioned fake-poet trying to heal his heart under the broad sky, but merely a man who wants to look at an unfamiliar world for a while.

And stap me, it will go hard with those who flout me or in any way incur my displeasure. For in my hand will be a staff the size of a house, which none but I can wield.

My itinerary will not be set down here in advance, for the almost babyishly simple reason that I have not got one.

If I strike a dull patch of country, or a bestially industrialised area, neither the loutish inhabitants nor the kings of commerce will see me for dust.

Nor shall I scruple to use the train or the motor-car in such circumstances, since I am under no vow to walk, and have no desire to make the thing a sheer torture by being obstinate.

It will be no good saying to me, "Oh, you fool, why didn't you go to the Outer Hebrides, instead of messing about on the Cheviots?" since my time is limited, or, "What? You were in Edinburgh, and did not describe such-and-such a spot! Didn't you even see the Thingamebob?"

Anybody who wants all that can get it out of a guidebook.

Let me add, as a last word, for the benefit of the Health Maniacs, that I am not having special hygienic boots made; nor shall I wear football breeches, or queer shirts, or load myself up with ground-sheets, thermos flasks, and all the rest of it.

Nor, I fear, shall I spring from my bed at 6 a.m. to do breathing exercises.

Adieu! Adieu! my native shore. . . .

IN THE TRAIN

Trust me to leave London at the really fashionable moment.

If, however, I had waited another few days I could have said to the porter, "What are the birds like up there this year, my man? Are they flying well? Steady with that creel, and mind the guns. They are loaded, in case I spy a bird from the train window. Put the worms and flies in the van, please—but keep them separate. Ah! How do, Sir George. Going up for a bang? The tang of the moors, eh? Yes, upon my word."

I write these winged words in the train which is taking me to Hexham, in Northumberland.

As to Hexham itself, it can go hang. You will get nothing out of me about it, because I am going to turn my fine nose to the Cheviots as soon as I am out of the train. I shall pause to look at it, and no more, taking in the old Abbey Church of St. Andrew, about which you all talk so much.

I am told that there is a fine view of the countryside from the monastic ruins west of the church-yard. I shall deign to investigate the matter, and to assuage your thirst for the truth.

I see, from the map that is spread out on the seat beside me, that I can make my way to the Roman Wall by paths. I shall cross it, sleeping to-night I care not where—but (if I can find such a thing) at an inn by the Tyne, on the way to Bellingham.

Some may wonder why I do not make for Otterburn, and the battlefield, and the memory of the Ballad of Chevy Chase, which moved Sir Philip Sidney, so he said, like the sound of a trumpet.

The reason is because Otterburn is on the main road, and also off the route I have chosen. My way lies west of that road and across country which, to judge from my map, is treeless, roadless, very hilly, and as wild as one could wish. The main road crosses my way northwards a few miles from Jedburgh, which is my objective.

There is in this carriage with me a man who, were I to allow my imagination to run riot, would persuade me that I was already embarked upon one of those strange adventures about which "Sapper" writes.

He is wearing thick blue glasses, and his hat is pulled down almost over his eyes. Beneath it, what is obviously a wig protrudes. He is huddled up in his corner, and I cannot tell, for the thickness of his spectacles, whether he is sleeping or watching.

What if I leap up, tear off wig and hat and spectacles and cry, "Aha! de Virolay again! I thought so!"—or, "Dirty Dan, by Jove! What have you done with Primrose?"; or, "Well, Schaufgotz, so we meet again!"

The worst of going on like this is that when you are wrong you look such a fool.

Perhaps the man is merely an editorial plain-clothes man, ordered to shadow me, and to see that I don't write all this in the "Temple Bar".

If that is the case, I will lead him a fine dance across the fells, until he screams to be recalled by telegram.

The only other occupant of my carriage is, I think, Something in the City. His eyes are as shifty as the eyes of a shrike, and I wouldn't trust him with a penny for his starving grandmother.

My instinct is to lean across, tap him on the shoulder, and murmur, "The game's up. Chuck it, while there's still time. I give you fair warning."

And he'd probably turn out to be a harmless violinist.

One good game when you are sick of the train is to begin to grimace at your fellow-travellers; sudden, sharp, diabolical grimaces. It may even lead to them pulling the communication cord, in which case you say, with dignity, "I am to blame for alarming these gentlemen. I have swallowed my watch."

After that there is even a chance that they will be made to pay the fine.

I am now going to sleep, and a murrain on you all.

HEXHAM

The rain was pelting down from a hopeless sky when I sprang, with a snarl, out of the carriage, and advanced through the cringing crowd.

When the chief citizens had been summoned to the market place, I addressed a few well-chosen words to them. "*There is one thing your town lacks*," said I, "*and that is some kind of statue of me. If I were you I should start a subscription at once.*"

"But what have you done for us," inquired a prominent shopkeeper, "that we should so honour you?"

"It is enough," I replied, "that I have paid a visit to your town."

It is, in truth, a happy, peaceful little place, and, as far as I can judge, the only bellicose element in it is a sect which has stuck up a notice over the door of a hall: *Fire and Blood!*

Well, if that is all they want, I can give them plenty of it, but I am in rather a hurry to get off towards the Border. So the marauding and the slaughter must begin at once.

The boasted view from the Abbey grounds wouldn't interest a blind ox, for the simple reason that there is nothing but mist to see.

This curse of mist has always robbed me of my great views. When I toiled up to the Faucille Pass to see the mountains of Savoy it was the same story.

I am dogged by mist wherever I go, and the psychoanalysts have probably got a Graeco-Latin name that fits the case.

Had I but brought my Strindberg or my Ibsen, all would be golden sunlight once more in my soul, but there was no room in my pack for them, without leaving behind my Proust and my dumb-bells. *Unthinkable!*

I am not at home in the taverns yet, because the dialect is very strong. Most people seem to be talking Lowland Scots, Scotch, and Scottish, or what you will.

One man, the easiest to understand, asked me if I intended to devote much time to the Roman Wall. I replied that I was up here to see about restoring it, as it seemed to be too easy to slip out of one country into the other.

He said, "Whoever puts that job in hand must have a lot of money."

Whereupon I hinted that the Government would pay for it.

That threw the whole assembly into a fury.

"*That will mean more taxation,*" said a gaitered farmer.

"But we have representation, don't forget," said I.

That pacified them a little, but they clearly thought the whole business was an unnecessary expense, and one man said "Passports, I suppose," in a surly voice.

One curious thing, which I have not seen mentioned anywhere in books. *The Hexham women all walk sideways.* They come at you on the pavement like footballers about to give you the shoulder.

Is this a physical disability? Is it a local tradition? Is it the latest Border fashion? Is it hatred of strangers? Is it stupidity? Is it a joke?

I can make nothing of it at all. The men walk about in a normal way. So do the children.

I shall have one more shot at the view from the Abbey grounds, but by that time these words will be speeding towards London, and it is possible that you will never know what I saw.

But if I have been baulked, so far, of a view, I have had one stroke of good luck. I see, in the local paper, enormous headlines about a "Rally of Hikers" somewhere near here.

I shall keep the name in mind and avoid it like the plague: creeping, if I can, unobserved up the Vale of Tyne.

I had no idea that Hexham was a great centre for the wool trade, and for the making of gloves. But this is so, and apparently there used to be a famous make of glove known as the Hexham Tan.

And now a sop to those who want to know about the Abbey. In style it is Early English—that is to say, it was finished in the twelfth century.

It contains a Sanctuary Chair or Frith Stool, a fine Rood Screen and a nine-foot monument of a Roman on horseback threatening a Briton.

Now are you happier?

The market-place pleases me greatly. There is an old Cross, and the people stand about and gossip in groups. The best buildings are of old grey stone, not unlike the grey stone of the Cotswolds—or, if you will, of Somerset.

The streets have not yet lost their character. That is to say, they meander. But I believe they are being widened and spoilt as quickly as possible.

I suggest the market-place for my statue.

And now it is high time to shake the dust, or rather mud, of Hexham off my boots, and to go forward boldly and with much noise towards the village called Wall; and so over the Wall and on up the Tyne Valley into what I am told is magnificent country.

Hexham, farewell. One day you will realise, little town, what manner of man you entertained.

STAND BY WITH YOUR BLOODHOUNDS

The moment I had left Hexham the mist rose with an audible sigh of relief. The result of this was that from the top of a hill above a village called Acomb I had a superb view of the little grey town carrying the huge Abbey upon its shoulders.

The great central tower dominated the whole landscape, and I immediately began to thank heaven for the sight.

It was doubly surprising, because Hexham under its hills looks like any English small town, but instead of the spire of the parish church, there is this monster challenging the sky.

On a bridge over the Tyne I met and talked with the first man who had the guttural "R" of Northumberland, but everybody had it after that, and they all said it was going to rain. And it did.

I kept to the road for a while, but when the rain began I trespassed, and discovered a little wooden shelter which a gentleman had built for his pleasure on the right bank of the river.

Here I sat watching the rain and the midges dancing on the water, and composed a piece of music called "The Dance of the Midges." Its lilt bored me after a while, so I emerged from the shelter and went on through thick undergrowth, terrifyingly large plants and beastly quagmires.

And for my pains I had to come all the way back, as the path was a cul-de-sac.

In comparatively high dudgeon, I took to the moors, which I christened George, Othello, or Abd-ur-Rahman, according to my mood.

At first they were no wilder than the Sussex Downs, with the same farms in wooded hollows. But after the Wall they became savage, and snapped at me as I passed.

But, stay. What of the Wall?

I found a bit of it in a small wood, and also the abutment of a Roman bridge, the heavy stones moss-grown, but still in place. It was a bridge that led across to a fort which remains to-day.

I sat down and looked at it for a long time, and thought of the pavement at Bignor, and then of all the relics of those conquering men up and down the world.

But I rose with a light heart, singing as I went "The Song of the Wall" which I had made up.

THE SONG OF THE WALL

When Hadrian built the Roman Wall
To keep the horrid Scots away,
He didn't build it long enough
Or high enough or strong enough,
And look at us to-day!

The business men come tumbling in
With rock-hewn brow and granite chin,
Leaping old Hadrian's garden wall
Like children come to play.

If I had built the Roman Wall
You wouldn't see a Scot to-day,
For I'd have built it quick enough,
And tall enough, and thick enough,
To keep them all at bay.

And every wandering mother's Jock
Might wander by his native loch,
The right side of the garden wall,
For ever and a day.

By the way, there is an inn called Hadrian's Hotel in the village named Wall. How much better it is to preserve the decencies than to call it the Splendid.

On the moors the plover cried; and the sound is like the creaking of a badly-oiled door. Let the ornithologists put that in their snares and smoke it. Also a bird with a call like a falsetto whinny, and a very long beak, rose from a hummock at my feet and made the day hideous with its noise.

What was marked on my map as a footpath was practically invisible. No rabbit could have followed it, and I discovered later that even the field-mice had to go in single file along it.

Here on the moors there were no roads, but only tracks from one farm to another, and little burns, and low stone walls. The whole landscape was in tune with the lowering sky, but the distances had none of those lovely misty blues that you will only see in Western Ireland.

A high wind was driving the dark clouds before it, and sudden gusts of rain swept against my face as I trudged on.

Then suddenly out came the sun, and I climbed over a rise and saw far off the ribbon of the river twisting between the meadows, and a compact village on its banks.

I shall not disclose the name of the village. Nobody nowadays should risk such a thing, with all these Scouts and hikers going about. I will only say that when I came into its streets I thought I was in Bolsano or Garmisch or Interlaken, or any other mountain centre.

Men with strong nailed boots passed to and fro, dressed as they pleased, and not in the silly walking uniforms of to-day.

The inn is a delight to the eye, and here I shall stay for the night. Even as I write, mound upon mound of meat is being trundled up the stairs for me.

On an old chest is set the candle that will light me to bed, and assuredly only happy dreams await him who lies down here to sleep.

So far I have drunk no notable beer, but when one is thirsty there is no time to worry about that.

Only two Boy Scouts have dared to come near me. I met them both on a road. One I threw into the Tyne, and the other I gave in charge for vagrancy.

The sight of these hobnailed boots is alarming. It looks like glaciers ahead, and I have sent a small boy to the village shop to buy me a length of rope and an ice-axe; an ordinary axe will do, however.

I have also warned the police that if I am not in any of the Border public houses to-morrow evening they are to send out St. Bernard dogs (or any dogs they can get hold of) to look for me. Expenses to be charged to Miss Betty Nuthall.

CROSSING THE CHEVIOTS

The lark was still snoring when I sprang from my bed, dressed hastily and prepared to cross the Cheviots by the path I had chosen. It was my intention to reach Jedburgh by nightfall   a stretch of between thirty and forty miles.

Outside my window I could see thin rain, and something told me, before I had looked at the sky, that I was doomed to kick my heels all day here. When I went outside my fears were confirmed. The sky was leaden, without a break and the rain was beginning to settle to a steady downpour.

The prospect of crossing lonely hills by an uncertain path in such weather appalled me—particularly as I should be soaked and dispirited before ever I began the crossing. I am still several miles from the beginning of the task.

Last night a man gave me two useful bits of information.

(*a*) You can cure a Cocker spaniel's cold by giving it snuff.

(*b*) If this ruddy Government were out we could start to get something done.

He gave me both these bits of information with hardly a pause between them.

The rain stopped at about 9.30, and cramming these notes into my pack, I paid my bill and started off at a breakneck speed, and I am at the moment sitting on a knoll about a thousand feet up. I can see right over the North Tyne valley to the distant pikes and fells of Cumberland—a magnificent view—wild, deserted, and with the way along which I have come winding across the heather.

A strong wind is blowing black and grey clouds south-eastwards, but they are very high, and I may escape more rain. A man I passed some miles back told me I had a good path all the way, and that it finally became a green road—one of the old roads, now disused, by which the coal carts used to go.

I cannot, of course, get to Jedburgh to-night, owing to the late start; and, furthermore, there is more up-hill business than I was led to believe. As soon as you get to the top of a rise, you have to plunge down to cross some tiresome but very beautiful burn. The air is full of the sound of running water.

I have never been in such a lovely spot in England.

Having rested myself, I shall move on.

And now the adventure is over, but you will not know the end of it till to-morrow.

The last human dwelling I passed will long be remembered. A woman who was leaning over a gate made a meal for me, and by that time I sorely needed it. I found it very difficult to understand what she or her husband said. And there was a little lad, whom they called Hob, who was completely unintelligible.

During my meal I consulted the map, and the strangeness of the names formed a song in my head.

THE SONG OF THE NAMES

By Cushat Cleugh and Scrathy Knowe
　　By Saughy, Scand and Skill,
Along the edge of Pepper Law,
　　And over Spithope Hill,
From Shielsknowe Stones to Peden Burn,
　　And under Dandie's Scree,
Along by Houx and Skidden Pike
　　There's not a man like me.

From Wheelrig Head to Hophills Nob,
　　From Lodden Bent to Skell,
By Butter Tofts and Arks Edge Rig,
　　And over Hindhope Fell,
Past Fawhope Shank and Huel Crag,
　　And out to Catcleugh Lee,
'Twixt Wether Moor and Corby Moss,
　　You'll meet no man like me.

GRAND CHORUS
Seek you from Pedlar's Shaw to Knock,

From Kiln Sike to Deerlee,
From Kielder to Jed Water Ford,
You'll meet no man like me.

I also made up a song for the refutation of the macrocephalous Swinburne, who said that even the weariest river winds somewhere safe to sea. Deadwater Burn winds nowhere safe to sea, unless it burrows, like the Mole near Guildford, or the Garonne in the Val d'Aran, and reappears somewhere else.

Anyhow the song says:

Unlike the Severn or the Thames,
The Avon or the Dee,
The waters of Deadwater Burn
Will never reach the sea.

Other rivers may be substituted to suit all tastes, as for example:

Unlike the Tagus or the Rhone,
The Oder or the Spree,

and so on.

After a good meal I set out again.

THE BORDER

As I went on after my meal the path mounted higher and higher until I seemed to be walking on the very top of the world.

A gale of wind buffeted me, and soon the rain came driving over the hills and valleys, which were dotted with sheep, looking like white snails you could pick from the hillside, as a woman in Galway once said to me.

The path became almost indistinguishable from the long grass and heather, and soon I was floundering along in boggy ground, and looking anxiously ahead, either for a break in the storm-clouds, or for some sign of a human being who might assure me that I was on my course still.

The day was far spent when I came down a soggy track, crossed by innumerable burns, and found myself on a hard road. Clearly I had come out of the hills too soon.

I dragged myself along—making but four miles in two hours.

While I was sitting under a wall to shelter from a violent rainstorm I saw, blundering towards me, a 'bus. It seemed to me to be the prettiest 'bus I had ever laid eyes on. I rose, shook myself, halted the 'bus, and got inside, and so my weary body was conveyed the last few miles into Jedburgh, like that of any ordinary hominoid.

It was after 6.30 when I was picked up, and I was ready for my dinner in Jedburgh.

Jedburgh is as lovely a little town as I know. For a man coming out of those high wastes, wet and dirty and weary, I can think of no happier harbour. It is small, neat, with an air of antiquity, and full of repose. Exhausted though I had been, I recuperated rapidly, and went out in the evening to look at the town—particularly at the Jed Water, which begins its life out on the desolation of the Kielder Moors, and enters Jedburgh under ancient trees. Above it are curious little cliffs of almost crimson sandstone.

I fell in love with Jed Water, and intend to follow it to-day until it falls into the Teviot.

The great shell of the abbey dominates the town, and I stood looking at the sky through the broken arches; and at the surviving rose-window.

There is a French air about the place. You come round a corner and find yourself looking at the pointed towers of the Loire country, or at a Mansard roof. Queen Mary had a house which stands to-day, with a garden running down to the river, and Bothwell is said to have visited her here. It is in Queen Street—and they have put red tiles on its roof!

Some day I hope to return to this restful little town, and walk about its streets.

The weather is again foul, but who cares about that? Certainly not you, sitting at ease in your comfortable office chairs, gossiping gaily together, and with a sound roof over your heads.

Ah! but do you not envy me, for I am about to go quietly along Jed Water, to find whatever there may be to find; to lie in little woods, musing; to leap streams; to sing as I go?

The beer is excellent, and the people appear to be exceedingly happy, making you welcome in bar-parlours, and saluting you in the streets.

Not one wireless instrument have I heard since I left Hexham, and if I can trust my map I shall not be plagued to-day, any more than I was yesterday, by motor-bicycles.

WALKING IS BEST AFTER ALL

If thou would'st view Melrose aright,
Go visit it by pale moonlight.
If thou would'st view Melrose awrong,
Go visit it by sharrabong.

Scott would be the first to forgive me for thus twisting his lines; since the whole place is stagnant with parties of tourists, and the streets are cluttered with cars.

But I cannot complain. I have walked from Jedburgh to Melrose by a way of my own, through high woods, and by tangled paths. Though the going was abominable, the trees kept the rain off me. And in the afternoon the sun came out to join me.

I said good-bye to my dear little Jed Water where she joins the Teviot, forded the Teviot with a shout, and found what was marked on my map as an old Roman road in the woods.

In the matter of the Teviot, I sang this little song:

For one who's crossed the Cheviots
A river like the Teviot's
*   A joke and nothing more.*
I'll simply take a single jump
And land in Ancrum with a bump
*   They'll hear from shore to shore.*

As a matter of fact, I missed Ancrum on purpose, and took to the woods.

I came under the shoulder of Pinielheugh, on top of which, striking the stormy sky, is an enormous thing like a lighthouse. It is the memorial of the battle of Waterloo.

Between 10.15 and 1.30 I passed five people, no inns, and about twenty million sheep. In Maxton I bought milk chocolate, and later on, when I struck another road, bananas at St. Boswells. From here I went by the Tweed along a path, giving up all idea of Dryburgh Abbey, where Scott and Haig are buried, because it was full of charabancs.

I had my first draught of ale near four o'clock, as an *optima* or *bonissima fide* traveller. One look at me, splashed from head to foot with mud, convinced the landlord of my good faith.

I must return to the Waterloo memorial. From the last hill, before the descent into Melrose, I looked back and saw it over all the miles between; and behind it, faint as mist, the giants of the Cheviots.

By the roadside, right under the Eildons, which are over 1,300 feet high, I found a stone marking the place where stood the Eildon tree. Here, says the legend, the queen of the fairies appeared to Thomas the Rymer. And here, will say a legend yet to be, the Girl Guides appeared to me.

Five of them came waddling along as I stood there. I will wager they were off to practise wood-craft or some other beastly modern priggishness.

Let others describe the Abbey. Its situation under the hills, by the river, reminds me of Tintern, but it is not nearly so imposing; perhaps because it is not so isolated.

There is a gale blowing, but the sun is out. To-morrow I hope to wander along by the Tweed to Selkirk, and possibly into Ettrick Forest. I am tempted to visit Yarrow also. They say it is very beautiful. But I shall go as I please, my only object being to have fun.

I find that travel on foot still fills me with intolerance for everybody except myself.

If I meet somebody in a motor-car, I curse him for an international financier—he is probably a traveller in biscuits. If a load of happy holiday-makers goes by in a motor-'bus, I curse them for a pack of savages. If I meet a man toiling along with his luggage on his back and a staff in his hand, I curse him for an affected fool.

It appears to me that I am the salt of the earth. But what a different tale I had to tell up in the Cheviots! Had you brought me a nice luxury-car, how I would have leaned back in it—and been sorry for doing so afterwards.

There is only one way to see anything or to have adventures. And that way is by going on foot; painfully, dirtily and happily.

I bought a mackintosh in Northumberland, and whenever I contemplate throwing it away the rain begins again. It is a hog of a thing, much too big for me, and trails like a dressing-gown. And when I enter towns the young people say: "Look at that poor old man in the big coat." The ribald among them laugh openly, until I make a threatening movement with my blackthorn staff.

A sound like a muffin-bell tells me that my oxen are cooked. Good-night, and sweet sleep.

When there is a six-course meal, all in small helpings, with a forty-eight hour wait between the courses; when you ask for a bit of bread, and it is handed to you between a spoon and fork, in case the fingers of any one who hasn't rowed for Leander should contaminate it; when a special maid is kept to put detestable flowers on the table; when there is an ostentatious and utterly ridiculous wine-list—what do you conclude?

You conclude—and you are right—that the English have been at it again, spoiling something good.

In the bar there were many and varied conversations, for those present were of all sorts. Somebody said: "Is it singular or plural?" One group was discussing Sir Patrick Hastings.

But the natives were talking about mushrooms. Them I gladly joined, and when asked why they were doing so badly this year I attributed it to the weather. I couldn't have done better. From that moment I was listened to.

They told me that a certain castle on a neighbouring hill was called somebody or other's Folly. I said I had heard that before. Whenever there is a castle on a hill, that same story is told. I have only once believed it, and that was when two men in the Jura told it me, with many details which I could verify. And it was actually called La Folie.

So I told them a story about the Devil meeting Wordsworth up above Tweedside, somewhere near Ettrickbridge End.

All the Highlanders I talked to before I set out on this walk sneered at the Lowlands, and told me I was a fool to waste my time.

I am glad I did not take their advice. The Highlands are probably more beautiful but I must do one thing at a time. And first I want to see the Lowlands, and to work towards the sea, and a part where, I am told, people do not go.

When I set out this morning a man in the doorway of a house pointed to my trousers and said, "A brush-down would take a bit of the weight off you," and immediately he fetched a brush and groomed me, crying "Shoh!" and hissing like an ostler.

This he did with so many accompanying gestures of pantomime that I staggered against the wall with laughter, in which he joined. And presently we were both roaring and holding our sides, to the disgust of two ladies passing by.

He told me also that King Arthur was buried under the Eildon Hills, and I said, "One day I shall stand on Carter Fell and blow my bugle, and he will rise and ride over the border to save England, and then it will be all up with Big Business."

The man with the brush considered this for a moment, with his head cocked like a bird's. Then he laughed again, and so did I—until tears streamed down our faces in the rain. A sight for the natives.

On leaving the Tweed, I waved it on its way, at the same time uttering an offensive rhyme. For my heart was away by another river that flows in blessed tranquillity beneath Irish mountains. The rhyme said:

> *There is a river under greyer skies,*
> *For which, in dreams, I strain my hungry eyes;*
> *Could I but see it now I should not heed*
> *A miserable trickle like the Tweed.*

I passed Abbotsford, where Walter Scott lived, and climbed into Selkirk that stands above Ettrick Water. Climbed is the word. It is like getting into Cassel or Poitiers. There is a fine statue of Scott, and a noble war memorial, whose quiet dignity might with advantage be copied.

I wrote some Scott poetry by the way:

> The abbot stood on Ailsa Rock,
> Nor scorned to hear the chieftain mock
> His hoary head, his tresses grey,
> Where erst the stricken tyrant lay.
> "Fling down my targe!" the Douglas cried,
> "Ere Athole sleep by Teviot side.
> No minstrel now, I ween, may draw
> On Roderick's crags the broad claymore,
> Since by Dunvegan's magic well
> King James has heard the passing bell."
> He ceased, and Moray's shaggy glen
> Gave back the living voice again,
> Till Stomach's henchman, bold Fitz-James,
> Had gathered Leslies, Bothwells, Graemes,
> And ridden over grey Glencairn
> With Lennox Dhu——

Perhaps that is enough.

And now I am in Ettrick Forest, hunting the wild boar, and making for a small fisherman's inn of which I have been told. The rain it raineth every day, and ahead of me the sky is black. More-over, the wind with which I have romped so long has dropped. Maybe I will build me an Ark on some high hill and invite the animals in—but not the warthog, who reminds me of the society hostesses.

I SAID: "I AM THE FISH"

It has been raining all day, and I might as well have walked in the river as on its banks.

But at the end of the loathsome day I found a delightful little fisherman's haven. When I pre-sented myself, filthy, soaked, and down-at-heel, they asked me if I had been fishing. I replied that I was the fish and that I would have welcomed a hook with a large lump of meat on it at any time during the day.

The countryside is desolate, the hills are anything between 1,100 and 2,400, but the mist reveals only about twenty of all those feet. Yarrow Water rolls placidly along, but it will be finer weather before Yarrow is revisited, for all the love I bear Gaffer Wordsworth.

However, fishermen are always good company, and if they lie one can always lie harder.

This is certainly the most desolate bit of country I have seen since the Cheviots and there will be no American dancing to-night, I fear.

The names of the mountains and farms are a sweet symphony: Snouthead, Nout, Ritty Rig, Dryhopehope, Witchie Knowe, Ugly Grain, Murt Grain, Damhead, Foulshiels, and so on.

I hear that Mungo Park was born at Foulshiels, which only shows that when a man walks he ought to haul a literary gent about with him, in order to trot out the literary associations. The little chap could follow by motor-car, so as not to hurt his feet.

"Come," said I to the fishermen, "what about another cast before bed? I will wager any man here a pair of mackerel that I will land the first grayling."

The bet was not accepted, and the only reply I got was a scurry of rain against the window in the rising wind. The fishermen were not of the boastful sort. They smoked peacefully, exchanging occasional words, and listening to my endless tales of prowess in far lands; nodding their heads knowingly, and smiling.

They wore down my ranting mood until I, too, lowered my voice. And some spell put us all into a Druid sleep. We grew drowsy, and their eyes seemed to me to have a goblin glint in them.

I began to fancy that I was benighted and that the place was faery, and might disappear suddenly and leave me standing alone among the barren hills in the stormy night.

Then one of the men laughed loudly, and all was human again, and I looked at their faces and was reassured.

So ended that day.

BURNS WAS THERE BEFORE ME

Somewhere in a high wood I began to grieve because the people of the neighbourhood have so little opportunity of seeing me.

The more I thought of it, the more saddened I became, especially when I saw a man looking up at the misty moon. What did he want to look at the moon for?

Had he but realised that perhaps this was his one chance of seeing me, he would have let the moon go hang.

So presently I wrote this very bad sonnet, groaning as I did so, and rolling my eyes unhappily.

> *The moon is out to-night on Kielder Moor,*
> *And so am I. Then who cares for the moon?*
> *The Cheviot folk have got her at their door,*
> *But I, alas, shall vanish all too soon.*
> *Why, any fool, at almost any time,*
> *Can see the moon, for what the sight is worth,*
> *But I, who make for you this silly rhyme,*
> *And spend my days in barging round the earth,*
> *May nevermore attack the border-side;*
> *And long years hence, old gaffers by the fire*
> *Will tell their children, with a smirk of pride,*
> *How I came striding by, from shire to shire.*
> *The moon will rise again on Hitherdon,*
> *To lift your hearts long after I am gone.*

I grow web-footed, like the alderman's pig, when he had dragged it about the St. Pancras baths every day for two months. It is no exaggeration to say that I have not been dry since I left Hexham.

And not only is there perpetual rain, but the air is growing colder and colder, until the teeth chatter like castanets. I expect icebergs in the rivers.

It will give you some idea of the deserted wastes that are my playground when I tell you that there are no golf courses. The people who mapped the district did it, I suppose, while sitting in their armchairs. What is called a forest, for instance, is a bare chaos of grey crags and mossy boulders.

As for the paths, the mappers shut their eyes and slammed down their mapping-pens, crying, "Let's say there's one here!"

I have no compass, but a goat followed me this morning, saying, "If you had a compass, you would see the idea of calling an inn The Goat and Compass."

Yarrow Water is but an infant, crooning happily, and the mountains are making me sick.

Even the cows laugh at me over the hedges as I go by. I hear them saying, "There goes another restless fool. Why can't he sit still in a field, and chew grass. Does any one ever see us tearing along like that?"

It occurs to me that there may be floods soon, in which case surely I shall have first claim to a boat, after all I have endured.

Yarrow Water has a very beautiful birthplace. It comes toddling out of St. Mary's Loch, a stretch of dark water from whose shores the hills rise like cliffs. I walked along by the loch and watched two stately swans riding the storm-ruffled water.

Then I went on to the Loch of the Lowes. Above it, on a grass mound, is a statue of James Hogg, the Ettrick Shepherd, and some verse of his about the solitude and grandeur of the two lochs.

I crossed a little bridge and refreshed myself at what turned out to be the last inn I was to find for sixteen miles. But those sixteen miles were through the best country I had yet seen. I was never lower than eight hundred feet, and as I went on I came to clearer weather and an absolutely deserted landscape. The air was full of the sound of falling waters, and little turbulent burns crossed my path from every direction.

So I plodded on down Annandale, until signs of human activity appeared once more, and at evening I entered the little town of Moffat, on the Annan, which has a statue of a ram in the market-place. The little inn where I refreshed myself was apparently visited often by Burns, who wrote on one of the windows a piece of verse.

I made a great meal, and was pleased to remark an Englishman who had dressed for dinner. The British Raj! The white man must keep his end up when he comes to these lonely outposts of Empire.

I could imagine him forgetting to shave one day, and a fellow-fisherman saying to him, "Moffat's got you, old man. You're going all to bits."

HOW I WENT TO GLASGOW FOR A DRINK

Dark clouds threatened more rain as I came out of Moffat, and started on a three-mile climb to the saddle by which I intended to cross into Clydesdale.

The view from the saddle was superb; a tumbling sea of dark hills stretching out to the horizon on every side. The rain held off, and, singing *Follow me Down to Carlow*, I went along at a tearing pace.

I came down on to a moorland road, which, the moment it saw me, began to climb again. As mile succeeded mile, the old trouble of the walker—thirst—descended upon me. Nor could I expect an inn, however closely I looked for it on my map. It promised to be another droughty day, with rain-water as the chief dish at the banquet.

I was going strongly onwards, still climbing, when a small motor-car slowed down, and a young man with a carefree face asked if I would like a lift.

I said I would gladly take one as far as the next house of refreshment.

"If you want a drink," said he, "Glasgow is about the nearest place. Jump in."

"How far is it?" I asked.

"About fifty miles," said he.

So I got in, and a very delightful journey it was. He told me that he purveyed animal medicines; or, in other words, cast physic to the dogs, cows, sheep, goats, and so on.

We passed the village which I had marked down for my night's resting place, and he assured me that 'bus or train would get me back to it, so that I could start off to-morrow according to my plan.

Suddenly, looking full at me, he said, "You are not a hiker."

"No, thank heaven," said I.

"Beachcomber is walking up north," he said.

"So I read," said I.

"Where have you come from?" said he. "Hexham," said I. "I am Beachcomber," "I suspected it," said he, "but I always thought of you as a tall lad with a sarcastic face."

After that we both enjoyed the joke, and he inspected my great blackthorn staff.

He dropped me at Busby, where the busby was invented, and I took a twopenny tramfare and went into Glasgow by Clarkston and Holmlea Road, to the Central Station. Here I bought papers, had my drink and some food, and found there was a train back to my night's lodging in two hours' time. So I went down to the docks and looked at the shipping, and contemplated going down the Clyde in a boat. But I dismissed the idea. The weather was too bad, and also I was expecting a telegram at the Crawford post-office.

And that is the story of how I went to Glasgow for a drink.

After a very tedious train journey I got back to my village, and while drinking a toast to myself in beer discovered a curious little children's railway that zigzags miles up into the mountains, to a place where there is a little inn. By great good fortune there is a train to-night, and I shall go by it, or perish miserably in the attempt. To-morrow I shall break the backs of several high hills on my way to the Nith Valley and Ayrshire.

And if any one complains that I am taking too many rides I will ask him to tramp the Lowland moors and mountains in wet weather for a few days, without a companion, and with no inns.

I have been amazed at the lack of inns. All the jokes about Scotsmen drinking seem to me to be pure bosh. They can't get the stuff. I have been in a small town where there was only one place licensed to sell drink!

And once more, if any one thinks I emphasise the need for drink, let him walk for a week in, lonely places in the rain.

It is pouring with rain again as I write these words, while I wait for the toy train. The glass, they tell me, is rising; but they have been telling me that day after day all along the way. I don't believe a word of it.

Probably my mountain inn is a myth. What care I? To-day has been comparatively restful, and I am good for anything that turns up. As for to-morrow—let all who care for their safety keep clear of me. I am eaten up with a longing for the coast, and the devil take these endless moors!

To-day, in the mist of early morning, I composed three Slav dances; admirable parodies, which I have been singing, on and off, all the day through. I have also composed a very heavy, gloomy,

Nordic thing called "Ibsen"; a brooding masterpiece, to which I shall set words while I am in my doll's train.

Good-night, then, my faithful and constant pests. It takes a man like me to be a man like me.

"A PARTICULARLY SILLY THING"

You left me waiting for a toy train, which was to take me into the hills.

It turned out to be what I had expected, one of those tram-trains that grunt along very slowly.

I left it at a place called Leadhills, so called because the hills are full of lead; and a dirty, dripping night it was to land in a mining village. But the inn turned out to be the perfect haven in such weather, and I was, needless to say, the only person there.

It boasts of being the highest in Great Britain, but a policeman in New Cumnock denied this hotly, and advanced the claims of one in Argyllshire.

Anyhow, it was high enough to be very cold. That night I slept the healthy sleep of a tired animal.

I made a very early start the next morning, as it looked like being fine for a short time, and I had a long way to go before I should be near shelter.

And I did a particularly silly thing, and one that nobody with my experience of hills would normally do. I tried a heather-track that seemed to wind up over the hills, in order to save the tedious journey by road.

It turned out to be a lucky shot, as far as the general direction went, but it was so boggy that I was perpetually forced to take to the heather, and make a détour, warily. I was soaked through to the knees in no time, but the sun came out, and I had the world to myself. And when I reached the top of a very high hill I saw the mist wreathing up over Nithsdale, and far away the uncovered summit of Cairnsmore, marked on my map as 2,600 feet high. Far away below me stretched Ayrshire, and behind the distant veils of mist the sea that was my goal.

How can I describe to you the horror of coming out of the grandeur and the silence into the stink and noise and vulgarity of the main road from Dumfries to Glasgow?

However, it had to be the road, with only mining villages to pass through. One of them was Kirkconnel, but if it was Helen's lea I will eat my hat.

In Sanquhar (pronounced Sanker) a temperance hotel bore the notice *Miss Sharp, Proprietrix*. Stap me! What of the classics, boys? Can I speak to the proprietrix, please?

In Sanquhar, too, a band played in the street—Scottish tunes, and no mongrel American muck.

It was hot and thundery, and when the euphoniumist picked up his great instrument it struck me that he ought to have a special tube fixed to it, and fill the thing itself with beer. Then, while his mates laboured at the task, he could be drinking peacefully.

The bandmaster, seeing his happy smile, would say: "Ah, there's an example to us all. A cheerful disposition."

And still the euphoniumist would drink while the others blew their insides out.

I could have done with a draught of strong wine on that road, and I sang dismally to myself:

> *Where is that tarry, stenching wine*
> *They gave me up in Aragon,*
> *As thick as mud.*
> *As dark as blood.*
> *Strong as the flood*
> *Of Aragon.*

It had a body like a horse,
It was great nature's second course,
You had to drink the stuff by force
In Canfranc, up in Aragon.

DO THEY BACKBITE IN AYR?

I met an old man in a wood. He was carrying a spade, and his speech was slow and emphatic, like the speech of many very old people.

I shall not attempt to reproduce his dialect.

I asked him if it would be fine.

"Fine enough, probably," he said.

And with that I should have passed on, but he said—

"Where are you going?"

"To Ayr," said I.

"Ayr," said he. "Oh, well."

I knew he had something to say, so I waited, while he leaned on his spade and looked me straight in the eye.

"To Ayr?" he said.

"Yes," said I, "to Ayr. What is it like?"

"I've nothing against it," he said, "but I'd never wish to see any friend of mine in Ayr."

"Why on earth not?" I asked.

"I've nothing against it," he repeated.

"What is the matter with Ayr?" I asked.

"I've nothing against it," he said for the third time. "But I wouldn't wish to see any friend of mine go there. Of course, that doesn't apply to a gentleman like yourself."

"Were you unhappy in Ayr?" said I.

"I never was in Ayr in my life," said he.

"Then why do you talk of it so?"

"I've nothing against it, but I have my reasons, the same as any one else. If I had my free choice, I'd not go there if I was you."

"But why?" I shouted.

"It happened forty-two years ago," he said.

I thought he would tell me of love lost long ago, but he said suddenly and vehemently:

"I had a friend."

"Well?" said I.

"It was forty-two years ago," said he, "and my friend went to Ayr, and he had not been there a day—not an hour—before they were backbiting; men, women, and children, all backbiting. And that's what's wrong with Ayr, in my opinion, though I've nothing against it. Backbiting."

"But what," I asked, "was all this backbiting about?"

"It was just backbiting," said he.

"But what had your friend done?"

"He got on the wrong side of them."

"Of whom?"

"The people of Ayr, I'm telling you."

It was like trudging through mud to get anything out of him.

"What made the people of Ayr backbite when your friend went there?" I said.

"He didn't pay his rent for two months," said the old man, "at some twopenny lodging place you wouldn't put an owl into, and they all began to backbite because he hadn't the money to pay for the dirty old place."

"It is possible," I said presently, "that the people of Ayr may have changed a bit in the last forty years. Perhaps they have given up backbiting now. After all, you say you have never been there."

His eyes narrowed, and he answered swiftly and fiercely:

"It is true that I have not been there, and I pray God I may never set foot in the place. But they're still backbiting."

"How do you know?" said I.

"Because I have a friend who went there three years back, and he said every one in the place was backbiting, and that the wee children were brought up to backbite, and as far as he could see, were taught nothing at school but backbiting.

"You have the whole of Scotland before you," he said, "and you must choose this place where they have been backbiting for forty-two years, and probably long before that, if we only knew. If I were a young man like you, and could walk, I'd sooner walk into the sea and be fished out dead than give these people something to backbite about. Why, you could get an omnibus up to Caithness, they tell me. But if you intend going to Ayr, I suppose you'll go there."

He ended on such a sad note that I was inclined to tell him that I had changed my mind. But I did not do so, and as I left him he turned to watch me.

When I looked back two hundred yards along the forest ride he was still staring after me sadly, dreading, I suppose, the terrible backbiting into which I was about to plunge.

MY FIRST FINE DAY

As to-day was the first really fine day, with hot sunshine, I am moved to say a word about the astounding regulations with regard to drink in this country.

They say that if you have come over three miles you are a traveller, and as such are entitled to a drink at any hour on Sunday.

But when you ask for the drink you are either told that the inn has only a six-day licence, and cannot serve you, or else you have to pay an extortionate price, after writing your name and address in a book and swearing that you have not drunk at any other place in the village or town!

The thing to do is to write, "Lady Astor, House of Commons." You will then pay one shilling for a glass of warm bottled beer.

No wonder the male population goes mad on Saturday nights.

All day, after an early Mass, I walked in the strong sunshine, going by footpaths and across fields. The most amusing encounter, now that I look back on it, was with a man who, in addition to speaking an incomprehensible dialect and having no teeth, had an impediment in his speech.

When I met him I was very hot and angry, and had been tempted to throw my pack away, so heavy had it become. I realise now that I made long speeches at this harmless man, all about liberty and free will.

It was a long time before he made me understand that he was an advocate of what is humorously called temperance. Could anything be more intemperate than forbidding people to drink after fifteen miles in a broiling sun?

A repulsive little boy in a farmyard shouted "Hiker" at me as I passed. And I shouted back, "My boy, don't you believe everything you read in the papers."

In the High Street here there is a thatched house called Tam o' Shanter's Inn, and I can see that I am in for a day wi' Burns to-morrow. His cottage is near here, and also the Auld Brig o' Doon. It is a pity I do not like his verse. Tom Moore could have beaten him at a song with both hands tied behind his back.

The man who served my meal told me I was very near the famous Prestwick golf course. I told him I had been round it in bogey forty-seven times since last July. After that he looked at me with awe, and I was served with the best.

He asked me if I was golfing at the moment.

I said, "No, I am going to break a fishing record to-morrow, and the next day I shall get, maybe, a hundred brace of pheasants."

He retorted that the season had not begun. To which I replied that I never waited on the season but took my birds as I found them, and shot them dead on any day of the year. "And serve them right," I added.

I then spoke to him of polo, and the difficulty of transporting one's ponies nowadays.

"Mine travel in a pantechnicon," I said, "driven by one of my men."

Later on I saw him whispering to his wife, and trying to reconcile my horrible clothes and broken boots with such a lordly life.

This morning I saw a big slag-heap against the sky, and my mind went back to the pyramid that used to stand up against the horizon on the Annequin road, on the way up to Cambrin or Cuinchy or Braddel's Point in 1915. And I remembered how we foot-sloggers used to swear that when the war was over we would never walk another yard.

To-day has produced no verse, if I except a malediction on the creature who stood in the door-way of a frowsy tavern saying, ad nauseam, "We hae na a Soonday licence. Gae tae Ayr"; and another malediction on a young man who, some days ago, when I was trying to get draught beer in a big hotel, said in an actress-voice, "They hev burtled beah. Esk therm for thaat."

I replied, "Oh, I say! Thenks most feahfullah, d'you know, and all thet sort of raat. But may darktah has ordered me common bittah, you know. One does feel it's such a boah."

Both my maledictions are unprintable, unless incorporated in a novel by a young woman.

BURNS—AND A BOWLING GREEN

Under a blazing sun, but with a thick haze on the sea, I came out of Ayr and walked to Alloway, the village of Burns.

From the meadows where he takes his repose I am sure the shade of the poet looks down and laughs at the things that are done in his honour.

The very 'bus that brings trippers to the place is called "The Bonny Lassie o' Doon."

Notices point the way to the "Banks of Doon," and to the Auld Brig, upon which a man in a bowler-hat stood with his camera ready. He offered to take my photograph, with the Burns memorial as a background. I said the honour was too great for a normal man, and begged to be excused.

There was a machine which, for a penny inserted into a slot, promised to show a portrait of the poet. Countless booths sold reproductions of the famous Nasmyth portrait, in all sizes from Tintoretto's "Judgment" to the head on a postage stamp.

There were Burns cups, Burns plates, Burns dishes, and every kind of souvenir to prove that the possessor had actually been to the place. And, as a culminating piece of fun, in the village that was bursting itself to honour the singer and drinker, the same stupid restrictions were observed. What on earth would their hero have made of such nonsense?

On my way up into the hills again I came across one of those incomprehensible people who seem to be sent to batten on me.

This man talked incessantly, and I kept on saying "Yes" and "No." Then I caught a sentence about a place farther on that was "airched wi, rosy-dendeerums owerheid." This sentence recurred frequently.

It was ten minutes before I understood anything else.

The remainder of the day was spent in exploring the coastal villages of Ayrshire and I had my meal in the town of Girvan, a kind of smaller Littlehampton.

The scenery is magnificent all the way along, as the hills come right down to the coast-road. You can walk by the strand, or by the hills, or by the road.

After Girvan I crossed what must be the lowest Pass in Europe. It was called Kennedy's Pass and beside it the Perche, that easy saddle that leads from the Roussillon to the plain of the Cerdagne, is a monster.

Imagine toiling slowly all the way up Piccadilly to the great watershed at Hyde Park Corner, and then descending dizzily to Knightsbridge. There you have Kennedy's Pass.

I passed a village where all the old people were leaning over the bridge and watching the water swirl along seawards. They were exchanging flippant remarks, like children. A very pleasant sight.

As I proceed upon my way, the high moors and mountains of Wigtownshire begin to stand up into the sky, and I propose to tackle them to-morrow, and to get as much of the climbing as possible done before the full heat of the day. The mist on the sea has been so thick that Ailsa Craig, the big rock about eight miles from the shore, was invisible from Girvan.

A steamer visits it every now and then, but I believe there is nothing much to see except the lighthouse.

As I was examining old tombstones in a churchyard I was handed a religious tract, and later on ran full tilt into another band playing religious music. One player was having the time of his life. He made no attempt to play his part, but simply did an air of his with own, all sorts of extra twiddles and twists thrown in.

Nobody seemed to resent this. Perhaps he was of importance locally, so that nobody would dare to criticise his whimsicalities.

In the village which I have chosen as my refuge for the night there is a bowling green. I have already visited it, and noted that nearly all the players were young men. For £4 you can be a life member.

While I was watching a game the local policeman did his round of the green, as though he knew that passion plays fast and loose with a man who indulges in this seemingly peaceful game.

I select for special mention a river called the Stinchar.

ADVICE TO WALKERS

I have had two days of as varied a landscape as any one could wish: glimpses of villages hidden among trees in deep valleys; great empty heaths and high boggy moorland; glens where you can lie in the shade of tall ferns and listen to the burn-water going over the boulders; flashes of blue sea between the shoulders of hills; low meadows under the mountains.

Yesterday I cut right through the hills without troubling to find a path, and only once was the ground dangerously boggy. The heather was a furnace under a sun that blazed out of a cloudless sky, and for seven and a half hours I met nobody but an occasional drover coming up some steep track, and whistling to his dog.

It was only in the evening that I discovered how far out of my way I had come—but what did that matter?

All the same, I have been wondering which is worse: to be grilled all day, or to be drenched with rain and buffeted by wind. I think the grilling is less unpleasant.

When I arrived at my inn last night a man said, looking at my pack, "Is that all the luggage you have?" For a moment I was tempted to give him the rough answer made by Berlimpon when the witch asked him if he could spare no more than one silver coin for an absolutely correct reading of his hand.

All the luggage! ALL THE LUGGAGE!

What more would he have me lug over the boiling heather, and up and down the stony mountains, and under and over the rocks, and this way and that way in the bog, and here and there through the brawling torrents?

Did he expect me to carry a trunk on my back like a porter, or to drag a suit-case by a thick rope wherever I went? Is it possible he had not heard that I was on my way, devastating the country on all sides?

On the other hand, my blackthorn staff has been much admired. And it had better be! One sneering word spoken of it, and all its old hedgerow life in Ireland comes back to its mind. In a moment the thin veneer of civilisation is lost, and it becomes the whirling staff of a conqueror.

As I toiled along in the sun yesterday, sometimes without so much as a boulder for shelter, I was thankful that I had learned the wisdom of wearing a hat. When I was younger and more foolhardy I entered Spain over the mountains bareheaded, and next day had sunstroke. I am not risking such a thing again.

In the inn where I stayed last night, at the village of Glenluce, I had one of those chance encounters that are the delight of haphazard travel. There was an elderly gentleman staying there, who was an expert on two things—bee-keeping and the mountains of Norway, and possibly on a third—Border history.

He talked vigorously and well, and told many good stories. We breakfasted together early the next morning, and then went our ways; he eastwards, I westwards to Stranraer.

It was but a step to Stranraer, but by ten o'clock the heat was terrific again. I deposited my pack and made inquiries about the boat that is to take me to Larne. From there I go by train to black Belfast, and then through lovely Dublin to the south. After a pause for breath I rush back to London prepared to burst once more upon a wondering metropolis.

Those who would do what I have done, walk for pleasure, have a double difficulty to contend against.

They must avoid, on the one hand, the parts likely to be visited by motorists; for the motorists' country means disfigured landscape; dull, noisy roads; bestialised inns or hotels, with bad-food, high prices, and fancy drinks.

On the other hand, they must avoid this new horror, organised walking, which is being boosted to death.

Between the two a careful man may steer. I, except when I was visiting towns like Melrose and Selkirk, or going, with my eyes open, to places with literary associations—I have kept clear of both dangers for a great part of the time; but only by going where there are no roads and nothing capable of being turned into a tea-shop for the scouts and "Ramblers," and so forth.

To while away the time before my boat sailed I went to Port Patrick, which is a rocky little seaside place.

They were launching the new lifeboat, and I watched the ceremony and the trial run.

It was too misty to see the mountains of Mourne, and after sitting on a rock and dangling my legs for some time I returned to Stranraer, and to the boat that is to carry so noble a burden to Larne.

Adios, pestilent public.

FAREWELL TO SCOTLAND

Long before my boat sailed out of Loch Ryan, I noticed as I paced the deck, figures that were no more than wraiths, moving to and fro on the quayside in the mist of dawn. And as I strained my eyes in the uncertain light, it became evident to me that they had gathered there to bid me farewell.

Presently, when the mist lifted a little, a tall, middle-aged man stepped forward, and began to speak in a full voice. He explained that he represented a large deputation from all the districts through which I had passed during my journey to the sea. He apologised for the shortcomings of each district, expressed his regret that I should have been inconvenienced by thirst, or annoyed by Boy Scouts and other pests and insects of the roads.

In fact, the deputation abased itself, and awaited my pleasure.

I stood upon the deck, idly twirling my great staff, and contemplating the bowed heads of the Scotsmen. Then I began to speak. I said:

"Lowland dogs——"

At my opening words, the bowed heads were raised, and all eyes were fixed upon me, expectantly.

"Lowland dogs," said I, "in my extensive travels up and down the world, it has ever been my custom to overlook the minor faults and shortcomings of those whom I honour with my presence. If I see an ugly landscape, I forgive it. If a mountain displeases me, I swallow my displeasure. If the inhabitants are repulsive I make allowances for the philosophy or the religion in which they have been brought up. . . ."

The silence was so intense that I distinctly heard a pin drop.

"But," I went on, "there is one abomination that I cannot forgive. My hand will be heavy upon the town or village which, in its sour-faced and stiff-necked Calvinistic priggishness, forgets or deliberately ignores those conventions of hospitality which Christian men have been wont to enjoy. I will not tolerate a barred and bolted tavern door. Reflect upon this, Lowland dogs, and mend your ways."

Then I sang to them, and so loudly that the wheeling gulls fled in panic to the open sea, the following song:

> O, thirsty are the Lowlands,
>   Where only cattle drink,
> Unless a man's prepared to swill
> Bog-water from a moor until
>   His belly's like a sink.
> Thrice-damned, despairing people
>   —(I read it in your eyes)—
> Abjure your long-jawed temperance men
> Who lure you to some beastly den
>   For milk and custard pies.
>
> O doomed and hopeless Lowlands,
>   Open your eyes and see
> How Christian men in Christian lands
> Are gripping mugs in hairy hands,
>   And drinking deep like me.
> Rise up, and end this humbug!
>   Fling wide the tavern door,
> And let us wallow at the bung,
> While all the noisiest songs are sung,
>   As oftentimes before.

As I ended my song, the Captain sent a sailor to ask me if it was my pleasure that he should cast off. I assented with a nod. Then, gazing pityingly at the people on the quayside, I bade them take heart and mend their disgusting ways before retribution fell upon them.

There was a sound of sniffing and sobbing, and then, as the boat began to move from her moorings and headed for the open sea, the deputation began to shuffle away by twos and threes.

The hills on the banks of the loch slipped by, the mist rose, and a freshening breeze whipped the water into little white-crested waves.

The boat sped on, and the watchers on the shore saw my figure diminish, until it was but a blob upon the horizon. The cheers of the schoolchildren, dressed up to see me off, grew fainter. Then I lay down in the stern, with my head upon my pack, closed my eyes, and waited for sleep.

(*Scene: Beachcomber's office. Tastefully furnished. On the Louis Quinze desk, with Jacobean legs, the ormolu clock has stopped. The tin daffodils in the marble vase need dusting. The red lacquer telephone is ringing shrilly. Enter Prodnose. He rushes to answer it.*)

PRODNOSE: Hullo! Ah, good-morning, Lady Cabstanleigh. No, we do not know where Beachcomber is. We have no news of him. What? No, I'm afraid I can't say when he will be mentioning your parties again. Of course, the loss of publicity is most trying for you. Yes, I will keep you informed.

(*He rings off. Enter Captain "Stag" Fauncewaters, Mrs. Wretch, Roland Milk, Dr. Strabismus (Whom God Preserve) of Utrecht, and others.*)

MRS. WRETCH: Where is he?

PRODNOSE: Nobody knows. Some say he was last seen, overcome by beastly architecture, in Belfast.

CAPTAIN FAUNCEWATERS: I shouldn't be surprised if he hasn't been mobbed for disturbin' the grouse on the moors in Scotland.

PRODNOSE: He would not do that. He is kindly at heart, in spite of all his blustering.

MRS. WRETCH: Well, I can't say I have had much kindness from him. He made fun of Miss Wizzle's novel.

(*The telephone rings. Prodnose springs to the receiver.*)

PRODNOSE: Hullo!

THE VOICE OF BEACHCOMBER:

> Ziste! Zeste! Pas d' chagrin,
> On rigole avec du vin!

PRODNOSE: What? Hey? Whoa! Where are you?

THE VOICE OF BEACHCOMBER: Aha!

PRODNOSE: Wait! Here, I say! Hi! Hi!

(*He agitates the thingamegig, but there is no reply. He rings up the exchange.*)

Where was that call from?

EXCHANGE: Wrrrong number!

PRODNOSE: No, no. It was the right number. Where was the call put through?

EXCHANGE: Sorry you've been trrrroubled!

PRODNOSE: Where was——

VOICE: But, Gertie, darling, I can't blackmail him yet. Give me time.

PRODNOSE: Get off the line!

ANOTHER VOICE: You will sell out, Sir George, if you take my advice.

ANOTHER VOICE: And bring my shirts to the club, Mason.

(*Prodnose dejectedly hangs up the receiver.*)

PRODNOSE (*awed*): It was his voice.

MRS. WRETCH: What did he say?

PRODNOSE: He was singing one of his coarse foreign songs. It's dreadful. What are we to do? (*Wrings his hands.*)

MRS. WRETCH: Was it a French song?

PRODNOSE: I think so.

MRS. WRETCH (*covering her face with her hands*): O-o-oh! Shame! Shame! A French song! O-o-oh!

(*Curtain.*)

(Scene: Beachcomber's office. The green glass armchair is still empty. Prodnose and Mrs. Wretch are pacing the room, distraught.)
MRS. WRETCH: Still no word of him?
PRODNOSE: None.
MRS. WRETCH: Well, may I lead off with my article?
PRODNOSE: Pray do, dear lady.

BIBLIANA

By MRS. WRETCH

It is not often that we book-reviewers make use of superlatives, but it is time we all said frankly that Miss Wizzle's "Notwithstanding Clarice" is what we have all been waiting for. Never has the soul of a girl been so ruthlessly bared, and in a style that would not have shamed Mrs. Humphry Ward. The book is colossal. Its impact stuns. It is dynamic, elemental, repulsive in its agonising strength. It——
PRODNOSE: I don't think Beachcomber would print this. I'm sorry.
MRS. WRETCH: But don't you like it?
PRODNOSE: I adore it. But he has such queer prejudices.
MRS. WRETCH: Oh, very well.

DISARMAMENT

By Ex-M.P.

It is a truism of modern life that nothing is worth fighting for, and——
PRODNOSE: Hi! Stop it! He would never allow this to be published.
EX-M.P.: But——
PRODNOSE: I know him better than you do. I'm sorry.

A NEW SUMMER DRINK

By PANSY STRANGEWAYS

("*Flutter,*" *of the* "*Evening Ramp*")

Take a pint of milk——

PRODNOSE: Whoa! I beg your pardon, but Beachcomber would never pass this sort of thing. Can you make it beer?

PANSY (indignantly): Certainly not!

PRODNOSE: He's not very keen on milk.

PANSY: I can easily dispose of my writings elsewhere. Good-day!

PRODNOSE (to Mrs. Wretch): This is a most difficult business. I don't know what we can put in I wish he'd return.

MRS. WRETCH: I think you're very silly to pay any attention to his likes and dislikes while he's away. Now's your chance to put in all the things he refuses.

PRODNOSE: Indeed, you do not know what he would do to me. He says such insulting things to me when he is angry.

At that moment a distant sound of cheering is heard. Prodnose leans out of the window. Cries of "God bless you, sir! Good old Beachcomber!" are borne to him on the breeze. Hastily collecting his things he runs headlong from the room to welcome his tormentor. As he passes down the corridor he has to dodge from side to side to avoid the groups who are strewing rose-leaves on the linoleum outside Beachcomber's office.

A
DICTIONARY
FOR TODAY

A

active: A term applied to the stock market.

adequate: Adjective applied by timid dramatic critics to the performance of an actor or actress whom they do not wish to offend.

advanced opinions: Any one who advocates the destruction of the religion or the morality of Europe is said to hold advanced opinions.

aesthete: Any effeminate young man who dresses queerly.

alcohol: Any drink with however small a percentage of alcohol in it.

amateur: One who plays games for the love of the thing. Unlike the professional, he receives no salary, and is contented with presents of clothes, clubs, rackets, cigarettes, cups, cheques, hotel expenses, fares, and so on.

amendment: Copy for the lawyers.

angel: A small dog.

animals, kindness to: Kindness to nice animals.

antimacassar: A ridiculous Victorian device by which men with oily hair were prevented from staining and ruining the backs of armchairs.

architect: Jerry-builder.

Arctic conditions: A cold day in England.

artistic: A woman is said to be artistic when she wears a bed-quilt with armholes pierced in it, sits on a round coloured cushion, instead of on a chair, and fills her house with young aesthetes.

ascetic: A teetotal, non-smoking, vegetarian millionaire.

audacious: A writer who sneers vaguely and in a muddled way at such institutions as Marriage and the Family is audacious.

authority: A writer who succeeds in getting the same article, with the wording altered slightly, published by several newspapers over and over again: as in the following sentence, "Mr. Jones, the great authority on women."

autobiography: A book of gossip about other people.

avenue: The scene of a politician's explorations.

axe: A Minister of the Crown or the head of a department of State is said to use the axe when, in answer to a demand for economy, he dismisses a liftman or a doorkeeper.

B

baby: (a) A motor-car.
(b) A grand piano.
(c) An American actress.

back to nature: Living in a motor-caravan during a heat wave.

baffle: A verb used in connection with the police. Whenever a crime is committed they are said to be baffled.

ballet: Acrobatics accompanied by pretentious music.

ballet, Russian: More fantastic acrobatics, accompanied by uglier and more pretentious music.

banned: An indecent book is widely advertised as banned when there is no other way of selling it.

bargain: Any article reduced from ten shillings to eight shillings, and worth half-a-crown.

beautiful: Adjective applied to the daughter of any woman prominent in the weekly illustrated newspapers.

beauty: A luxury which can be bought at certain specified shops in the West End of London.

beer: A drink made of various chemicals in various proportions.

bijou: A French noun meaning jewel. When applied, as an adjective, to the English word residence it means any very beautiful little house.

biology: A department of novel-writing.

bogus: See Company Director.

bohemian: A young man or woman who sits on the floor at a party until some one offers him or her a lift to another party; any one who likes to eat kippers and drink flat beer after, say, 4 a.m.

bombshell: The omission of a cricketer from a team.

bottled at the château: Bottled in the laboratory.

boundary: The margin of a cricket-field.

boyish: Adjective applied to girls.

brewer: An almost obsolete word. It now means chemist.

British boxer: Jewish boxer.

British modesty: Saying that, although we are superior to other peoples, we never mention that superiority.

bronze: Word used to describe the colour of a woman's skin, after she has been lying in the sun for a week or two.

busy: Idle. Adjective frequently used to describe rich women who have nothing to do, as in the following sentence: "Lady —— is one of the busiest women in London these days."

C

cabinet: A gramophone.

Caesar: The name of a dog or a racehorse.

California: A district in the neighbourhood of Hollywood.

Capitol: A film theatre.

Capri: The name of a house in any suburb or seaside place.

careless: See "Hesitation."

carnival: An indoor cocktail party on ice.

caustic: Adjective applied to the wit of magistrates and judges, as in the sentence, "The judge then asked who was this gentleman, Mussolini, who appeared to be an Italian?"

ceremony: An official reception given to a Channel swimmer, or a distribution of prizes to boy scouts.

champagne: Any fizzy drink in a night club or a cabaret show.

champion: One who plays games well.

chaperon: This word, now obsolete, has been traced to a barbarous old social custom of the days when young unmarried girls were supposed to need protection. The chaperon was a hideous figure who hovered near her charge, and interfered with self-expression. The result, nearly always, was an inhibition and an ensuing inferiority complex.

charity: Humiliating the aged and infirm by putting them into institutions.

chattel: A woman who so far humiliates herself as to marry, to remain faithful to her husband, to have children and to manage her home, is known as a chattel.

cheers, deafening: An ovation given, under compulsion, by schoolchildren, to any one for whom the traffic is disorganised.

christening: Pouring champagne over a ship.

civilisation: Something possessed only by England, Prussia, Scandinavia and the United States.

civilised country: The civilised parts of the world are England, the United States of America, North Germany and Scandinavia.

clandestine: Well-advertised; adjective usually applied to the visit of an American film star to London; or to a fashionable wedding, widely photographed and described.

clean-up: A system employed by the police to get rid of undesirable night-clubs. The clubs are closed, and may only be opened again under new names.

clear-cut: Any policy of the government, e.g., the present policy with regard to disarmament.

clue: What the police find when they fail to arrest a criminal.

colony: A group of artists or cranks.

companionate marriage: Free love.

competition, unfair: The attempts made by small shopkeepers to do business after the big multiple stores are closed.

confession: The widely advertised publication of the intimate details of somebody's private life.

conquest: A noun used to describe man's control over some element which he can never hope to control such as the sea or the air.

conservative: The dullest party of the season.

contemporary thought: Anything anybody cares to say against traditional Christian morality. The expression is used frequently by dramatic critics in defence of dirty plays.

continental gaiety: Building more teashops at English seaside resorts.

contract:
(a) In business a contract can only be broken by the consent of both parties.
(b) In marriage, either party can break the contract without the consent of the other.
(c) A game of bridge.

controversy: A polite comment made by one person on some trivial statement made by another in a newspaper.

Corinthian: A member of a football team.

courtesy: True courtesy belongs to one who addresses an inferior in a hearty manner, hinting that he too is, in spite of appearances, a human being.

cradle: A cage full of workmen.

creation: A woman's hat or frock.

creator: An author who invents a character in a novel; as in the sentence, "We look forward with confidence and excitement to the next work from the inspired pen of the creator of Daisy Brown."

creed: Political opinions.

criminal: Adjective applied to the conduct of a woman who allows herself to become plump and attractive.

crisis: See Garvin, J. L.

critic: Anyone who boos a boxer or applauds a footballer.

cross swords: When two writers argue they are said to be crossing swords.

culture: Anybody who learns a number of facts by heart either from a book or at a course of lectures is said to have acquired culture.

D

dago: Any Catholic foreigner.

dancing: (a) Ball-room dancing; the couples either walk slowly round the room, or wriggle about on one spot in the manner of savages, (b) Stage dancing; the man flings the woman against the scenery, swings her round, holding her by the heels, half strangles her, or balances her in ridiculous positions on his shoulder or on his head.

darling: A conventional mode of address, corresponding to the "Mr. (or Miss or Mrs.) So-and-So" of our fathers.

Darwinism: See Queen Anne.

deal: An understanding whose existence politicians deny, and whose terms they do not intend to keep.

debacle: Defeat at cricket or tennis.

debate: Backchat and patter.

decent: Like ourselves, as in "A decent fellow."

decree: The verdict of a divorce-court judge.

defeat: Massacre of oppressed by oppressors.

de luxe: Any article which has these two words attached to it will cost you about ten times as much as the same article without these two words.

desecration: The South Downs are said to be desecrated when a petrol-station is put up on a hill where there is a parking-place for motor-cars.

Dickensian: Adjective used to describe (a) snow at Christmas, (b) very long novels.

dignity: A ridiculous, pompous Victorian quality.

disarmament: Conversations between politicians about the next war.

disillusioned: When a married woman discovers that her husband objects to her spending her life in dance-clubs, she is said to be disillusioned.

dome: (a) A building in Brighton.
(b) A café in Paris.

downfall: Defeat at cricket or football.

Drake, spirit of: A reference, usually made by business men, to the famous pirate.

drastic: The steps which each political party is always going to take with regard to unemployment are called drastic.

drink: Obsolete word meaning beverage.

dud: Anybody who does not explode, in the manner of the excitable young people of to-day.

duel: A game of tennis; or a few moments of backchat in the House of Commons.

E

economy: Cutting down other people's wages.

edict: A statement about bathing-dresses, made by town councillors.

efficiency: Mistaking the means for the end.

Elizabethan: See Tudor.

elusive: Adjective applied to overpowering French perfumes.

emancipated: Adjective applied to any young girl who leaves home and keeps to regular office hours.

England: Eleven cricketers.

epic: A horse-race.

epicure: One who likes eating badly-cooked food in overheated, noisy restaurants.

epigram: Any sentence spoken by anybody who is in the public eye at the moment.

estate: A miserable collection of jerry-built bungalows and villas facing the sea.

evidence: Anything anybody tells a Commission of Inquiry.

evolution: Natural selection.

exodus: Departure for seaside.

F

facilities: Facilities for divorce.

facing facts: Not facing facts.

fair: An exhibition of machinery at Olympia.

The Fall: Autumn.

fan: An enthusiast.

Fascist: Bolshevik.

festival: (a) One week's cricket at Scarborough; (b) One month's Wagner at Bayreuth.

festive: Any one who goes to a night-club, cabaret or noisy and vulgar restaurant is festive.

fiasco: See Parliamentary Commissions.

fighting spirit: Being beaten in a game without howling, cursing or attempting to injure your opponents.

fire: A gas-heater or electric stove.

fitness: A national quality which has increased year by year, and has at last culminated in yo-yo.

flag: The implement used to mark the holes on a golf course.

flowers: Domestic ornaments made of glass, rubber, paper or velvet.

flying squad: A special contingent of police whose business is to arrive at the scene of a crime shortly after the departure of all those connected with it.

folk-music: What the band plays in Prague or Budapest, in return for champagne all round, or cash down.

food: An obsolete word meaning diet.

francophil: See Snowden, Lord.

freedom: The right to do whatever one pleases.

friend: A dog; as in the following sentence: "Mrs. Brown and friend."

G

Gainsborough: A film company.

galaxy: Five or six actresses.

gate: The figures of attendance at a football match.

general: (a) a cook; (b) a motor-omnibus.

gentleman: A cricketer whose initials are printed together with the word Mr., every time he is referred to.

genuine: An adjective usually applied to antique furniture. When so used, the word signifies that a certain piece of furniture has been prepared so skilfully that it will deceive even collectors and experts. Antiques that are not labelled genuine will only deceive the general public.

gesticulation: Any movement made by a foreigner.

getting there: Getting anywhere.

gifted: An adjective used to describe the daughter of any society hostess. See also beautiful, popular, talented.

gipsy: One who stains his or

her face and begs on Epsom Downs.

glamour: A noun of contempt used by book reviewers when it is suggested that there are things worth dying for.

Godmother, Fairy: Words used by the Medical Officer of Health for the L.C.C., in referring to the L.C.C.

good enough for "Punch": Any remark made at the tea table by a small girl to a clergyman.

government: See House of Commons.

graceful: The contortions of girls on tennis-courts are said to be graceful.

grounds: Excuse for divorce proceedings.

H

hairpin: A dangerous turn on the road.

hard-headed: Any business man who repeatedly escapes detection is called hard-headed.

Harlequin: A footballer.

harvest: A spate of novels at the beginning of a publishing season is known among reviewers as a harvest.

hearth: An open space containing a gas-fire.

hell: Mr. Warwick Deeping's word for his "loss of faith in his essential, inevitable self."

herald: A dressmaker who imposes a new fashion upon women is called a herald of whatever it may be

hero: One who breaks a speed record.

hesitation: When a pedestrian, in trying to cross a road, finds motor vehicles coming at him from every direction, at a high speed, he makes use of what is called hesitation.

highbrow: One who has to pretend that he prefers three hours of Strindberg to ten minutes of Billy Bennett.

higher criticism: Saying that Homer and the Song of Roland were written by committees, Shakespeare's plays by Bacon, the Gospel of St. John by anybody but St. John and so on.

historic: Adjective applied to a meeting of Boy Scouts or Girl Guides.

history: See Wells, H. G.

home: An institution for the infirm or aged.

home-loving: Any actress who is photographed in some one else's rock-garden is described as home-loving.

Homer: An American name.

honest: A man who has not actually been caught red-handed in any dishonest act. When there is nothing whatever to be said about a politician, he is called honest.

honour: A term used in playing bridge.

hops: An old-fashioned ingredient of beer, before the custom of using chemicals came in.

hours: The day is divided into three periods: before hours, hours, and after hours. Hours themselves are the time during which it is permissible to drink in a public place. The House of Commons has only the period called "hours", because it made the law itself.

human: Adjective applied to a novel, as in the sentence: "It is a human story, brilliantly told."

humdrum: A word used to describe people who prefer their own home to other people's homes; and even to restaurants and night clubs.

humility: A man who pretends he is no good at games, when really he is an excellent player, has true humility.

I

ideas: Dangerous things; as in the sentence, "Putting ideas into his head."

idyll: A photograph of a crowded reach of the Thames, each punt having its gramophone in full blast, is described as an idyll.

improvement: Pulling down an old building and putting up a new one.

indefatigable: Women who keep on giving parties are said to be indefatigable.

independence: A state attained by women when they all began to dress and walk and talk in the same way.

indispensable: Anything any one wants to sell you.

instantaneous: The effect of

any patent cough mixture is always instantaneous.

institute: One stage further on towards perfection in the matter of country inns.

institution: Workhouse.

intellectual drama: Strindberg, Ibsen, Pirandello, Toller, Tchehov, Bjornson, etc.

invasion: The arrival in England of Mr. Jones the American golfer.

island: A small piece of land surrounded on all sides by traffic.

K

Kid: The Christian name of nearly all prize-fighters.

knight: One who is honoured for great service (not always of a military nature) rendered to the State.

L

Lady Godiva: Any girl who takes part in a pageant, and sits on a horse, wearing a large wig and a bathing costume.

latin instability: Any refusal by the French to be talked out of their convictions.

library: The room where the murders take place.

lido: A wooden building and three tents by the side of the Serpentine.

lift: Obsolete word meaning elevator.

litter: Any object left lying about which is too small to be offensive. The word is never applied to petrol-stations, advertisements, bungalows, etc.

logic: An unfair means of winning a verbal dispute; a decayed branch of scholarship, which all sensible men discarded long ago.

love: No score at tennis.

lowbrow: One who prefers ten minutes of Billy Bennett to three hours of Strindberg.

lyrics: The words of songs in musical comedies and revues.

M

majestic: Adjective used as a name for hotels and film theatres; anything very large.

maligned: Any public character about whom the truth is told is said to be maligned.

mandate: The right to exploit and bomb from the air the inhabitants of another country.

manners, bad: Forgetting, on arrival, uninvited, at a dinner or dance, to introduce your hostess to the people you bring with you.

manners, good: Leaving a dinner or dance, to which you came uninvited, without making a fuss.

marathon: Doing anything for a long time; e.g., dancing for twenty-four hours on end, or sitting in a tree for a week, or going round a racing track until you fall asleep.

margin: Profit or loss made on a business transaction.

martyr: One who (a) foregoes good food and drink in order to look thin; (b) suffers from rheumatism.

massacre: Defeat of oppressors by oppressed.

mass production: The putting into practice of the doctrine that quantity is more important than quality.

Mayfair: A small district with a very large population, comprising all those whose names are mentioned in society gossip, all titled people, and all those who are photographed for the weekly illustrated papers. They all drink cocktails all the time.

maypole: Synthetic butter.

Mecca: A sacred place, as in the phrase: "Lord's, the Mecca of cricket-lovers," or "Wimbledon, the Mecca of tennis-enthusiasts."

medical treatise: See novels.

medieval: A term of abuse.

medium: A man or woman with strange powers in the dark.

millennium: See Utopia, Golden Age, etc.

milton: A patent medicine.

mineral: A teetotal drink.

miracle: A piece of good acting.

mission: A purpose of uplift. In contemporary American criticism Rabelais is described as a man with a mission. (See Ch. IX, "The Therapeutics of a Laugh," in Mr. S. Putnam's "Rabelais.")

modern comforts: A hotel is said to possess modern comforts when every bedroom has central heating, a telephone, thin walls, uncomfortable chairs, and a skylight above the door, through which shines, all night, a blinding electric light.

monogamy: An obsolete word meaning a fidelity complex.

Moulin Rouge: The famous Parisian meeting-place of penniless artists and Bohemians from the Latin quarter.

movement: A noun usually applied to any activity of cranks, such as walking about naked, living on nuts, and so on.

musical: Any one who sits through a long stretch of Bach, or an evening of Wagner, is musical.

N

naiad: A girl who bathes at Southend, Bognor, Bournemouth, etc.

Napoleon: Any very rich business man.

national government: A system of Coalition by which the most notorious men of one party without a policy are replaced by the most notorious men of three parties without policies.

natives: Inferior people who stay in the country, and perhaps even in the village where they were born.

naughty: Obsolete word, once applied to children, and now meaning neurotic.

neurasthenic: Any child who is what used to be called naughty. Science has discovered, in our own time, that children's bad manners or bad habits are due to their "nerves."

neutral: Waiting to see which way the wind is going to blow.

new light: The discovery of an unimportant letter from one dead bore to another dead bore is said to throw new light on one or other or both of the bores.

new thought: Writing like Miss Gertrude Stein.

no exit: A sign indicating the most convenient way out of a building.

Nordic: Belonging to the superior Protestant culture.

nursery: A place in which flowers are brought up and cared for.

nutritious: Adjective used to describe any particularly repulsive chemical food.

O

odyssey: When a popular hostess makes a trip to the Continent it is called an Odyssey.

old master: Any picture, painted by a long-dead artist, for which an American collector is prepared to pay a big price.

old-world courtesy: Any exhibition of good manners, such as showing respect and deference to ladies, opening doors for them, taking off the hat to them, and so on.

omnibus: A great mass of fiction collected into one volume.

one-way traffic: A system by which the traffic goes round in circles, and dashes off at a tangent in any direction.

open-minded: Empty-minded.

opposition: Keeping up the game of Parliamentary Government.

order, point of: An excuse for a riot at a public meeting.

Orient: A football team.

output: The only thing that really matters in the manufacturing world.

outspoken: Adjective applied to sordid details in a novel; also to any book which advocates complete chaos in the department of morals.

P

pageant: A sort of charade organised by women.

palace: Any large and over-decorated building, preferably a film theatre.

pandemonium: Noun used to describe a scene in the House of Commons when two members squeal at each other, in defiance of the Speaker.

panel: A Government medical service.

paradise: Noun used to describe the Riviera when the whole gang is there.

park: A space reserved for motor-cars.

passionate plea: When a politician says that we need international peace, or more policemen, or no speed limit, he is said to be making a "passionate plea."

patron: Any one who goes to a theatre or a picture house.

pavilion: (a) a place in which people sit to watch cricket; (b) A hall at the seaside where concerts are given.

peace pact: A formula decided upon by a committee.

pedestrian: Anybody who is knocked down by a motor-car.

Pericles: A town in America.

permanent: Used chiefly of the wave in a woman's hair, which lasts for a few months.

persecution: Not allowing people to go about naked.

pessimism: Any reference to India, Egypt, South Africa, war, unemployment, over-taxation, etc., etc.

picnic: A meal of tinned food eaten in a motor-car by the roadside.

pilgrim: One who comes south for a football match.

pint: Glass containing about ¾ pint.

pirate: An omnibus.

plays, censorship of: The system by which a play likely to have a harmful effect on Christian morals may be performed only on Sundays.

pleasure, the life of: Eating the same food with the same people, hearing the same music, and staying in the same kind of hotel in all the international resorts of Europe.

pledge: The daily promise of a political candidate.

pluck: A verb denoting the removal of a lady's eyebrows.

policy: A term in use among insurance agents.

port: Any liquid resembling port in colour.

portrait: An expensive photograph.

pot-luck: Taking whatever happens to be in the tin.

preach: When a father objects to his daughter drinking and dancing all night, and being insolent to anybody outside her own set, he is said to be preaching.

prestige: A nation acquires or loses prestige by beating or being beaten by other nations at games.

pride: Vanity.

priceless: Adjective used to express admiration for anything that is within the reach of all but the smallest purse; e.g. a film-play.

priest-ridden: Adjective used to describe the state of affairs in those countries where the Catholic Church is said to have no power any longer.

primitive: Any hotel is primitive which is without running water, electric light and telephones in every room; and has no cocktail-bar, dance-floor, swimming-pool; and no loud-speaker in the lounge.

prince: Any exiled Russian.

private dance: A dance to which only those who know, or know of, some one who has been invited, can gain admittance.

problem: A noun used almost always in connection with women's clothes, as in the phrase, "The dress problem."

prodigy: A child who plays the piano when he ought to be asleep in bed.

progress: A system by which everything new is better than the thing it supersedes. All history teaches us that the world is slowly advancing towards a millennium. This constant improvement may be noticed to-day in, say, the department of Architecture.

propaganda: What the other side says.

prophet: Any one who says that anything will happen.

provocative: A reviewer's adjective for any book, when his other adjectives have been used up.

public servant: A Government official, e.g. a tax-collector.

pugilist: A business man who is occasionally compelled to box a round or two in the interests of his business.

pugnacious: Anybody who fails to agree with opinions expressed in the usual small talk at a dinner-table.

pyramid: An enormous monument erected in the desert by the Pharaohs, in order to prove that the English are the Lost Tribes of Israel, that the world will end in A.D. 2574, and that Bacon wrote Shakespeare's plays.

Q

quaint: Adjective used to describe the customs, manners, dress and architecture of a foreign nation.

Quixotic: Any one who attacks an existing evil.

R

rabid: Adjective applied to (a) Tories; (b) Teetotalers.

raid: When members of the police force visit a night club, it is called a raid.

the Real Paris: Those places in Paris to which English residents take English visitors to meet other English residents.

recluse: A man who cuts down his social engagements while he is writing a novel or a play. See hermit, anchorite, etc.

reduce: A word used by women to describe the process of becoming angular.

reform, electoral: A system by which an elector who dislikes two candidates will be able to vote for both of them.

release: The liberation of a film.

religious: Teetotal, kind to animals, and opposed to war and games on Sundays.

remote: A place with only one big modern hotel. See also "Off the beaten track."

repression: Exercise of the will in the province of morals.

reverence: The emotion felt by the normal Englishman in the presence of a county cricketer.

revelation: Public confession by an actress of some important thing in her life—e.g. her ambition to play "Hamlet," or her preference for dark men.

revels: A party given in a restaurant or night club, when drinking is allowed to go on an hour or two longer than usual.

revolt: Noun used to describe the action of an M.P. who becomes sick of his party, and chucks it in to join another.

rights: Certain privileges claimed by women, e.g. equality with men in all branches of activity.

ringcraft: A boxer is said to possess ringcraft when he knows exactly which illegal tricks he can employ without being warned by the referee, or barracked by the spectators.

robbery: Any price charged for any article abroad is said to be robbery.

romantic: One who holds any philosophy but the extreme materialistic.

rotarianism: Making a religion of Big Business.

royalty: What writers expect from publishers.

the rush hour: That hour during which the traffic is almost at a standstill all over the West End of London.

S

sacred: Adjective used to emphasise the duty of voting during a parliamentary election.

safe: A hiding-place for valuable jewels or papers, the lock of which can only be manipulated by the owner, and any burglar who happens to be on the premises.

salesmanship: The art of badgering people into buying things they do not want and even making them think they do want them, and have always wanted them.

saloon: A motor-car.

sanctum: The study in which a politician or a writer works.

San Remo: Popular name for a villa or bungalow in an English suburb or seaside resort.

scientific data: A series of minor hypotheses leading up to a major hypothesis.

scientific fact: Any hypothesis of popular science.

secret: Anything told by a society woman to a man whom she suspects of being a gossip-writer.

secret wedding: When the prospective bride and bridegroom are not photographed together every day for a month before the wedding, the wedding is called a secret one.

security: Shares in something that will go bust sooner or later.

self-control: Obsolete Victorian word for repression.

self-determination: The right of any people to govern themselves. Except those out of whom we hope to make money, or those of whom we are afraid.

self-expression: Doing whatever you please. A parent who punishes a child is said to be interfering with its self-expression.

self-starter: A piece of machinery that may or may not work if you start it.

set sail: To start a journey in a Trans-atlantic liner, or a cruise in a motor-yacht.

settlement: See concession.

she: A personal pronoun used in speaking of a motor-car.

shop: Obsolete word, meaning store.

shop assistant: Obsolete word for salesman.

shrine: A holy place. Communists are said to "worship at the shrine" of Karl Marx. See "Worship."

shy: Adjective applied to a man or woman who does not call you by your Christian name five minutes after having met you for the first time.

slogan: A vulgar catch-phrase to advertise a patent medicine.

slum: A neighbourhood in which poor people have their homes.

slum-clearance: The destruction of poor people's homes to make room for film-theatres or 'arty' flats with garages.

social duties: The struggle to get notorious people to attend a dinner party or a cocktail party.

social service: Compulsory education, at the taxpayers' expense, for all those who would be happier and better without it.

social work: Meddling with the poor.

solemn: Dull.

spartan: One who bathes in the Serpentine during the winter months.

spirit: A voice in a dark room, saying that uncle is well, and the weather fine.

Spurs: A football team.

squeamish Victorian: Any elderly person who has preserved a certain degree of reticence, and even defends self-restraint.

sterilisation: Mutilation of the poor.

stoic: A dyspeptic millionaire on a diet.

straitlaced: Anybody who has a rigid moral code is called straitlaced.

strenuous life: Phrase usually applied to those who play games excessively.

strike: Lockout.

strong: An adjective of praise applied to any repulsively and brutally ugly piece of sculpture or to any unintelligible picture.

strong, silent: These adjectives, which always go together, are applied as an indication of great qualities to a man with an immobile face who has nothing to say on any subject.

strung, highly: Any child in need of a sound thrashing is said to be highly strung. See also temperamental.

stuffy: An adjective applied to Victorians at home; also descriptive of a certain Victorian atmosphere which is unfavourably compared with that of modern centrally-heated rooms.

subtle: All psychology is subtle.

subtlety: Involved nonsense in a novel.

summer time: The time during which all clocks are one hour fast. A modern invention admired greatly by those who support the mechanistic theory of life.

superstition: Noun accompanying the adjective mediaeval.

surprise: Every marriage of every film-actress is a surprise.

sylph: Any woman of less than elephantine proportions.

symbolism: Anything in art which is unintelligible to the normal man.

T

table: Football scores.

tactics: Methods employed by a football team to defeat its opponents.

take in: Americans, on their way, let us say, from Paris to Madrid in a luxury train, are said to "take in" the Pyrenees during the trip.

temperance: An intemperate hatred of drink.

thought, modern: Infantile emotionalism.

the drink question: The problem of how to make it impossible for a working man to get a glass of beer.

thrill: A fatal accident.

time: The word of command used to dismiss people from public-houses.

time-worn: Any theory that is distasteful to you.

toleration: Toleration of evil.

tourist: Anybody who is not in your own party abroad.

trance: A mental state in which a man or woman, sitting in the dark, knows what is taking place not only in this world, but in the next.

transition, period of: When critics are tired of saying the same thing over and over again about a writer, they announce that he is going through a period of transition.

traveller: One who tries to sell things.

triumph: Noun used to describe any new American film.

troop: An old military word now applied to Boy Scouts and Girl Guides.

truth: There are two kinds. a) An old truth; i.e., a stupid, out-of-date superstition. (b) a new truth; i.e. the latest guess of science.

Tudor: Designation of any cottage in the country that has a crazy pavement, blackened deal "beams", an old coaching lantern in the porch, and the name carved in Gothic lettering on the gate.

U

ukase: A pronouncement made in Paris on the subject of women's clothes.

unassuming: Any nonentity in the public eye, about whom there is nothing to say, is called unassuming.

unbiased: Having no convictions.

understanding, an: Any international banking arrangement.

undying fame: See Bradman, the cricketer.

united: Adjective applied to a football team.

unprecedented: Every scale is unprecedented.

unsurpassed: Any politician's knowledge of anything he talks about is said to be unsurpassed.

V

vagabond: Noun used to describe a man who has enough money to spend his time travelling all over the world.

valuable: Adjective used to describe any report prepared by a Parliamentary Committee or a Royal Commission.

variety show: A standardised programme of American turns, with the names of the performers and of the songs altered occasionally.

vigil: Waiting in a queue to see the first night of a new play.

village amenities: Compulsory folk-dancing, etc., etc., etc.

virtue: The cardinal virtues are Punctuality, Physical Fitness, Smartness of Appearance, Cleanliness, Teetotalism, Playing the Game, Kindness to Nice Animals.

virtuoso: A term frequently applied to musicians. It signifies the ability to play a piece of music so cleverly that the audience exclaims, "This is what the composer meant."

vista: Something that is opened up.

vitamines: Something that appears and disappears at the command of Science. It is found, and not found in certain foods. Slang abbreviation for "Here today and gone tomorrow."

vivid: When a girl writes a novel in which the characters talk like drunken bargees her work is called a vivid picture of life as it is.

vulgar: Adjective used by Mr. H. G. Wells to describe Napoleon's contribution to history.

W

warning: When a motor vehicle is travelling so fast that it cannot pull up quickly enough to avoid knocking down a pedestrian, the horn is blown. This is called a warning.

wayfarer: Any one who takes a motor-tour abroad, and then writes a book about it.

wedding, secret: A wedding that is reported more widely and at greater length than other weddings.

whimsical: Anything said or written by Sir James Barrie.

win: Obsolete word meaning win through.

wings: (a) Part of a motor-car or aeroplane; (b) Exit and entrance for actors and actresses.

wit: Any public man who tells a story or repeats a joke is a wit.

witticism: Any joke, whether stale or fresh, funny or dull, made by a man or woman in the public eye at the moment.

world-peace: A state of affairs which would make it possible for the international moneylenders to get even more power than they possess at present.

I am basking in the Parisian sunlight, drinking my Pernod, and watching the cosmopolitan crowd passing up and down the boulevard.

From my table I can see old *père* Nichaud, the doyen of the Poupouists, and a disciple of Apollinaris, who taught me how to draw mackerel with my eyes shut.

Ah, Lolotte has just entered. Lolotte, the little dancer from the *Brebis Qui Tousse*, who used to shoot plums off the trees with a rook-rifle—how long ago?

With her is handsome young Fujiyama, the Japanese artist, and Dolmen, the dour Cornish poet who strangled La Folie with his braces at the corner of the Rue des Mauvaises Odeurs.

"Garçon!"

Surely I know that *voix*.

Assurément! It is "Gop," the wicked caricaturist of the *Calviniste du Nord,* the go-ahead paper that first printed Dubosc's explanation of Proust.

We greet each other.

"*Tiens, mon vieux!*"

"*Et vous?*"

"*Pas mal.*"

"Gop" married the widow Colifichet, because he owed her four months' rent. He and Puant are the authors of "*Bonsoir, Nou-Nou!*" the new revue at the Alouette.

He was a wild young man in his youth, this "Gop," and used to drop eggs from the top of the Eiffel Tower.

At a corner table, in the shade, Manon, from the *Grands Augustins*, is talking to Mathilde Mercredi, the *soubrette* from the *Samaritaine*. "Tic" greets them. He is smoking one of his long Cuban cigars at the wrong end, and his trousers are patched with leading articles from the "*Ami du Peuple.*"

"*Hé, Manon!*"

The slim girl starts, and looks up.

"*Mais . . . tais toi!*"

Here comes Tric-Trac, who sells his own songs at ten sous the kilo every evening in the Place Pigalle. They say he has written an opera in which he makes use of only three notes.

Ah, now for a real Bohemian—Paradis, in his velvet coat and black trousers, with his pale, dirty face and eyes that burn like live coals. He is dying, they say. He sleeps in the day-time, and drinks all night, but if he cared he could be a great artist.

Paradis was brought up on his father's estate in the Morvan, but he ran away to a publisher's (the modern equivalent of running away to sea) and managed to get a novel published. It failed, and he did no more work.

His father makes him a handsome allowance, and he lives in the Rue Chat Maigre with Tortoise, the poet, and Beaugras, the etcher.

At a table on the pavement I note Van Kuypers, the Dutchman. With him is La Grenouille, who sits for Garnache. When he becomes excited he pours his coffee into his coat-pocket and takes off his boots. They say that he has a crayon frieze running round the lining of his hat, representing a boar-hunt in the forest of Quercy.

La Grenouille sleeps in a canoe which is anchored to the side of a big swimming bath, but she keeps a mole in a fur glove suspended from the ceiling.

The sun sinks. The café teems with life.

Ah, Paris!

A clock in the Rue Manet strikes six-thirty, and I think of those words of de Gourmont.

Abuse

PRODNOSE: Do you know, I would rather be wading through wet clay than reading you?

MYSELF: Well, what is to prevent you wading through as much wet clay as you please? I don't want you hanging about here, I can assure you.

PRODNOSE: Steady, now, I am one of your readers, and you cannot afford to be rude to me.

MYSELF: You miserable, wall-eyed, sheep-faced, spavined, long-eared, lily-livered pig, I care less than nothing for you and your rotten little opinions.

PRODNOSE: Anybody can be rude.

MYSELF: Go ahead, then, wart, if you have the courage.

PRODNOSE: I will not be drawn into an undignified brawl.

MYSELF: Undignified brawl! If I had my way, you'd be dragged head-first into an inn and dipped into ——'s ale, which is the worst in England, until you screamed for mercy.

In The City

The Bumblethorpe Loan is bad tactics. The early trustee issue, already over-subscribed in some quarters, is to be released for repayment of the special redeemable stock, in short-term loans on ordinary holdings. Securities released on corresponding profits could very easily be used at exchange rates, by covering short falls. But this is not being done. Why? Simply because those who might balance the offering of dollars have not the guts to support at lower levels the demand for cumulative preference releases. It is all part of the mania for sale by tender, and the sooner the surplus is bought back and absorbed by the bears, the sooner some shrewder manipulation will enable the supporters of revaluation to resume aggressive exchange of sterling.

Dr. Strabismus at Salzburg

The Doctor was dissecting a fish in the laboratories of the Baumgartner Museum at Salzburg yesterday, when some friends called to carry him off to the opera. He absent-mindedly stuffed the fish into his pocket.

The anaesthetic wore off during the second act of *Faust*.

The fish, a large whiting, leaped from the Doctor's pocket and out of the private box on to the stage.

Marguerite dived, and brought off an exceedingly difficult catch, throwing Mephistopheles off his balance as she did so, and pushing Martha against the scenery.

Amid cries of "Safety Faust!" the diva flung the fish back, but it struck the ledge of the box and rebounded into the orchestra, where the conductor stunned it with one blow of his baton.

Next day it was eaten, *en colère*, by the Mayor.

WAGNERIANA

Wagner summoned his charwoman.
'Look here,' he said angrily, 'I can write my name in dust on this piano!'
'It's a grand thing to be so educated,' replied the charwoman.

ANOTHER CANTO

Monsieur Ezra Pound croit que
By using foreign words
He will persuade the little freaks
Who call themselves intellectuals
To believe that he is saying
Quelque chose très deep, ma foi!

THE OLD REFRAIN

Nothing short of a comprehensive scheme of national planning will solve our problems.
                                                    (Captain H. Macmillan, M.P.)

Like the refrain of an old music-hall song these words danced before my delighted eyes. This kind of thing used to be said once a day by politicians a year ago, until the Prime Minister overdid it. But now here it is again, and I welcome it as comic relief.

It is a good sentence to play with. You can make it into the main theme of an oratorio; or you can use it as the chorus of a song. For instance:

She sat in an old-world garden
Alone, at the end of the day,
And softly the shadows gathered,
As thus to herself she did say:

Chorus (*loudly*):

Nothing short of a comprehensive scheme of national planning will solve our problems.

Or,

Where the wood dips down to the hollow,
Two lovers stood in tears,
The sorrow of parting lay o'er them,
And the pain of the passing years.
As the tears splashed over their clothing,
Like healing summer rain,
Each clasped the hand of the other,
And sang this sweet refrain:

Chorus (*rudely and offensively*):

Nothing short of a comprehensive scheme of national planning will solve our problems.

WHY MR. GLADSTONE WORE TROUSERS

The Chancellor of Melbourne University said the other day: 'So long as a man can put his trousers on without sitting down, he is not old.'

The real sign of old age is when you have to lie down to put them on.

With smart men these questions do not arise. Two valets hold the trousers, and the man is lifted up by two other valets, and then slowly lowered into them, as a packing case is lowered by crane into the hold of a ship.

Ruskin used to lie on his bed and raise his legs in the air. Then his man, standing on the bed, used to more or less pour the trousers over his legs. Sometimes they fell too swiftly, and got muddled into a heap above the knee. But it was all one to jolly Jack Ruskin.

Gladstone tried this method once, but the valet got the legs crossed while lowering them. Gladstone said, 'I appear to be squinting somewhat,' and sent for an oculist. The oculist said, 'My dear Prime Minister, do you expect me to make a pair of spectacles for you to wear on your legs?' 'No,' said Gladstone. 'Well, then,' said the oculist.

It was only when Gladstone tried to walk that he realized what had happened. He fell over, of course, and hurt his arm. The doctor came, and after examining him said, 'Mr. Gladstone, why cannot you put on your trousers like any normal man? If you would only do that, these mistakes would not occur. You might have broken your neck.'

'I might wear knickerbockers, of course,' said Gladstone.

'I don't see that that would make much difference,' said the doctor. 'Knickerbockers have two legs, you know, just as much as trousers.'

'Yes,' said Gladstone, 'but there's less of each leg.'

'I know,' said the doctor, 'but the legs can get crossed, all the same.'

'Then stap me,' said Gladstone, 'I'll stick to trousers.'

And he did.

Ruskin used to raise his legs in the air

TAIL-PIECE

'Let me give you some more chicken, Mrs. Burghersh.'

'Thank you, Mrs. Renton, just a mouthful!'

'Mason! Fill Mrs. Burghersh's plate.'

CADS AND SWINE

CHAPTER I

MY ARRIVAL AT NARKOVER

'I say, you chaps, here's the new kid. Let's tar and feather the little swine.'

Those were the first words I heard, when I arrived, small and unprotected, at the great public school that has turned out so many of our statesmen.

I shrank back appalled, while the ringleaders went off to fetch the tar and the feathers. When they returned, there was a junior master with them.

'If you don't jolly well help to hold him down, sir,' said one of the bigger boys to him, 'we'll tell old Denbury where to find those marked cards of yours.'

The master blenched, but had no choice in the matter. I was rapidly tarred and feathered and thrown into a coal-cellar. There I passed my first night at Narkover, a victim to bitter thoughts; hungry, cold, and terrified of the rats that scampered over the coal. And my father had told me that was to be the best time of my life!

Early next morning I was released by a monitor who had a grudge against the gang who had imprisoned me. He made me give him all my pocket-money, and an IOU for £20 as well.

Weary and sore, I crept into the study which I was to share with a boy named Glass. As I opened the door, I saw, through the smoke-laden atmosphere, a crowd of boys collected round a roulette table.

CHAPTER II

SETTLING DOWN

It did not take me long to settle down in my new surroundings. I soon discovered which masters were easy to bribe, which boys were willing to act as 'fences', that is, receivers of stolen property, and how to make use of a few clever methods of cheating at cards.

On my first visit to the school night-tuckshop a very exciting thing happened. Kaussmann, whose parents were very wealthy, had arranged to have a cabaret show sent down from London. The girls arrived, disguised as natives of Narkover, and were smuggled into the tuckshop that night, with the help of a master who had been caught house-breaking by a boy in his form.

Everything was in full swing, and I, with a group of new boys, was sitting at a table laden with wine and spirits, when suddenly the place was raided by old Tamplin, the mathematics master, a very pious fellow. He took our names and told us to clear out, but imagine our delight when one of the girls who had been dancing in the chorus shouted out:

'Well, if it isn't little Mopsy-Wopsy!'

Tamplin was very much taken aback, particularly when she hinted that there were certain passages in his life of which she could give a glowing account to the headmaster. So Tamplin took it like a sportsman, and joined us in a drink.

'We shan't get any more sermons from him,' said Marston minor to me as we left the tuckshop.

CHAPTER III

THE PILHAMPTON MATCH

The great football match of the year was the Narkover-Pilhampton game, and I was lucky enough, while still in my first year, to be one of the fags told to collect the various bribes paid in advance by the Pilhampton team.

Here, as a digression, let me protest against recent attacks on the fagging system. In all my four years I can recall only eleven deaths from fagging. And in one of those cases the fag brought it on himself by knifing a prefect during a game of bridge in the school chapel.

I remember my house-master saying to me: 'The Pilhampton bribes don't seem to be coming in very well.' But he cheered up the next day when we got £10 from the Pilhampton coach, who had exacted a promise in writing that we would expel our goalkeeper for theft before the match. I was told to get someone to steal a marked fiver, and conceal it in the goalkeeper's locker. Unfortunately he caught me concealing it, and if I hadn't possessed a letter of his confessing to the murder of a new boy, there would have been no end of a row. But he played in the match after all.

Narkover won the match by two goals to one. Our captain's father, a very wealthy man, managed to conceal a big cheque in one of the lemons served at half-time. A Pilhampton man found it, and they all slacked for the rest of the game.

After the match we all sang school songs.

> . . . *The old game, the bold game,*
> *The best game of all.* . . .

Even now I hear those young voices. . . .

CHAPTER IV

MY BAD LUCK

One of the things we all looked forward to was the Sunday sermon in the chapel. Here, surrounded by the invisible ghosts of great men long dead, we listened to words of consolation and hope. The subjects were various, among the favourites being the evils of gambling, the straight bat in life, the wickedness of giving away money to beggars, the need for clean hands and faces, and good clothes, in life's struggle, and so on.

I remember one Sunday, when a roar of laughter drowned the opening notes of the hymn. The headmaster, in pulling out his handkerchief, had produced with it two aces. They were retrieved by another master and handed back with what must have been a ribald jest, for old Dr. Smart-Allick scowled at him and made as though to hack his shin.

We were supposed to read quietly in our studies on Sunday evenings, but most of us played cards, or smoked, and talked. One evening, when our house-master had gone out to bribe the local police to hush up a rather bad case of window smashing, we decided to break open his desk and steal any loose money he might have. But we found that some fellows from the headmaster's house had forestalled us.

One of them, who had been swindled out of his share, turned informer, and for two days we had detectives from London prowling about the school buildings. And it was one of them who found a ring belonging to our house-master's wife in my locker. It was planted on me, of course. I got into serious trouble and had to promise to reform myself at once. By bad luck, only the next day I was caught trying to forge another fellow's name.

Chapter V

I GET MY COLOURS

During my third year at Narkover the captain of football hinted to me that he would have no objection to my playing for the school if I could find the cash for my colours. There was some opposition at first. One of the forwards, Gill, had been promised fifty quid by someone who wanted his colours, so it became obvious that I should have to find a bigger sum before my name would be considered. After some thought, I decided to employ a chap named Phelps.

Phelps was our best card-sharper, and for a small commission he agreed to get into a game with some of the richest boys. The trick came off, but Phelps 'squealed' because somebody paid him an enormous sum to tell all he knew. The headmaster sent for me, and told me to try to win my colours honestly.

I went away very miserable, but fortune had not deserted me. A chap called Denton sold me a letter written by the head prefect to the headmaster's eldest daughter. I took the letter triumphantly to the head, who promised to help me in the matter of the colours.

He was as good as his word. He expelled my most dangerous rival (the fellow who had bribed Gill) on a trumped-up charge, and I was given my colours at last.

Chapter VI

TIME PASSES

At the end of my third year, with only one more year to go, I began to understand something of the tradition, the *esprit de corps*, of Narkover. I found a deeper meaning in the words of our school song:

> *Straight be thy bat,*
> *Aye, straighter year by year . . .*

And when the old boys returned I realized how love of the old place had twined about their hearts like ivy. How we cheered them! One was a famous blackmailer, leader of a gang of stock-brokers in the City; another had done time for bigamy, and we gazed with awe upon him; a third already had three names, which he varied according to the company he found himself in. But to us he was always Schmeltz the boy who was said to have doped the St. Leger favourite while still in the Upper Fifth. For breaking bounds he was caned, but the headmaster gave us a lecture on the value of initiative in life.

What was it, I asked myself, that bound us all together, and brought the tears to the eyes of even the most hardened criminals among us? What was it that made the junior mathematics master give back the pocket-case he had pinched from one of the parents? What hidden magic made him play the game, in spite of temptation?

I worked harder in my last year. A master who owed me money for cards got me a set of new cribs, which increased my marks by leaps and bounds. I also began to tire of the clumsy house-breaking expeditions, and the crude cheating at games, and to apply myself more to the subtler kinds of chicanery. I remember a lecture that made a deep impression on me. The headmaster said, 'If you smash into a house, shoot the occupants and make a get-away, you will lift, perhaps, a little money and some valuables. But if you stick to big business, and operate from a well-furnished office, you will probably die a duke.'

> *Straight be thy bat,*
> *And clean thy starched collar. . . .*

Chapter VII

At the beginning of my fourth and last year I was made a prefect, and consequently found myself comparatively well off financially. Naturally we bigger boys had much more opportunity for pulling off big jobs than the youngsters, and the masters were more inclined to come in with us on a good thing. I remember that three of us even managed to float a bogus company, and collected a large sum from new boys who had wealthy parents, and then more from the parents who were annoyed at their sons being involved so early in non-paying propositions, and did not want the thing made public.

Time wore on, and my last term arrived. I found myself becoming very sentimental at the thought of being separated from my friends. Finally came the last days, and I cannot resist quoting here part of the farewell address of dear old Smart-Allick, the headmaster.

'Some of you,' he said, 'may have cheated at cards. Well, we've all done that. Some of you may have forged a friend's name to a cheque, or lied to get him into trouble. Ah, but that was only your baser selves. Above the stratum of villainy is the pure gold of a Narkoverian, unalloyed, assayed in the fires of comradeship on field and in class-room. . . .'

While these noble words were being spoken, I was almost nauseated to see a fellow-prefect quietly rifling the note-case of the boy next to him, albeit with tears in his eyes, for he, too, was leaving that term.

'The whole world,' continued the head, 'is now your cricket pitch. Go forth, and score bravely. Your names are engraved upon the great heart of Narkover.'

We filed out into the dusk, singing softly the words of the school song that has welded old Narkover boys together all the world over.

NARKOVER SCHOOL SONG

When we who played for Narkover
 In happy days gone by
Are parted by the piteous foam
 And, 'neath an alien sky,
Recall the glad, the joyous time
 When youth was at the spring,
God grant that in our hearts may chime
 The song we used to sing:

Refrain:

 Straight is my bat,
 Aye, straighter year by year,
 Life's googlies spin,
 Break out, break in,
 But I can have no fear.
 Loud comes the call
 Across the world to me,
 I laugh at Fate
 My bat is straight
 As e'er it used to be.

When we who played for Narkover
 Are laid beneath the loam
May breezes bear to us once more
 Some echo from our home,
May we recall the hour of pride,
 When life was on the wing,
And boys who played to save the side
 Were not ashamed to sing:

Refrain:

 Straight is my bat, etc.

Bosha, the Indian mystic, has arrived in England to show us the Way of Dar Chumbi.

Bosha's method of imparting knowledge is to makes faces. Each expression has a significance, and the key is kept by his disciple, Mme. Stilfandi, once a prominent woman member of the Tulse Hill Bingers, a curious masonic sect.

I asked Mme. Stilfandi how she was converted to the Way of Dar Chumbi, and she closed her eyes and moaned: 'Life is but a Preparation. We must all go through the Ivory Door. Love is the Key. And all Being is Conscious.'

At this point Bosha made a hideous face, and one of his disciples, an Oxford rowing blue, said to me, 'The Master is feeling Sick.'

* * *

Bosha the Mystic made the Six Constructive Faces of Bohuddas Tai in the Sheldonian at Oxford, as announced.

There was only one interruption, by a Mumbojumbanist, who asked loudly what was the constructive value of a grimace in these troubled times.

Mme. Stilfandi was understood to say that the face was the index of the soul.

The Mumbojumbanist then confessed that he had once pinched his little brother; after which he cried, and was tenderly removed by officials.

Bosha then went on making faces.

The Six Constructive Faces of the Bohuddas Tai

DR. SMART-ALLICK AT NARKOVER

I HAVE always thought that the only really up-to-date school for young ladies was St. Ethelfrith's. The headmistress, who is the popular Miss Topsy Turvey, insists on the girls painting their nails in the school colours, and nightly attendance at the school night-club is compulsory for all girls, to whatever religious denomination they belong. She herself joins the midnight bathing class.

Her theory is that by letting youth express itself freely one eradicates repressions.

The school is in the neighbourhood of Narkover, and rumour has been busy lately coupling the names of Dr. Smart-Allick and Miss Topsy Turvey.

The Doctor was informed yesterday that a certain amount of gossip was connecting his name with that of the ravishingly beautiful headmistress of St. Ethelfrith's.

The Doctor said: 'I'm too old a hand to fall for a schoolmarm. Though, mark you, I won't deny that I pinched her ear in a picture house on one of our half-holidays; an action of small significance when one considers the infinite variety of horseplay possible to patrons of the celluloid world.

'The suggestion that I distracted her attention by a show of affection in order to acquire a temporary lien on her handbag is an insult to my intelligence. I'd got hold of the bag long before we entered the picture house. I said it was too heavy for her to carry. When I gave it back it was a good deal lighter. Ha, ha!'

Last night the draw for the Narkover sweep took place. Dr. Smart-Allick is one of those conscientious headmasters who believe that no task, however trivial, should be delegated to an inferior. He therefore wrote out all the tickets himself, put them in the large basket, shuffled them, and even drew them himself. He also called out the results.

At the end, he announced, with pardonable pride, that he himself had drawn every horse. 'As your headmaster,' he said, "this makes me very happy.'

It was afterwards discovered that every name in the hat had been Smart-Allick.

'Away with tradition,' cried the headmaster. 'A modern age requires modern methods, and the devil take the hindmost. Clarkson minor, if you don't stop grousing I'll knock your head off, you nasty little beast!'

Miss Topsy Turvey was yesterday asked to say something about her friendship for Dr. Smart-Allick.

She said: 'The proximity of the two schools, of course, throws us together a good deal. I look upon the Doctor as a very serious-minded man. With regard to the ridiculous incident of his pinching my ear in a picture house, I really do not see why a busy headmaster should not have a moment's relaxation now and then.

'As to the actual pinching, it was done in the friendliest way, and without any of the impudence or ribaldry which one is accustomed to associate with such a jaunty gesture.'

Asked if she would permit the Doctor this liberty again, Miss Turvey blushed, and said that she preferred not to answer.

Pressed for an answer, she said: 'It is difficult to say. One gets carried away.'

She is said to be deeply distressed at the suggestion that Dr. Smart-Allick has a wife in every school. She intends to make inquiries, and in an outburst yesterday spoke of going to Swindon (where her mother lives) to forget.

She has received anonymous letters warning her not to take Dr. Smart-Allick too seriously, as he is not the marrying type.

Interviewed yesterday, Miss Turvey said: 'I believe the influence of a good woman would do wonders for him.'

When told of this the Doctor said: 'If I thought she was a good woman I wouldn't waste a moment on her. No good woman would have picked up those card-tricks I showed her as quickly as she did. Why, two nights ago the delightful little rogue got hold of the ace I was about to palm, and so turned the tables on me. She'll make a first-class sharper if only she applies herself to the game.'

Topsy was taking the Upper Sixth at St. Ethelfrith's in Deportment when suddenly through the open window of the class-room vaulted Dr. Smart-Allick.

'Are you alone?' he hissed in a mock-dramatic tone.

'Of course I'm not,' said the astonished lady, pointing to the twenty-seven girls on the benches.

'Send all these creatures away,' said Smart-Allick.

The headmistress gave a gasp of horror.

'Have you been drinking?' she asked.

'Of course,' retorted the pedagogue. 'Haven't you?'

'Please, please go,' implored the headmistress, her mortar-board all awry with emotional strain.

'First,' said the Doctor, 'I must take toll of those ruby lips.'

He advanced towards her, and the girls began to titter. They laughed more loudly when a quart bottle fell from his pocket and smashed in pieces on the floor.

'Girls, you may go,' faltered Miss Turvey in a feeble voice.

She watched them file out, and then turned to remonstrate with the intruder.

Alas, a headier wine than love had lulled him into a hoggish slumber. He lay curled up on the window-seat, muttering, 'Six to four on the field.'

The headmistress walked out of the room with her chin in the air.

A reporter, with that delicacy and refinement which endears the journalist to all people of judgment and taste, has succeeded in interviewing Topsy, and asking one or two direct questions.

'Miss Turvey,' he asked, 'would you call Doctor Smart-Allick a drunkard?'

The beautiful dark eyes of the lovely young headmistress flashed angrily.

'Certainly not,' she said. 'As a student of psychological phenomena I should call him bottle-conscious and possibly alcohol-minded, but I am sure he is unacquainted with the baser forms of alcoholism.'

'Did he break into your school the other day?' asked the reporter.

'No,' said Miss Turvey.

'He did not enter the classroom by the window?'

'Certainly he did,' replied the headmistress. 'But as I had left the window open, the question of breaking in does not arise.'

'Was he intoxicated?'

'There is more than one kind of intoxication,' retorted the siren of St. Ethelfrith's, with a roguish smile.

'But you do not deny that he spoke of taking toll of your ruby lips?'

'Such a proposition,' answered Miss Turvey, lowering her eyes, 'does not necessarily argue that my visitor was alcoholically unbalanced.'

'But a quart bottle fell from his pocket, Miss Turvey.'

'He had hoped,' replied the headmistress, 'to be asked to stay to lunch.'

'The bottle was full, then?'

'From a hasty glimpse of the damage, I should say that very little had been drunk. A mere hasty swig—er—gulp on the way over from Narkover.'

Miss Topsey Turvey was among those in the pavilion with Dr. Smart-Allick the other day, during the Narkover match against Rugton. The boys seemed to be more interested in their popular headmaster than in the cricket, and when Dr. Smart-Allick rose to go into the changing-room to explore the possibilities of the note-cases of the visiting team, it was seen that the beautiful headmistress laid a restraining hand on his arm, and appeared to whisper something urgent.

The Doctor laughed and pinched her cheek playfully, while one of the little scholars made a book on what would happen next.

The Doctor's haul was evidently a good one, as shortly after his return from the changing-room a messenger was sent into the town and returned with champagne.

Asked if she had anything to say, when the match was over, Miss Turvey replied, 'We are just good friends.'

'How she can talk such rot after all that bubbly,' said the Doctor, 'is more than I can fathom.'

'I know I'm only a foolish little thing,' said the lovely Topsy, 'but I can't see how you can have had such phenomenal luck in the Derby sweep.'

'Fragrant morsel,' replied the pedagogue, 'I know the ropes, every strand of 'em. Yours, fair charmer, to bring solace to jaded mankind as the evening shadows fall. Mine to charge into the hurly-burly, to pick up what's going. Hesitate, I pray, to mix the domestic with the bohemian.'

'They say,' ventured Topsy, 'that I am not your first love.'

'Measured by acreage,' replied the Doctor, 'my wild oats wouldn't feed an old one-eyed cob. Come, dusky siren, what is a peccadillo more or less in the great infinity of time?'

'Is bigamy a peccadillo?' asked Topsy firmly.

The Doctor's face fell.

'What rat has been squeaking?' he thundered. Then, with a laugh, he went on. 'If it be true that I have contracted unions here and there, I will divorce the hussies in batches of six. You are my lodestar. Come, accord me the nectar of those ruby lips.'

Topsy was taking the Upper Sixth at St. Ethelfrith's in poetry, when she was observed to be overcome with some strong emotion. She had just read some lines which may have vividly recalled to her the headmaster of Narkover. The lines she was reading aloud when her voice faltered and broke were the following, of Wordsworth:

> He spake of love, such love as spirits feel
>   In worlds whose course is equable and pure;
> No fears to beat away—no strife to heal—
>   The past unsighed for and the future sure.'

Curiously enough, at almost the same time Dr. Smart-Allick was taking the Upper Sixth at Narkover in poetry. He quoted a passage, and appeared to be deeply struck by its implications. The lines that so moved him were these, of Pope:

> To heirs unknown descends the unguarded store,
> Or wanders, heaven-directed, to the poor.

The parents of the young gentlemen of Narkover and of the young ladies of St. Ethelfrith's, as well as the governing bodies of both these academies, are growing restive. They feel that unless the beautiful young headmistress and the wayward headmaster are soon made husband and wife, discipline will go to the devil, and the moral tone of each school deteriorate rapidly.

The Doctor has always been too interested in financial questions to devote time to trifling with the affections of single ladies, but on this occasion, as he himself so aptly puts it, 'the little guy with the bow and arrow has plugged me bang in the heart.'

What, then, holds the Doctor back from a proposal?

Surely there can be nothing in the preposterous story that Mrs. Smart-Allick is a name borne, stubbornly if not proudly, by twelve or thirteen ladies of varying age, station, and place of abode.

Pray heaven this may be but the wagging tongue of rumour!

'Twelve or thirteen wives! What delicately nurtured girl could stand for such a thing?' as Thérésia Cabarrus said to her old nurse.

The governing body of Narkover School is much disturbed by a report that Dr. Smart-Allick recently invited the lovely headmistress of St. Ethelfrith's to sit in the classroom while he was taking the Upper Sixth in card-sense.

Apparently Topsy was installed in an arm-chair by the side of the Doctor's desk, and one of the boys who is in the pay of the governing body reports that from time to time the Doctor would pause, lose the thread of his sentence, and turn to stroke the cheek of the visitor.

When the lady said, with a blush, 'Not in front of the boys,' the Doctor dismissed the class with a wink, crying 'That's all right by me, peach-blossom.'

The governors have drawn up a resolution, in which they state that 'Dr. Smart-Allick's conduct would be more suitable to a dubious dance-hall than to the storied classroom of a great public school. It is, therefore, our painful duty to entreat the Doctor to moderate his transports, and to confine trivial and unseemly dalliance to those moments when youthful and impressionable eyes are safe from the shocking spectacle of unlicensed fondling.'

Dr. Smart-Allick, in his reply, expressed great surprise that these estimable gentlemen should 'endow a merely conventional caress with all the wild debauchery of the Court of Nero.'

He went on:

'A reader of this correspondence would find it hard to believe that the casual tweaking, and, possibly, momentary pinching of a school-teacher's ear should arouse a tumult of such proportions. I hasten to inform these excellent gentlemen that the dormitories of Narkover are devoid of dancing girls, that no pagan music proceeds from the flutes of those entrusted to my care, and that baths in wild asses' milk are still a comparative rarity within our precincts.

'Nor do I pelt adventuresses with roses in school hours. I would but add this: If it should ever become necessary for me to spill the beans I reckon that I know enough about the governing body to ruin it within six hours. *Verb. sap.*'

Topsy has written to the governors of Narkover School as follows:

Gentlemen—(if such you be, which I very much doubt from information in my possession, supplied by my friend Dr. Smart-Allick)—Gentlemen, the degradation of your minds may well be imagined when one realises that you have made a pagan mountain, resounding with licentious revelry, out of a quiet Victorian molehill.

If you require your nominee for a headmastership to be an anchorite, how comes it that you have no provided him with an inaccessible cell upon some windy Atlantic headland? Must a pedagogue, then, astonish his hosiers by ordering none but hairshirts? Must he forgo the pleasures of the table for a disciplinary diet of ground glass? Fie, gentlemen! Live and let live.

After all, it was my ear he pinched, and if anybody has a right to complain, it is I, the unprotected woman. Let us hear no more of this ridiculous affair. Forbear, I beg of you, to sully the fair name of friendship with the foul breath of suspicion.

I honour the Doctor as a chivalrous friend, and I hope I know enough not to permit occasional familiarities to one who would take advantage of my normal love of honest fun.

Miss Topsy Turvey received later a visit from a lady who was a stranger to her. The lady gave no name.

'It would only give her a nasty jar if she knew,' she said to the servant.

The lady was shown in.

'To what may I attribute the pleasure—?' began Topsy.

'Who said anything about pleasure?' snapped the visitor. 'You're very thick with Smart-Allick, aren't you?'

'We certainly see a good deal of each other,' said Topsy.

'Well, if you'll be warned by me,' said the visitor, 'you won't see any more of him.'

'I can take care of myself,' answered the headmistress haughtily.

'You little fool,' hissed the visitor. 'It's not you he's after. It's your dough.'

'And who are you who thus deign to warn me?' asked Topsy.

The visitor lowered her bleary eyes.

'One whose fortune, wisely invested, once meant the whole world to that infamous pedagogue,' she retorted. 'Are you worth much?' she next inquired.

But Topsy was crying softly. In her mind's eye she saw her idol the headmaster's hideous feet of clay. They stuck out a mile.

Dr. Smart-Allick and his love were talking in the rose garden at St. Ethelfrith's. The air was still, the moon was full.

'Tell me, Smarty, have there been other women in your life?'

'Delicate water-lily, I cannot lie to you.'

'Well?'

'I would rather keep silent, my dainty bird of Paradise, upon so weighty a matter.'

'But—but you haven't ever actually been married?'

'Sweet morsel, enchanting may-bud, in his time a man plays many parts. If I have now and then lent the glamour of my name to this or that member of your delightful sex, 'twas but a passing whim, naught but a passing whim, devastating lodestar.'

'Oh, you are false, false, false! Where are they now?'

'Seven in gaol, two at large under assumed names, one on the run, one in Australia,' replied the Doctor briskly, ticking them off on his fingers.

Topsy wept softly.

So strong, however, is the call of love that the Doctor and Topsy met again the next night in the rose-garden at St. Ethelfrith's.

'No, no. Come no nearer, heartless Lothario that you are.'
'Exquisite bud of May, can you not let bygones be bygones—including that provocative widow from Hunstanton?'
'Oh, Smarty, how can I know that you will not, even when we are one, desert me for some more exotic blossom?'
'When we are one? What can my delicious baggage mean by that?'
'Why, when we are married, my cruel Adonis.'
'What have I ever said, ineffable distraction, that would lead you to believe me capable of offering such a base insult to one so like the driven snow? I, who am smirched with a myriad conquests, dare scarcely raise my dazzled eyes to the blazing sun of your beauty and goodness. And you speak of marriage!'
'I understood that our troth was plighted.'
'Plighted my foot, my old cockyolly bird! There must be some mistake.'

The voices ceased. The Doctor strode from the garden. In his heart a bell tolled, and he heard on the breeze a fairy melody which said, 'Suppose she starts the breach of promise racket?'
The forlorn Topsy gazed disconsolately at the moon, and wondered how much money it takes to mend the heart of a fond and foolish headmistress.

On yet another night they met in the rose-arbour.
'Devastating lodestar, I am sure you understand that I have too much decency ever to ask you to become engaged to me with all these so-called Mrs. Smart-Allicks round the place.'
'Heartless Don Juan, do you think a girl such as I would have consented to meet you without a chaperon, had she not believed your intentions to be honourable?'
'But, tiresome enchantress, you have no proof that I ever proposed marriage to you.'
'None, false one. I destroyed all your letters, as you bade me.'
'Excellent morsel! Entrancing elf! Thoughtful witch!'
'But stay, there was that telephone conversation which was overheard by my head monitor Agnes Hauticourt.'
'Thunder and lightning! How could she have overheard it?'
'There's an extension in the monitors' Common Room.'
'Triple damnation! Intoxicating viper, what have you done?'

The Doctor strode from the garden, his strong features working nervously.
Topsy smiled in the darkness.

Dr. Smart-Allick has received the following letter from Mrs. Turvey, of Sea View, Swindon.
MY DEAR DOCTOR SMART-ALLICK,
Though I have not the pleasure of your acquaintance, your name is frequently on my daughter's lips. I am an old woman, and wise in the ways of the world. Naturally my daughter's future is a

matter of great concern to me. Now, Doctor, you also are a man of the world and will understand what I mean when I ask if your intentions are honourable.

Sometimes a man does not realise that what for him may be a mere fancy is for the girl a very grave affair. Topsy tells me that you held her hand recently. I trust that this was rather the poetical prelude to the full blast of romance than the careless gesture of a Don Juan. Pray reassure me, my dear Doctor.

I remain,

Yours truly,

EMMELINE TURVEY

To which he replied:

Mrs. Turvey, honoured madam, your solicitude does you credit as a mother. Your suspicions do you discredit as a woman of the world. Your daughter's honour is as dear to me as my own, and if you start any of the breach of promise stuff, I'll blow the whole gaff, and tell you just where you get off.

Your daughter and I are just good friends. Should any warmer emotion supersede this idyllic comradeship, rest assured that it will be kept within the bounds of respectability. Just you keep out of this.

Yours faithfully,

GEORGE SMART-ALLICK

Topsy has refused to see the Doctor any more.

A note which he threw in at the classroom window said: 'Exasperating blossom, why do you keep me on the white-hot gridiron of doubt? What has your own little pedagogue done to make his own little lodestar so cruel and cold? Give me a sign that I am forgiven, irresistible icicle.'

Miss Turvey was seen to be most upset, and was distinctly heard to tell the class that Queen Elizabeth burnt the cakes at the battle of Omdurman.

But she vouchsafed no answer to the despairing swain.

The death was announced yesterday of Mrs. Emmeline Gascoigne Turvey, widow of Francis Mulsington Turvey, at Sea View, Sebastopol Terrace, Swindon.

It is understood that her large fortune goes to her only daughter, Topsy, at present headmistress of St. Ethelfrith's, Giggling-on-the-Hill.

I was the first to bring the news to Dr. Smart-Allick, of Narkover.

'Poor little thing,' he said.

'Do you still love her?' I asked.

'More than ever,' said the Doctor fervently.

Among my correspondence yesterday was a letter from somebody who tells me that Topsy Turvey is on her way to Ireland, where she hopes to hide herself successfully from Dr. Smart-Allick.

The doctor is stated to have said in public, 'Now that I know she is rich I need not hesitate to offer her the protection which every heiress needs in these lawless days. Furthermore, there are certain fortunes which, by their magnitude, are so enticing that even shrewd business men are prepared to risk a breach of promise action, and the consequent overhead charges.

'I don't know quite what Topsy's little game is, but it can hardly be a coincidence that she dropped a slip of paper bearing her destination. I intend to follow her if necessary from Leopardstown to Baldoyle.'

Yesterday Dr. Smart-Allick and Topsy motored out of Dublin to Killiney. They sat on the hillside, and once more the beauty of the headmistress went to the pedagogue's head like wine.
'Exquisite witch,' he said, 'if an unworthy man might—'
'Yes?' she said expectantly.
'Might venture to speak of his devotion to one so unspeakably fair—'
'Yes?' said Topsy encouragingly.
'Could I but hope,' continued the Doctor, 'that she whom I worship would one day give me leave to call myself her protector—could I but dare to aspire—'
'Yes?' said Topsy, with feigned eagerness.
'If she would but turn her rose-pink ear to attend to my humble suit.'
Topsy lowered her eyes.
'Are you proposing to me?' she asked softly.
Dr. Smart-Allick started violently, and darted a quick look at her face. Once more he shied.
'Not yet, delicious lodestar,' he cried triumphantly, like a man who has locked the bailiffs in the scullery, and escaped great peril for the moment.
Topsy frowned and said it was time to go back to Dublin.

Overheard in the lounge of a Dublin hotel:
'Fragrant lodestar, to be with you for an hour is sheer, undiluted essence of Paradise. What must it be to be with you for ever?'
'To know that, Smart, dear friend, a man would have to try the experiment.'
'Ah, provocative rosebud, happy the man for whom such a lot is reserved. Yet who could dare to aspire, delectable sprite?'
'He who dares nothing gains nothing.'
'Delicious rogue, I dare not take this as an invitation to me to lay bare my heart. Yet—yet—tell me, ineffable witch, is there anyone else?'
'And if there were not, impetuous wretch?'
'Then would I—'
'Yes?'
'Then would I cast myself at your feet, and utter the hot words that are seething inside me. Despair of my soul, will you—won't you—that is, could you ever consider me as your—'
'Say the word, my dearest friend.'
'As your—loyal and devoted friend and—as your true friend, I mean?'
'Nothing nearer?'
'As your—husband? Will you marry me, Topsy, angelic tormentor?'
'Give me a day or two, dear one. Write to me tomorrow.'

Topsy received the following letter from Dr. Smart-Allick, at her Dublin hotel, last night:
INTOXICATING LODESTAR,
I retract no word of what I said to you at the hotel. But I think it would be foolish and rash to take any hurried steps—not that I do not burn to see you enthroned as Narkover's châtelaine, but because evil tongues, wagging untimely, might well suggest that an indecent haste had made me

prefer the pursuit of my own bliss to a nice regard for the feelings of one so recently bereaved—and bereaved to what a tune, if I may drag money into the affair!

Dastardly rumour might even attribute to me some faint hankering for a share of your good fortune—which, I admit, would come in nicely, the public-school business not being what it was. Let us, then, my rosebud, do nothing without forethought.

I count the seconds till I may once again bathe myself in the radiance of that glance.

Yours for better or worse,

GEORGE

The astute headmistress replied:

WICKED ONE,

Your cautious approach to what I had deemed to be the haven of your hopes does more honour to your head than to your heart. *Honi soit* is a maxim I have ever instilled into the girls of St. Ethelfrith's. Why care if others impute evil motives, when you are secure in the knowledge of your own integrity? Is not love enough? Or has solitary reflection cooled the ardour which I thought I discerned in your lightest word? Tell me, in black and white, that you wish to marry me, or I shall go back to Swindon, there to immure myself in a convent, beyond the reach of cruel and predatory men. Reassure me, dear George.

Your anxious lodestar,

TOPSY

Topsy is anxiously waiting to hear from Dr. Smart-Allick. She has not seen him since he proposed to her the other day.

'I expect a letter,' she said to-day, 'by every post, as he promised to put his proposal on paper. You see, a verbal proposal is not much good to an unprotected girl. The man may repent of his action when he gets home. In that event it is very comforting for her to have written evidence of the seriousness of her swain's intentions, in order that she may keep him up to scratch.'

'But do you really love this man?' I asked.
'That is not for a girl to say,' replied the headmistress, rather foolishly.
'What exactly does that mean?' said I.
'One's feelings are sacred,' she answered.

Inquiries at Dr. Smart-Allick's hotel in Dublin revealed that he had passed a very disturbed night. He had paced up and down the corridors, calling frequently for stout, and waking up the other guests by torrents of oaths.

All are agreed that there is something on his mind, especially as he appeared at breakfast wearing two waistcoats but no coat, and with his braces hanging down behind him—to the perpetual peril of his trousers.

Dr. Smart-Allick later disappeared.

When Topsy heard no more from him, she became anxious, and throwing the conventions to the winds, went round to the hotel where the Doctor was staying. To her amazement and chagrin she was told that he had gone suddenly, leaving no address behind him.

On receiving this damnable news the lovely headmistress reeled back as though buffeted by a succession of thunderbolts. All the colour was drained from her face, and muttering, 'Oh, the unmitigated scoundrel,' she was about to leave the hotel.

At that moment a chambermaid handed her a torn and crumpled piece of paper, which had been found in the grate, suggesting that perhaps it would help her to solve the mystery. Topsy glanced at the paper and read: *Oh, Topsy, indeed I meant what I said. I want you to marry me at once, my ineffab—*

Here the writing, which looked like something scratched with a charred stick by a child in a tertian ague on a mountain-top in December—here the writing broke off, as though some powerful emotion had intervened and rendered the scribe's task hopeless.

With a smile the headmistress put the incriminating scrap of paper in her handbag, and walked out of the hotel.

INTERLUDE

Prodnose: Recently you went out of your way to insult the public. You are always telling us that we are idiots.

Myself: And so you are.

Prodnose: Does it ever occur to you that it is out of us that you make your living?

Myself: Exactly. Could there be a better proof of your imbecility than that you will actually pay to read a lot of bosh, day after day? Think of all the fun you might be having instead of straining your eyes. I think it is this incessant reading which gives you that half-frightened, half-dead look. You are nothing better than a heap of fish. Not only do I dislike you; I despise you.

Prodnose: But—

Myself: Go, before I kick you downstairs.

Dr. STRABISMUS

A NEAT INVENTION

Dr. Strabismus (Whom God Preserve) of Utrecht has invented a series of mouse-traps whose aim is 'to wear the mouse out psychologically.'

The mouse sees a bit of cheese and suspects a trap. But it is dummy cheese, and the mouse says to itself, 'Nobody would set a trap with sham cheese, because no mouse would risk its life for such a thing. Therefore there is no trap.'

In walks the mouse, brushing aside the sham cheese, and bumps against a bit of real cheese. 'This must be the trap,' says he, and at once retreats and saves himself.

He finds, all around him, other traps, some baited with real and some with sham cheese, and he grows tired and nervous, until finally he takes a bite at a bit of sham cheese which has been smeared with poison.

BRACEROT

The Doctor is said also to have invented an extraordinary weapon which will make war less brutal. It is described as a very powerful liquid which rots braces at a distance of a mile.

This liquid, which is sprayed out of a sprayer, has no ill effect. It smells like a spring morning. But it is deadly to the material from which braces are made.

Within an hour of an attack by this liquid—which is heavier than air—the braces begin to rot; and finally disintegrate. The air becomes full of the rustle and plop of falling breeches, and the hapless infantrymen find that their movements are impeded by the descended garments.

Also, the idly flapping shirts give them a sense of inferiority.

An experiment was tried in a field near Aldershot, but the wind changed, and a group of interested Staff officers had to waddle hastily to cover behind a lorry, where they remained until spare braces had been brought from Aldershot.

A certain major, whose trousers had fallen over his horse's head, was thrown into a garbage heap. He is now seconded to a Highland regiment.

Several foreign Governments have become interested in the new Strabismus invention for rotting the braces of an army in the field.

The story of how the invention, called Bracerot, was introduced into Germany is not without interest.

A very beautiful spy, as blonde as an egg and Nordic to the finger-tips, dropped her handbag in front of one of the uniformed Storm Milkmen. He retrieved the fallen gewgaw, and she at once told him a ghastly story of the oppression of the Nazis who were being prevented from seizing power in Pomorze, that ancient Prussian territory.

He took the story to the Great High Shock-Council of the Weldgeführengebundgeschlucht-verein.

A special parade was announced in Berlin, to demand the return of Pomorze to the Reich. The Führer himself mounted a rostrum to address the assembled troops.

But what is this? His sensitive nostrils twitch. The air is full of a sweet aroma, and at his first barbarian shriek all hands are raised in the Nazi salute.

Imagine his mortification on hearing a crash of falling trousers, and finding himself confronted with rank upon rank of bony knees.

Holding up his own trousers, he took refuge in his car and drove away, but the troops, being Prussian, did not budge. They remained at the salute, with their breeches about their ankles, because their officers were too confused to give any word of command.

Not a smile illuminated those wooden faces.

And who, you ask, was the spy? Reader, it was—but, no! That is a State secret.

The Prussian Reich is now considering a new kind of steel braces, which would resist the inroads of Bracerot.

Professor Grossvolk has already produced a pamphlet in which he proves that ordinary braces are effeminate and un-Aryan. 'The braces of a Prussian should be of the finest, hardest steel, to match his indomitable soul.'

Mr. Eden is to go to Peking to ask representatives of the Chinese Admiralty whether steel braces ought to be considered as protective armour, if they exceed a certain width. After that he will go to North Borneo to ask the Albanian Foreign Secretary who started the European war, and why.

And then he will go to Carlstad to ask representatives of the Swedish Women's Co-operative Industrial Federation why Prussia has torn up another treaty. A representative of Bracerot, Ltd. will accompany him.

The Great High Prussian Storm-and-Shock Commander has issued an order that during the present epidemic of Bracerot every Nordic man is to wear two pairs of braces, and to carry a third pair of Emergency Braces in his knapsack.

When he feels his braces disintegrating he is to sing a patriotic air, salute with one hand, and adjust the Emergency Braces with the other.

General Goering said yesterday:

There are weaker Non-Aryan races who may imagine that an Aryan can be made to look undignified if you deprive him of braces. Our reply is that the old Norse gods never knew what braces were, and if necessary we will dress like them, in monstrous nightshirts. The Latins, softened by luxury, think that no man can go into battle with his trousers down. Trousers or no trousers, it is our mission to save Europe from Shintoism, and I—

PHWOOSH! Down fell his Nordic breeches.

The spy who succeeded in introducing Bracerot into Prussia seems to have discovered how easy it is to make the pompous and foolish Boche look even sillier than he is.

At a mammoth meeting in Berlin to protest against the existence of the Polish Army, the principal speakers suddenly felt their trousers loosening, and had to disappear hurriedly. At another meeting to protest against the existence of the French Army, three very high officials were subjected to the same humiliating experience.

Later in the day a march-past of Storm Troops, held on the occasion of the protest against the continued occupation of Switzerland by the Swiss, had to be discontinued. As each battalion drew level with the saluting base its breeches fell with a rush.

But as for me, would that I were in Perpignan, at the Sign of the Golden Lion.

A long memorandum, drawn up by some of the most prominent men in Prussia, suggests that belts should be substituted for braces. These belts would be coated with a certain chemical capable of resisting Bracerot, and nullifying its effects.

At the first test, in a field outside Berlin, the trousers of the savants fell with the customary crash.

The same thing occurred at a mass demonstration in favour of the return of the French Channel ports to the Reich.

I learn that Prussia will on no account join any conference unless a guarantee is given that disarmament shall apply first and foremost to Bracerot, which saps the fighting spirit of even Nordic fools. The English reply will be that the manufacture of large quantities of Bracerot stimulates the braces industry, and does not necessarily make a nation bloodthirsty.

Prussia maintains that the deliberate rotting of braces constitutes an act of aggression. She refuses to be encircled by the brace-rotting nations.

CONTRETEMPS IN THE BILLIARD ROOM

A pathetic story lies behind the latest experiments of Dr. Strabismus (Whom God Preserve) of Utrecht, in the matter of growing hair on billiard balls.

Some years ago the Doctor was staying at the country house of a certain Colonel Sopper. The Colonel and his most intimate friend, General Tumult, liked to play billiards together after dinner. Both were bald and short-sighted.

The Colonel was a small man, and had often been tapped on the head by the spoons of short-sighted guests at the breakfast-table. One night he laid his head on the edge of the billiard table to judge an angle, and the General potted him rather hard.

The mistake was taken with great good nature by the Colonel, but when it happened every night, he grew tired of it. It was then that the Doctor designed wigs for the balls, in order to distinguish them from the heads of the military gentlemen. But it was observed that the wigs fell off when the balls were struck.

So the Doctor tried to grow real hair on them, but without success.

General Tumult was also bald, as I have said, and one day while he was dozing in the Cavalry Club a subaltern painted a map of India on his head. Even with his hat on you could see Allahabad on his forehead for several days.

TAKE IT OR LEAVE IT

Dr. Strabismus (Whom God Preserve) of Utrecht has invented a small circular spoon, with a hole in the middle. Through this hole the cook can look at whatever she is about to stir.

The spoon has no handle, so that when looking at, say, porridge, through the hole, the cook must hold the spoon by the rim of the circle. When the actual stirring is to begin, a handle can be fitted to the spoon, or else an ordinary spoon can be used.

'If you're in one of your saucy moods, Major, you'd better stay outside.'

ANOTHER TRUE STORY

The story of the man whose baldness made him so shy that he was allowed to wear his hat in a police court reminds me of the man whose nose was so ugly that he was allowed to wear a false one.

The jury laughed at him, and he hung his head and scraped the floor with his foot. Off dropped the false nose, and a roar of laughter smote the mildewed walls of the court.

He was too shy to pick up the nose, but a little girl stole forward and retrieved it. At this gracious act the laughter turned to tears, and somewhere at the back of the court a lonely violin played 'In a Monastery Garden,' while women wept aloud and men blinked to keep back the tell-tale drops.

The magistrate lay sprawled across his desk, his shoulders heaving like the body of a sleeping hedgehog. A police sergeant drew his sleeve across his eyes, and four hundred love-birds, released from a cage in the weighing and robing room, fluttered harmlessly about the rostrum.

Meanwhile the little girl, whose name was Agnes, was stroking the grizzled head of the prisoner and murmuring in his cauliflower ear gentle words of affection. And so an old man's heart came softly into haven at the close of a summer's day.

Years later, when time had silvered the golden locks of Agnes, and the man with the false nose had gone to that bourne from which no hollingsworth returns, the sweet benefactress, routing in an old cupboard, found a false nose among the family papers. Memory at once touched her with its fleeting wing, and she remembered the smell of the courthouse, the bowed head of the prisoner, the courteous old magistrate. And as she raised her tear-stained face she thought she saw the man with the ugly nose sitting on a cloud and playing upon a golden harp that air which had drawn them together. Fervently she clasped her hands and pitched headlong in a swoon. Graham, her trusty old family butler—

PRODNOSE: Won't that be enough?

MYSELF: As far as I'm concerned, I wish I'd never started it.

CAUSERIE DE SAMEDI

Once upon a time there were two fleas, inseparable companions, and ambitious, as fleas are wont to be. In the course of time, as fleas will, they became millionaires. And what do you think they bought with their money? A fine upstanding dog.

ADVERTISEMENT CORNER

A young traveller in wire-netting was bitten by a gnat on the side of the head, while sun-bathing at Littlehampton. When he attempted to put his bowler on he found that the inside of the crown pressed on the bite, and hurt like fury. So he had to wear the hat almost over one ear, and was, of course, sacked by his employer. Two days later his employer, while sun-bathing at Frinton, was also bitten by a gnat—and also on the side of the head. He, too, had to wear his bowler almost over one ear, which made him *understand the other fellow's point of view*. He sent for the young traveller, reinstated him, and made him sales-manager. Which shows that a little thing like a gnat-bite may start that fermentation of the milk of human kindness which is the secret of happy co-operation between employer and employee. For one gnat-bite on the head makes the whole world kin. So start to-morrow being kind to gnats, and then, perhaps, they will bite *you*.

(Advt.)

COME INTO THE KITCHEN

(With Mrs. Whelkstüffer, author of 'The Truth About Mutton,' 'Blancmange and I,' 'Roast and Be Damned!' etc.)

Take a cauliflower. Tear it to bits. Sift it through a sieve into a copper pan. Drop cheese on to it. Serve cold. This is Cold Cauliflower Maîtresse d'Hôtel.

THE 'NARKOVERIAN'

I have received the first number of a new school magazine, the *Narkoverian*, produced by the Narkover boys. It is full of good things. I like very much the idea of the gallery of famous old Narkoverians 'who have shed lustre upon their alma mater.' Number One, who appears in this issue, is Sir Harry Gutkin, and the short biography runs as follows:

Gutkin, Sir Harry (alias Fred Whitlow), company promoter, s. of late Tom Clutch, m. Millie Rathouse. Vice-President Washington Irving Society. Took prominent part in Anglo-Korean mines incident of 1919. Shot in back 1920. President (until imprisoned) of Scottish Diamond Mines, Inc.; chairman Hungarian Lighthouse Development; secretary Sahara Irrigation Co., Ltd.; treasurer Oxford and Cambridge Oil Co.; hon. treasurer (until imprisonment) Turkish Sardine Trust. Clubs: Senior Hunted Financiers, Junior Beetle. Hobbies: cards, dice, roulette. Address: c/o Solomon Basch, 819 Scoggs Street, Whitechapel.

A RUMOUR DENIED

I am asked to deny once again the rumour that Lady Cabstanleigh is to be floodlit. I have a letter from her solicitors, Messrs. Robb, Steele, Pilfer, Pilfer, Robb and Steele, on the subject. Here is the important passage:

. . . Our client, though of generous build, can in no sense be said to constitute a public monument or other edifice or structure, within or without the meaning of or by the Act. The floodlighting of human beings cannot be held to be the prerogative of any company, society, guild, syndicate, board, committee, sub-committee, league or omniumgatherum whatsoever. In the case of demiseizin, replevin, or mayhem on the high seas, a warrant of restraint may be applied for under article 64 of the Seasonal Restrictions (Incomplete) Act of 1868.

BIG WHITE CARSTAIRS AND THE M'BABWA OF M'GONKAWIWI

BIG WHITE CARSTAIRS has been busy preparing a list of the names of African chieftains who might be invited to attend the Coronation celebrations in England. The most picturesque personality on the list is the Yubwa of Yubwabu, who stamps all his letters with the skull of a warrior dipped in boiling dirtibeeste's-milk cheese, and has thick hair on the soles of his feet.

His grandfather travelled 4,000 miles through dense jungle to meet Livingstone near the Victoria Falls. After a journey of eight months he arrived at the meeting-place, only to find that he had missed Livingstone by fourteen minutes. He ran after him, but was too tired to go far, and so he and Livingstone never met.

Livingstone was told the story years later at a reception given by Lady Berrington. He laughed a good deal.

If the Coronation festivities include a processional march of the representatives of the Empire, will the M'Babwa of M'Gonkawiwi be included? And will he insist on being accompanied by Ugli, the witch-doctor and perhaps by Jum-Jum, the sacred crocodile? A special committee of M.P.s is meeting at the House of Commons to consider these questions.

There is a feeling in some quarters that if one curious potentate and his entourage are to be honoured, then the claims of others must be considered. And that brings us to the fascinating question of what is to be done with the Wug of Noonooistan and his Holy Apes, Buruwo and Buruwa; with the Baffomi of Gopahungi; with the Padalu of Pokmo; with the Hereditary Snevelinka of Ridolulu and his Dancing Bear; with the Bhopi of Sliwiziland; with Mrs. Elspeth Nurgett, M.B.E., and her corps of Swuruhi Girl Guides; with the yellow harbourmaster at Grusti-wowo Bay; with Hijiwana, the Queen of the Waspidili pigmies; and with Plakka, the roving ambassador of the Nopi of Buttabuttagatawni.

A message from Big White Carstairs has reached the Colonial Office. It says that the M'Babwa of M'Gonkawiwi insists on marching through London, so that people may see him. His party which will accompany him on the march, is to include Jum-Jum the sacred crocodile, Ugli the witch-doctor, eighteen wives, thirty-eight devil dancers, forty-one pigmies, a sorcerer, an astrologer, four idol carriers, six head-hunters, a dwarf wrestler, the Zimbabwe Wanderers cricket team, the Umpopo United football team, Mrs. Roustabout, the missionary, the old tribal hedge-hog, a mad spearman, a baboon, a herd of dirtibeeste, and a native actress.

The M'Babwa of M'Gonkawiwi, who has hitherto taken no part in the controversy which is raging over his visit to England, broke his silence yesterday with a strong expletive much used by his tribe. When Carstairs told him that the Great White Mother Over the Sea might not be too pleased to welcome Ugli the witch-doctor and Jum-Jum the sacred crocodile, the M'Babwa said, 'Ufganoola.' A rough translation of this would be, 'I hope you and your Great White Mother may be roasted over a slow fire of dirtibeeste's wool.' He later insisted on bringing his team of devil dancers, his eighteen wives, his magicians, and his pigmy poisoners. Carstairs at once cabled to the Colonial Office as follows:

M'Babwa threatening bring devildancers wives magicians poisoners stop what action advised stop.

The Colonial Office cabled back:

Impossible include poisoners magicians wives devildancers in official welcome stop must come as private tourists stop.

There has been a spirited correspondence between Big White Carstairs and various Government departments on the subject of the visit for the Coronation of his Serene Highness the M'Babwa of M'Gonkawiwi, M'Gibbonuki, M'Bobowambi, Zimbabwe, and the Wishiwashi hinterland, comprising Wowo, Nikiwawa, Wibbliwambi, M'Hoho, M'Haha, M'Tralala Zogomumbozo, Moponambi, Nambipambi, and Sockemondejaw.

In answer to the application for an invitation, the Colonial Office wrote to Carstairs:

. . . We have been unable to find some of the places mentioned as being under the jurisdiction of his Serene Highness on any map. Nor have we been able to trace a ruler with such a title as the M'Babwa claims. Is the M'Hoho mentioned in your report the M'Hoho near Zumzum or the M'Hoho near Wodgi? Should he travel as the ruler of the places mentioned he will be allotted a seven-and-sixpenny seat in Shepherd's Bush. If, on the other hand, he travels as Mr. Posworth, we can promise him nothing nearer than Slough High Street. The suggestion that he should bring with him a tribal witch-doctor and a sacred alligator is not favourably viewed. There is no accommodation for witch-doctors or animals, though doubtless the latter could be temporarily accommodated at Whipsnade, and the former in Bond Street, in the parlour of Mme La Zophitella, star-gazer. . . .

Carstairs replied:

. . . Of the utmost importance not to offend the M'Babwa. Discontent among the tribes in his territory might mean a rising of the Slobga pygmies and the Ushawiri head-hunters. Could not the sacred crocodile be held up at the Customs until a doctor's examination had certified some infectious disease? As to the witch-doctor, why not get him into some Mayfair set? Plant him on the rich women as a new craze. They've never met anyone who can foretell the weather from the entrails of a goat. . . . Most of the M'Babwa's possessions are not on any map yet, but the M'Hoho mentioned is the one near Wodgi. . . . You can't put him as far off as Slough. There'd be a rising here . . .

The Colonial Office has just been thrown into as fine a state of panic as ever seized a flock of Limousin sheep by another despatch from Big White Carstairs.

It appears that the M'Babwa of M'Gonkawiwi has assimilated huggermugger and helterskelter and hotcherypotchery a certain amount of Western usage—just enough to make things awkward for everybody. He has, for instance, determined to travel to England as plain 'Mr. Hurst,' while his wives have been saddled with the names of English football teams, such as Oldham Athletic, Sheffield Wednesday, and so forth. Ugli, the witch-doctor, is to travel as Herr Goethe, and Jum-Jum, the sacred crocodile, as Fido. Carstairs has pointed out that this is not the right procedure for the occasion. But the M'Babwa is as stubborn as a Numidian goat. Furthermore he insists on wearing his cricket cap (Zimbabwe Wanderers) while in England.

Yesterday Miss Whelkstone (Soc., Wriggleminster) asked the Minister of Transport whether the system of lights applied to sacred crocodiles. The Minister replied that he did not anticipate that the crocodile would be allowed to go out unaccompanied. Major Thruster (Con., Thostle-hampton-with-Buckett) said he thought foreign visitors would get a very queer idea of the Empire if they found the hotels and restaurants filled with the magicians and devil dancers of dubious potentates. The Home Secretary, or someone made up to look like him, said that His Majesty's Government had never at any time contemplated filling hotels and restaurants with magicians or devil dancers. There would, at most, be a round dozen, and arrangements were being made to shove them on to the Boy Scout organisations.

Miss Wilkinson: Shame!

Miss Rathbone: Yes, shame!

The Speaker: Will you two ladies kindly stop talking rubbish?

Mr. Hatt (Lib., Pomphbury): In the event of the M'Babwa of M'Gonkawiwi seeing fit to include cannibals in his suite, will the Board of Trade give an undertaking that no foreign visitors will be eaten?

Miss Rathbone: Are they to eat the English, then?

Miss Wilkinson: Yes, are they to eat the English, then?

No answer was given.

AT THE BOARD OF AGRICULTURE AND FISHERIES

Memo:

What is all this about an African chief and his crocodile? What are we supposed to do?

Memo:

It's a sacred crocodile. I don't see where we come in.

Memo:

What do you mean—'sacred'?

Memo:

I don't know. I suppose they worship it.

Memo:

If so, it comes under the Established Church. Better pass all this correspondence on to the Home Office.

Mrs. Wretch, supported by the P.E.N. Club, Auntie Edna's International Pacifists, Mr. Aldous Huxley, Mrs. Wurfie, and the Neo-Liberal League, is making a last frantic appeal to the Home Office to keep the M'Babwa of M'Gonkawiwi out of England. From a photograph in her posession she has established the fact that he wears a black shirt. But Big White Carstairs has cabled: 'That is not a shirt stop it is his chest stop.' Mrs. Wretch, however, is still convinced that he is a Fascist, and that his mission is to annoy Professor Laski, and to carry on secret propaganda against the National Liberal Club.

Unless the Home Office can be persuaded to act, the M'Babwa will arrive in England shortly.

The following statement was made in the House yesterday with reference to the M'Babwa of M'Gonkawiwi:

Unless our dusky cousin from overseas intends to appear in London naked to the waist, the blackness of his chest should not give offence to that progressive and enlightened part of our population which, very naturally, sees in this colour an organised international menace to progressive Liberalism and enlightened Marxism.

Dear Sir,

Much as I love our great British Empire—I had a cousin once who was rescued from drowning by an Australian—I do not see why the M'Babwa of M'Gonkawiwi should be given facilities for seeing the Coronation when so many white people will not be able to see it. Furthermore, by extending hospitality to an animal and a witch-doctor, we are carrying democracy to absurd lengths.

I learn that an official of the R.S.P.C.A. has objected to the sacred crocodile Jum-Jum being lodged in an aquarium, where it would have to mix with ordinary animals. It is further pointed out that much cruelty is needed to train a crocodile to be sacred, and the suggestion is that if the beast comes to London it should be looked after by a Mrs. Gespill, whose lodging-house in the Camberwell Road is a haven for creatures of the deep, including the toothless shark from Dumeira, captured by Rear-Admiral Sir Ewart Hodgson during manoeuvres in the Red Sea.

Asked yesterday whether the M'Babwa of M'Gonkawiwi, etc., had a seat reserved for him at the Coronation, Mr. Ramsay MacDonald said: 'What we have to do is, at present, according to what we can do, is to see that in the allocation of seats, that is, of seats for various people at the Coronation, is to see that the seats are sufficient. The question of the M'Babwa being allowed to have his crocodile Jum-Jum next to him is a question which must be decided by those who are competent to make such a decision, that is, by those who have the competent authority to make a decision on this matter. Such decisions can only be made by the people who can make decisions of this sort in such matters, not otherwise. What we have to do is to see that this is done, or to see that somebody does it, who can do it, in such a matter, I think.'

Mrs. Borgholz asked to-day in the House whether it is a fact that the chest of the M'Babwa of M'Gonkawiwi is really black, and if this is not Fascist propaganda designed to prevent the British public from knowing that he wears a black shirt. It is suggested in progressive quarters that Miss Wilkinson and Miss Rathbone and Canon Ball should make a journey of investigation to find out to what extent Fascism is prevalent among the M'Gonkawiwi tribes.

A sad voice interposed: 'But who will pay for the trip?'

Another voice replied, 'The Moujiks, Ltd., Travel Agency.'

The affair of Carstairs, the M'Babwa, and the Colonial Office has reached such gross proportions that the Colonial Office has ceased attempting to push the whole thing on to the Board of Agriculture and Fisheries, on the plea that Jum-Jum, the sacred crocodile, is a beast to be dealt with by that department.

Meanwhile Carstairs has received the following letter from Lady Cabstanleigh:

Dear Major Carstairs,

I trust you will forgive the liberty I am taking, but a mutual friend of ours, young Hoofe of the Colonial Office crowd, tells me there is some hitch about one of your local big pots bringing his witch-doctor to England. I understand the fellow's name is Ugli. Is he more of a witch than a doctor or vice versa? Well, I thought I might help you all out by putting the fellow up while he's here. What does he eat and drink? Will he have dress clothes? I suppose he's not utterly savage—not that one really cares, but there'll be a sort of bishop in the house, and I don't want any exorcism stuff. And I hope he can behave decently. I mean, I've never forgotten that Rumanian gipsy singer who bit the neck off a magnum of Yquem 1904. By the way, I suppose he's plumb black. If he's yellow I shall unload him on to Sybil, who loves 'em yellow ever since she was rescued from a snake by a Chinese chef. But it turned out to be jaundice. Forgive me for bothering you. . . .

Carstairs has replied to Lady Cabsanleigh's offer to accommodate the witch-doctor:

Dear Lady Cabstanleigh,

I'm afraid the witch-doctor Ugli would be rather a handful for you. He chants incantations all night, picks his teeth with his spear, and lights bonfires whenever he can. One does one's best, but all one's efforts to make him change for dinner have so far failed. He simply doesn't seem to understand, and, under his influence, even the M'Babwa himself won't go beyond a dinner jacket and a black tie. He seems to think a white tie is some sort of symbol of the domination of the white races—as indeed it is. For these reasons I hesitate to put him on to you. And he might start sacrificing one of the ladies to Bok, the headless god of the Boopi jungle. And then the bishop you spoke of would have to intervene, I suppose. And you couldn't have the papers getting hold of a story of human sacrifice at Cabstanleigh Towers. I'm rather inclined to get him into some quiet hotel in Kensington, where the retired Army and Naval officers might be able to manage him . . . . I understand that the Galashiels Aquarium has offered to house Jum-Jum, the sacred crocodile, temporarily.

Professor Roosch, Tollemache Professor of Comparative Folk-Lore at Oxford, has written to the Colonial Office to point out that the housing of the sacred crocodile Jum-Jum in the Galashiels Aquarium would most certainly be resented all along the lower Poopoo, and might start a Garumpi, or holy crocodile war, since Jum-Jum is supposed to be a kind of deity. To which the Galashiels Aquarium replied that they already have a sacred codfish from Bali and that it is treated just like any other cod, except that on the occasion of the first full moon after August Bank Holiday it is exchanged for a dwarf jelly-fish in the Bodmin Aquarium, according to a proviso in the will of the donor, Captain Marabout.

Carstairs landed at Southampton from the *Megatherium* yesterday morning. He was met by his mother, and motored straight to his home near Brocklehurst. His mother said, in an exclusive interview, 'I am so glad to have my son home again.

'It is so good to have him back. Naturally I am delighted to have him back home again, and to see him again. It is so good to see him back that I am overjoyed to have him with me once more, and to have him back again, so that I can have him home again.

'I am so glad to see him back again, and so glad that he is home once more. It is so good to have him back, and to see him home again once more. I am delighted to have my son back home, and to see him again. It is so good to see him back home, and I am delighted to have him back.

'Naturally I am very glad to have him with me once more, and to see him back. And I am overjoyed to be able to have him home with me again, and to see him once more, now that he is back home again with me. It is so good to have him back home again and to see him back.'

Carstairs said, 'Everyone has been most frightfully decent, and I must say I think everybody's been awfully good.

'Naturally I am fearfully glad to be back home again with my mother, and to see her again, now that I am back home again once more. It is so good to see her again, now that I am back home, and I'm naturally pretty pleased to be back again, so that I can see her now that I am home again with her once more.

'It is frightfully good to be home again with my mother, so that I can see her, and I am awfully glad to see her now that I can be back home again with her again.'

ERRATUM

In my article on the Price of Milk, 'Horses' should have read 'Cows' throughout.

OLD BADHAT ARRIVES

A Challenge to Youth!

We have all had enough of the infant prodigy. There should be a hearty welcome for a new arrival in London, a Turkish violinist named Badhat, who is said to be more than a hundred years old. He plays very little, and very slowly, as by the time evening concerts begin he is half asleep. For this reason musical critics, who are generally half asleep themselves, have had a certain difficulty in judging his playing.

For his first appearance last night he chose two short pieces of his own composition. The first was almost inaudible, owing to the feebleness of his bowing and his constant drowsy pauses. In the middle of the second piece he fell asleep for a few minutes, while the auditorium was hushed, at first with embarrassment and later with kindly goodwill towards the poor old man.

He awoke after a time, and resumed his fiddling, but his yawns announced that he was fighting a losing battle.

Two bars before the end attendants carried him to his bed in the changing room.

I will now print a criticism of the Turkish virtuoso's first appearance in England from the pen of one of London's foremost musical critics.

OVATION FOR TURKISH VIOLINIST

My musical critic writes:

In 1887 Cosima Liszt wrote to Hirsch, 'All my life I have thought that Kabbitch played the Rondo Capriccioso too slowly. Now, at the age of ninety-four, I am not sure he was not right.' I could not help remembering this as I listened to Badhat, the most considerable violinist Turkey has sent us since Ayoub. There is a kind of patina about his playing which brings out the middle-distance of the melody, and by the very slowness of his tempo he conjures up the slowly moving camel trains of his Asiatic home. Vladimir Skraping takes seven minutes and thirty-one seconds to play Drischin's *March of the Men of Sobelsohngrad*. Badhat last night took nineteen minutes, which would lead one to believe that the men of Sobelsohngrad were as somnolent as this centenarian violinist. Yet one forgets everything in the long-drawn sweetness of the final bars. Badhat, who has been playing for more than ninety years, can never have played better than last night. At the end he was awakened by the applause of a frantic audience. It was not very sporting of them to demand an encore. Only a snore responded.

BADHAT AGAIN

Badhat, the centenarian Turkish violinist, appeared again at the Bœotian Hall last night. He was to have played a new Hungarian tone poem called 'Bitten by Jackals,' which won the Prix de Helsingfors two years ago. But Badhat fell asleep while the pianist was playing the interminable rubbish which introduces the composition. When they awoke the old man, he shouted drowsily for sherbet, and then went to sleep again. The audience's money was given back grudgingly, and Badhat was taken back to his hotel in a cab.

WICKLEFIDGET

I thought I was safe in inventing, two days ago, the name Praggsley Wicklefidget as an example of a fantastic name which nobody would claim. I was wrong.

Dear Sir,

The attention of our client, Mr. Praggsley Wicklefidget, has been called to a paragraph in your column of 23rd November. Mr. Wicklefidget himself, his unmarried sister, Miss Anne Wicklefidget, his aged grandmother, Mrs. Veronica Wicklefidget, his married sisters, Mrs. T. H. Fobcraft and Mrs. Buttery Darter, his aunt, Mrs. Euonima Nurgle, his fiancée, Miss Celery Seeking, and many other relatives and friends, have been, not unnaturally, considerably upset at this gratuitous reference to the family name in a newspaper with a circulation of nearly five million. Our client, therefore, has instructed us to demand a full apology for what he cannot but regard, at its mildest, as a grave lapse of taste. Yours faithfully.

Haggisberg, Cutacross, Pipperby, Tufteigh, Wallow-Wallow, Twosafrock, Murmurhurst, Owtch, and Candleson.

MY REPLY

Dear Messrs, Haggisberg, Cutacross, Pipperby, etc. etc. etc.,

I do not believe in the existence of your client. I do not even believe in the existence of your firm. I see no reason why you should believe in my existence. So the whole thing becomes mere nonsense. Good day.

Yours faithfully,
Conworthy Bwilph.

THEY BOTHER ME AGAIN

Dear Sir,

If you will look up your Nackstone on Smigony and Validification, you will find that a plea of non-existence is no justification of rebuttal and rebiliment. You exist. We exist. Our client Mr. Wicklefidget exists. And, as Mr. Justice Cocklecarrot ruled in the famous case of the Peruvian Tin-Openers' Association and Mrs. Whackstraw versus Miss Norma Raggett and the South-Northern Railway: 'Where existence can be proved it must be assumed to be a reality.' We therefore repeat, on behalf of our client, the demand for a full apology.

Yours faithfully,
Haggisberg, Cutacross, Pipperby, etc. etc. etc.

MY REPLY

I have instructed my solicitors, Messrs. Teamarch, Beerbody, Awlbutt, Fawfinger, Udge, Gackork, Plithwith, Emerl, Spivingham, Rathit, Oomes, Spickmarl, Pernott, Tylidge, Polie, Toothwood, Dioneer, Dogling, Headwaters, Vistigo, Morrid, Hundive, and Knickerstick to offer an apology to all concerned, except Miss Celery Seeking, who, being only Mr. Wicklefidget's fiancée, is still only a Seeking, and not yet a full-fledged Wicklefidget.

Within a few weeks everybody will be talking about 'Thunderbolt' Footle, the new discovery of that greatest of British boxing promotors, Scrubby Botulos.

Mr. Botulos said yesterday, in an interview, 'Here, at last, is the genuine article. He's very handsome, dresses well, and has a number of good books at his lodgings. I have worked out a preliminary programme. I'm going to fix a fight with someone not too good. The Thunderbolt will win, and we shall then have no difficulty in getting him on to the films. During the making of his first film he will become more or less engaged to an actress—or, better, to a society girl. That will keep his name before the public, and there will be no need to tire him with too much fighting. The idea of calling him Thunderbolt before he has done any fighting is to get the public to realise how good he's going to be.'

Mr. Botulos then distributed photographs of the new world-beater, showing his enormous muscles, which, said Mr. Botulos, 'are harder than iron, and bigger too.'

I understand that a fifteen-round contest has been fixed up between 'Thunderbolt' Footle and 'Slugger' Faxafloi, the man-eater from Iceland. It will take place some time within the next year, if Footle's theatrical and film and concert engagements permit. Footle said yesterday, 'I shall not train much. I don't have to. My dancing keeps me fit. And, anyway, one blow will finish the fight. He won't know what hit him.'

It is rumoured that Footle is engaged to be married to Miss Mae West. But he said yesterday, 'We're just good pals.' Miss West said, 'Where does he get that stuff about being good?' Meanwhile the Thunderbolt is being sued for breach of promise by a friend of his publicity manager, Joe Bulgetti.

Mr. Billy ('Haunch') Venison, the boxing critic, said yesterday, 'It's difficult to say much about the Thunderbolt till we've seen him fight. He'll have to fight somebody sooner or later. That yarn about how he can smash through a six-foot wall with his bare fist doesn't impress me. It is told of every British heavy-weight. I know that wall. It's a cardboard one, kept in the training quarters and photographed with a hole in it.'

'I SHALL WIN'

('Thunderbolt' Footle)

The Thunderbolt's manager, Scrubby Botulos, announced yesterday that the fight between his man and Faxafloi will have to take place very soon, because the film and cabaret people are not inclined to give good contracts to an unknown boxer. 'The pooblic,' he said, 'was not interested in a singer or a dancer until he will be have won a fight or two. What we was have got to get is that our man Footle shall have been proved to be a chimpiron.'

Footle said: 'The fight's as good as over. He won't know about it until the hospital surgeon brings him round. He won't know what hit him. I'll just give him one jab. He needn't bother to come into the ring. I'll just knock him through the ropes. You may say that I shall win easily by a knockout in the first second of the fight.'

The boxing critic, Billy ('Haunch') Venison, said: 'It's difficult to say anything until one has seen the fighters at work. I think that Footle should win unless Faxafloi proves too much for him. The same may be said of Faxafloi, only vice, of course, versa.'

Asked by his publicity manager whether the newspapers were to be informed that he had a deadly right or a deadly left, the Thunderbolt said, 'Everything about me is deadly. I'm dynamite from head to foot. He won't know what hit him.'

Faxafloi said, 'I shall win. He'll never know what hit him. I've got a load of dynamite in each fist.'

Informed of this, Footle said, 'I shall win. I've got more dynamite in my little finger than he'll ever have in his whole body. He won't know what hit him.'

Informed of this, Faxafloi said, 'I won't have to hit him. Just a flick. I'm dynamite. He'll never know what hit him.'

Asked what his tactics would be, Footle said, 'I won't need any. Just a tap and he'll be in the doctor's hands for a year. I'm made of dynamite. He won't know what hit him.'

It was announced at Footle's headquarters to-day that the Thunderbolt had strained his throat while fulfilling a crooning engagement at a cabaret. But he was out in the afternoon, skipping and being photographed. Later he dislocated his thumb with a savage blow at the punchball, which bounded back, struck him on the head, and knocked him down.

'He is a real fighter,' said Scrubby Botulos. 'He doesn't seem to know the meaning of defence, he's so aggressive.'

The Thunderbolt said, 'I shall win. He won't even guess what hit him.'

'Even if he did guess he wouldn't believe it,' sneered an onlooker.

Mrs. Dietrich, when asked if she would attend a film with the Thunderbolt, said, 'You can say we are just pals. I hope to meet him soon.' Joan Crawford, when asked if there was anything in the rumour of her affection for Footle, said, 'I have never met him, but we are just good pals.' Constance Bennett said, 'I've never heard of him. We are just pals, that's all.'

'Thunderbolt' Footle, Britain's new heavy-weight boxer, has signed a contract to appear as Faust in Gounod's opera. A daily paper has acquired the rights of 'The Story of my Fights,' which will not be published until he has done some fighting. Meanwhile he is still training for his fight with Faxafloi, the mystery heavy-weight from Iceland. Owing to the calls upon him for making gramophone records and being photographed at parties, the Thunderbolt will probably have training quarters in a large flat off Piccadilly. To-morrow he is skipping in Hyde Park for United International Films, Ltd. It is hoped that before his training is over he will appear at the first night of a new film with Mrs. Dietrich.

'Thunderbolt' Footle was knocked out four times yesterday, once by each of his sparring partners. His trainer said, 'Thunderbolt wasn't really trying, and he wasn't ready, and the sun was in his eyes. You can tell what he's made of by what he said when he came to in his dressing-room. He said, "He'll never know what hit him. I'm dynamite. That's what I am. Dynamite." '

Rumour is still coupling Footle's name with that of Miss Mae West. 'You may say we're just pals,' he said yesterday.

Asked what his tactics would be in the fight with Faxafloi, he said, 'I won't need any. I shall just come out of my corner like a whirlwind on the stroke of the bell. One blow will finish it.' At last Britain seems to have a champion.

Faxafloi appears to be a grim young man. He can't croon, doesn't like dancing, and doesn't want to be an actor. 'In fact, all he can do is fight,' said his trainer.

The fifteen-round contest between 'Thunderbolt' Footle and Rink Faxafloi, the Iceland Wizard, will take place on Monday night. The hour has been changed from nine-thirty to eight-thirty, because the Thunderbolt has a cabaret engagement later in the evening. Footle said yesterday, 'I shall win. He won't know what hit him. Then I'm ready for Louis, Schmeling, Baer, Farr, one at a time or all together. I'm set for the championship, and you may say that I consider it an honour to bring glory to British boxing.'

Scrubby Botulos said, 'I'll be surprised if that Icelander even gets out of his corner to begin the fight.' And 'Haunch' Venison, the boxing critic, said, 'The fellow with the most dynamite in his

fists is going to win. It's always been my experience that, in a heavy-weight fight, the winner is the one that can put the other fellow down for the count. If I had to hazard a guess, I should say this fight will be no exception to that rule.'

England is talking of nothing but the forthcoming big fight to-night at Burlington House. Has Britain at last found a native champion? Will this, Footle's first fight, put him at one bound in the forefront, etc. etc. etc.?

A round-by-round description of the fight will be broadcast, the running commentary being in the capable and experienced hands of Mr. Guy Babblebotham and Mr. Hardleigh A. Mouse. ('Slop' of the *Sporting Chance*.)

Footle took things quietly yesterday, to avoid becoming stale. He lay in bed and read Upchurch's *Pragmatism and the Endocrine Gland*, while his publicity manager wrote thousands of telegrams wishing him good luck, signed by such celebrities as Rabindranath Tagore ('Sock him, feller!'), Mae West ('May victory smile upon you!'), Gabriele d'Annunzio ('Atta Thunderbolt!'), the League Council ('Geneva is with you, cully'), the Southern Railway ('May the decenter man win'), and Rear-Admiral Sir Ewart Hodgson ('Lots Road is watching you').

Hardly had my little pen come trippingly off the paper at the end of that last sentence, when a news agency message was handed to me by my assistant under-secretary.

The fight is postponed! Not enough people have bought seats. Lack of interest is attributed to the fact that Footle has not become engaged to any actress. So, in order to lose as little time as possible, the publicity manager has got him engaged to that tiresome old-stager, Boubou Flaring. As I write this, they are being photographed together. He is saying, 'Boubou is just swell,' and she is replying, 'Thunderbolt's a great guy.' And already seats are being bought like hot cakes. So it is unlikely that the postponement will be for more than a day or two.

To-night the British hope, Footle, will meet the Iceland Man-Eater, Faxafloi, in a fifteen-round contest at Burlington House at 9.30. The running commentary by Mr. Guy Babblebotham and Mr. Hardleigh A. Mouse will be broadcast.

Footle is said to have developed a curious back-hand swing which will prove deadly. He said this morning, 'I shall win. Probably a knock-out in round one. I'm dynamite.' Faxafloi said, 'I shall just rub him into the floor with my heel.'

'Haunch' Venison, the boxing critic, said, 'If you ask me, I should say that the man who can hit hardest, stand up longest, and prove himself a winner will win the fight. If it doesn't end in a knock-out there will probably be a decision on points. A dead-heat is hardly likely. Nor is a draw without a verdict. Both men will have to box. And the result—well—wait and see.'

THE BIG FIGHT BROADCAST

If you buy a debenture or any other form of loan capital your asset cover will cooee wheeeee squunk. . . . We are now taking you over to Burlington House to listen to the big fight between 'Thunderbolt' Footle and Faxafloi. . . . Mr. Babblebotham and Mr. Hardleigh A. Mouse are going to describe the fight for you. . . . Well, here we are. Burlington House is packed. I don't think I've ever seen such a crowd, have you, Mouse? No. Ah! You hear that cheering? Somebody's just come in. I think it's the French Ambassador, isn't it, Mouse? . . . No. I think it's Jack Hobbs. . . . Oh. Right. And here's—surely it's—isn't it Lady Cabstanleigh, Mouse? . . . No. It's two bankers. . . . Oh. Right. The ring is filled with famous boxers, and the referee is introducing them. I can see Louis, Schmeling, Neusel, Foord, Farr, Max Baer, J. H. Lewis, Wilde, Dempsey, Tunney, Beckett, Carpentier, Harvey, Thil. . . . Hullo! What's happened? Oh, you heard that roaring. Footle has arrived, but he can't get into the ring owing to the mob of famous boxers. And here comes Faxafloi now. They'll have to clear the ring. . . .

Footle looks magnificent in his blue dressing-gown with golden dragons on it. Faxafloi is wearing a green dressing-gown with red spots. He looks very fit. I'm sure we all want to see a sporting fight, but that doesn't prevent us from wanting to see a British victory. I think they both look pretty fit, don't you, Mouse? . . . Of course they do. Why wouldn't they? . . . Er—I've just heard that Lord Towcher is somewhere among the audience. . . . Now, we'll be off soon. The gloves are on, and the referee is just making his little speech to the two men. Faxafloi looks very cool. Footle is grinning, and he is evidently the idol of the crowd. . . . There goes the bell for the first round. . . .

Footle has rushed from his corner like an express train. No wonder they call him 'Thunderbolt.' Faxafloi looks puzzled. Footle was in such a hurry to get at his man that he apparently had no time to aim a blow at him when he came within striking distance. Faxafloi has side-stepped and Footle has crashed into the ropes. Ah! He's coming back. He's certainly doing all the attacking so far. Full of spirit. Hullo! He's slipped. He's down. He's up again. He's a bit dazed, and has aimed a wild blow in the air. Faxafloi is at the other side of the ring talking to his seconds. He seems amused. Don't know why. Footle's coming for him again. What spirit! He's still doing all the attacking. If one of those blows connects! Now they're face to face. The bell just saved Faxafloi from one of those terrible swinging punches.

Round II.—Footle's changed his tactics. He's more cautious. Neither man has landed a blow so far, but if the fighting spirit counts for anything, the first round was Footle's. Hullo! Faxafloi has moved forward. He's hit Footle hard under the chin. Footle's down. One—two—three—four—five—six—seven—eight—nine—ten. Out! Faxafloi wins. The crowd is going mad. Booing, hissing, screaming. The verdict is evidently unpopular. But I must say I think Faxafloi won without a doubt. Don't you, Mouse? . . . I think so. Oh yes. But it was rotten luck on Footle, . . . He's come to. Phugh! He's in a rage, kicking and scratching. Faxafloi came over to shake hands, but Footle shouted something at him, and then burst into tears. The crowd is cheering him for his plucky effort. . . . We are now taking you over to Morecombe Bay Casino to hear Squelch Rongero's Band. . . .

In his dressing-room Footle said, 'I wasn't feeling well at the start. The lights were in my eyes, and I thought he was going to foul me. I'm confident that I was the better man. It wasn't his blow that knocked me out, it was the impact of my head on the floor of the ring. I'm ready for Louis or Schmeling now. I wasn't fairly beaten. I won the first round on points. I think I slipped just before he hit me in the second round. I was just going to hit him with all my might when it happened. I wasn't well, and my gloves weren't put on properly. I had him beat, then I slipped up. I don't think he hit me at all. My shoes were slippery, and the floor was dangerously slippery, too. I think I won on points.'

SHIPPING NEWS

Lady Cabstanleigh was blown two miles out of her course yesterday.

THE PICK OF THE PROGRAMME

There is apparently some controversy on the recent enterprising and audacious broadcast of a man sifting cold porridge through a cardboard sieve while standing inside a safe. Nothing like this had ever been attempted before, and several million listeners are doubting whether what they heard was really the porridge going through the sieve, or merely sounds made in the studio by somebody rubbing a thin slice of ham against a tin disc, or perhaps only a gramophone record. It is vastly important that the British public, which is the most cultured and intelligent public in the world, should know what it is getting for its money. It is a dangerous policy to try to fob it off with anything but the very best in the way of entertainment. If it is announced that real porridge is to be sifted through a real sieve, then real porridge should be sifted through a real sieve.

I speak bluntly, feeling that I represent the democratic feelings of 23,734,117 decent, cricket-fearing men and women.

FOULENOUGH AGAIN

Only one false note was struck at the great gathering of the McMuckies of McMuckie at McMuckie Castle, McMuckie. Members of forty-one septs attended. Even the McFlooties of McFlootie were there. The chief of the clan, the McMuckie of McMuckie, wore the enormous tartan clarsach in which his ancestors fought at Bannockburn.

During the dancing of a twenty-twosome reel it was noticed that one of the dancers was wearing the wrong tartan.

'Who are you?' asked the McMuckie sternly.

'I am the McBagpipe of McBagpipe,' replied the stranger, making a pass at the chieftain with a four-foot stick of Edinburgh rock.

A chase began, but the stranger got away. But before he had dashed out through the castle kitchens, more than one rosy cheek bore witness to a hurried salute from the gallant McBagpipe.

AND YET AGAIN

Lady Cabstanleigh's 'Pageant of Beauty,' a series of tableaux in aid of the Public Schools, was wrecked by a tiresome occurrence.

The tableaux were presented in the ballroom of her London house, but something went wrong. At first the spectators thought it was lack of rehearsal. Later they changed their opinion.

The first tableau represented a Dance of Nymphs in the Glades of Parnassus. Some of the loveliest young society girls, in exquisite Greek draperies, posed as nymphs, but when the curtains were parted a male figure in shooting tweeds reclined in their midst. This man, resting on one elbow, held to his lips a large quart bottle of ale. He remained motionless, but the effect of the tableau was ruined, and the curtains were quickly drawn.

The next tableau showed Actæon and his Hounds in Pursuit of Diana. But the hounds had been outpaced by the same gentleman in loud tweeds, who was discovered kneeling and offering Diana his quart bottle.

There was a rumpus behind the scenes, and presently Lady Cabstanleigh announced that Captain Foulenough had been ejected.

Far from it. The third tableau, Nausicaa and her Maidens playing Ball, was ruined by the same tweed-clad figure offering one of the maidens a football.

SEESAW

Dear Sir,

We three have noticed in your column, if such may we call it, we hope, a number of letters about phenomena in restaurants. Sir, we are the three Persian gentlemen who played seesaw in the lounge of the restaurant. It was upon the belly of the fattest of us, Risamughan, that the plank (from a sugar-melon tree of Kermanshah) was gently but firmly laid. Then Ashura and I, Kazbulah, sat one at each end of the plank, and the sport, as you English call it, began. Sir, we beg to state that we did not do this to advertise anything except our own extreme happiness. For, sir, we were going home to our own families in Filthistan, the gramophone company for which we had the honour to act as night-watchers having gone burst. So, sir, we played seesaw for fun in the nearest place we could find. And, sir, one day, if we ever return from Persia, we hope to play seesaw again in that most hospitable restaurant. And, sir, P.S., it does not at all hurt Rizamughan's belly, since he wears a thick cork bathmat, with 'Welcome' written on it, under his shirt—a souvenir from our boarding-house, sir, in the Cromwell Road. Astonishing good luck, sir, and remember us as

The Filthistan Trio.

AN ADMIRAL PROTESTS

Dear Sir,

It seems to me regrettable that, at a time when we are endeavouring to attract foreign visitors to London and to make a good impression on them, our restaurants should be turned into bear gardens by idle Persians with nothing better to do than play seesaw in the lounge. No doubt all the other eccentrics of whom we have been hearing lately will claim happiness as their excuse—I refer to the absurd waiters who formed the word Flobbo, to the Japanese lady who hung from the chandelier, and to the brown-haired quintuplets who played leapfrog. One would hesitate to blame the Persian gentlemen if they had stuck to orthodox seesaw. But this laying of planks across people's bellies is going too far. If the clien-tèle of a fashionable restaurant is to be at the mercy of any eccentric Persian who cares to play the fool, it is time we gave up the pretence of being civilised. I enclose my card.

Yours faithfully,

Ewart Hodgson, Admiral (Retd.)

THE CIRCULATION DROPS

Dear Sir,

I have countermanded my order for the 'Daily Express,' which I have read since 1869, twice every day, and am now taking the 'Ironworker's and Riveter's Morning Laugh.' When it comes to publishing stories about Persian gentlemen playing seesaw, every decent Englishman must protest. 'The Ironworker's and Riveter's Morning Laugh' hasn't much circulation, but it is young and go-ahead, and gives away flannel pen-wipers with a coloured supplement about Australia every Monday morning. And one is not ashamed to let the servants see it. I am sorry for this. Your shipping news was the best in England, but I draw the line at Persian horseplay in English restaurants.

Yours truly,

Sidney Herbage.

The Case of the 12 Red-Bearded Dwarfs

Mr. Justice Cocklecarrot began the hearing of a very curious case yesterday. A Mrs. Tasker is accused of continually ringing the doorbell of a Mrs. Renton, and then, when the door is opened, pushing a dozen red-bearded dwarfs into the hall and leaving them there.

For some weeks Mrs. Renton had protested by letter and by telephone to Mrs. Tasker, but one day she waited in the hall and caught Mrs. Tasker in the act of pushing the dwarfs into the hall. Mrs. Renton questioned them, and their leader said, 'We know nothing about it. It's just that this Mrs. Tasker pays us a shilling each every time she pushes us into your hall.'

'But why does she do it?' asked Mrs. Renton.

'That's what we don't know,' said the spokesman of the little men.

Mr. Tinklebury Snapdriver (for the plaintiff): Now, Mrs.—er—Tasker, where were you on the afternoon of 26th January? Think carefully before you answer.

Mrs. Tasker: Which year?

Mr. Snapdriver: What?

Mrs. Tasker: Which year?

Mr. Snapdriver appeared disconcerted. He consulted his notes and one or two books. Then he whispered to a clerk and consulted another barrister.

Mr. Justice Cocklecarrot: Well, Mr. Snapdriver, which year?

Mr. Snapdriver: Am I bound to answer that question, m'lud?

Cocklecarrot: It was you who asked it, you know. (Roars of laughter in court.)

Mrs. Tasker: M'lud, I think I can tell him the year. It was 1937.

Cocklecarrot: Why, that's this year. What then?

Mr. Snapdriver: Where were you, Mrs. Tasker, on the morning of 26th January 1937?

Mrs. Tasker: I called at Mrs. Renton's house to leave a dozen of red-bearded dwarfs with her.

Cocklecarrot: Had she ordered them? (Howls of laughter.)

The court then rose.

This extraordinary case was continued yesterday. The first sensation came when Mrs. Tasker submitted a list of over seven thousand people whom she wished to call as witnesses. Counsel for the defence, Mr. Bastin Hermitage, was about to read the list when Mr. Justice Cocklecarrot intervened.

Mr. Justice Cocklecarrot: Is it necessary to call all these people?

Mr. Hermitage: I believe so, m'lud.

Mr. Justice Cocklecarrot: But surely they cannot all be connected with the case. For instance, I see here the name of a Cabinet Minister. Also a well-known film actor. What have they to do with these dwarfs?

Mr. Hermitage: I understand that some of these dwarfs claim to be related to the Cabinet Minister.

Mr. Justice Cocklecarrot: And that distinguished sailor Rear-Admiral Sir Ewart Hodgson?

Mr. Hermitage: I understand he knows one of the dwarfs.

(Sensation in court.)

After lunch there was a brisk passage when Mr. Snapdriver, for the prosecution, threatened to call more than twelve thousand witnesses if counsel for the defence called seven thousand.

Cocklecarrot: Come, come, you two. This is becoming farcical.

Hermitage: It is a bluff, m'lud. He hasn't got twelve thousand witnesses.

Snapdriver: Here is my list, m'lud.

Cocklecarrot: Yum. I see it includes two Cabinet Ministers and an entire football team. (Sarcastically): I suppose they, too, are related to the dwarfs.

Snapdriver: So I understand, m'lud.

Cocklecarrot: (in a ringing voice): Who on earth are these astonishing little red-bearded gentry?

Hermitage: I think Admiral Sir Ewart Hodgson could tell us that.

Cocklecarrot: Very well. Call him. We are wasting our time.

Mr. Snapdriver, cross-examining, said, 'Now, Sir Ewart, will you, as a distinguished sailor, be good enough to tell the court what you know of these dwarfs, of whose persistent interference, Mrs. Renton complains?'

There was a hush of expectation as the admiral adjusted his spectacles, produced a sheaf of papers from an attaché case, and began to read the following:—'By the might of the Navy our Empire was built up. By the might of the Navy it must be protected. Britannia did not rise from out the azure main merely to sink back into it again. The salt is in our blood, and—'

By this time the court was filled with wild cheering, and several ladies waved small Union Jacks.

Mr. Justice Cocklecarrot: Yes, yes,

Sir Ewart, but what has this to do with the case?

Sir Ewart: The future of our Navy —(cheers)—is the concern of us all (cheers).

Cocklecarrot: Really, I shall have to clear the court if this goes on.

Mr. Snapdriver: I beg leave to enter a residuum, with jaggidge.

Cocklecarrot: Don't talk rubbish.

Mr. Snapdriver: Now, Sir Ewart, do you know these dwarfs?

Sir Ewart: Dwarfs or no dwarfs, Britannia's bulwarks are her great ships. (Cheers). See how they churn the farthest seas, their enormous prows cleaving—

Mr. Snapdriver: Please, please, Sir Ewart, try to confine your remarks to the matter in hand. Do you or do you not know these dwarfs?

Sir Ewart: I should be sorry to allow my acquaintanceship with dwarfs, giants, or anyone else to distract my attention from Britain's need to-day—a stronger Fleet. (Cheers.) Britannia, Mother of Ships, Queen of the Deep, and—

Cocklecarrot: Mr. Snapdriver, why was this witness ever called?

Mr. Snapdriver: It was a subpoena.

Cocklecarrot: In demurrage?

Mr. Snapdriver: Yes, and in toto.

Cocklecarrot: Oh, I shall have to grant a *mandatum sui generis*.

(The case was then adjourned.)

The hearing of the case was continued to-day. Mr. Justice Cocklecarrot said: 'So far, hardly a mention has been made of these dwarfs. We have heard a long speech about the British Navy, and there has been a brawl in the canteen about the cost of coffee and sandwiches. It is not thus that the majesty of the Law is upheld.'

Mr. Tinklebury Snapdriver: I apply for a writ of *tu quoque*.

Mr. Bastin Hermitage: And I for a writ of *sine mensis*.

Cocklecarrot: Ah, that's better. That's more like the Law. I well remember in the case of the Pentagon Chemical Foodstuffs and Miss Widgeon *versus* Packbury's Weather Prophecies, Ltd., Captain Goodspeed intervening, a colleague of mine laid down that—however, let

us to the matter in hand. I understand, Mr. Hermitage, that you intend to call the Tellingby fire brigade. May I ask why?

Mr. Hermitage: They had been summoned to Mrs. Renton's house to extricate a child's head from between her chestnut fencing on a day when Mrs. Tasker arrived with the dwarfs. The chief of the brigade will tell us that Mrs. Tasker pushed the little men into the hall as soon as the maid, Agatha, had opened the door.

Fire Brigade Chief (from back of court): No, I won't!

(Consternation. Laughter. Cheers. An Asiatic carpet-seller is thrown out.)

Mrs. Renton told her story yesterday. She said:

I was resting after lunch in my boudoir, when the maid, Angelica, informed me that some gentlemen were in the hall. I asked her who they were, and how many. She said she had counted twelve, but that she had never seen any of them before. I said, 'Do they want to see me?' And Angelica said, 'I don't think so.'

Very mystified, I went into the hall. My first instinct was to laugh. Imagine the effect of seeing a group of twelve red-bearded dwarfs, each fingering his little round hat nervously. I said, 'What can I do for you, gentlemen?' The spokesman answered nervously, 'Mrs. Tasker pushed us in here,' 'Why?' I asked, 'We don't know,' replied the spokesman.

Mr. Bastin Hermitage: I suggest they were an advertisement for Red Dwarf Horseradish Sauce.

Mrs. Renton: I don't eat horseradish sauce.

Cocklecarrot: Perhaps they wanted to make you eat it.

(Laughter and ribaldry in court.)

After lunch Rear-Admiral Sir Ewart Hodgson was called again, by mistake. But before the mistake was discovered he told the court that the new Navy scheme to provide longer hammocks for tall sailors would be worthless unless shorter hammocks were provided for small sailors. Mr. Justice Cocklecarrot suggested that all this was irrelevant. But Sir Ewart replied: 'Not at all. If these dwarfs were in the Navy they would be completely lost in the new hammocks.'

Cocklecarrot then said, 'It seems very difficult to keep this case within the realm of common sense. There are no red-bearded dwarfs in the Navy, so let us hear no more of this.'

When the hearing of this case was resumed and the court had assembled, Mr. Justice Cocklecarrot expressed his dissatisfaction with the progress made with the case. He said that the business of the court, which was the administration of justice, was being continually held up by irrelevancies, and he recommended to both counsel rather more expedition. 'We must keep to the point,' he said.

And at those words a piercing scream rang through the court. A woman was seen to be standing on a bench and pointing at one of the dwarfs.

'It's my Ludwig, my own little son Ludwig,' she cried. 'Ludwig, Ludwig, don't you know your mother?'

There was no answer.

'Well, do you or don't you?' asked Cocklecarrot impatiently.

'My name is Bob,' said the dwarf with slow dignity, 'and I am an orphan. I was left on the doorstep of a house in Eaton Square. In a basket. A month later both my parents died.'

'How do you know?' asked Cocklecarrot.

'I read it in the paper.'

'You read it?' shouted the judge. 'Why, how old were you?'

'Thirty-one,' said the dwarf. 'It happened last year.'

'Do you ask the court to believe,' interrupted Mr. Hermitage, 'that at the age of thirty-one you were put into a basket and left on the doorstep of a house in Eaton Square? Who carried the basket?'

'Two friends of my mother,' said the dwarf.

'Were you covered up in any way?'

'Oh yes,' said the dwarf, 'with an old travelling-rug.'

And what happened when you were found?'

'The lady of the house fell over the basket when she came out to go to a dance. She thought it was the washing, and had me carried in by the back entrance. The maids had hysterics when I got out of the basket, and, of course, I had to clear out. So I went to Nuneaton to seek employment; and it was while working there for a haulage contractor that I met the lady who afterwards became my wife, and a dearer, sweeter creature—'

'All this,' interrupted Cocklecarrot, 'has nothing whatever to do with the case. Mr. Hermitage, please try to confine yourself to the matter in hand. The whole thing is becoming impossible.'

A scene occurred after lunch, when the dwarf was asked whether he had ever served in the Navy. He burst into tears and said, between sobs, 'Ever since I was a little fellow—well, I mean, ever since I was even smaller than I am now, I longed to be a sailor. I always wore a sailor suit. But my eyesight made my dream impossible of fulfilment. And now, of course, it is too late. There has always seemed to me to be something wonderful in the surge of the waves and the roar of the wind. Then there is the comradeship. I tell you, after such ambitions, it is difficult to resign myself to being pushed through doors by ladies like Mrs. Tasker, for no apparent reason.'

At this point Cocklecarrot intervened impatiently, and the dwarf left the witness-box, still sobbing. A lady who shouted 'I'll adopt the little dear' was asked to leave the court.

Another ludicrous scene occurred while Mr. Tinklebury Snapdriver, for the prosecution, was cross-examining Mrs. Tasker.

Mr. Snapdriver: Your name is Rhoda Tasker?

Mrs. Tasker: Obviously, or I wouldn't be here.

Mr. Snapdriver: I put it to you that you were once known as Rough-House Rhoda?

Mr. Hermitage: No, no, m'lud, Rough-House Rhoda is another lady, whom I propose to call—a Mrs. Rhoda Mortiboy.

Cocklecarrot: What a queer name.

A Dwarf: You are speaking of my mother.

(Sensation.)

Cocklecarrot: Is your name Mortiboy?

The Dwarf: No. Towler's my name.

Cocklecarrot: (burying his head in his hands) I suppose she married again.

The Dwarf: What do you mean—again? Her name has always been Towler.

Cocklecarrot (groaning): Mr. Hermitage, what is all this about?

Mr. Hermitage: M'lud, there is a third Rhoda, a Mrs. Rhoda Clandon.

Cocklecarrot (to the dwarf, sarcastically): Is she your mother, too?

The Dwarf: Yes. My name's Clandon.

Cocklecarrot: I think, Mr. Snapdriver, we had better proceed without this Rhoda business. My nerves won't stand it.

Mr. Snapdriver: My next witness is the artiste known as Lucinda—a Mrs. Whiting.

(Everybody looks at the dwarf.)

Cocklecarrot (with heavy sarcasm): And, of course—

The Dwarf: Yes, she is my mother.

Cocklecarrot (roaring): Then what is your name, you oaf?

The Dwarf: Charlie Bread.

(Laughter and jeers).

Cocklecarrot: Clear the court! This foolery is intolerable. It will ruin my political career.

Mr. Snapdriver: Now, Mrs. Tasker, you do not deny that on several occasions you drove these dwarfs, a dozen of them, into Mrs. Renton's hall.

Mrs. Tasker: That is so.

Mr. Snapdriver: What was your motive?

Mrs. Tasker: I wanted to drive the dwarfs into her hall.

Mr. Snapdriver: But why? Can you give me any reason? You will admit it is an unusual occupation.

Mrs. Tasker: Not for me. I've done it all my life.

Mr. Snapdriver: You have driven dwarfs into other ladies' houses?

Mrs. Tasker: Certainly.

Cocklecarrot: Where do you get your supply of dwarfs?

Mrs. Tasker: From an agency. Fudlow and Trivett.

Cocklecarrot: Extraordinary. Most extraordinary.

Mr. Hermitage: Now, Dr. Spunton, is there, to your knowledge, any disease which would account for Mrs. Tasker's strange habits?

Dr. Spunton: There is. It is called rufo-nanitis. The spymtoms—

Mr. Hermitage: Symptoms.

Dr. Spunton: Yes, spymptoms, but I always put a 'p' before a 'y'.

Cocklecarrot: With what object, might we ask?

Dr. Spunton: I can't help it, m'lud.

Cocklecarrot: Do you say pyesterday?

Dr. Spunton: Pyes, unfortunatelpy. It's hereditarpy. Mpy familpy all do it.

Cocklecarrot: But why 'p'?

Dr. Spunton: No, py, m'lud.

Cocklecarrot: This case is the most preposterous I ever heard. We get nowhere. The evidence is drivel, the whole thing is a travesty of justice. In two weeks we have done nothing but listen to a lot of nonsense. The case will be adjourned until we can clear things up a bit.

Dr. Spunton: But I was brought all the wapy from Pyelverton.

Cocklecarrot: Well, go pyack to Pyelverton. Goodpye, and a phappy pjournepy. Pshaw!

The hearing was held up for a long time today, when the Deputy Puisne Serjeant-at-Arraigns discovered that, owing to an error of the Chief Usher of the Wardrobe, Mr. Justice Cocklecarrot had emerged from the Robing Room with his wig on back to front. According to an old statute of Canute (Op. II. C. in dom:reg:circ.: 37. Cap. 9 pp.: gh: od: ba: ha: 26, per Hohum 46: 98 (e). Tan: 64 by 36: zh: vos: H. Mid: sub rosa 49) the wig must be changed round by the Bailiff of the Wards. So they sent a messenger to bring him from Gregson's Dive. When he arrived he had forgotten the words of the prescribed ritual, and instead of taking Cocklecarrot's left foot in his right hand, he took his right foot in his left hand, thus invalidating the whole tomfoolery.

Meanwhile a brawl was taking place outside the court. A lady bearing a banner which said, 'Litigate, Don't Arbitrate,' was accidentally pushed off the pavement by the dwarfs, who had come in a large motor-car.

When Mrs. Tasker arrived, she held a newspaper in front of her face, thus enabling the unwary Press photographers to advertise the *Hunstanton Daily Courier.*

The dwarfs were cross-examined to-day. At least, one of them was cross-examined.

Mr. Hermitage: Your name is Howard Brassington?

The Dwarf (in a deep, loud voice): It is no such thing.

Mr. Hermitage (consulting his notes): What is your name, then?

The Dwarf: Stanislas George Romney Barlow Barlow Orchmeynders.

Mr. Hermitage: Two Barlows?

The Dwarf: Why not?

Mr. Hermitage: You are a night watchman.

The Dwarf: Why not?

Cocklecarrot: Mr. Porchminder, you will please answer yes or no.

The Dwarf: No.

Mr. Hermitage: Where were you on the night of 10th April?

The Dwarf: No.

Cocklecarrot (to counsel): Apart from retaining fees, would it not be better to speed up this case a bit?

The Dwarf: Yes.

Cocklecarrot: Send him away. Call Mrs. Renton.

Mr. Hermitage: Speak your mind, Mrs. Renton, speak your mind.

Mrs. Renton: I will. I accused Mrs. Tasker of driving a dozen redheaded dwarfs into my hall. She admits she did it. The dwarfs say she did it. Well, what more is there to be said? What are we waiting for?

Cocklecarrot: Mrs. Renton, you do not understand that certain formalities—er—the Law has its own way of doing things.

Mrs. Renton: And that is why I have to come here day after day to listen to all this irrelevant foolery—speeches about the Navy, arguments about a dwarf's mother, fuss about dates, and so on.

Cocklecarrot: I am the first to admit that there have been irregularities and delays in this case, but—

(A dwarf shouts loudly, 'M'lud! M'lud!' Cocklecarrot and Mrs. Renton exchange glances.)

Mr. Hermitage: Well?

The Dwarf: I think I'm going to be sick.

Mrs. Renton: That is about the only thing that hasn't happened in this case so far.

Cocklecarrot: Usher! Remove that dwarf.

Cocklecarrot: The time has, I think, come for you, ladies and gentlemen of the jury, to consider this case on its merits.

Foreman of Jury: And what, sir, would you say were its merits?

Cocklecarrot: What would you?

Foreman: We have not so far understood one word of the proceedings.

Cocklecarrot: I must say there have been moments when I myself seemed to have lost touch with the real world. Nevertheless, certain facts stand out.

Foreman: For instance?

Cocklecarrot: I will not be cross-examined by my own jury. You are here to deliver a verdict, not to question me. You have heard the evidence.

Foreman: Was that the evidence? All that horseplay?

Cocklecarrot: If this continues I shall discharge the jury, and the case will be heard all over again with a new jury. Stop those dwarfs singing! This is not a music hall.

When Mr. Justice Cocklecarrot continued his attempts to address the jury, interruption came even sooner than before.

Cocklecarrot: Now these red-bearded dwarfs—

Chorus of dwarfs: M'lud! M'lud! M'lud!

Cocklecarrot (testily): Well? What is it *now*?

A dwarf: We object to being called red-bearded. Our beards are not red. (Sensation in court. The dwarfs, standing up in line, are seen to have dyed their beards bright yellow. Laughter breaks out.)

Cocklecarrot: This is a very foolish trick. There is no law to prevent a man dyeing his beard any colour he pleases, but the question arises whether a beard of bright yellow is not perilously near contempt of court.

Mr. Hermitage: But, m'lud, surely the colour of the beards of these gentlemen is not material to the case.

Cocklecarrot: I will not be led off into another idiotic argument. If they come in on stilts it is not material to the case, but it is contempt of court.

'Now then,' continued the learned judge, 'let us hope that there will be no more of these interruptions. For though the law must be impartially administered, and everybody given an equal chance, yet there are certain restrictions which must be imposed upon merely irresponsible behaviour. These dwarfs—

A dwarf: Small gentlemen is a more polite description of us. It is not our fault that nature has been niggardly in the matter of inches. Why should a dwarf be funnier than a giant?

Another dwarf: Yes, why?

Cocklecarrot: If you two small gentlemen have finished your conversation perhaps I might be permitted to proceed. (Sarcastically) Have you any objection?

A third dwarf: Some of us haven't said a word all through this case.

A fourth dwarf: There is a tendency everywhere to bully the undersized. Yet in the eyes of the law we are citizens like everybody else.

A fifth dwarf: And proud of it.

(The other dwarfs cry, 'Hear, hear!' Uproar breaks out. Cocklecarrot sighs heavily and shrugs his shoulders.)

Cocklecarrot (to the jury): Perhaps I may be able to continue my address to-morrow.

Next day Mr. Justice Cocklecarrot endeavoured once more to deliver his summing up in this remarkable case. 'What the jury has to decide,' he said, 'is whether Mrs. Tasker deliberately drove those dwarfs into Mrs. Renton's house, or rather into the hall of her house; whether the maid Célestine—

Mrs. Renton: Angelica.

Cocklecarrot: What?

Mrs. Renton: Angelica.

Cocklecarrot: What do you mean, Angelica? Why do you keep on saying Angelica?

Mrs. Renton: It is my maid's name.

Mr. Heritage: It is her maid's name, m'lud.

Cocklecarrot (angrily, but with a show of patience): All right, then, Angelica. Now—

Mr. Snapdriver: Perhaps there is another maid, called Célestine, m'lud.

Mrs. Renton: No. The other is Minnie. (Roars of laughter.)

Cocklecarrot: There may be forty maids. I am speaking of Angelica. Now what the jury has to decide is whether this maid—er—Min—er—Angel—er—Cél— Whether this maid Célestine—

Mrs. Renton: Angelica.

Cocklecarrot (dropping his head in his hands and speaking wearily): Mrs. Renton, will you please allow me to say what I have to say? The name of the maid is immaterial.

Mr. Snapdriver: But, m'lud, Célestine was on holiday at Bournemouth at the time.

Mr. Hermitage: My learned friend means Eastbourne, m'lud.

Mr. Snapdriver: My learned friend is right. Eastbourne.

Cocklecarrot (satirically): Well, now that this very important matter has been settled, perhaps we can continue, unless someone would like to tell me that Minnie was at Blackpool.

A Dwarf: If it comes to that, I myself have been to Blackpool. (Howls of laughter.)

Cocklecarrot (regarding the dwarf with rage): That is most interesting and most relevant.

(The court rises for lunch)

'I intend,' said Mr. Justice Cocklecarrot, 'to make a supreme and almost despairing attempt to sum up this most curious case. Therefore, if anybody has any questions to ask, let them be asked at once, so that I may be released for my next case, that of Hungarian Lighthouses, Ltd. *versus* Miss Myra Keekie.

Several Dwarfs: We're in that, too.

Cocklecarrot (with heavy sarcasm): I cannot tell you how delighted I am at the prospect of having you with me again. May I ask how you small gentry come to be involved in such a case?

A Dwarf: We are Miss Myra Keekie. It is we who wrote the famous letter cancelling an order for twelve hundred and thirty lighthouses.

Cocklecarrot: All this seems to be quite clear and straightforward. It looks as though I am in for another month of tomfoolery. Hungarian lighthouses, indeed! Why, Hungary—

Mrs. Renton: May I implore your lordship not to start this case before mine is disposed of?

Cocklecarrot: Oh, certainly, certainly. Now, where were we? Hum. (With sudden anger.) It is these damnable small gentlemen who keep on confusing the issue.

Sun streaming through a water-bottle and glass on the judge's desk set a light to papers.

(News item)

Mr. Justice Cocklecarrot, informed of this accident, saw an excellent way to deal with the case. He cunningly set alight to all the papers relevant to the case—if anything can be called relevant to such a case—by manipulating the water-bottle and the glass. He then fed the flames with his wig and various bits of wood which he kept in his pocket. Within an hour the court was burnt down.

The following letter speaks for itself:—

Dear Sir,

As you are aware, I recently played a small but not unsensational part in the Dwarf Case. I flatter myself that I conducted myself more as an ardent supporter of a strong Navy than as a witness for or against anything in particular. I now learn that the case is to be tried again, owing to some technical flapdoodle or other. May I take this opportunity of stating as publicly as possible that, if I am called again, I shall to the best of my ability once more defend the Navy? What these dwarfs did or did not do is no affair of mine. To-day we are concerned with more important matters. For there can be no safeguard for the peace of Europe until our British-built warships lie keel to keel across every knot of the seven seas, and until every port of the habitable globe harbours a British submarine.

Yours faithfully,
Ewart Hodgson (Rear-Adml.)

COCKLECARROT'S NEXT CASE

It was learned late last night that the case of Miss Ruby Staggage *v.* Broxholm Hydraulic Laundries and Others will come up shortly for hearing before Mr. Justice Cocklecarrot. Miss Staggage is said to be the trade name of a firm of rocking-horse makers, who are suing the B. H. Laundries for the complete ruination of sixteen yards of washable twill used in making coverings for the tails of the horses. Pending dead-freight, demurrage, charter-party, copyhold, and aznalworratry, Mr. Chowdersleigh Poss will appear for the plaintiff, and Mr. Charles Honey-Gander for the defendants. The case will be heard in court number 19 of the Probate, Agriculture and Fisheries Division. Miss Boubou Flaring, the famous actress, will be on the jury, and is asked not to start the autograph business while the case is being heard.

The Case of the Rocking-horse

Cocklecarrot: Having regard to the curious nature of this case, I think there should be an appeal under article 6 of the Statute of Giminy and Bocage.

Mr. Poss: Under Statute Law, m'lud, refraction must be proven.

Cocklecarrot: Aye, an' it be not proven, there is always the right of multiple cozenage.

Mr. Honey-Gander: Ultra vires?

Cocklecarrot: Of course. *Sine die.* Tutamen being implicit, with or without barratry, responderia and plonth, except in municipal law.

Mr. Poss: And wivenage, in lieu of direct mandibility?

Cocklecarrot: Not concurrently with external vapimenta. Merely in plenary copyhold.

Mr. Honey-Gander: M'lud, a tort being the source of a private right of action, in common law, as distinct from equity, matrimonial, Admiralty, agricultural or piscatorial jurisdiction, *alterum non laedere*, I suggest that classification, *per se*, under the Employers' Liability Act of 1897, as in Wivenhoe *v.* Spott (1903 A.C. 274) becomes a matter of malicious nuisance, *sic utere tuo ut alienum laedas*, in which case follopy is self-evident. For instance, a turtle's egg in the Galapagos Islands—

Cocklecarrot: Quite, quite, Mr. Honey-Gander. Let someone else develop the thing for a bit now.

Now, my office being *jus dicere*, if not *jus dare* (see Hopkins *v.* Tollemache), it would be some considerable advantage to me to know what this case is about. Nobody, so far, has thought of mentioning such a thing.

Mr. Honey-Gander: M'lud, we have first to decide whether common usage or commercial usage is the more convenient instrument for developing and expanding a statute law.

Cocklecarrot: I don't see why we have to go into that now.

Mr. Poss: M'lud, if a contract is unenforceable, as in Miss Fancy Fimple *v.* The Gaiety Theatre, Buttery-on-the-Vile, then, and not till then, the interchangeable nature of judicial procedure becomes, morally speaking, paramount. Now by the Bills of Exchange Act (1876) twill was included in the category of perishable goods. But if perishable goods are used to wrap the tails of rocking-horses they become, by mansuetude, imperishable, because the tail of a rocking-horse, of which the wrapping is an integral part, is a structure and not a moving fixture.

Cocklecarrot: How can a thing be both perishable and imperishable?

Mr. Poss: Only the Law can tell us that, m'lud.

The second day of the hearing of the Rocking-Horse case quickly produced a sensation. Cocklecarrot asked Mr. Honey-Gander, counsel for the defendants, what the twelve red-bearded dwarfs could possibly have to do with the Broxholm Hydraulic Laundries, and how they came into the case. Mr. Honey-Gander made the sensational reply, 'M'lud, I understand that these gentlemen have a controlling interest in these laundries. In fact, they are Broxholm Hydraulic Laundries.'

Cocklecarrot: Then why do they call themselves 'Others'?

Mr. Honey-Gander: I believe, m'lud, that there are others connected with the laundries.

Cocklecarrot: Red-bearded dwarfs, too, I will wager.

Mr. Honey-Gander: So I understand, m'lud.

Cocklecarrot: How many?

Mr. Honey-Gander: Forty-one, m'lud.

Cocklecarrot: Merciful heavens! Call Miss Staggage.

Mr. Honey-Gander: Your name is Elvira Staggage?

Miss Staggage: No, sir. It is Amy Clowte.

Mr. Honey-Gander: But—

Miss Staggage: Elvira Staggage is my trade name.

Mr. Honey-Gander: I see. You own a rocking-horse factory?

Miss Staggage: No, sir. I act for the real owners.

Mr. Honey-Gander: And who are they?

Miss Staggage: A number of red-bearded dwarfs, sir. I see them over there.

(Sensation in court.)

Cocklecarrot: This is quite intolerable. These dwarfs are plaintiffs and defendants in the same case. The thing is without precedent. What on earth are they up to, suing themselves?

Mr. Poss (for the plaintiff): They maintain, m'lud, that in their capacity as hydraulic launderers they have swindled themselves in their capacity as rocking-horse manufacturers.

Cocklecarrot: This is really insane. I must adjourn the case for a day or two. It is without precedent, I repeat.

An attempt was made to resume this case on the next day, but since the twelve red-hearded dwarfs are both plaintiffs and defendants, Cocklecarrot was rather at a loss as to how to proceed. He had, however, discovered a precedent in volume XVIII of Blitherstone, the case of a Miss Frack, who brought an action for libel against herself. Miss Frack was a novelist who, to obtain publicity, wrote a novel under the pen-name of Miles Euston, in which she said that Miss Frack, one of the characters, was a thief and a forger. She was awarded damages against herself, and was in the papers for three days, which sent her sales bounding up.

Matters were complicated, however, by the dwarfs entering a plea of Cujusmodo. Nobody had ever heard of this plea, until one of the counsel unearthed it in the third year of the reign of Henry II. There the matter rests at present.

'The present position,' said Mr. Justice Cocklecarrot, 'would appear to be this: A body of twelve red-bearded dwarfs, in its capacity as a firm of rocking-horse makers, is bringing an action against itself, in its capacity as a hydraulic laundry, alleging that a twill covering for the tail of a rocking-horse was destroyed by the said laundry. But the position is complicated by the fact that the horse in question has no tail. It is, therefore, difficult to see how any case arises. Nor is the matter clarified by regrettable horseplay.'

A Dwarf: Rocking-horseplay, I submit, your reverence.

Cocklecarrot: You will kindly address me properly or not at all.

Dwarf: Not at all what?

Cocklecarrot: What do you mean, 'what'?

Dwarf: No. What do *you* mean, 'what'?

Cocklecarrot: What I said was— oh, go to the devil!

'The time of this court is valuable,' said Cocklecarrot, as four of the dwarfs carried in a large canvas cake, opened it, and released an actress who began a slow dance in the well of the court.

'Valuable to whom?' queried a dwarf.

'To the public,' replied Cocklecarrot.

'The public,' answered the dwarf, 'would far rather have all this foolery than the usual dull nonsense of cross-examinations and long speeches. See how they are all laughing.'

And, indeed, the packed court was shaking with laughter.

'Take that actress away,' shouted Cocklecarrot, and the girl flinched back in mock alarm. And at that moment paper snow fell from the ceiling, and a dwarf cried, 'Ah, do not turn our little sister out without a roof to her mouth. Have mercy, daddy.'

Cocklecarrot laid his head in his hands and groaned audibly.

The court had to be cleared owing to the roars of ribald laughter which greeted the appearance in the witness-box of the twelve red-bearded dwarfs all in a heap. Their names were read out amid growing uproar. The names appeared to be: Sophus Barkayo-Tong, Amaninter Axling, Farjole Merrybody, Guttergorm Guttergormpton, Badly Oronparser, Churm Rincewind, Cleveland Zackhouse, Molonay Tubilderborst, Edeledel Edel, Scorpion de Rooftrouser, Listenis Youghaupt, Frums Gillygottle.

Cocklecarrot: Are these genuine names?

A Dwarf: No, m'worship.

Cocklecarrot: Then what's your name?

Dwarf: Bogus, m'ludship.

Cocklecarrot: No, your real name.

Dwarf: My real name is Bogus, your excellency.

(At this point the court had to be cleared)

The case was held up again after lunch while the twelve red-bearded dwarfs were photographed, some riding the rocking-horse, which they had brought with them, others stroking it, and yet others crawling beneath its mottled belly and crying 'Peep-bo!'

Cocklecarrot: But this horse has no tail. I thought the whole case was about a length of twill to cover the tail?

First Dwarf: M'worship, it is a guinea-horse.

Second Dwarf: Yes, your grace. If you hold it up by its tail, its head drops off.

Third Dwarf: With a bang, your ludship.

Fourth Dwarf: We have a bicycle, too. And that has no tail, either.

Fifth Dwarf: It's a guinea-bicycle.

Sixth Dwarf: The handlebars are made of lard, as a precaution.

Cocklecarrot (savagely): Against what?

Chorus of Dwarfs: Burglary, sire.

Cocklecarrot (groaning): What in Heaven's name is all this nonsense about?

Mr. Honey-Gander: I confess, m'lud, the case is developing along unexpected lines.

Cocklecarrot then suggested that this ludicrous case, which need never have come into court, could easily be settled if the dwarfs (in the person of the hydraulic laundry) would apologise to themselves (in the person of the rocking-horse firm) for having destroyed a twill covering for a non-existent tail. The dwarfs lined up, six a side, and apologised in chorus. They then left the court singing *Moonlight and Mrs. Mason.*

Cocklecarrot said afterwards, 'I am hoping that my next case will not include these tiresome little gentlemen. I think I am about due for a bit of straightforward stuff, without all these distractions and fooleries.'

The Dwarfs Again

The action brought by the Phinehas Cupper-Harsnett Trading Company and the National Mortgage Indemnity Agency against Mrs. Wharple, Mohammed Brown, The Constructional Rebate Pitcher Plant, Maracaibo United, and Cicely du Bois for recovery of stamping costs has been settled out of court. Much to the relief of Mr. Justice Cocklecarrot, who discovered that the whole business was another family quarrel of the twelve red-bearded dwarfs.

'These little gentlemen,' said Cocklecarrot, 'seem to have invented a new kind of litigation. They are continually bringing actions against themselves or each other under the names of fantastic companies or individuals, none of whom appears to have any existence save on paper. The object of all this is still obscure, but there are those who hint at international ramifications, and believe that we are witnessing an attempt to make British Justice look even sillier and beastlier than it is.'

Recently the twelve dwarfs bought a female singing-mouse called Royal Gertrude on the hire-purchase system —ninepence a year for fifty-one years. The mouse broke its foot against a sugar-tongs, and, instead of singing, bawled. Only the first ninepence has been paid, and the dwarfs are claiming the money back. The firm of Hustington and Chaney, importers of singing mice, refuse to take the mouse back or refund the money, and the Boycott Japan League is organising a mass-meeting of novelists and professional agitators to petition for the deportation of the mouse to the island of Capri, where a mouse-lover, Miss Webbe-Ffoote, has offered to house, feed, clothe, and educate it.

The situation seems to await the experienced touch of Mr. Justice Cocklecarrot.

(All join in the general laughter, and the court adjourns for lunch.)

The case of the polo pony was held up after lunch for a considerable time while an experiment was made in court. A candle was lit by the puisne serjeant-at-arraigns and the polo pony was brought in in a loose box. It was led out, and on its back were the twelve red-headed dwarfs, bowing to right and left, and grinning.

'What are you doing here, you dwarfs?' asked Cocklecarrot angrily.

'We were passing,' replied the ringleader, 'and so we looked in. Quite like old times. This pony is the model for a new rocking-horse we are constructing. We have, alas, no money to spend on books of anatomy, and so we have to study from nature. A polo rocking-horse ought to be just the thing for a child of wealthy parents. Ah! We cannot all be wealthy. When we were small, we had but one hat between us. Did we, you ask, wear it in turn, or huddle all our heads beneath its sheltering crown, like ants under a mushroom? Your curiosity shall be rewarded, judge. We never wore it at all. It rotted in a shed, unworn. And yet, sometimes when the spring wind blows, we remember that old hat and tears well unbidden to our eyes. So, when a weary heart—'

With a great roar of rage Cocklecarrot sprang erect. 'Clear this damnable court!' he bellowed.

(He then repeated the trick with the water-jug and the sunshine, and burnt the court down.)

The Case of the Polo Pony

Yesterday, before Mr. Justice Cocklecarrot and a mixed jury, the case was continued in which Mrs. Heaulme (née Parsons) is seeking to restrain her neighbour, Mr. Cawley, from keeping a polo pony in a disused railway truck near her conservatory. Mrs. Heaulme alleges that when the conservatory window is open the pony, Fido II, breathes on the flowers, and sometimes on guests who come to tea. Mr. Cawley maintains that the pony is so young that his breathing would not blow out a candle.

Mrs. Heaulme: Who cares whether he blows out a candle or not?

Mr. Jedbind (for the prosecution): Are you in the habit of having tea by candlelight in your conservatory in April?

Mr. Faffle (for the defence): I object, m'lord.

Cocklecarrot: Objection over-sustained.

Mr. Faffle: Meaning what?

Cocklecarrot: Fire ahead—er—proceed.

Mr. Cawley: A polo pony is not likely to know whether there is a lighted candle in a conservatory or not.

Mr. Faffle: Is it not as natural for a pony to breathe as anyone else?

Mr. Jedbind: An old pony breathes just as much as a young one.

Cocklecarrot: Or a middle-aged one, eh?

Song

The Captain stood on his bridge alone,
   With his telescope to his eye,
The ship she was sinking rapidly,
   As the storm went howling by.
He saw the rush for the lifeboats,
   And he noticed a peer old and grey,
Then a sailor approached and saluted,
   And thus to the peer he did say:

     Chorus:
Pray take my place in the lifeboat,
   'Tis a gesture I willingly make,
Since I fagged for your nephew at Repton,
   It's the least I might do for his sake.
And when next, sir, you're seeing your nephew,
   Pray sing him this short refrain:
'Piddock minor went down like a Repton man,
   And gladly he'd do it again.'

AMONG THE NEW BOOKS

Brittle Galaxy. By Barbara Snorte.

A colourful and courageous attempt to put the point of view of the artist misunderstood in a world of wars and rumours of wars. Dalton Sparleigh is the eternal figure of the hero who is the centre of his world, and regards his own personality as the most important thing in life. 1,578 pages of undiluted enthralment.

Groaning Carcase. By Frederick Duddle.

A very delicate and tactfully written plea for old horses, against a background of country-house life. It is fiction made more compelling than fact by one who seems to be right inside the horse's mind.

Splendid Sorrow. By Walter Fallow.

Was Ernst Hörenwurst, adventurer and rake, the Margrave Friedrich Meiningen of Hohefurstenau-Lebensbletter? Mr. Fallow, in his new historical romance, has no hesitation in leaving the question unanswered.

Tricks With Cheese. By 'Cheesophile' (of the *Cheese World*).

The author appears to be able to make everything, from a model of the Palace of Justice in Brussels to a bust of his aunt, out of cheese. A good book for the fireside.

Fain Had I Thus Loved. By Freda Trowte.

Miss Trowte has been called by the *Outcry* the Anatole France of Herefordshire. There is an indescribable quality of something evocative yet elusively incomprehensible about her work. The character of Nydda is burningly etched by as corrosive a pen as is now being wielded anywhere.

No Second Churning. By Arthur Clawes.

An almost unbearably vital study of a gas-inspector who puts gas-inspecting before love. Awarded the Prix de Seattle, this book should enhance the author's growing reputation as an interpreter of life's passionate bypaths.

Pursuant To What Shame. By Goola Drain.

All those who enjoyed Miss Drain's romantic handling of a love-story in *Better Thine Endeavour* and *Immediate Beasts* will welcome this trenchant tale of an irresponsible girl who poisons her uncle. A famous tennis player said, before he had even seen the book, 'In my opinion Miss Drain is unique and unchallengable. Her command of words is a delight.'

MY OWN DEAR PAGE (For My Own Dear Public)

Do, please, write to me, all of you. Then I shall feel I know you, and we can get together and contribute our little effort towards the betterment of this weary world.

A dear old great-grandmother, by the fireside, in the winter mists. Her face is furrowed by time and care, but in her heart is wistful tranquillity.

Those words, spoken by the girl next to me on the bus, made me realize what a power for good a conscientious journalist can be. I at once rang up a dear little old lady who lives in such a lovely little cottage near Chertsey. She was out, so I went out into my garden and looked up at the stars.

That girl on the bus haunts me. One day she may be somebody's great-grandmother. Will she remember the bus, and the journalist who just longed to be decent to somebody's great-grandmother?

Let us, you and I, try to be what we might be. 'Nothing,' said Emerson, 'is difficult to do when once it is done.' Everywhere I go I see people who are longing and yearning, as I am at this moment, to *understand*. For if we can but understand, then our problems and difficulties fade like snow before the sun.

I wish you could see my charwoman's mother. Such trust, such confidence, such bravery. Oh, why must the world be full of crime and cruelty, when there is this love and understanding waiting for us, if we only get together?

Soon spring will come like an army with banners. What are we going to do about it? Please, please try to realize that I want to help. To-morrow I will tell you how a girl called Ann cried despairingly yet happily as we stood side by side by a cab shelter and watched, through the park railings, a small bird murdering a worm. Through her tears shone faith and hope, and for her the dark winter of discontent was over. She was on her way to marry a stoker from Christchurch. And I said to her: *'Be happy, and then everyone else will be happy. Tears are the jewels on time's fingers, and all our troubles are but chaff before the wind.'* I think, I hope, I pray that my words helped her a little.

She told me, as we stood on the terrace, gazing at the moonlit sea, the most harrowing story I have ever heard. It was a love story, but the love was thwarted, and all her world was Dead Sea fruit in her mouth. I longed to bring comfort. I said: *'Never laugh at people who tell you that every cloud has a silver lining. It is literally true. Try to concentrate on the lining instead of on the cloud. There is a sweetness in sorrow which softens shattered souls, and in suffering we learn to understand.'* I spoke eagerly, for I knew what she was feeling. And when she turned her face to thank me, I knew that somehow, stumbling blindly, I had been of use to a fellow creature. And suddenly my world was irradiated with beauty. So true is it that a good deed, however small, is God's golden boomerang. It bounces back and blesses the doer.

Of all those millions who wrote to me in reply to my appeal, I think I understand Mrs. Hoofe best. Mrs. Hoofe, of Leytonstone, says: *'Nothing in my life has helped me more than what you said about your charwoman's mother. I think many of us forget that charwomen have mothers. The hurly-burly of daily existence takes toll of our tender thoughts. It was not thus with my mother's sister, Mrs. Towty. She always had a kind word for charwomen's mothers. So I just want to thank you.'*

Thank *you*, Mrs. Hoofe. This morning the grass in my tiny garden seems greener than ever before, and all because of our deep understanding.

All day long I have been thinking of Mrs. Hoofe. One day, when the silvery mist is clothing our mellow London in a garb of sombre gossamer, I shall take a bus along the lonely way to Leytonstone. For I do ask you to believe me, and I am not ashamed to ask it on my bended knees, that Leytonstone is only every other place under a different name. And its folk are our folk, just like you and I. They laugh and suffer and die like us. And love, too, touches Leytonstone with its daffadown wing.

She was playing Beethoven – just a silver-haired lady at an oh so little piano. My thoughts took wing. I seemed to see you all, my readers, and somehow we were all smiling through our tears because we were together, and understood what the music was struggling to say. And I said deep down in my heart, *'Joy and agony are but two sides of the same medal'*. And echo wove a soft answer on the loom of peace.

Stop Press: Financier Caught by Nose in Rat-trap says, 'Cheese Makes Him Sick.'

LA RUSTIGUZZI ARRIVES

Among the polygot singers arriving now for the Opera season is Emilia Rustiguzzi, who sang so loudly in Milan last year that the orchestra had to be enlarged by 324 instruments. Few laymen (and fewer clergymen) realize that the whole art of opera lies in a nice (or, perhaps, nasty) balance between the human voice and the orchestra. The more noise the one makes the more noise must the other make. But a tactful conductor always lets the orchestra win. That explains the surprise with which musical critics record that 'Her voice, now and then, soared above the orchestra, and her words were audible in all parts of the auditorium.'

Well, La Rustiguzzi is not one to take a mere mass-attack lying down. We shall need the largest orchestra in Europe to drown her. It is said that she once blew the slates off a potting-shed while singing one of Grieg's lullabies in a garden at Pisa. And if you hate this kind of thing, there is always the Royal Academy and Cowes. With my do-re-mi-fa, and I know not what else.

'Follow My Lieder'

Emilia Rustiguzzi sang a number of exquisitely melancholy *lieder* at Lady Cabstanleighs' party last night. So powerful was her voice that a picture of the late Lord Cabstanleigh, in the uniform of the Pathan Guides, slipped from its moorings and crashed on to the head of Mrs. de ffoux-Hermitage. So thick, however, is that shapely skull, with its prominent bump of stupidity, that no damage was done, except to the picture. The deaf Mrs. Owle sprang from her chair during one of the diva's top notes, crying, 'I hear! I hear!' But it was during the singing of Bootzs' 'Schlaffzimmer' that the thing became intolerable. The police, thinking that mad butchers had occupied the house for slaughter purposes, arrived with documentary proof that a clause in the lease stated that cattle must not be slaughtered on the premises. There were laughing explanations, and the fun went on.

It is not likely that Emilia Rustiguzzi will appear in opera for at least a week. So loud is her voice that the orchestra will have to be enlarged. This will be done by cutting off a row or two of the stalls. When Banger, the Swedish conductor, asked her to take a passage more quietly at rehearsal the other day the diva cried: 'Corpo di Bacco! Civitavecchia! Poldinetta! Fango che sale! Fuori i Barbari! Do you think I am a crooner?'

Meanwhile she has been much annoyed by a musical critic's remarks. This critic wrote, 'We have not yet had an opportunity of hearing Rustiguzzi, of whom so much is expected, but if rehearsals are any indication of her powers it is perhaps permissible to remark that St. Pancras Station is looking for someone to announce the northbound trains.'

(*To-night: Broccoli in 'Trovatore'.*)

RUSTIGUZZI'S ISOLDE

It is now almost certain that Rustiguzzi will play Isolde to Ravioli's Tristan. There will be a specially augmented orchestra – 334 instruments more than the usual ration, and mostly trombones. This will probably be the first occasion on which the untrained voices of the rich women in the audience will have had to take second place. Musical critics are beginning to ask themselves whether quality is not after all better than quantity. Further, Rustiguzzi has developed a tiresome habit. When she has emitted a resounding yell, and draws in her breath with a noise like the November tide receding over the shingle at Kemp Town, she is apt to whistle through her teeth. And as everything she does is on a huge scale, this bitter east wind between her teeth takes the listeners' attention from the yelling and summons expectant cabmen from all streets within a mile of the Strand.

Rash conductors who put up umbrellas while she is singing will only have them blown inside out.

(*To-morrow: Scampi in 'Maraschino'.*)

REHEARSAL

There was a rehearsal at Covent Garden yesterday. Emilia Rustiguzzi tried some of her loudest shouting, and, as luck would have it, the same day had been appointed for an auction of a job lot of vegetables within a bowshot of the Opera House. So that when Rustiguzzi opened her great throat and began to yell Senta's ballad, everybody who is anybody in the vegetable world heard her and thought the auction had started. Then might you have seen a pretty concourse, for there came tumbling up all the potato porters and broccoli pushers and tomato carriers and cabbage shifters and bean shovers. They were followed by the basket balancers, melon tasters, apple twisters, orange gougers, peach peelers, pea grafters, endive sloggers, onion runners, chive drivers, and parsley pickers. The whole swarming mass of men and women came crowding towards the noise, and, drawn by the magic of art, invaded the Opera House, where they began to bid in raucous voices. The louder they shouted, the louder roared the happy diva, and the louder played the orchestra. It was just like the real thing.

LA RUSTIGUZZI HITS OUT

So abnormal is the voice of Emilia Rustiguzzi that yesterday, during a rehearsal at Covent Garden, a deputation of distinguished jugulocologists, laryngophobes, gulophiles, gutturopsychiatrists, and what not, from many countries, called upon her to examine her throat. They knocked her down and knelt on her, while an Asiatic specialist took an X-ray photograph of her capacious gullet. They probed her throat, pulled her tongue, peered at her teeth, jabbed her with little spiked instruments, hit her on the side of the head with the flat of their hands, twisted her ears and tapped her broad-acred back with hammers made of reinforced bdellium. Whereupon the singer, without warning, pushed open her great maw and let them have a note or two of 'Rienzi', the last and noisiest of the Tribunes. And as she sang there came such a storm-blast from her mouth that the faculty was blown about the room like a lot of withered hazel-leaves on a hillside. A little Greek foreman cutter and slasher, 'the only one in this street' who earned a whack on the jaw from a dude whose trousers were fourteen inches too short, was flung against a door and rebounded like a wet sack filled with verdigris. And a pompologist from Breslau, where Cecil Rhodes was born, was blown against the ceiling.

'That will teach them,' yelled Rustiguzzi, 'to interfere with an artist.'

FORCEFUL SINGING

There has been another row. Ragomir Burlasch, the tenor, complains that there can be no illusion of reality in singing with Emilia Rustiguzzi. She makes such an infernal din that it is impossible to pretend to the audience that you are in love with her, or that it is any use trying to sing a duet with her. Yesterday, when she turned on Burlasch with a roar of love, he staggered back against the castle door and strained his shoulder. He said it was like being fired out of a gun's mouth. And he is particularly angry with the critic who said that in the subsequent duet 'Burlasch was inaudible.' He said afterwards, 'No singer on earth could have been audible. This woman is simply wrecking opera.'

A photograph of the muscles in her back during an aria will be found in the index.[1]

'Emilia Rustiguzzi,' I wrote, 'is, perhaps, the only living singer who can fill Covent Garden.' Unfortunately, there appeared immediately underneath this statement the mysterious words, 'Threepence a ton for the first thousand tons.' Yesterday I received a letter which ran as follows:

The attention of our client has been called to a paragraph in 'By the Way.' (The paragraph is then quoted.) While we are fully aware that the words used may bear a favourable construction, our client considers that among the ignorant the sentence might be taken to refer, not to the beauty and popularity of our client's voice, but rather to her gross tonnage. The words which follow would seem to bear out this construction.

I have replied:
Dear Sirs,
I can assure you that when your client is singing I shut my eyes and forget her enormous proportions. To me she is a mere singing bird. Preferably a little corncrake.

---

[1] Under 'Nostrils, sham, see glass eyes, dummy.'

SEVEN PART SONG

Soprano: When that the rain doth lightly fall——
Basso: When that the rain
Tenor: When that the rain
Falsetto: When that the rain
Treble: When that the rain
Contralto: When that the rain
Alto: When that the rain
All: When that the rain doth lightly fall
Treble: In tavern cool I lie me down
Basso: Me down
Alto: Me down
Tenor: Me down
Soprano: Me down
Contralto: Me down
Falsetto: Me down
All: In tavern cool I lie me down.
In tavern cool, in tavern cool,
I lie me down, I lie me down,
In tavern cool I lie me down.

INTERRUPTION

Prodnose: What is the good of printing that without the music?
Myself: What music?
Prodnose: The music to the song.
Myself: There isn't any music.
Prodnose: Then what is the point?
Myself: There isn't any point.
Prodnose: But why print it?
Myself: To fill up space, you fool.

A NERVE-RACKING MASTERPIECE

The third volume in the *Huntingdonshire Cabmen* series is published this morning. No higher praise can be given to it than to say that it is worthy of its predecessors. An age devoted to pleasure-seeking and cheap sensation is, perhaps, inclined to underrate the importance of this exhaustive list of cabmen's names. But an attempt has been made in this new volume to counteract any tendency to dullness by abandoning the usual alphabetical order. Thus it is with a pleasant shock of surprise that one finds, on page 231, 'Jelf, E. N., Barlow, D. J.' Such happy juxtapositions as this stimulate the interest of the reader, and give a semblance of narrative to what the undiscerning might call a mere catalogue of names. The volume concludes with 'Henderson, N.', and leaves one wondering whether there will be other Hendersons in Volume IV, promised for the autumn season. One would like to quote the whole book, but perhaps the following excerpt will give a taste of the quality of this monumental work:

Chance, B. Harris, Arthur. Kermode, S. S. Vale, P. Manton, W. R. Caldecott, R. Lister, Tom. Robinson, B. L. Robinson, E. T. Prout, V. Garrison, F. J. Sladder, T. W. M.

The juxtaposition of two Robinsons is a masterpiece of style, as daring as it is unexpected. But in justice it must be said that this volume contains nothing as memorable as the amazing 'Baines, H. Baines, L. T.' of Volume II.

A CHORUS OF PRAISE

Some unsolicited opinions of *Huntingdonshire Cabmen* Vol. III: 40,000 *copies sold before the proofs were ready.*

(The publisher)

A major event. One had not realized that there were all these cabmen in Huntingdonshire.

(The Dean of Canterbury)

Democracy's ringing answer to the Dictators.

(Professor Harold Laski)

We approve of it. It should be in every home.

(Miss Wilkinson, Sir Stafford Cripps, and Miss Rathbone)

TAIL-PIECE

From that moment she never looked back.

(From Mr. Lot's 'Life and Times of Mrs. Lot')

The Case of Juliette Milton

(from the Chronicles of Mr. Justice Cocklecarrot)

A Mrs. WEBCROSS writes to me as follows:

Dear Sir,

I have seen it stated in the 'Cardiff Bugle' that the fairies now appearing at the foot of Knockfierna in County Limerick are the celebrated red-headed dwarfs who have made Mr. Justice Cocklecarrot's life a hell. This is not so. The twelve little gentlemen are at present my lodgers, and I have no complaint to make of them, apart from a tendency to bawl for second helpings of meat (which are not included in our board), and a readiness to flirt with my pretty boarder in the most outrageous manner. In the term 'flirting' I include ear-pinching, eye-rolling, lip-smacking, nudging, giggling, and even, upon occasion, Sudden Embracing in the passages. But my object in writing to you, sir, is to put it on record that neither I nor the late Mr. Webcross has ever harboured fairies, either knowingly or unknowingly.

Believe me, sir,
Yours respectfully,
(Mrs.) Lottie Webcross.

THE TWELVE DWARFS

Dear Sir,

We, the undersigned dwarfs, desire to bestow our heartiest approval upon the wise and timely letter of our dear and revered landlady, Madame Webcross. We are not Little People in the fairy-tale sense of the words. We are merely small in the human sense of the word. As to flirtation, when you are as small as we are, and red-haired into the bargain, you have to take your fun where you find it. Full many a furtive kiss changes hands, or rather mouths, without Church and State rocking on their foundations, and if
there is a jollier pastime for a spare moment in a corridor than the tweaking of some alluring ear, we, the undersigned dwarfs, would be glad to hear of it. Evil be to him who thinks evil, say we. Horseplay is no more out of place in a humble boarding-house than in the gilded mansions of the great, and a loving heart is just as likely to beat beneath the ready-made waistcoat of a lodger as beneath the braided and double-breasted garment of a loftier Lothario. All this we say, well knowing that one of our number, Churm Rincewind, is even at this moment encircling with adventurous right arm the provocative waist of Juliette, the sylph-like diseuse who, after bringing down two houses a night at the Old Victoria in Oldham has, bird-of-passage-like, made her temporary nest in No. 8, adjoining the linen cupboard.*

We are, sir,
The Twelve Dwarfs.

THE PRETTY BOARDER REPLIES

Dear Sir,

As the 'pretty boarder' referred to by Mrs. Webcross in her letter to you, I should like to take this opportunity of denying the statement made by a dwarf of the name of Churm Rincewind to the effect that he put his arm round my waist. All that happened was this. Mr. Rincewind put a small ladder against me while I was reading a letter. He mounted the ladder and kissed the tip of my right ear. Thinking he was crazy I pushed him away, and he fell from the ladder and hurt his wrist. I understand he is claiming damages. The whole incident is too foolish to be taken seriously. One does
not expect to have ladders put against one in respectable boarding-houses, nor to see a grinning face on the top rung.

Yours truly,
Juliette Milton.

I learn that the red-bearded dwarf, Churm Rincewind, who fell from a small folding ladder on the third-floor landing of Sea View boarding-house, Chelsea, while kissing the ear of Miss Juliette Milton, is bringing an action for damages. The case will come up for hearing shortly. The judge will be Mr. Justice Cocklecarrot. Miss Milton said yesterday, 'The whole affair is too ludicrous to discuss. My solicitor tells me that there has never before been a case of a small man planting a ladder against a lady, and then bringing an action because he is pushed away and hurts his wrist.'

The nearest approach to such a case was when a man-about-town tried to throw a brass curtain-ring over the head of one of the giraffe-necked women from Burma. He mounted a ladder to get a better aim.

MRS. WEBCROSS GIVES EVIDENCE

The hearing began yesterday, before Mr. Justice Cocklecarrot (with full jury), of the case in which Mr. Churm Rincewind, a red-bearded dwarf about town, seeks to recover damages for an injury to his wrist, sustained when he fell from a ladder which he had mounted for the purpose of kissing the ear of a young lady boarder at Sea View, Chelsea (proprietress, Mrs. Webcross). Mr. Tinklebury Snapdriver was for the defence, Mr. Graham Gooseboote for the prosecution.

Mr. Gooseboote: You are Hermione Webcross, proprietress of the boarding-house known as Sea View?

Mrs. Webcross: I object, m'lud.

Cocklecarrot: What—to the boarding-house?

Mrs. Webcross: It is not' known as' Sea View. It *is* Sea View.

Mr. Gooseboote: And what sea, may one ask, does it view? The Pacific?

Mrs. Webcross: Properly speaking, there is no view of the sea, as we overlook Delton and Mackworth's Cycle Accessories. But the name handed down by my late mother, Clara Webcross, is Sea View.

Mr. Gooseboote: Very well. Now, Mrs. Webcross, do you encourage your male boarders to make overtures to your female boarders?

Mrs. Webcross: Certainly not. My house is not a co-educational road-house.

Mr. Gooseboote: Then how do you explain the fact that one of your boarders, a lady, was kissed on the ear from the top rung of a small ladder in broad daylight?

Mrs. Webcross: It was the exception that proves the rule. It might happen to anyone.

(The court then rose for drinks.)

JULIETTE CROSS-EXAMINED

Miss Juliette Milton, dressed in a four-piece gabardine of moiré tussore with green revers and crotted manchlets, was cross-examined yesterday by Mr. Gooseboote.

Mr. Gooseboote: I suggest that you yourself helped to place the ladder up which your assailant climbed.

Miss Milton: No. I can get plenty of kissing without having to act as a sort of builder's mate.

Mr. Gooseboote: No doubt, no doubt. Er—did you in any way extend your ear, in order to make the dwarf's pleasant task easier?

Miss Milton: I am an actress, not a contortionist. I cannot move my ears at will.

Mr. Gooseboote: Not even a fraction of an inch, in order to avoid an unorthodox salutation?

Cocklecarrot: May we see this ladder?

Mr. Snapdriver: Certainly, m'lud. It is here. It shall be passed up to you.

Mr. Gooseboote: With your ludship's permission, I would like to try an experiment.

Cocklecarrot: With the ladder and the lady's ear? Fire ahead. I'm sure the whole court envies you.

(The court then rose for more drinks.)

Mr. Gooseboote was half-way up the ladder, which he had leaned against Miss Juliette Milton, and was already stooping to her ear, when cry rang out.

Rincewind: M'worship, I object. Why should the learned counsel be allowed to do with impunity what I am being prosecuted for doing without impunity?

Cocklecarrot: It is in the interests of justice.

Miss Milton (blushing): Not entirely, I hope.

Mr. Gooseboote (beaming at her): No, of course, not entirely. There is the human element.

Cocklecarrot: That element, Mr. Gooseboote, must be strongly controlled in a court of law. The present experiment with an ear should be scientific, cold, detached. Meaning no slight to the—er—quite obvious charms of the lady.

Miss Milton: Thank you, m'lud. You are all most kind. It is so difficult for a lonely girl——

Rincewind: In every reconstruction of a crime that I can remember it was the accused who was given the leading part.

Cocklecarrot: There is no question of a crime in this case. It is no crime to—er—fondle such an ear.

Rincewind: Then why am I here?

Mr. Snapdriver: To claim damages, you fool, for a sprained wrist.

(The court then went rushing out for drinks.)

Mr. Gooseboote: Now, Mr. Rincewind——

Rincewind: Sir. Yours to command.

Cocklecarrot: Please, please, Mr. Rincewind.

Rincewind: With pleasure, m'ludship.

Cocklecarrot: Please do not speak until you are questioned.

Rincewind: I was under the impression that I *was* being questioned.

Cocklecarrot: Oh, very well. But try not to interrupt or to waste the time of the court. Pray proceed, Mr. Gooseboote.

Gooseboote: Now, Mr. Rincewind, how do you account for the fact that you fell from the ladder without Miss Milton pushing you?

Rincewind: Emotion.

Gooseboote: What do you mean—emotion?

Rincewind: It is difficult to balance on a ladder while indulging in dalliance and gallantry, as you probably know.

Gooseboote: The experience has not yet come my way.

Rincewind: Live in hope, cully, live in hope.

(The court then rose as one man and dashed madly for the canteen.)

Mr. Snapdriver: I put it to you, Mr. Rincewind——

Rincewind: Put away.

Snapdriver: What?

Rincewind: I said 'put away'.

Snapdriver: Put away what?

Rincewind: That's what you were going to tell us.

Cocklecarrot: Come, come. This is ludicrous. Mr. Rincewind, you must endeavour to refrain from interruption.

Rincewind: Your wish is law, Big Chief.

Cocklecarrot: Would that it were.

Rincewind: Were what?

Cocklecarrot: Law.

Rincewind: Oh.

Snapdriver: Now, I put it to you, Mr. Rince——

Rincewind: Now we're coming to it.

Snapdriver: M'lud, this is impossible.

Rincewind: He's losing his nerve.

Cocklecarrot: I shall have to fine you for contempt.

Rincewind: All the dough in the world wouldn't pay for my contempt of this court, not meaning any offence.

(Sensation. The court is cleared.)

SENSATIONAL DISCLOSURE

Cocklecarrot: This case seems to have got out of hand. We are here to consider the claim for damages of little Mr. Rincewind, who fell from a ladder while kissing the ear of the plaintiff, Miss Juliette Milton. Mr. Gooseboote, learned counsel for the defence, has repeated Mr. Rincewind's experiment with success. Mr. Snapdriver, learned counsel for the prosecution, now demands to follow suit. Well, if we are all going to reconstruct the case so realistically, we shall be here for weeks. But I cannot for the life of me see what these experiments, dangerously pleasant in themselves, can possibly prove. Miss Milton, did you push Mr. Rincewind off the ladder?

Miss Milton: No.

Cocklecarrot: Then you encouraged his advances?

Miss Milton: Certainly not. He is so small. I did not see him until he kissed me.

Cocklecarrot: Do you ask me to believe that you did not notice that you had a ladder leaning against you?

Miss Milton: Of course, I noticed it, you bl——m'lud.

Cocklecarrot: Then why did you leave it there?

Miss Milton: Must I answer?

Cocklecarrot: Of course you must.

Miss Milton (shyly): I thought it might be someone else coming up it. (Sensation.)

COCKLECARROT SUMS UP

Mr. Justice Cocklecarrot said: 'As it seems quite impossible to conduct in a normal manner any case in which these little gentlemen are involved, I suppose I may as well make a kind of summing-up. If the jury think that Mr. Rincewind was pushed from the ladder, they will consider his claim for damages reasonable. If, however, they are satisfied that he was not pushed but fell, as it were, of his own volition, their duty is clear. One thing that has struck me as odd about the case—apart from the interludes of lunacy which we have all deplored—is the fact that Miss Milton awaited the marauder, calmly allowing a ladder to be laid against her, as though she were a wall. She must have heard the approaching steps of this little bravo, and descried his face as it was advanced menacingly towards the goal of his unlawful whim—I refer to the perilously beautiful ear of the defendant. Now, Mrs. Webcross has assured us that ladder-gallantry is not part of the everyday life at her boarding establishment, yet Miss Milton expressed no surprise when she felt the ladder against her body, nor when she saw this little gentleman's moon-face gazing up at her. I am puzzled; and I am bound to add that the two learned counsel have merely confused the issue by their prodigious display of idiocy and incompetence. I will end on that note. It is for the jury to make what they can of all this nonsense.'

Life at Boulton Wynfevers

When I was head aquarium keeper at Boulton Wynfevers, the commodious Tudor residence of the seventeenth Baron Shortcake, we had goldfish in every room. "Travers," my master would say to me, "have you changed the fish-water in Lady Katharine's room?" or "Travers," he would call from the minstrels' gallery, "are the fish in the Hon. Guy Clobbock's room eating well?" or, "Travers," he would yell from the gunroom, "the fish in Lady Muriel's boudoir are making so much damned noise I can't hear myself eat."

We had one fish that snored, and we always put it in Lord Thwacker's room, and told him it was the ghost of the ninth baron.

*   *   *

It was my duty as head aquarium keeper to keep an eye on all the different kinds of fish in our aquarium, and every night, before retiring to bed, Baron Shortcake expected me to report that all was well. The men under me had to count the fish, and then I would hand a slip of paper to my master, with the figure written on it. He always feared that some might escape—an impossible contingency, since the fish were in tanks and were watched night and day. I once ventured to ask the Baron where the fish could go to if they escaped. He answered: "Travers, fish are queer customers. They might break out. I wish to run no risks." One night he roused the household saying he had dreamed that a China Sea pterolotl had escaped, and was not satisfied until I had shown him the little beast asleep among weeds in his tank.

*   *   *

Towards his eightieth year my dear old master became an even greater goldfish-addict than before. He filled the house and grounds with goldfish, and I, as head aquarium keeper, was often called to flick the fish off people's clothes, or to drive them from the dining-hall table.

One evening, when sprats Melba were on the menu, Lady Thrashurst ate six sleeping goldfish by mistake. They had crept on to her plate. The consciousness of her error brought her to her feet with a roar of shame and anguish, and so energetically did she wriggle and squirm as the rudely awakened fish struggled in her throat that my master, recalling the Eastern dances of his youth, shouted an Oriental oath and clapped his hands.

*   *   *

On the morning after my old master had lost £73,000 in IOU's to a guest, we sold the entire Boulton Wynfevers collection of goldfish to a lonely old lady who had just cut her niece out of her will. From that day the Baron changed. He would wander listlessly from room to room, calling the absent fish by name and starting guiltily if he thought he saw a movement in the empty bowls.

He would sit late at his dinner, and would often call for me to repeat some story of the fish, saying, "Travers, tell them about that time when the two Burmese Rovers got down the back of Lady Felspar's dress," or "Travers, do you recall how that little devil Silver Slipper drank a glass of my Meursault on the night of the fire?" or, "Travers, I do not think Sir Arthur knows the story of how Tiny and his gang got into the Bishop's hot-water bottle and tickled his feet." And he would sigh and say, "Those were the days."

* * *

They were, indeed, the days. Once a year the grounds were thrown open to the villagers and their friends, and the London papers would send photographers and reporters. The Baron was usually photographed standing between two of the biggest bowls, and little girls dressed as goldfish would curtsey to him and present him with an album in which to stick snapshots of his favourites and prizewinners.

Twelve years running we won the Shires Cup for the smartest turn-out, and the fish always got fresh water and an extra meal—not to mention a playful flip on the back from the beaming owner.

I still treasure the photograph of myself standing between my master and Lady Mockett and holding up Jellaby Wonder II by the tail.

* * *

Deafness troubled my old master considerably towards the end of his life. I remember an occasion on which he was entertaining the Lord Lieutenant of the County to dinner. He, also, was deaf. He suggested to Lord Shortcake that the craze for tropical fish was dying out.

"By topical," said my master, "I presume you mean fashionable." "I don't agree," rejoined the Lord Lieutenant. "I think they are unfashionable. They are aliens in any aquarium." "Who are aliens?" asked my master. "No, no," said the Lord Lieutenant. "Not us. I said the fish." "Damn it," hotly retorted Shortcake, "what fish are you talking of?" "No, no," said the Lord Lieutenant, "not us. I said the fish." "What?" roared my master. "Do you mean *all* fish?" "Well, they *are* all fish, aren't they?" said the Lord Lieutenant angrily.

* * *

As the evening wore on and the port in the decanter sank lower and lower, the two deaf men groped for an understanding. When the Lord Lieutenant spoke of flying fish, my master thought he had said "frying fish." He grew enraged at the idea of frying valuable specimens of his collection. "But surely," said the Lord Lieutenant, "you keep flying fish?" "I do no such thing," replied Shortcake, "and if I did I should do it in the kitchen, not in the aquarium." "That's the first time," said the Lord Lieutenant, "I ever heard of anybody with an aquarium in his kitchen." "Besides," said my master, "you couldn't eat most of them, even if you fried them." "There you are!" said the Lord Lieutenant, "what's the good of flying fish?"

* * *

Nothing annoyed Lord Shortcake more than an obvious indifference to his goldfish. He would say to a guest before retiring. "You will find your bowl in your room. Don't disturb the fish more than is necessary."

The tactless guest would sometimes grin and say nothing or even show surprise, as though he were unused to such a thing. But what my dear master liked was to get some such reply as: "Oh, but how very thoughtful of you! What breed are they? How many? What age? Certainly I will not disturb them."

On one occasion a young lady of title, on receiving the parting information and admonition went into screaming hysterics, which infuriated my master. "Does she think they are mice?" he asked me several times.

* * *

On another occasion a stupid dowager cried: "What! Real goldfish?" "Have you ever seen goldfish that weren't real?" snapped my master. "But, do you mean *real* goldfish, like the ones in bowls?" she continued. "Damn it all, madam," said my master, "I don't know what kind of goldfish you have been used to, but there's no nonsense about mine."

"But why in the bedroom?" asked the dowager. "Why on earth not?" countered Lord Shortcake. "What odds is it to them what room they are in?" "Well, I shall put them outside the door," said the dowager. "You can do that with your boots, but not with my fish," said my master. "Why not," he added, "fill your boots with water and put them in the bowl with the fish instead?" The dowager considered this for a while, and then left the room in high dudgeon.

* * *

I would not like my readers to have the idea that life at Boulton Wynfevers was all goldfish. There were days when my master became profoundly dissatisfied with his hobby. "Travers," he would say to me, "these damned fish never *do* anything. They roam round their bowls, but anybody can do that."

It was my task on such occasions to comfort him by referring to the sheen on their coats, or their efforts to look intelligent when shouted at, or their value as ornaments. "Bah," he would say, "I prefer a good bloater. You can, at any rate, *eat* a bloater." I would then point out that you can't keep bloaters in bowls all over a house. "Quite right, Travers," he would say, "one must make allowances." And he would add: "It takes all sorts to make a world."

* * *

Curiously enough, my old master was always afraid of fire destroying his fish. An Indian law student had once told him that goldfish are terrified of fire. That is why, during the winter, their bowls were always placed as far from the fires as possible. And he even asked the chief of the local fire brigade to submit a plan for dealing with an outbreak of fire among the fish. This gentlemen said: "Oh, but they're safe enough. They're in water." "So are ships," said the Baron, "but they catch fire." There was a fire-alarm in every room, and, I, as head aquarium keeper, had to wear a fireman's helmet and carry an axe on windy days.

* * *

My dear old master, in spite of the immense wealth which enabled him to own the largest private aquarium in the shires, was a simple gentleman at heart.

Though he had a first-class chef he would never eat fish. He said to me one day: "If I collected cows, and kept on eating beef, I should feel like a murderer. Same with fish. That is why I never shoot pheasants."

But he was very fond of a plain boiled egg, and always kept the shells. Out of these he would make what he jestingly called "Small porcelain bric-a-brac." These were so fragile that no maid was allowed to dust them. They were kept on a mantelshelf in his dressing-room. And if he broke one, he would glue the pieces together again. I remember one ornament which he called a frigate in full sail. He used matches for the masts and calico for the sails. One day it disintegrated in the bath and disappeared with the bath water, to his chagrin.

* * *

Lord Shortcake collected stamps as well as goldfish—but only English twopenny stamps. He had no interest in foreign stamps, which, he said, should be left to foreigners. He had many albums filled with twopenny stamps, for he said that no two stamps were the same. Often a bored guest would be forced to admire the contents of these albums, and if he said: "But they all look the same to me," my dear old master would reply, "That is because you don't study them enough. All Chinamen look the same to many Westerners, but they are really all different."

* * *

It was the duty of my master's secretary, Aubyn Spicecraft, to keep every twopenny stamp which arrived with each day's post. Lord Shortcake showed no interest in the contents of his letters. He would ask, at breakfast, "How many of our well-known twopennies to-day, Spicecraft?" And, according to the answer, he would smile or frown. Sometimes Spicecraft would venture to remark that there was a letter from a relative or a dear friend. My master would then reply, "Well, what odds, so long as it's got the jolly old twopenny stuck to it, eh? Give me the stamp, I always say, and anybody can have the letter, eh?"

My dear old master was of so kindly a nature that he was easily victimised. He was asked once to stand for Parliament, the member for the constituency having died. On his inquiring what they would like him to stand as, a go-ahead member of the local football club said, "Why not the Gold-fish candidate? Better treatment for our dumb friends, and all that. Good publicity value."

My old master replied that goldfish were not dumb. He said they mewed very faintly, at certain seasons. Otherwise, he said, he was prepared to present the case for better treatment for all fish to the representatives of the nation.

* * *

Lord Shortcake was actually preparing his election literature when a friend told him that if he got up in the House and talked about goldfish he would be laughed at. "Through me, then," he said, "they would be laughing at the fish. I will not do it, eh?"

The newspapers, of course, ran the Goldfish candidate for all they were worth, but my dear old master could be stubborn when he wanted to be. In a final interview he said, "I think I can best serve the interests of fish by abstaining from the rostrum of public life, eh?"

* * *

Among my duties at Boulton Wynfevers, as I have stated, was the counting of the goldfish. Every night, before the household retired to bed, I had to hand to my dear old master a slip of paper with the total figure written on it.

The figure was always 13,874, since every dead fish was replaced at once, from a reserve tank, by a living one. But Lord Shortcake always took the thing seriously. He would say, "Hum! 13,874. Not bad, Travers, not at all bad, eh?"; or "By George, Travers, 13,874, did you say? Pretty sound figure, eh? "or "Bravo, Travers, we're keeping it up, eh?"

Once I wrote 13,847 by mistake, and my dear old master made me count them all over again. "Slippery little devils," he kept on saying. "Can't be too careful."

* * *

When the house was full of guests the counting had to be done while they were out of their rooms. I had to hang about the corridors and seize my chance. And I well remember going into the Queen Elizabeth room in the east wing to tot up the denizens of that particular bowl and hearing a scream. A young lady was arranging her hair at a mirror, and when I had explained my intrusion she said, "It doesn't ring true, my man," and, turning to her maid, she said, "Germaine, lock up my jewels and give me the key." Such base talk made me hang my head in shame, and under my breath I cursed the day those goldfish were born.

What struck me as so silly was that I had no need to count them. I knew the figure by heart, as the shrewd reader will have guessed.

* * *

My master's own personal bowl, in his bedroom, was stocked with the best of the fish, and I shall not be likely to forget the night when the lights fused and a certain bishop blundered into the room, mistaking it for his own, and plunged his right foot into the bowl. Candles were brought, but one big beauty was missing. My master surprised the bishop by saying, "I think Wonder of Arden is hiding in your gaiter." The bishop had to remove his gaiter, and out jumped the fish and slithered into a corner of the room. Lord Shortcake and I rounded it up and replaced it in the bowl. But it was an anxious night, and at two a.m. my dear old master beat on my door, shouting, "I think I hear a stray fish in Sir Arthur's room." It was a false alarm.

* * *

During the summer months it was Lord Shortcake's custom to entertain on a large scale. But the younger among his guests resented the lack of swimming pools, since every possible piece of water, ornamental or otherwise, was reserved for the goldfish.

One cocksure young lady said one day, "Shorty, old hog, why not clear out these fish and give us a break?" My dear old master flushed with anger. "Those fish," he said, "can do nothing but swim. You, my dear Poppy, have other accomplishments—or haven't you?"

I had strict orders to see that nobody dived into the main pond, and a large notice warned human beings to respect the privacy of the fish.

* * *

I remember the ghastly silence when, at dinner one night, a jovial young peer said, "Any fishing down here, Shorty?" After a moment my dear old master replied, "What would you say, Flinge, if, while you were lying in your bath, a beast came and fixed a hook in your throat and hauled you out?" Young Mr. Flinge gaped. "Don't sort of get the idea," he said. "What are you talking about?" "A parable," said Lord Shortcake, "a mere parable. If the cap fits shove it on." "What cap?" asked Mr. Flinge, "I say, I don't know what you're talking about." But my master had summoned me from my place next to the third butler, and now shouted loudly, "Keep him from the fish, eh?"

* * *

When I announced to my dear old master that Polly Cragge, one of the parlourmaids at Chealvercote Grange, the residence of Lord and Lady Hoopoe, had promised to marry me, he at once asked, "Does she understand about goldfish?" I said that we had not discussed that subject much. To which he replied that marriage with a head aquarium keeper meant something more than a passive interest in his work.

He even sent Lord Hoopoe a bowl of fish, in the hope that Polly might become fond of them. He received in return a note from Lord Hoopoe which said, "I take it that the present of goldfish was meant for someone else. I return them herewith." They were at once sent back to Chealvercote, where a groom fed them to an Irish wolfhound.

* * *

Our engagement dragged on, because Polly took a violent dislike to the goldfish at Boulton Wynfevers. Every time we were together, my dear old master would track us down and get us into the aquarium. He kept on asking us to guess what he was going to give us for a wedding present. We would pretend not to know, and he would chuckle and say, "Why, six dozen spankin' fine goldfish, eh?" And one day he gave Polly one of his Golden Marvels. To humour him she took it back to Chealvercote, where it escaped and was found half-dead in Lord Hoopoe's tobacco pouch, which he had offered to the rural dean. Polly was sacked and broke off our engagement. For a while I found it difficult not to hate the fish.

* * *

Among frequent visitors was a cunning lady in straitened circumstances, the handsome widow of a ne'er-do-well. How she wheedled my dear old master in order to get into his will! She who did not know a whale from a lobster, would simulate a deep interest in the goldfish, crooning over them, stroking them, and pretending to recognize each individual fish. It was only when she mistook an Orange Wonder for a Tawny Perfection that Lord Shortcake smelt a rat. But she even went so far as to crowd her bedside table with books about goldfish and once wrote a poem about King Sam, one of our prize specimens, which began: "Round and round and round and round, he swims without a human sound, sparkling here and sparkling there, what does he know of carking care?" My old master had this framed and hung in the aquarium.

* * *

My late lamented mistress, Lady Shortcake, who died in 1938, had often been accused of feigning interest in goldfish in order to keep my old master in good humour. But is it likely that any lady of her attainments could have stooped for 61 years to such deceit? And how can anybody simulate an interest in goldfish? The only member of the family who actively disliked the fish was the third son, Stanley. "There must be some bad streak in the boy," my old master would say. "It isn't natural. He's not a Shortcake." His own excuse, that he was bitten by a Yellow Peril in boyhood, was never taken seriously at Boulton Wynfevers. "Pah," my master said once. "If they were only bigger I'd put my head in their mouths without a tremor."

* * *

The thought of Lord Shortcake with his head in a goldfish's mouth was too much for one of the young butlers. His chest heaved with inward laughter, and an entire dish of peas, about to be offered to Lord Hoopoe, slithered down the ear-trumpet of the Dowager Lady Garment, who had just placed the instrument in position in anticipation of some outrageous compliment from her neighbour. The cascade of peas against her leathery old ear drew from her an eldritch shriek. "She might have awakened the fish," said my master calmly, when it was all over, and she had apologised to Lord Hoopoe for smacking his face.

* * *

Aubyn Spicecraft, my dear old master's secretary, was one of those secretaries who must fold a newspaper before handing it to anybody, so that it has to be unfolded again before being read. This, he said, gives an employer the idea that he is independent and can look after himself. That is why, he would say, employers always unfold newspapers so pompously.

Lord Shortcake was interested only in stories about goldfish. If there were none in the papers, he sent them out to the servants' hall. It was Mr. Spicecraft's task to mark with a blue pencil any such

stories, and then to cut them out and file them after my master had read them. In addition to this, we subscribed to a press-cutting agency, which sent us all references to goldfish.

* * *

It was Spicecraft, of course, who took down at dictation and typed my dear old master's monumental work, "A History of Japanese Crossbreeds," in eight volumes, with coloured plates of every kind of odd goldfish known to mankind. I cannot resist quoting its closing words, which hang above my Aquarium-Keeper's Diploma as I write. "And so, reader, we say farewell to goldfish. May everybody find such constant companions upon life's thoroughfare as I have found. For this world is but a bowl, where we poor mortals blunder round and round until our brief day is done. Nor, with all man's boasted brains, can he rival in beauty the little fish which has been the subject of my humble work. Gentlemen, I give you the toast: Goldfish!"

* * *

Here is another anecdote which shows the loveable simplicity of my master's character. One Christmas there was a party for all the children of the neighbourhood at Boulton Wynfevers. A Chinese conjurer (a Mr. Sam Thickett) was engaged. His first trick was to make a bowl of goldfish disappear. This so annoyed Lord Shortcake that he stopped the performance, crying, "Find them at once." The conjurer began to produce the missing fish from the ears and pockets of the children. My master beckoned me from the room and said, "Travers, this must be stopped." So the magic lantern was brought in, and we had "Glimpses of Jamaica" (Miss Grabbing at the piano).

* * *

It was for some time my dear old master's ambition to have a film made about the life of a gold-fish. But he always fell out with the film people over the question of a plot. He said that no plot was needed, and that no human beings should appear.

He told one producer, "I know what you mean by human interest, eh? Thousands of Hawaiian dancing girls." "What's wrong with Hawaiian dancing girls?" asked the producer. "I want an English picture of animal life," replied my master, "and no jungle stuff, with mad escapes." He insisted that the title should be "Goldfish," and not "Little Wonders of the Deep," which, he said, suggested a lot of dwarfs diving for pearls. Nor would he have any incidental music. "The picture itself must hold the attention," he said.

* * *

Finally the film was made by a week-end guest at Boulton Wynfevers, and was always shown after dinner. It was simple and beautiful. It showed the fish swimming round and round in the bowl, without any commentary. There was one tense moment when it looked as though the fish might turn and swim round in the opposite direction. At this point my master would grip the arms of his chair until his knuckles were white. But the fish, after a moment's hesitation, decided to go on as before. Then Lord Shortcake would give a contented sigh, and say loudly to the guests, "You see? The little beggar didn't reverse after all, eh?"

* * *

My dear old master was very forthright in his views on art. When a famous portrait-painter came to Boulton Wynfevers to paint him, he said bluntly, in my hearing, "Mark this, sir, none of your confounded cubist portraits. I'm not a three-cornered tomato on a yellow banjo, even if I look like that to you."

The artist, who painted the conventional glossy portraits at £2,000 a go, was taken aback. "And," continued Lord Shortcake, "I want a background of goldfish in bowls. Bring the fish out strong. Idealise 'em, if you like. But don't call the thing 'Sunset on a Dead Horse'."

* * *

Once a year Lord Shortcake's team of house-party guests played a cricket match against the village. My master himself captained his side, and showed those qualities of gay absentmindedness and *laissez-faire* which were the despair of his friends. While fielding, he could not resist talking to the ladies, and often sat down among them, or took the arm of one of them and paced up and down with her. When he bowled, he never would admit that he had had a complete over. "Now, umpire," he would say, "can't you *count,* eh?" And he never yielded up the ball without a laughing protest. "Oh, well," he would say loudly, "if *that's* your idea of six balls, eh?" One young and timid umpire once let him have his fling. He bowled fourteen balls, and then said, "Come, umpire, I've had my six balls. You may call 'Over,' eh?"

* * *

Lady Shortcake, though not sharing her husband's passion for goldfish, was a handsome and stately lady of the old world. Her main interest was her rose garden.

But there came a clash when a rose was called after her. Her lord and master had already called a goldfish after her, and though she assured him that nobody could ever mistake the one for the other, he implored her, for the sake of appearances, to write to the authorities and get the name of the rose changed. This was done, and the bloom in question is now Mrs. Hufnagle.

* * *

My mistress also liked to play the harp, which instrument she never mastered sufficiently to play a melody. But very beautiful she looked as she allowed her fingers to roam at will over the golden wires, humming an air the while.

* * *

Lord Shortcake was nothing if not unmusical. But that did not prevent him from singing "Asleep in the Deep," in a very loud and raucous baritone, whenever he was bored. Sometimes, in his absent-minded way, he would commence this lugubrious ditty at the crowded dinner-table, without warning. It was then his helpmeet's task to recall him to reality by making some such observation as "Ernest, your tie is very nearly back to front," or "My dear, no Albert Hall stuff, I beg," or "Shorty don't break out yet."

Once, when he was a young man, he went to a concert. A lady had just begun to sing when my master shouted, "We don't want any coal to-day." He always referred to that as his best joke.

* * *

Lord Shortcake's widowed sister, Lady Bursting, was a frequent visitor. She had a singing mouse given to her by a friend and we had to be very careful of it. It was fed on the choicest morsels of cheese, which so amused my master that one night he gave it some port. That night the singing was distinctly husky and out of tune, and when put out for its run before being shut up for the night, the mouse staggered along the terrace and finally fell down the steps into the rose garden. There a stray cat got it.

To console his sister, my master wrote an epitaph for the mouse.

> *Alas for Henrietta's mouse!*
> *It was the pet of every one in the house.*
> *But the cat pounced like a couple of retrievers,*
> *And that was the end of the pride of Boulton Wynfevers.*

* * *

Lady Bursting's attitude to the ubiquitous goldfish was very peculiar. She affected to be unaware of their presence in the house. When her attention was called to them, she would say, non-committally, "Oh, *those*. Yes." Nothing would induce her to talk about them, or even to look at them. My master used to say, "That woman goes through life with her eyes shut. Anybody would think there were no fish in the place." As aquarium-keeper I felt myself included in her lack of interest, and once, when she found my peaked hat on a table, she picked it up between finger and thumb as though it had been a putrid rat. Doubtless she had some deep-seated hatred of goldfish which she cloaked with a veneer of apathy.

* * *

Lady Shortcake was deeply interested in folk-dancing, and we always had a village team in her lifetime. The only time my master became aware of this was when, returning one early spring morning from bird-watching on the banks of the Bottlemere, and about to let himself in by the back door, he ran into Angelica, one of the parlourmaids. She was dressed up as Queen of the May. He asked for an explanation. On being told that she was on her way to the maypole, he thought she was referring to a local inn. "How long have you had this dreadful habit?" he asked. "I only began it last year," said Angelica, "to please her ladyship." "What on earth do you mean?" roared my master, so loudly that one of the guests, a Miss Fowler, opened her bedroom window, and cried, "Can't you two make less noise?"

*   *   *

At breakfast, Lord Shortcake said to my mistress, "My dear, I met Angelica going to the Maypole. She had the impudence to say she did it to please you." "Of course," said Lady Shortcake, "she's one of my most promising pupils." "Pupils?" bellowed my master, "Am I mad? Since when have you been giving lessons in drinking?" Lady Shortcake drew herself up frigidly. "Who said anything about drinking?" she asked. "What else is there to do at the Maypole?" asked my master. "They dance round it, you oaf," was the reply. Lord Shortcake blinked unhappily, and murmured, "I give it up."

*   *   *

Ah, the old days at Boulton Wynfevers!
In a can of freshwater fleas intended as food for our fish, my master found one large flea, which he kept in a matchbox. He called it Polyphemus, because he said it had one large eye in the middle of its forehead. Nobody ever verified this, as the box was kept in a cupboard in the gun-room.
The flea died there, and Lord Shortcake said, somewhat inconsequently, that if only people would mind their own business these things would not keep on happening. Pressed by her lady-ship for an explanation of so strange a saying, he replied, "Shut up there in its box in the gun-room, it stood no chance." "Well, who shut it up?" asked Lady Shortcake. "Somebody had to," answered my master, "to stop everybody peering and fussing."

*   *   *

"I believe," said Lady Shortcake, "that it was just an ordinary flea." "I trust, my love," replied her husband, with an old-world inclination of the head, "I trust that my Lady Shortcake's experience of ordinary fleas is so negligible as to preclude the possibility of her being a competent arbiter in the matter."
"Vulgarity," retorted my lady, "cannot be cloaked by a spate of words."

*   *   *

On one occasion a facetious young man, when the salmon was being served at dinner, said loudly to Lady Trowell, "What next? Ho! Goldfish and chips." Lord Shortcake gave him a look in which pain and anger fought for mastery. "I was only joking, sir," said the young fool. "Had I believed you to be speaking seriously," replied my master, "I should have shown you the door." An awkward silence fell, and then silly old Mrs. Fotherick-Dowler said heartily, "And a very fine door it is, Shorty, if I may say so." "Jolly good show!" said a man's voice lower down the table. For everybody was trying to tide things over. "Did you see Hobbs at the Oval in 1924?" came from a gaunt man. "That was the year Myra married that gadget Helmsley," screamed a woman's voice. But Shortcake sat glumly listening to jokes about his fish.

*   *   *

When the house was empty of guests, my master and mistress would often play a game of billiards after dinner. If the fish were quiet, I generally acted as marker. And a gloomy occasion it was. Lord Shortcake's bad eyesight and lack of skill prevented him from scoring any points, save by an occasional fluke. Lady Shortcake's eyesight was good, but she was an even worse player. And nothing less than a hundred up would suit them. Most of the scoring was done by misses, and towards the end of the game the cloth was nearly always torn by some savage and despairing stroke of my master's. What made things worse was that my master would tender advice to her ladyship before each stroke. After the stroke he would rebuke her, and outline her faults. And always, when the game ended he would say, "I wasn't on top of my game to-night, Henrietta."

*   *   *

I seem to hear their voices now. . . . Travers, the jigger for her ladyship. . . . Travers, I'll trouble you to chalk this damnable cue. . . . Shorty, keep quiet while I aim. . . . Henrietta, my love, can't you manage a bit more spin? . . . You aimed at the wrong ball, Henrietta. . . . Travers, kindly read out the score as it stands at the moment. . . . There, Henrietta, I've left you a perfect sitter, all you have to do. . . . My dear girl, you're playing putridly to-night. . . . Take your hand off the table, Shorty. I can't see the pocket. . . . Travers, you aren't chalking my cue enough. . . . Women are no good at billiards. . . . RRRRRP. . . . Curse the cloth, it's always tearing!

DIPLOMATIC COURSE

Quoting a recent dictum that "There should no longer be any room for gentlemen in the diplomatic service," Dr. Smart-Allick has decided to prepare some of his more promising pupils for a diplomatic career.

A recent examination paper is worth quoting. One of the questions was:

How would you, as an Ambassador in a foreign capital, set about procuring an interview with the Minister for Foreign Affairs of the country to which you are accredited?

One of the answers was: "I wood send a beutiferl wumman to elure him into my clutches."

Here are one or two more answers:

"Sanbag him in a loanley ally."

"Get old uv some inkeriminating letters and blackmale im."

"Brake in to his ministery and hold him up at the point of the ruvvolver."

"Get him into a game of whist behind locked dores."

"Pertend to be his long lorst unkil."

"Dissgise meself as a gass inspekter cum to read his metre."

MY SECRET

Somebody asked me yesterday how on earth I manage to get all the news for my column in order to keep it up to date in these difficult days.

I explained that it is only with the greatest difficulty that I can keep this column so astonishingly topical. It means being prepared, at any hour of the night or day, to receive the latest message from a news agency or a correspondent. That message then has to be checked, since I am very careful of my reputation for strict accuracy. I allow nothing to appear under my signature which has not been verified.

IT IS NOTHING, I ASSURE YOU

My questioner then went on to point out that very often I seem to get exclusive stories. How, he asked, is it that you so frequently steal a march on your colleagues and other newspapers?

As modestly as I could I explained that I was merely trying to do my duty as a good newspaper man, and that my successes were no doubt due to my flair for news. "See," I exclaimed, "just a moment ago I got this. I am sure you will see it nowhere else. It is worth a paragraph to itself.'

OARSWOMAN TCHAIKOVSKY DRAMA

Mrs. Prentle, of 2 The Villas, Horsepot, celebrated her 143rd birthday yesterday, surrounded by her 398 grandchildren. Though still vigorous, Mrs. Prentle persists in calling herself the oldest Etonian, and thinks that she rowed for Eton against the M.C.C. in 1812, with Tchaikovsky as cox. Mrs. Prentle has never seen a train, and thinks that the modern girl plays too much croquet.

(*Beachcomber News Service.*)

PRODNOSE'S UNWORTHY SUSPICION

Prodnose: Did it never occur to your questioner that it would be by no means impossible to invent that kind of ridiculous story?

Myself: I resent that remark. I resent it for myself and for the traditions of decent journalism. And I know I have all Fleet Street, and perhaps (who knows?) even Bouverie Street, behind me.

MARINE HOUSE

I have unearthed a very nasty piece of gossip. It is being said that Mrs. Wretch, before her marriage, and at the time when she was the belle of Wugwell's Circus, once spent three days at Marine House. It was at the time when she was the lady who had to balance a glass of port on her nose for a seal to drink from. And rumour says that she beat the seal to it five nights out of six. Rumour says also that her exotic charm had such an effect on Mr. McGurgle that he slipped her dainty morsels when the châtelaine was not looking. But one day, at supper, the châtelaine *was* looking, and winged words flew to and fro at the festive board.

This was, of course, long before Colonel Wretch, eyeing her from the three and six-pennies, marked her down as his mate.

COLONEL WRETCH PROTESTS

From Colonel Wretch's secretary I have received the following statement:

Colonel Wretch has been much distressed at further references to that period of Mrs. Wretch's life which was not wholly unconnected with Wugwell's Circus. There are circuses and circuses. The Colonel cannot insist too strongly that Wugwell's was something more than the usual vulgar entertainment. The Colonel also begs to doubt whether Mrs. Wretch was ever a guest at Marine House. As one of the leading performers, she stayed at the best hotels. The Colonel would also like to point out that Wugwell was not the sort of proprietor popularly associated with circuses. He was a man of culture and savoir faire, spoke German, and had been, I believe, at a public school.

NOBBY JELLIFER BUTTS IN

Dear Sir,

The gent calling himself Colonel Wretch seems to think Wugwell's was a sort of Oxford University. Let me tell him, as the man who balanced a midget on each hand to the tune of "Hearts and Flowers," that we was a real slap-up circus and no nonsense. Wugwell could speak German because he was once in a team of German acrobats. As for his public school, the nearest I ever heard of his getting to one was the time he and Alf Sandley and Mabel Catstone was chucked out of an inn near Eton, Mabel having told the landlord that he had a face like Sauchiehall Street, Glasgow, on a wet Monday morning. As for Mrs. McGurgle and Marine House there was places we dossed that would have made her place look like the casino at Monte.

Yrs. faithfully,
NOBBY JELLIFER.

A STRONG MAN'S LOVE

Dear Sir,

Many circus-goers, I flatter myself, will remember the Strong Man of Wugwell's. It was me. At the end of our show I had to support on my chest a human pyramid. And the loveliest rose in all that pyramid was the Equestrian Belle, Appassionata. Often I would pinch her smooth ear as she passed me on her way to the ring, and if stolen kisses are sweetest, the twelve or fourteen I pilfered in quick succession on the afternoon when the tiger mauled the milkman near Bedford will remain deeply inscribed in memory's tablets. I feel sure the Colonel, who is now sole heir to her ruby lips, will not grudge me my theft, nor the lady regret the folly of an idle hour.

I subscribe myself,
SULIMAN BEN RASCHID.

MRS. WRETCH PROTESTS

Dear Sir,

I have held my peace while my bohemian past has been dragged up, not through snobbery, as the mistress of Wretch Hall, but to spare my husband the indignities of public controversy. The gentleman who revealed that he embraced me (for mere purposes of equilibrium) went far enough. But when it comes to kisses stolen by an even more shameless colleague, I must protest. Suliman may have grazed my profile in the give and take of circus camaraderie, but to suggest that I submitted to "twelve or fourteen kisses" is to exaggerate grossly. The layman is apt to think of a circus as a hotbed of free and easy debauchery. In all my time at Wugwell's nothing occurred to bring a blush to my cheek—if I except an occasion when Wugwell himself called me a roguish morsel, an expression which meant no more than it said.

Yrs. faithfully,
UTTA WRETCH.

MR. McGURGLE'S PREJUDICE

Mrs. McGurgle asks me to point out that Marine House drew its clientèle chiefly from solid commercial travellers and holiday parties, and rarely had dealings with the Stage or Circus. The late Mr. McGurgle, she adds, had an objection to stage folk, whom he thought flighty and unstable. This prejudice was based on an unfortunate experience, when a tragedian who was a guest at Marine House came down the chimney at four in the morning with a bottle of stout in each pocket. Mr. McGurgle said, "My love, if a serious actor behaves like this, what would music-hall people do?"

THE EXPLANATION

Dear Sir,

As the tragedian referred to by the late Mr. McGurgle as having come down the chimney at four in the morning, with a bottle of stout in each pocket, I should like to say that it was Christmas time, and I was doing a Father Christmas act to amuse the guests. I would add that the fact that fate has called some of us to portray upon the boards characters of a serious type, does not prevent us from harbouring human feelings. I played Silas Root in "The Waif of Castle Perilous" 4,378 times (including once before a Prince of the Blood), but off the stage I liked to relax.

Yours truly,
LESTER DAVENANT.

MRS. McGURGLE PROTESTS

Dear Beachcomber,

Tongues are once more wagging. The whispering campaign about helpings is under way. Some people do not seem to know that there is a war on, and expect meat and gravy to be ladelled out as in peace time. I flatter myself that we at Marine House have always preferred quality to quantity, even in normal days. The lately deceased Mr. McGurgle used to say to me, "Florrie, my dear, one thin slice of tender meat, cooked to perfection, is better than a thick lump of inferior stuff, burned to a cinder." But some houses I could mention do not seem to have realised this elementary truth. Our quantity may have diminished, but our quality remains at the same high standard. If there be sceptics, let them glance at the compliments in our Visitors' Book.

Yrs. truly,
FLORENCE McGURGLE.

WHAT THE LODGERS THINK

Dear Sir,

The other day I was at pains to take up Mrs. McGurgle's challenge, and to examine her visitors' book for signs of satisfaction. Here are a few entries at random.

The hash here contains everything except the furniture. Thanks a lot. F. Upchurch.

The Government can have my mattress for old iron. Connie Gray.

Judging by the smell, I'd say the walls are papered with cabbage. Ernest Cullett.

If the noise in No. 8 is a gentleman snoring, then 'I don't care if the 9.10 from Eastbourne passes through my room every thirty seconds. H. Cragg.

Need I say more?
JOSEPH PUDKIN.

MRS. McGURGLE AT BAY

Dear Sir,

Mr. Pudkin, whose acquaintanceship I have not the pleasure of knowing, has merely picked out derogatory messages from the Marine House visitors' book. Here are a few of a different kidney.

A real home from home, and

the landlady of our dreams. Tom and Sid.

Such a relief not to be warned that Worcester sauce is an extra. Phyllis Tile.

> Any one who burgles
> Mrs. McGurgle's
> Is in for a treat
> If he pinches her meat.

Honest injun, that meat was a knock-out. Charlie Kilburton.

A DEFENDER

Dear Sir,

Atta la belle McGurgle, Queen of Marine House, Empress among landladies and the rosy apple of every worth-while lodger's eye. Nobody who has ever seen her as I have, shovelling out the cabbage with a Bottyshelly smile, could find fault with her establishment. Beauty, as the poet hath it, draws us with a single hair. Well, what price the McGurgle mop? Enough to draw a ten-ton barge, I'll swear. But no more, lest I lay bare my heart. Ouch!

> Yrs. to a T.,
> GEO. MASON.

THE TEST

Dear Sir,

The test of a boarding-house is whether you can get away with the kipper trick. You nail a kipper under the dining-room table. If it has not been discovered and removed at the end of a week, the house is badly run. If otherwise, then it is a well-run establishment. May I say in all friendliness that Florrie McGurgle herself un-nailed my kipper within four hours on the only occasion when I tried to carry out this test. Facts speak for themselves.

> Yrs. truly,
> WILLIAM BOZZING.

MRS. McGURGLE PROTESTS

Dear Sir,

I have never been considered the shy little mouse that can't take care of herself, but I must say that if my late deceased husband, Mr. McGurgle, were among us still, some of the insults and innu-endoes used lately would have been either unheard or crammed back down the throats of the utterers. I affirm, and can bring proof, that nobody ever nailed a kipper under the table at Marine House. Our clientell, I am proud and happy to state, is not of that low standard of ethics. Any attempt to nail a kipper anywhere would be detected at once, since from my chair at the head of the table, I am able to keep every patron under kindly but keen observation.

> Yrs. truly,
> FLORENCE McGURGLE.

MRS. McGURGLE DEFENDS HERSELF

Dear Sir,

Mr. Kidd's complaint that he could find no literature at Marine House is mere carping. There is a public library two minutes away, in Lampeter Street. The late Mr. McGurgle always said that the duties of a good hostess consisted of sending her clientell to bed happy and decently replete. He did not add that copies of the classics should be popped under their pillows—though he was ever one that liked a good book in season, and I have seen him under-line in pencil any phrase that appealed to him. When he died his books went to his sister, who, owing to poor health, needed recreation. In conclusion those who have gathered round the fire on a winter's evening at Marine House for a conversatziony will, I think,

admit that no book was needed to enliven the occasion.

> Yours truly,
> FLORENCE McGURGLE.

MR. SHELLGROVE'S TESTIMONY

Dear Sir,

Mr. Kidd's search for a book to read at Marine House surely stamps him as belonging to what I may call the older element among lodgers. We youngsters have other fish to fry. It was at Mrs. Hawks-weed's establishment, Sea Nook, that I met my better half, and I am thankful that there were no books to mar our courtship. Nor did I ever hear any lodger ask for such a thing, being occupied, as we were, with apple-pie beds, sponges over doors, snakes and ladders, choruses round the piano, blind man's buff, hand-reading, and so on. The only lodger I ever saw with a book was a martyr to liver, and read himself into a stupor every night.

> Yrs. truly,
> TED SHELLGROVE.

MRS. HAWKSWEED JOINS IN

Dear Sir,

I have not the pleasure of Mrs. McGurgle's acquaintanceship, but permit me to state that I seem to recall Mr. Shellgrove as the watery-eyed gentleman who courted, while under my roof, the lady we used to call the Beefeater, owing to her capacity for polishing off a plate of beef before the others had even reached for the mustard. The martyr to liver, who Mr. Shellgrove saw with a book, would be Mr. Sprott, but he only pretended to read to distract attention from the bags under his eyes. And if he had a book he must have brought it with him. Any

book that ever got left about was pounced on for wedging doors or windows. So I can sympathise with Mrs. McGurgle in hating the very name of books, recalling as they do unsociability, gloom and a lot of ideas any lodger is better off without.

> Yrs. truly,
> OLIVE HAWKSWEED.

ANOTHER TRIBUTE

> Once in the long ago,
> Rashly I fear,
> Sweet Flo McGurgle, I
> Fondled your ear.
> Brief was my dream of bliss;
> My heart's delight,
> Side-stepping daintily,
> Led with her right.
>
> I still recall your blush
> When, with a shout,
> Old Mrs. Huxtable
> Counted me out.
> SID TARPER

ANOTHER MEMORY

> 'Twas tea-time at old Marine House,
> And I made a remark on the geyser,
> Which dribbled all over the place,
> And was known far and wide as a wheezer.
>
> The landlady gave me a look
> Which said, plain as words,
> "How I hate yer!"
> I replied, without pausing to think,
> "McGurgle by name and by nature!"
>
> That night when the supper came on,
> Our landlady's face it was wooden,
> And I was the one, you will guess,
> That got the fag-end of the pudden.

(Edgar Trick, sometime lodger at Marine House.)

TAILPIECE

If false whiskers became fashionable, fewer men would shave, since there would be no point in being clean shaven under false whiskers.

Dame Sybil Thorndike

DO HER EARS FLAP?

Girls with large, haphazard ears need that little something which will keep these important features to their moorings. No man wants to dance with a girl whose ears flap like broken shutters. Ear-poise is now more important than ever. In these days of stress restful ears are what men want, not the ears that break the windows on each side of an alley on windy days, nor the ears that create a breeze like the flippers of a great fish. Consult Mme Zaphroma, who will tell you the secrets of the ages. Many a marriage has been wrecked by incessant ear-movements in the home. How often has the tired City man, craving peace by the fireside, been driven to despair and madness by the restless ears of his mate. Bicycle clips, hat guards, strong leather bags have all been tried in vain. The smart girl goes to Mme Zaphroma for the fifty-guinea course of ear-control.
Tackle those ears now!

(Advt.)

A LOVE SONG

(for six zithers and a balalaika)

When love comes to the braceplug setter
The braceplug setting stops.
He makes an appointment with the girl,
Then off to her he pops.
And they wine and dine the season through,
Till he gets to know her better,
Then he offers her the hand and heart
Of a jolly loving braceplug setter.

Refrain:
He called his sweetie Grapefruit,
And now he's in disgrace,
He called his sweetie Grapefruit,
Grapefruit, Grapefruit,
For every time he squeezed her,
She hit him in the face.

ON THE AIR

THE TRUTH ABOUT THE BUCKET

(Cretins' Hour)

We are now introducing to listeners Mrs. Vumper, who will tell her story. Mrs. Vumper. Well, when I saw the bucket I said to Mr. Vumper, that's my husband, I said, Charlie, that's his name, Charlie, I said, I do really believe that this bucket is empty. Oh no, he said, it can't be. So we both went closer, and I must say I was surprised to see water in it. It's cold, said my husband, dipping his hand into it, and him being one that likes warm water, I knew he wouldn't mistake it. So I said yes, it's cold water all right. And then we went to see my daughter, Clara, who's in service with Mr. and Mrs. Miller, but she wasn't there, owing to it being her day off. So we came back, and the bucket had gone. Thank you very much, Mrs. Vumper, I suppose you were very much surprised to see the bucket gone? Oh, yes, I said to Charlie, well that does surprise me. Thank you, Mrs. Vumper. Good night.

The Brains Bust

. . . "And here's a letter from Mrs. Weevil, of Pitney, asking which end of a carrot is the nearest. What do you think, Joad?" "Well, I should say that it depends on what you mean by nearest. Nearest to what? Or to whom? Eh, Huxley?" "Er—Yes. I don't think I quite understand the question. Obviously one end of a carrot must be nearer to a given something than the other end, unless one presupposes equidistance in the part of both ends." "I disagree with you there, Huxley. Nobody presupposing equidistance would have propounded the problem of which end is nearest to something. And evidently the use of nearest presupposes more than two ends. Of two ends one can be nearer. Of three or more one is nearest." "Ah, yes. I concede you that point, Joad." "Ha-ha-ha." "Ha-ha." "As chairman I rule that a carrot can have only two ends. Ha-ha-ha." "Aha-ha." "Ha-ha." "We ought to get a donkey to help us." "I forbear to make the obvious comment. Aha-ha-ha." "Ha-ha." "Ha-ha-ha-ha."

"Now here is a question from Miss Gowpe, of Boxton. Miss Gowpe asks: 'Does a sparrow blink because it wants to or because it must?' Huxley?" ". . . Well, aha, I don't quite know what the question means, but it is an ascertained fact that the sparrow's fibula is under its nosket-pilve. This may tend to promote blinking. The Aztecs . . ." "Joad?" "I entirely disagree with Huxley. Sparrows don't blink. They cannot blink. They have no eyelids. And the fact that they have nothing to blink with proves that they cannot blink. Of course, a certain kind of sparrow blinks with its ears . . ." "Joad means the Polynesian sparrow, but those are not its ears. They are the remains of external fins. . . ." "Tee-hee, I really think, aha, well, er—who would want to blink, anyway, unless he had to, I mean, aha, tee-hee, ahaha. . . ."

THE DUTCH FIG FESTIVAL

We are now taking you over to the toothpick factory, where Mrs. Delage will tell you something of this fascinating process. Here is Mrs. Delage. First of all the wood is selected. It must be the best quince-wood. The wood is dried and then sent to the hardening room to be hardened. It is then cut into lengths and rolled. Faulty wood is rejected. Then the newly cut lengths are split into picks. These are sharpened into little points at the end and sprayed with a galvanising mixture. They are then wrapped in Tasty paper wrappers, which have been stamped with the name of the factory. From that moment it is but a step to the tables of hotels and restaurants, where the tough and resisting instruments first come into contact with the human tooth as such. You have been listening to a description of the making of toothpicks by Mrs. Delage. As there are forty-seven seconds left before the ping-pong commentary we have time for a few bars of Schumann's Unfinished Symphony. Da-daa-da-daa-da-da-da.

AGONY CORNER

If the girl who stuck her head through the balusters of Battersea Bridge, in the hope that the fire brigade would come to rescue her, will communicate with the gentleman who tugged her free by the legs, she will learn that you don't have to be a fireman in a tomfool helmet to be sorry for a girl who can't think of any other way of getting asked out to a discreet supper of devilled bones.

NEWS OF WOMEN'S INSTITUTES

Moggs Cross:

Mrs. Gowling delivered a breezy lecture on Unvarnished Leather, with Miss Coupleday in the chair. The lecture was much appreciated, and the chairman, moving a vote of thanks, said she was sure they all wanted peace. Mrs. Curl, seconding the vote, said it was astonishing how little the average man or woman knew about unvarnished leather.

Bigfoddle:

The cake-weighing competition was won by Elsie Spoon. Miss Gwelville presented the prize, a ticket for the Flower Show, and said she hoped that Elsie would not follow in the footsteps of a girl she had heard of, who guessed nineteen tons as the weight of the cake.

Chumsey:

Mrs. Spoilworth gave a talk on quilts, which, she said, played a large part in the internal economy of the home. She ventured to think that we were about to see a quilt revival. This, she added, laughingly, would be good news for quilt-makers.

Hotel Superbe v. The Filthistan Trio

Mr. Justice Cocklecarrot

The action in which the Hotel Superbe is endeavouring, for purposes of publicity, to recover damages from the Filthistan Trio was begun yesterday before Mr. Justice Cocklecarrot in Court 4 of the Probate and Fisheries Division.

Cocklecarrot, in his opening address to the jury, began, amid frequent laughter:

"This curious case turns on the unorthodox activities of three Persian visitors to this country—"

Whereupon Kazbulah interrupted thus:

"May I please your lordship's grace, I object to the word unorthodox in connection with see-saw. There is nothing in our religion to say that see-saw is unorthodox."

Cocklecarrot: Objection sustained. I was not using the word unorthodox in a religious sense. It is possible that expert authorities on the game of see-saw might describe the actual method employed in your case—I refer to the laying of the plank on the belly of one of you—as unorthodox.

Rizamughan: In Persia this form of see-saw is exceedingly common, O judge, yes.

Cocklecarrot: But we are here concerned with what you were doing in England.

Ashura: He is right, O Rizamughan.

Cocklecarrot: You must not talk like that in this court. I am not here to be criticised.

Ashura: Not even favourably, O judge?

There was no reply.

Cocklecarrot then resumed:

"Whether or not the use of the belly—"

Foreman of the Jury: M'lud, one of our number, a sworn juror, Mr. Muffler, objects strongly to the public utterance of the word belly.

He suggests that stomach is the word.

Cocklecarrot: Really, sir, I am the best judge of what words can or cannot be used in this court.

Rizamughan: We have no objection to the word stomach, O judge.

Cocklecarrot: You have not been asked to express any opinion, Mr. Rizamughan.

Ashura: Is not a law court a rendezvous of free expression of opinion, O lordship?

Cocklecarrot: Certainly not.

Kazbulah: But is not your excellency freely expressing his opinion?

Cocklecarrot (with angry patience): I happen to be supreme here. I am, so to speak, above the law. I *am* the law. Your attitude is contempt of court.

Ashura: Oh, yes.

Cocklecarrot: Yes what?

Ashura: We have great contempt of court.

(*Cocklecarrot then bowed his head in his hands and there was silence.*)

Mr. Justice Cocklecarrot, in another address to the jury, said yesterday:

"We have here a case of three grown-up men playing the childish game of see-saw in the lounge of a restaurant, and playing it in such an unusual manner that ferrets were loosed apparently without any definite object. What we have to decide is at what precise moment and to what precise extent see-saw played by two Persians seated on a plank balanced on the belly of a third, and involving the peregrination of ferrets, may be said to contravene any accepted code of behaviour, or any written or unwritten law of the land. There is no precedent for such a case. The nearest parallel is the case of Ibstock *versus* Prancing, in which an antique dealer sought to restrain a night-watchman from filling the holes on a miniature golf-course with diminutive turtles. But the cases are not very similar—" At that moment the three Persians cried repeatedly, "Rashmiak!" Nobody knew what they meant, and after a hasty consultation with counsel the court rose with a bad grace, Cocklecarrot having ordered that the meaning of this word should be discovered.

Mr. Justice Cocklecarrot continued his fourth address today. He said: "This case seems to me to fall under two headings. It is really two cases. First, there is the question of the see-saw playing in the lounge, and then the question of the ferrets. I am tempted to say that it is a ferret-able maze of intrigue—" (Laughter).

Rizamughan: There was no vegetable.

Ashura: And no maze.

Kazbulah: And no intrigue.

Cocklecarrot: You gentlemen must really restrain yourselves. You are not in Persia now. If there are any more of these interruptions I shall have to take the steps which the law allows in cases of this nature.

Rizamughan: But, O Lord, this is a court of law, and we are the culprits.

Cocklecarrot: The defendants.

Ashura: Halt, O lord, we are not defendants. We are free men.

Cocklecarrot (with weary patience): Your interests are being looked after by your counsel. He will speak for you when the time comes.

Kazbulah: He will be too late, O Lord, thou thyself having got at the jury.

Cocklecarrot: This is monstrous! Mr. Snapdriver, kindly keep your clients in order. The court will now adjourn for twenty minutes. The case will then proceed normally—I hope. *A pretty girl at the back of the court:* What a hope!

The case of the Hotel Superbe *v.* the Filthistan Trio was bogged down yesterday for many hours, owing to the discovery of a misplaced comma in the Puisne Warrant (*ex delicto* and *quasi ex delicto, post Moselle ergo propter Moselle*). The Clerk of Arraigns and Torts pointed out that a stay of refringement might be granted, as in the case of the Burlington Tortoise Farms, Ltd., *v.* Mrs.

Amber Duckforth and Betty the Parrot, but that, if this were so, or not, the obligation of wrongful assumption of partial liability would fall like a ton of rock on the plaintiffs, slander of title and fraudulent competition being assumed *in toto* wherever proven or non-proven, unless, howbeit and albeit, collusion or collusions could be adduced from the behaviour of those who happened to be there at the time of the offence, the offence, for present purposes, being assumed to have been committed, or to have been about to be committed by some parson or parsons unknown.

"Malpractice!" cries the uninstructed reader.

"Not necessarily!" retorts the Law, and sends the uninstructed reader hotfoot to the famous case of the Billericay Bilberry-Canning Syndicate *v.* Heckwondwike Football Accessories, the Bank of Honduras, and Professor Felix Burtaway.

There the matter rests at present, as the actress said when she smeared the stockbroker's face with decayed vegetable refuse.

Another important technical detail held up the hearing of the case yesterday. The words fee simple, a term used in the Law of Real Property, had crept into the brief of Mr. Honeyweather Gooseboote. There followed a long argument as to whether, in the registration of deeds of conveyancing, the abstract of title is an abstract of the deeds themselves or of public record.

Mr. Snapdriver: It is immaterial, this case not being concerned with a deed of conveyancing.

Mr. Gooseboote: I yield that point. Nevertheless the question arises, am I justified in assuming that a term which occurs in my brief can be ignored at will—see Vesey 468 Wodenholme *v.* Cherry-pip.

Cocklecarrot: Come, come, Mr. Gooseboote, the words fee simple in your brief quite clearly refer to some other case. The Statute de Davis (51 Edw.III c.19,1334), dealing with tenants in fee tail, by a clerk's error, is precedent enough for you. Or do you hold it to be sporadic?

Mr. Snapdriver: I suggest, M'lud, that livery of seisin covers it, as in Mrs. Gullett *v.* HMS Contemptible.

Mr. Gooseboote: But I find in my brief also the apparently meaningless phrase "inter alia".

Cocklecarrot (sarcastically): Are you sure you have your brief in court—or is it the script of a music-hall turn?

(*Loud laughter, fruit-throwing, and cat-calls*).

The case was adjourned yesterday owing to an accident as unfortunate as it was unforeseen. Mr. Honeyweather Gooseboote, counsel for the prosecution, while leaning over to whisper to Mr. Tinklebury Snapdriver, counsel for the defence, dislocated his elbow. Mr. Snapdriver, in trying to rectify the damage, got the elbow stuck in his mouth, and could not withdraw it. Mr. Gooseboote left the court, walking sideways, with his elbow clamped tightly between Mr. Snapdriver's jaws. The sight of the two learned counsel shuffling gingerly towards the exit, to all intents and purposes chained to each other by these unusual bonds, was too much for the public. Loud and prolonged laughter filled the court for twenty minutes.

Mr. Honeyweather Gooseboote today read an appeal from his clients, the management of the Hotel Superbe, asking whether it would not be possible to do something to expedite the hearing of the case. Mr. Justice Cocklecarrot said, "This is most irregular. The law must take its course. The unfortunate incident of the trapping of one learned counsel's elbow in the mouth of another learned counsel has held matters up somewhat. There have also been technical difficulties, and misunderstandings, but—"

At that moment a cry rang out. Mr. Gooseboote, in leaning forward to speak to Mr. Snapdriver, had somehow got the latter's elbow in his mouth again, and was unable to dislodge it. Officials tugged in vain, and once more the two learned counsel had to leave the court, the one sideways, the other chained to him by the imprisoned elbow. Mr. Justice Cocklecarrot said, "If you two gentlemen cannot manage to keep your elbows out of each other's mouths you will have to surrender your briefs to less unfortunate practitioners. Such ludicrous clumsiness can do nothing but bring down upon the Law the ridicule of the public Press."

A doctor was called, and after examining the two counsel said that in his opinion the accident was a manifestation of certain psychic forces of which medicine as yet knew nothing. He said it was a clear case of Gumford's disease.

The case of the Hotel Superbe *v.* the Filthistan Trio was about to continue today—if I may use the word of a case which can hardly be said to have begun—when a police official, by order of Mr. Justice Cocklecarrot, approached the two learned counsel, to request them to sit far apart, in order to avoid accidents. But, *hélas*, it was too late. Once more, for the third and presumably lucky time, Mr. Honeyweather Gooseboote, in bowing to Mr. Tinklebury Snapdriver, had got the latter's elbow (including coat-sleeve and shirt-sleeve) stuck in his jaws, and was unable to dislodge the offending morsel.

There was uproar in the court. The fire brigade was summoned, and many junior narks heaved and tugged in the best Metropolitan Police tug-of-war traditions. When the fire brigade arrived, expanding ladders were run up, water poured in great volumes all over everything, shrieking women were carried in and out, windows were smashed with hatchets and ambulance men practised first aid on a half-drowned charwoman. Hysterical members of the public clambered on to the judge's dias, poised themselves uneasily, and dived on to horse blankets held below by a posse of bookies. Doubtful characters "saved" important documents and bits of furniture, which were piled on taxis and driven away into the unknown.

Mr. Justice Cocklecarrot then pointed out that there was no fire, and the court rose shakily.

Mr. Honeyweather Gooseboote: Your name is Kazbulah?

Kazbulah: O lord, yes, it is my name please.

Mr. Gooseboote: You must answer yes or no.

Kazbulah: Yes or no.

Cocklecarrot: The learned counsel means that you must say yes or no.

Kazbulah: My gracious worship, I did indeed say yes or no.

Mr. Tinklebury Snapdriver: No, no. You must answer either yes or no to all questions.

Kazbulah: Even so. Very well, I say either yes or no to your questions, O Lord.

Mr. Gooseboote: Is—your—name Kazbulah?

Kazbulah: Either yes or no. I reply even as bidden, oh, please.

Mr. Snapdriver: I don't really see how the thing can be put more clearly to him.

Mr. Gooseboote: Anyhow, we know it's his name. It's a mere formality—

Cocklecarrot: Mr. Gooseboote, you will kindly remember that the law rests on legal formalities. The procedure must be adhered to. We know his name, but we are bound to go through all this rub— all this. We cannot take it as read. Lunch will now be taken. The court will rise.

Mr. Gooseboote: M'lud, I should like to call Mr. Groundswell, the proprietor of the Hotel Superbe.

Cocklecarrot: Call away! You don't tell me we are actually getting on with this case! Why, we've only been at it a mere three weeks or so!

Gooseboote: Now, Mr. Ground-swell!

Cocklecarrot: Mr. Snapdriver, kindly keep your distance. We don't want any more elbow stuff.

Gooseboote: Now, Mr. Ground-swell, tell us what happened on the day in question.

Groundswell: Ough ough wurgh wurph ough erph ough wurgh wurgh erph ough—

Snapdriver: This is not a foreign national anthem. My client was last night stung on the roof of the mouth by a hornet.

Cocklecarrot: Well, is there an interpreter?

Gooseboote: M'lud, it's not a foreign language. You can't have an interpreter for noises due to a sting in the mouth.

Cocklecarrot: Well, then, you must cross examine someone else, Mr. Gooseboote. How long will he be in this state?

Snapdriver: The doctor says about a month, m'lud, failing further cala-mities.

Cocklecarrot (gloomily): Oh.

An atmosphere of tension was noticeable in the court today. Every time Mr. Snapdriver even glanced towards Mr. Gooseboote there was a universal intake of breath which sounded like high tide at Dungeness. At one point, when the two learned counsel leaned towards each other, Mr. Justice Cocklecarrot uttered an involuntary cry: the elbow specialist, who is in constant attendance, sprang to his feet and whipped out his gibboscope and his mometer; a police officer drew his luncheon in mistake for his truncheon; the Clerk of the Arraigns and the Puisne Serjaunte-at-Arms closed in tenderly but menacingly: the public shouted warnings.

The relaxation and relief after the false alarm were such that several ladies fainted, and a small com-mercial traveller went off into shriek-ing hysterics. A quantity of flock fell from the roof, prompting Cockle-carrot to ask who was tearing mattresses to pieces up there. By the time calm was restored, and the elbow specialist had diagnosed ulnitis and compound cubititis, it was found that in the general mix-up and to-and-fro caused by the mattress-tearing up aloft, Mr. Gooseboote's elbow was again firmly wedged between Mr. Snapdriver's jaws.

There the elbow rests at present.

Mr. Justice Cocklecarrot said yes-terday: "In all my years of experience at the Bar, I have never before known a case to be held up because the elbow of the counsel for the prose-cution was jammed between the jaws of the counsel for the defence. How such a ludicrous accident occurred, it is not for me to say. I can only express mild astonishment that two grown men could be the victims of such a monstrous piece of idiocy. The elbow, I am glad to say, has now been removed, and the two counsel will, I understand, be ready to take their places in court tomorrow. The medical report speaks of shock sus-tained by them both. I should like to take this opportunity of saying that when the elbow of one counsel gets stuck in the jaws of another, if any-body is entitled to suffer from shock, I should think it is the unfortunate judge who is trying the case. It will be my task in future to ensure that a distance separates the two protagon-ists sufficient to make a repetition of this ridiculous incident impossible."

A Legal Tangle

Mr. Justice Cocklecarrot's recent ruling in the matter of non-ferrous stair-rods has been called into ques-tion by older men in longer wigs. One of them pointed out that if a stay of demurrer is granted (*cestui qui veult*) without barratry or replevin, corres-ponding to responderia, the onus then rests on the plaintiff to prove ullage in demi-seisin, according to Stathers: *De Maiestate inflatissi-morum*, cap. VI. sec. 14 in which botulage is shown to be perse-quential and aetatulous, see also Murrain: *De Absurdissimis curat lex*, and other frolics of a seaside magistrate.

How then may we reconcile the capillamentary or perukial rights of the Law with the grisquillatory tendencies of these *Glires Justitiae*, these dormice of justice, as Mrs. Westlake has so aptly named the mountains of pomposity and empti-ness?

Glancing through Eggilbird's *Per-petratio Imbecillatis, vol. IX*, I find the case of a man who became web-footed through the drinking of strong ale during the summer solstice (with Agrippa already entering the Sign of the Hairy He Goat and Compasses) and failed to assert broffage during a nine-week hearing at the Market Harborough Assizes (Mr. Justice Otter Up). This forms an interesting sidelight on the much debated ruling of Cocklecarrot in the matter of non-ferrous stair-rods, *et alia mobilia secundum artem*. For then, as now, there rose a great clamour of the people, demanding the explanation of *quod sensu percipi non potest*, and battering of court doors with cries of "*Ut dummodo!*" and "*Tamquam imperfectis!*" and other snacks and driblets from Porridge's" Common or Garden Law for the Common or Garden City Masses", with a thumping great index and a foreword by a bottle-nosed Hindu from the Inner Temple.

But stay! An injunction *ab loco*, and pending

Fraxin	supprasition
vellum	aerial rights
dortmany	yardson
cludder	mivvick
aspen-traverse	techy
greengroan	abulbol
orchimandry	frank albacy
grossness	adequitio
evellience	firmatio
porgole	relt
gripe	double relt
initial outlay	gaming light
toggo	
gurney	
teleolo	

must, of its own *exquisitio*, be supposes to pre-suppose *abhinc* and *abhunc*.

But what does Acrocorinthus the Achaean say in his *Lorica Asinorum* or Breastplate of Dolts? He says that usucaption comes by priority of tenure and usufaction by prescription, as the lady barber of Toulouse discovered when the mayor set up a sheep-dipping accountancy in the manicure hall, on the plea that his grandfather had built the house. "Vacant possession", he cried, throwing the barbering furniture out of the window. And when the barberess countered with a plea of rebuttal and malvoisinage, the mayor came back on her with a plea of *vaccerosus quidam*, or the madman's vademecum. Her reply was a plea of arbitrage and *lusio*. And the pleas flew to and fro as thick as starlings, until the mayor died some forty-one years later, leaving my lady in possession,

but barely able to walk, see, eat, smell or jog the bottle.

We are faced then with a *linea anfracta* or zig-zag, which Blackstone characterised as an unruly use of a retuded right, as in the sudden changing of skin by a *cobra versipellis*, in a time of decrescent wind from the south-east, the same having nineteen facets, like the Sociman woman who made a haybag of her nose by piercing it with a fish-hook at the broad end nostril by nostril, as a goat breathes. But Ethologus the Mimic, in his Jurisprudence for Zenophobes, says that agrimony, once proven, may be taken as mere splutter or word-froth, and no more worthy of the courts of law than the shaking of a jelly, or the spooling of a cochlear on a midden on Septuagesima Monday. So, in the clause *ne venator impune* or let not the huntsman with impunity strangle hounds at bay, we touch the core of the whole imbroglio, and at once spring back and take to our heels, leaving but a drift of dust to tease the flies.

Try This on Your Flute

The Defence Act came up against a difficult problem last night. A man was wheeling a cow with handlebars fitted to its head, but no rear light, along a road. Further, he claimed that the road was not a road, but a path. When asked if the cow was a bicycle, he said that without a rear light it was a cow but *with* a rear light a bicycle. Then, removing one handlebar, he flashed a torch, and claimed that half a cow without a rear light was the same thing as half a bicycle *with* a rear light. The officials said that, as the torch was flashed *in front* of the cow or bicycle, or rather half-cow or half-bicycle, or bicycow, the question of a *rear* light did not arise. Then, countered the man, if the question of a rear light does not arise, it makes no appreciable difference whether the thing wheeled is a cow or a bicycle, or rather a half-cow or a half-bicycle. No *appreciable* difference, admitted the officials, but *a* difference.

The whole matter was then referred to Mrs. Whackstraw at the Ministry of Fiddlemeree and Foddlemeroo (GL 648, c.IV. 19). She passed it to Clara, her hideous niece in M.T. 7c iii. 24H, who put it in Isabel's "Unanswered" basket, where it was found by Tony, and thrown at Sybil and Nita.

And tomorrow the department is to be inspected by an under-secretary! Tea and buns and forced laughter. Miss Copple, I must congratulate you on the efficiency and keenness of your staff. Wow!

The case of the man who put handlebars on a cow after dark and wheeled it without a rear light is more serious than I thought. It is having our old friend repercussions, and Mr. Justice Cocklecarrot has been called in by the Government.

Last night Cocklecarrot explained, with his customary lucidity, that if a cow with handlebars is a bicycle, within the meaning of the Act, then a bicycle with four legs instead of two wheels is a cow, within the meaning of the Act. Again, quoth he, if a torch flashed in front of a cow is claimed to be a rear light on a bicycle, then a torch flashed behind a bicycle is a front light on a cow. And still further, averred he, if a cow with one handlebar is half a bicycle, then a bicycle with two legs is half a cow. All, all within the meaning of the Act. What Act? Almost any Act you like to mention as in the case of the Princess Rhama-Bul-Bhag *versus* Orkney Rolling Stocks and Mr. Cosmo Fewtrass, in which Mr. Justice Spaddlewidge held that a rhinoceros driven along a railway line is not rolling stock merely because a cloud of red, sulphurous smoke issues from its ears. But the same rhinoceros—let us call it Travers*—may be held to be rolling stock if it be used to draw a train, however small and dirty. All, all within the meaning of that thrice accursed Act.

Proceedings in the inquiry into the case of the cow driven without a rear light were held up yesterday when a

* Or Bestwick.

177

man carrying a crate of stockfish entered the court, placed a bowler on a stove, filled the bowler with eggs, and shouted, "If only I had some water to heat, I could boil these eggs."

There was silence for a moment, then Lord Climbertooth said, "No doubt, my good man. But what has this got to do with us?"

"Think yourself too good to eat a boiled egg, eh?" yelled the man.

"Not at all," said poor old Climbertooth, who has lived on chemical biscuits for years. "But one is still at a loss to see—"

But the man had collected his belongings and left the court.

"All this," said Cocklecarrot, "probably has some recondite connection with our case."

The hearing of the test case of the cow with handlebars was continued today behind closed doors and shuttered windows, and consequently in an atmosphere so thick and putrid that the wigs of the learned gentlemen came uncurled and hung over their faces like dirty door mats, thus impeding the flow of balderdash.

Mr. Justice Cocklecarrot confined himself at first to the remark, "You cannot milk a bicycle." This weighty decision, based as much on instinct as on a knowledge of farming and cycles, was followed by an irrelevant story of a girl who got damages from a railway company because, when she was visiting an aunt at Martinmas, a young porter at King's Knuckletooth unloaded a cow instead of her bicycle. Lord Climbertooth, who told this story, was asked to elucidate it, but refused, under an old statute of Henry III *de fibistulatione fibistulationarum*, which says clearly—but no matter.

Then rose, in all his majesty, Mr. Justice Cocklecarrot. From a capacious pocket he produced Exhibit A —the tell-tale handlebars which had been affixed to the cow's head. The sensation among his colleagues could not have been greater if he had been a bobbing Chinaman with hands in sleeves, smirking with delight at having extracted from an empty goldfish bowl the flags of all the nations.

Mr. Justice Cocklecarrot yesterday startled the legal world by announcing that "in law there is no such thing as a cow. Therefore what Mr. Poote drove along the lane without a rear light was a bicycle."

"But," interrupted Lord Grangecroft, "if it wasn't a cow, it does not follow that it was a bicycle. Everything that is not a cow is not necessarily a bicycle."

"For instance," mumbled Lord Climbertooth, "a porcelain cup."

"One rarely drives a porcelain cup along a lane, with or without a rear light," replied Cocklecarrot testily.

"How does a porcelain cup come into this matter?" asked Lord Bowglie dreamily.

"I only mentioned it as an instance," retorted Lord Climbertooth.

"An instance of what, might one inquire?" rasped Cocklecarrot.

"Oh, I forget," grumbled Lord Climbertooth, "it's immaterial."

At that moment Lord Maspberry cried out in a feverish nightmare, "I can't move! They are pouring porridge over me!" and awoke, gasping and clutching at his wig.

Cocklecarrot, sighing deeply, began once more, "Granted that what was driven was a bicycle and not a cow, then—"

But the words froze on his lips, as a trap-door in the roof opened, and down a thick rope slid a dusky sailor. Giving the name of Onslow, he said he was looking for a ship.

There was a slight dust-up in the cow case yesterday. Lord Climbertooth—by the way, it may be as well to say a word or two about some of the personalities of the case before going further and faring far worse.

Lord Climbertooth, Law Lord since 1884. Amateur billiards champion of Whitstable 1915. Collects pottery and etchings.

Fred Kittawake, man-about-town, in love with *Yakma du Plessis de Roye-Guenegand*, Turkish woman barrister, married to a French nobleman, and secretly in love with

Arthur Foolworth, pepper magnate, openly in love with

Nicolas Gawke, Customs Official, with permanent toothache, in love with

The Hon. Enid Brass, "Birdie" of the Censorship Department, in love with

Monty Bullingdon, skating assistant at the Palais de Glace de Beulah Hill, in love with

Margaret Spoole-Driffett, golfwoman, dog-fancier, card-sharper and owner of the Mustapha Turkish Baths at Clovelly.

(Hats by Maison Drosch. The giant toothpick in Act II lent by the Handelsbond Timber Company. Choreography by Commissarmutsky. Paper show by the Tawlom Valley Pulping Trust.)

A very, very old "legal luminary", who has not hitherto taken any part in the inquiry into the Defence Act relative to the driving of a cow without a rear light, yesterday broke his silence with notable murmurs. It was ascertained that he was endeavouring to say something when he raised his heavy, and oh, so foolish, face from his well thumbed copy of Roxton on Torts. Eagerly all bent towards him, out of respect for his great reputation and venerable appearance. But it was soon realised that this old man was still wrapped in the past, and once more conducting some case of decades gone by, when he said testily, "My verdict is that the cheese belongs to the man who recognised it."

"And the cow?" inquired Cocklecarrot sarcastically.

"If there is a cow involved," said the aged fool, "you must enter a plea of *beatus ille qui procul negotiis*, as in Connie Waterson versus the North Kent Sewage Development Trust, Dame Tramplemore intervening."

There the matter rests at present.

General indignation has been expressed in many quarters at Mr. Justice Cocklecarrot's attempt to "reconstruct the crime". A cow was brought into court, the windows were darkened, and the man who drove the cow, Ernest Poote, was asked to repeat his performance. Unfortunately the cow, a young and foolish one, ran hastily about in the darkness, knocking things over and causing panic. When the lights were flashed on the cow was on the dias, breathing easily and rhythmically into Lord Climbertooth's face. This is the first time a Lord High Attorney of Appeal and Prosecutor General At Large has had his face publicly breathed into by a cow.

Commenting on this case, a leading weekly says: "It is difficult to see what has been proved by this ludicrous experiment. It is, perhaps, safe to say that to be exposed to the promiscuous breathing of beasts is by no means an every day occurrence in the life of a Law Lord. Nor is the legal profession likely to recruit young men of the best type if it can hold out to them no more honourable prospect of useful service to their country than an experience which may be had for the asking by any illiterate herdsman who has the witlessness to permit one of his charges to breathe upon him. It is to be hoped that we have heard the last of a case which reflects no credit on British justice."

TODAY'S NEWS

Orang-Outang Kisses Plumber

Dead Fish in Mayor's Wardrobe

Egg-Throwing Baronet Detained

Bubbles from Meat are Invisible
says Gas Man's Daughter

Shot a Fungus Off Own Nose
—Chemist's Mad Feat

CAPTAIN FOULENOUGH IN THE FUR TRADE

Now there lived in a secluded Bayswater square a widow of singular beauty. She was on Captain Foulenough's visiting list, and when the ugliness of the world oppressed him he would look in on her for a cup of tea and a talk.

This widow's attractions suddenly became greatly enhanced, when Foulenough remembered that she possessed an enormous cat with a very fine, silky coat. His visits grew more frequent, and the lady was touched to observe that the Captain was at great pains to win the good graces of the cat and frequently remarked on the quality of its coat. "Jeremy, Jeremy," he would say musingly, "what a fine cat you are."

One day this widow, whose name was Lynette Owlesleigh-Frome, said, "Too terrible all this cat-stealing one reads about in the papers." The Captain sat as though turned to stone.

"The man who could steal a cat" continued Lynette, "ought to be shot. Don't you think so?"

"No death is too good for such a man," replied Foulenough in some confusion.

"You are very kind to Jeremy," said Lynette.

"Were he your ape I would still cherish him, my dear," said the Captain.

"But you like him for his own sake?"

"Oh, rather," said the Captain, with a treacherous smile, adding, "While these cat thieves are about, perhaps you would like me to take care of Jeremy?"

"Oh, I couldn't part with him—but if danger really draws near this neighbourhood I will ring you up."

"And I will be here to take him within the hour."

The Abduction of Jeremy

Two days later—and no wonder—Captain Foulenough received an urgent telephone call. A cat had been stolen from the house on the right of the widow's. Two more from a house on the other side of the square. Within the hour the Captain had arrived in Bayswater, and, while fondling the hand of the tearful widow, he graciously consented to remove Jeremy from the imminent danger. "I hope he won't have changed much when I next see him," said Lynette. The Captain made no reply, but popped Jeremy in a small bag and drove away in high fettle.

Maison Katzphur

Many a simple lady must have asked herself in perplexity, "But how can Katzphur Ltd. *possibly* afford to sell an ermine cape for £1 : 3 : 4?" The answer is—or was—in Tavistock Square: a nice plump pussy answering to the name of Pouchy.

Again, she might say, "How do they do it? Where on earth does this sable wrap, at £1 : 14 : 2, come from?" Dear lady, it comes straight out of a sack. That sable wrap less than a week ago was Bozo, pride of Lower Tungmere Street. Then Fred, hard (and often) bitten trapper, saw Bozo one dark evening, and pounced.

A sensitive girl, who had begun to suspect the truth, said the other day, "You know, every time I put on my mink coat, I think I hear a cat miaowing."

I hope I have made it clear that Foulenough himself takes an active part in what, in the trade, is called trapping. One of his favourite disguises is that of a gaunt spinster named Miss Birdie Belchambers, Hon. Treasurer of the Catsmeat Guild. In this disguise he swoops in the name of humanitarianism. But he prefers to operate among the well-to-do, and to return to Katzphur with half a dozen prize-winners purring in his sack. There was a tense moment the other day when a maid, handling his overcoat clumsily, ejected from a side pocket two-thirds of a mackerel. "Been to a fish auction," said the Captain. "Must have got tangled up in my coat. Certainly didn't buy it." "Just the thing for Raven," said the maid.
Raven is now a sealskin stole.

I am not going to pretend that Captain Foulenough knows anything about running a fur business. But that is where Manon Caramel comes in. La Caramel was once the toast of the Brebis Qui Tousse, in the Place Pigalle. She is now the Captain's general manager at Katzphur House, or, as it is more properly called, Maison Katzphur. As Foulenough says of her, she can wear two and twopence-worth of tomcat's pelt as though it were worth a film star's ransom. The popularity of Turkish cat as a new kind of fur is due to her. But between you and me, the first consignment on the market was merely the result of a large haul on a dark night at the lower end of Church Street, Stoke Newington.

Some more Furs

"He said he had called to test the telephone," said the lady, speaking breathlessly to the police officer. "He had the words 'Telephone Service' on the ribbon round his hat, and he jangled the instrument and kept on saying 'Hello, hello, hello!' Then he asked me to get him a small bit of thread for the nozzle, and when I came back he had gone, and there was no sign of Topsy. Her basket was empty."

'He said he had called to read the gas-meter. He seemed such a nice man, and stooped to stroke Palmerston, and muttered, 'Sweet little creature'—adding, rather impudently, 'Two sweet little creatures,' and staring at me saucily. He held the cat and stroked it while he read the meter. He then asked me to get him a bit of paper and a pencil, and when I returned he was gone. And so was Palmerston."

"Where are you going with that cat?"
Captain Foulenough, hugging a stray picked up in Elmgrove Crescent, felt his spine grow cold as the gruff voice behind him repeated the question. Turning, he confronted a policeman.
In his jauntiest manner he replied, "Ah, officer, it's you. I was on my way to the police station with this poor little creature. I found it over there. Seems to be lost. With so many cat thieves about these days, one cannot be too careful."
"That's right, sir," said the policeman. "And I think I recognise that cat. I'll return it to the owner, if you'll hand it over."
And the Captain, making the best of a bad job, gave up his latest acquisition.

"He was such a nice, kind gentleman," said the cook at No. 14. "He came down the street distributing the most delicious morsels of fish to all the cats he could see. And he spoke so kindly, too. He said to me, 'Ah, cookie. Good morning to you, my dear cook. And how are we this morning? And—why, bless my soul, do I not see a cat there?' 'Yes, sir, it's Pippy,' I replied. Then he called out, 'Ho ,there, Pippy, what about a nice tasty snack of fish, eh?' And he held out a morsel. Of course Pippy went up the area steps two at a time. And, just to tease Pippy, he retreated up the street. We haven't seen Pippy since, but he'll come back. He was such a nice, kind gentleman."

No Catch

When Mrs. Fossdyke (Connie to us) came into the drawing-room, she was surprised to see her visitor, Captain Foulenough, standing like an awkward schoolboy, with the cat Barlow half in and half out of his capacious pocket. "Such pretty tricks he has," said the Captain, "clambering in and out of my pocket. Twitsy-witsy, then, come up, my beauty." The cat emerged, licking its lips, and rapidly finishing a morsel of fish.

"You good kind de Courcy," said Connie, "I do declare you keep fish in your pocket for my cat." "It's nothing, I assure you," said Foulenough, flushing uneasily, and darting a dirty look at the cat. "One must do what one can for the sweet pets," he added bitterly as Barlow left the room, and thus eluded the managing director of Maison Katzphur.

A Near Thing

"Miaow!"
The lift-man glanced at the Captain. The Captain affected indifference.
"Sounded like a cat," said the lift-man.
"What did?" asked Foulenough, conscious of the bulge in his overcoat pocket.
"Sounded like a cat," repeated the lift-man. "Probably Miss Armitage's lost again."
"Probably," said Foulenough, who had just made a call on Miss Armitage (Phyllis to us).
"Miaow!"
Foulenough developed a hacking cough a second too late.
"Might be a wireless gone wrong somewhere," he said.
"No," said the lift-man, "that was a cat."

The Get-away

All the way to the ground floor Foulenough sneezed, coughed, spluttered, and stamped his feet, to drown further plaintive sounds.
"Miaow!" and very loud.
"Seems to be in the lift," said the lift-man.
"Sounded to me further away," said the Captain, beginning to sing loudly.
"Hark," said the lift-man.
"So–oftly fall the shades of nigh-ight," bawled the Captain.
As the lift reached the ground floor, Foulenough sprang out, crying, "Late for my appointment," and took to his heels.

The lift-man stood rigid, listening. At the end of five minutes he said, "Bah! No cat 'ere. Must 'ave been my imagination."

Exit Pomfret

Captain Foulenough was the centre of a curious scene at a dinner-table in Kensington. The conversation, ably guided by our hero, turned to cats.

"The whole secret of managing cats," said Foulenough, "is to get them to trust you. They then attach themselves to you." At that moment Pomfret entered the dining-room and miaowed ingratiatingly. Foulenough slipped his hand into his pocket and produced a handful of fish. The cat was his friend from that moment. "He seems to have taken a liking to you," said the foolish hostess. How truly she had spoken she realised when Pomfret's basket was found empty the next morning.

And thus did Katzphur Ltd. acquire another ermine stole, or borrowed, as Foulenough preferred to put it.

Agents for Katzphur

It has come to the notice of the police that Katzphur employs a number of lonely spinsters as agents. They move about the big towns saying, "Oh, dear, if only I had a cat to keep me company in my lonely room." That is why so many maiden ladies of rueful appearance are seen daily entering the palatial Katzphur building with bulging sacks on their backs.

A Foolish Woman

"Captain! In war-time! I really must not accept such beautiful sables from you."
"See how they become you, dear lady. See how——"
Miaow!
"Why, Captain Foulenough, just look at Rosieposie! What is it, pussy darling? There, then, did they, umumumsicums. She seems to be angry. Look at her arching her back at you! And look at her sniffing my sables. Woowoowoo then, did its little selfikins. Don't claw my sables. Rosieposie! Down, darling, down! Was ums want a stroky-poky in its backsywacksy then. What the devil is the matter, you little fiendypiendykins? Must you really be off, Captain? Oh, well, a million thanks for the furs—ouch! Drat this little wretch. Seems to have a grievance against my sables."

Business v. Pleasure

Beauty draws Captain Foulenough with a single hair; but which beauty? Miss Lavinia Gratcham, with her lustrous chestnut curls, or her cat, Moompie, with its glossy black coat?

For the first time for weeks, pleasure and business are having a tussle in the heart of the managing director of Maison Katzphur. Every time he strokes Lavinia's cheek, she purrs, thus reminding him of the primary object of his visit. Every time he strokes the cat, it is again Lavinia that purrs, so happy is she to see her Moompie treated with affection. "It would break my heart," says Lavinia, "if anything happened to Moompie." And, though the Captain is not at all reluctant to break her heart, he would prefer to do it in a more romantic fashion.

So, between the two purrers the Captain hesitates. When he contemplates that prize cat (Battersea Baths Diploma 1936, St. Neots Medal 1937, Crawley and Southdown Senior Grade Medallion 1938, Mrs. Roughouse Cup 1939, Chelmscote Trophy 1940), he remembers that he is a business man. But when he looks at Lavinia, he remembers that he is a human being first, and a fur magnate afterwards. Meanwhile choice titbits for Moompie continue to be charged to the firm as overhead expenses.

"Six days," said Manon Caramel, "you have been working on that Kensington champion, Moompie. The results to date are a smear of lipstick on your collar, powder on your coat sleeve, a rapid rise in overhead expenses, a dreamy look in your eye, and the initials L. G. scribbled all over the rough proof of our new catalogue. Those initials might stand for Lavinia Gratcham."

"Or Lloyd George," said the Captain, with an attempt at jauntiness. "My dear Caramel, the road to a cat lies often through the heart of its mistress." "By-pass it," snapped Manon irritably.

He Hesitates

Betting in the fur trade is about even. Whenever Foulenough glances at Moompie, lying by the fire, he feels that he is looking at one of the little Princes in the Tower. Conscience gnaws him with its iron teeth. And his evil genius whispers, "What a lark it would be to sell this lovely lady a fur coat made out of her own cat." And, "Oh, dastardly trick!" whispers his Better Self.

Every day he calls, and every day he leaves, with an empty bag. "That cat at the Kensington address," says Manon Caramel, "seems to be giving you a lot of trouble." "She's not a cat," flashes back the Captain angrily, thinking of Lavinia. "Oho!" says Manon. "Is that the way the wind blows?"

Meanwhile the Captain has bought a gay ribbon for Moompie's neck. "Don't pull it too tight," says Lavinia, "you might hurt the darling." "Over my own dead body," retorts the gallant fur-trader with feigned ardour. "Ah, Moompsie-Woompsie," murmurs Lavinia. "There, then," adds the Captain, tweaking its ear. And then, in a firm voice, "Are you never afraid of thieves?" "Thieves?" cries Lavinia, clutching her amethyst ring. "Cat thieves," says the Captain. Lavinia grows pale. "I was only joking," says the Captain, brushing an imaginary crumb from his sleeve, and affecting nonchalance. "Damn it," he mutters under his breath.

"Would you take Moompie?" sighed Lavinia.

"Would I!" echoed the Captain, rubbing his hands.

Crisis

"Moompie has been stolen!"

In these words Lavinia greeted the Captain, who started guiltily, as though he had done the deed himself.

"Oh, what beast in human form can have done so vile a thing?" cried the Captain, when he had recovered. "Probably Fred—or one of our directors," he added, to himself.

"What am I to do?" blubbered the beauty, twisting her handkerchief nervously. "Shall I inform the police?"

"I shouldn't do that," said Foulenough hurriedly, "not till we know which firm stole—I mean, who—er—well, you see, I mean, we've nothing to go on."

"He was stolen in the night, poor mite," said Lavinia. "Joe, for a fiver!" said the Captain to himself.

A Cunning Plan

During this painful scene, Foulenough was wondering whether he could persuade Katzphur Ltd. to restore the cat—if it was one of their men who had stolen it—and thus appear as a hero in the eyes of the lady.

"I will myself pull certain wires," he said to her.

"You mean you will get Moompie back?" simpered Lavinia.

"I cannot promise. But I have some influence in—er—high quarters."

"You darling!" cried Lavinia.

"Same to you with knobs on," replied her cavalier grinning broadly.

The Trick

Foulenough, ill-at-ease, faced Manon Caramel.

"That—er—Kensington cat, Miss Gratcham's, er—have any of our chaps hauled it in?" he asked.

"You bet. You were working too slowly."

"Is it—is it a fur yet?"

"No."

"Then it must be returned."

"What are you talking about?"

"She's on the trail."

"You mean you squeaked?

"Oh. no. But—the fact is, she's got onto the police, and said she suspected us."

"You dirty rat! You sold us!"

The trick worked. Katzphur Ltd. fell into a panic. And that afternoon the Captain, beaming and heroic, returned Moompie to the delighted Lavinia.

"How did you do it?" she cried.

"Gang of thieves," said Foulenough. "Got the Home Office on to 'em. Nothing, really. Only too glad to be of service."

"You darling!" said Lavinia.

"That's the tune!" crowed Foulenough.

Moompie stolen again

"Moompie's been stolen again!" cried the beautiful Lavinia.

Foulenough muttered something under his breath.

"I've rung up the police," said Lavinia.

Foulenough swore silently.

But when the police officer arrived and said that a firm of furriers, trading as Maison Pussikote, was suspected, Foulenough's heart sang. Pussikote was Katzphur's biggest rival. This should ruin them.

"If the beast—the dear cat is returned," said the Captain to Lavinia, "you'd better let me keep it in safety for you. It's an old trick—er—an old method of security practised by cat-owners nowadays."

Foulenough's Triumph

And so the skilful managing director of Maison Katzphur was able to rejoice over the ruin of Maison Pussikote, convicted of cat-stealing; and also to acquire Lavinia's champion, Moompie, by taking the animal into protective custody. His duty to the firm outlasted his love for Lavinia, and by the time he reported to her that Moompie had been run over and killed by a fish-lorry the silky coat of the famous cat was already swathing the broad back of a vulgar hoyden. By that time also the Captain had his eye on three monster Siamese, the property of a trusting and foolish old lady at Parsons Green.

Thanks to Snibbo

DEAR SIR,—For many years I thought there was a little Persian milkman in iron trousers riding a zebra round my room. Then I was recommended to take Snibbo, and I have not seen that little Persian milkman since.—(*Signed*) F. TOGGLETON.

[If you suffer from little Persian milkmen, mice in tartan overcoats, yellow gasworks with bristles all over them, neuralgia, depression, or boils, write for the free Snibbo Booklet, recommended by 123,784 doctors]

Mrs. Wretch and the Circus
Fun at Wretch Manor

MRS. WRETCH writes to me: "Noticing the name of Wugwell's Circus in your column, I recalled my early days with that excellent show, before I married the Colonel. Only the other day we received a visit from the Human Snake (a Mr. Ernest Parblow). I had no time to explain who he was to my husband, and you may imagine the Colonel's surprise when, in the midst of a discussion on Colonial policy, Mr. Parblow, in sheer good nature, began to twist himself round his chair, with his legs round his neck. 'My dear sir,' said the Colonel, 'are you unwell?' For answer Mr. Parblow turned his head back to front and tied himself round a side-table. 'It's a fit, a seizure, a stroke,' said my husband. 'Call Dr. Cricklade.' But I disabused him, and he tried to enter into the joke—rather awkwardly, I fear. He said he thought it all rather pointless and in very bad taste."

Ordeal by Beard

Colonel Wretch was reading his correspondence yesterday in his study at Wretch Manor, when a lady with a massive black beard beckoned him on to the lawn. Somewhat startled, he went out to investigate. "I come to plead with you," said the lady, "for the return of your wife for a week or two. Wugwell's Circus needs her." The Colonel, who had never spoken to a bearded lady before, was highly embarrassed. "My dear sir—er—madam," he said, "it is out of the question. Those days are over." Whereupon the lady began to cry, and the Colonel found himself saying "There, there, now," and offering his handkerchief. At this moment the wife of the Lord Lieutenant of the County strolled up the drive and stopped in amazement at what she saw. By the afternoon it was all over the neighbourhood that Colonel Wretch had a bearded lady in his life.

Lady Grimwaters to Colonel Wretch

MY DEAR NEPHEW,—One hopes that what one hears about you and a certain bearded lady is but idle gossip. You may remember that when you were injudicious enough to woo your circus wife, both I and your uncle warned you that her old friends of the ring might cause you considerable embarrassment. But neither of us suspected that you would be careless enough to get your name coupled with a grotesque performer, who, I understand, has no talent but the unenviable ability to grow a beard at will. Pray write to me to reassure me. There has, as you know, been no scandal in our family since your great-aunt Euphemia ran away with the Italian glass-blower. And you know how that turned out. —Your fond aunt, HORTENSE.

Mrs. Wretch to Mr. Wugwell

DEAR HILDEBRAND, — Over and over again I have told you that my circus life ended when I married Colonel Wretch. Your repeated efforts to persuade me to return, even temporarily, are an embarrassment to me in my social activities, as some of my committees think I am not wholly serious-minded. One lady has got hold of a picture of me standing on your shoulders and enticing a large ape to drink from a beer-bottle. Imagine the effect of that coming into the middle of an appeal for women ambassadors. Furthermore, it is impossible to explain away to my husband the no doubt well-meant incursions of my erstwhile companions. If Anselmo must pay a call, need he run barking between the vicar's legs? Don't ask me to make a "come-back" any more. La belle Zaboula must be but a memory.— Yrs. sincerely, UTTA WRETCH.

From Mr. Wugwell to Colonel Wretch

. . . If the exquisite mountain who is now your missus will not come to her old pal Mahomet H. Wugwell, what about me coming to the mountain? In other words, old boy, if my eloquence can turn the scale, will you abide by your wife's verdict, and take your beating like the bold old Corinthian you are? Failing that, what about you lending the grounds of Wretch Manor for a few performances? Nothing knocks the public like a dash of circusdom in a truly rural setting. And we could give one day's proceeds to your local Fish Zoning Week. I await your reply before coming to pay a formal call. I may say I've asked Madame Goulash (she of the sweeping beard) to lay off you. . . .

Colonel Wretch to Mr. Wugwell

. . . You do not understand. The world in which my wife now moves is never brought into contact with people who do aerobatics on horses or intercept seals' food. She is called upon to meet people who do not know that such things go on, and, when they are told of it, either close their eyes to it, or write letters to the paper to get it stopped. Five centuries of settled life have perhaps given me an excessive aversion from the haphazard existence of the circus ring. I can never forget, moreover, that an uncle of mine had a boyish passion for a knife-thrower's colleague, and got two wicked-looking knives in the leg one Michaelmas Day at Chichester. . . .

From Mr. Wugwell to Colonel Wretch

SIR,—While fully appreciating your hesitation in being asked to release your missus for her old equestrian act, I must point out that an honoured member of our troupe, Mimosa Mamie, Queen of the Tightrope, is, in her more private capacity, the wife of a respected chiropodist of Bury St. Edmunds, who is also on the local Conservative Club catering committee. Nor would your missus be asked to perform anything derogatory of her county position, such as throwing fish to the seals. All we ask is that she should make three tours of the ring, standing with one leg on the back of Wandering Willie and the other on the back of Bangor Bucks, ending with a leap into the arms of the clown, Romulus, who squirts her with soda water and kisses her cheek loudly.—Yrs. obediently, HILDEBRAND WUGWELL.

Colonel Wretch to Mr. Wugwell

DEAR MR. WUGWELL,—Does it not occur to you that, for the kind of thing you have in mind, my wife is rather out of practice? When she rides, she does not ride two horses at once, with one leg on the back of each, nor do the responsibilities of her position as my wife include leaps into the arms of clowns, to be followed, as I understand from your missive, by an exchange of noisy kisses and horseplay with soda-siphons. I must also ask you not to send emissaries to my home. Yesterday, as I was discussing a local matter with our vicar, a pygmy came up the avenue on a huge tri-cycle. He announced in a loud voice that he was the Whirling Midget, Anselmo Amantinelli. And he crawled between the vicar's legs and barked. Forgive me for not finding this very edifying.—Your truly,
ARTHUR WRETCH.

Mr. Wugwell to Colonel Wretch

. . . Suppose we were to cut out the clown's kisses and the soda-water squirting, would you let your missus ride the two gees? Or, failing that, what would be your reactions to her appearance in sequins on the back of Monty the seal, the idea being that she beats him to the food flung from the audience? Or is that too comic for a county bigwig? After all, this holiday circus is as much part of the war effort as motoring about inspecting rabbit-clubs or whatever it is she does. Mine is the hand that fed her in the old days, and are you going to join her in biting it now, just because I'm not a member of your hunt? As man to man, what about it, Colonel?

From Halma the Wizard to Colonel Wretch

SIR, Perhaps you would let your old woman, who was erstwhile one of us, officiate as the girl who whisks the yellow handkerchief off the gold-fish bowl when I shoot at the foot-lights. She would wear a startling costume, and would also cry "Hup" in a musical contralto when I throw her my mortar-board. My act is altogether more refined than most of the others in our show, and I'm sure you would not consider it beneath your old bag of mischief's dignity to assist me, especially as I once had the honour of being in the same human pyramid with her in a set-piece at Gosport. I enclose photo. She is the lady whose left foot reposes on my forehead.—Yrs. to a T, FRED HALMA.

Mr. Wugwell to Colonel Wretch

. . . Your letter gave me an idea. Why should not you and your missus appear together? You could take the place of the clown who is to catch her as she jumps from the two horses. It would look very gallant, and you need not squirt her with soda-water. Just a gag or two. Or perhaps you might produce an egg from her ear. We would bill the pair of you as Colonel Bonzo and La Belle Zaboula, or something of that sort. Nobody need recognise you, as we would make you up as a Cossack with red whiskers and a large spade-shaped beard. What do you say to it? If it appeals to you, as a horsy man, meaning no offence, just let me know. . . .

LIFE AT BOULTON WYNFEVERS

I

ONE of Lord Shortcake's many hobbies was amateur theatricals. The choice of plays at the Manor was somewhat restricted since my dear old master was convinced that Nature had cast his lady for the part of a large and dignified Empress. If there was no Empress in the play chosen he became angry. On one occasion he made so bold as to edit a well-known comedy. He added, here and there, the words "Enter the Empress", but nobody took any notice. Latterly, the moving spirit of these productions was a young man called Enoch Broodie, whose doctrine appeared to be that nothing mattered in a play except the lighting and the scenery and the costumes. Since Lord Shortcake belonged to the old-fashioned school, there were many loud disputes.

II

My old master liked the plays performed in the hall at Shortcake Manor to be of what he called the "breezy, open-air-style". He used to shout over the breakfast table, "We don't want any of this sex nonsense here." The result was that the characters invariably wore tennis clothes and carried rackets. I remember an occasion when the hero had to embrace the heroine. Both of them suggested that the rackets should be left behind for this scene. But my master roared, "Damn it! We don't want any Continental foolery. Kiss her and get it over, but don't drop the racket." Although he never presumed to act as official producer, his advice was so noisy and so continuous that everybody used to give in to him in the end.

III

Enoch Broodie, whose tastes were "advanced", found it very difficult to give rein to his modernist ideas in an atmosphere of tennis and golf and cricket. He once spent four days experimenting with a deep shadow that was to fall from the corner of a summer-house. "What's all this?" cried Lord Shortcake. "A new idea with shadows, sir," said Broodie. "Shadows be hanged!" shouted my master. "We want the audience to see what is going on, don't we? If this is one of your confounded artistic ideas, keep it, my boy, for when we produce Ibsen—which will be after my death, I can tell you." Sometimes a bit of dialogue would puzzle my master. Then he would say, "We must cut out all this highbrow stuff, Broodie. I don't understand it, so why should anybody else?"

IV

On one occasion my master consented to take a small part in a play. All he had to do was to enter from the left at the end of the act, in the character of a sporting peer, and, accepting a cigar, say, "Thanks awfully." But he made so much fuss over rehearsing this that the play was held up for weeks. He insisted on playing it very, very slowly. "This part," he said, "must suggest dignity. It's no good rushing on like an American salesman, grabbing a cigar, chewing it, and tearing off again. And I ought to say a bit more, otherwise it looks as though I only entered the room to cadge a cigar. How about my saying, 'Jolly weather, eh?' or something like that? And somebody ought to offer me a light. I only look an ass with an unlit cigar and the curtain coming down so soon afterwards."

V

At the first performance of the play in which Lord Shortcake made his appearance as a sporting peer, he took matters into his own hands. When his cue came he walked on slowly, accepted the cigar, and said, "Thanks awfully." The guests moved towards the French windows, and the stage manager prepared to signal for the curtain to be lowered. But my master had other plans. He began to talk to everybody about the weather, and while they all stood awkwardly wondering what to do next, be began to tell a racing story. The stage manager made violent faces in the wings, but my master kept that curtain up three minutes, and got a round of applause when he said, "What is this weed I am smoking? A Stinkadora, I presume."

VI

The day at last came when Lady Shortcake had the chance of playing an Empress.

To my master's delight it was decided to produce a farce called "Sailors Do Care", with a character in it called the Empress of Ruritania. He at once informed Lady Shortcake. She, however, when she had read the play, refused to make her entrance in a washing-basket carried by ratings. So the script was changed, and Lady Shortcake was to appear dressed like Britannia, and holding a trident. This had nothing to do with the play, and it made the rest of the cast laugh so much that the whole idea had to be abandoned. Instead, my mistress played the Bognor stowaway, Alice, and had to wear a straw hat inscribed on the band with the words "H.M.S. Loveaduck". Only her ladyship's dignified bearing saved this situation.

VII

Lord Shortcake was very keen on a little incidental music in our productions. But as his taste was for the old-fashioned valse, it was not always easy to please him. For instance, one year we were doing "Invisible Footsteps", an exciting thriller. Enoch Broodie suggested that during the big robbery scene a few sinister bars should be played softly. But my master wanted a valse called "Mignonette". When Broodie said that such music was unsuitable, and would make the audience laugh, my master replied, "It is the play that is unsuitable to the music, not the other way round." Mr. Broodie did not know what on earth to say to that, and the matter hung fire.

"Let me try to understand your point," said Enoch Broodie, "You say that this play is not suitable for the valse 'Mignonette'. Surely you mean that it is the valse which is out of place?" "Not at all," snapped Lord Shortcake. "Then," said Mr. Broodie, with a wry smile, "why don't we just chuck the play and have the valse instead?" "Well, why don't we?" replied my old master. At which Mr. Broodie began to tear his hair. Presently, with infinite patience, he said, "Can't you see that *any* valse is ridiculous for such a play, and particularly for a robbery scene, even if played softly?" "Softly be hanged!" replied my master. "We want the audience to hear it. It must be played loudly." Mr. Broodie, uttering a scream, retired from the controversy.

VIII

At a full-length rehearsal of the thriller the valse "Mignonette" was played during the safe-breaking scene. Broodie was beside himself with rage, and the cast and spectators all began to laugh. "There!" shouted Broodie. "Can't you see that the whole scene is ruined? How can anybody take it seriously with that absurd music being played? That's the sort of music to suggest home-sickness, or mother-love, or something." Whereupon Lord Shortcake said, "By George, old man! An Idea! Why not interpolate a line or two to explain the music? Why shouldn't the crook

191

pause as he is about to blow the safe and say, 'Ah, my dear old mater'? Something like that, eh?" Broodie swore silently and walked away.

IX

Once—and once only—Lord Shortcake was put in charge of the off-stage noises. The play was a love story, and included a thunderstorm. My master was given a poker and a big sheet of tin, and taught how to do distant thunder, and then how to suggest thunder close at hand. But on the night of the production he became confused in his cues. The heroine had just said, "How still is the summer night, Arthur, in this remote arbour. One could hear a pin drop." At that moment Lord Shortcake gave the sheet of tin the works. He fairly belaboured it, and all sounds on the stage were drowned, while the audience rocked with laughter. In the next act the hero said, "Mélanie, how close the air is today. Ah, didn't I hear distant thunder?" And at that moment my master pressed the motor-horn which should have been heard in the first act.

X

My dear old master tried his hand, once in a while, at almost everything connected with the theatrical productions at the Manor. I shall never forget the occasion when he took charge of the stage lighting. The lights swung and jumped all over the stage. On this occasion we had a well-known actress down from London, and do what she could, she was unable to get into the limelight. Everybody else got the light full in the face from time to time, but she remained in shadow. She angrily glared up at Lord Shortcake, high in the wings, and he, forgetting that a moving scene was in progress, shouted loudly, "What is it, my dear? Anything wrong?" Lady Shortcake, in the opposite wing, signalled to him to keep quiet, but he shouted even more loudly, "What is it, my love? Speak up!"

XI

When Lord Shortcake acted as prompter there was always trouble. He interrupted the slightest pause as a sign that somebody had forgotten the part, with the result that his resonant interruptions gave the impression that he was playing all the parts in the play, though invisible. This was all the more annoying because my old master rarely spoke in quiet tones. And he obviously thought that the prompter should shout his promptings; so that his voice was nearly always louder than the voices of the company. Add to this that he frequently lost his place in the script, and shouted the wrong words to the wrong player. I remember once, during a scene in which a mother was reproving her son for his extravagance, there came a pause. She had just said: "Is it horse-racing, Paul?" when my master's voice was heard bellowing: "Sugar, Mrs. Earle? Two lumps?"

XII

It was Lord Shortcake's custom to give a regular banquet to the performers every year, after the play had been produced. He himself toasted them in a short speech, which never varied. I can almost hear him now. "Ladies and gentlemen, it has ever been my aim to season the rigours of country life with a pinch or two of Thespian frivolity. The Swan of Avon has said, 'The whole world is a stage'. Allowing for exaggeration, one may say that there is an actor—or shall I say actress—ha!—in the heart of every man. Well, here in our small corner we do our damnedest to make the words of the Swan come true. Ladies and gentlemen, I give you the toast, the Shortcake

Dramatic Society, coupled with the names of all its members." After that a village girl presented a bouquet to Lady Shortcake, with a curtsey, and my mistress said, "Thank you, my dear," and patted her head.

XIII

The untiring efforts of Enoch Broodie to give a more serious turn to our Dramatic Society were stalwartly combated by my old master. "We're not trying to improve ourselves or anyone else," he would say, "we're having fun." The idea of applying such a frivolous word to the Drama made Broodie very miserable. And when he pleaded for "Plays with some sort of intellectual content," Lord Shortcake would wag his finger and say, "I smell Ibsen. Not on your life, Broodie. Over my dead body. Damned plays about demented sewage inspectors and whining women." "Have you read any of them?" Broodie would ask. "No need to," my master would reply. "Can smell 'em in the next county. Don't have to be bored stiff to know what would bore you stiff. Modern poppycock. Give me a straightforward play that any fool can understand."

XIV

Once, at Christmas, it was decided to produce a pantomime—"The Sleeping Beauty". But, here again Mr. Enoch Broodie, as the producer, came up against Lord Shortcake's old-fashioned views. Broodie said that nowadays there must be topical songs, and suggested a popular one of the moment, called "Shuffle off to Buffalo". My old master asked what on earth this had to do with the pantomime. "Why Buffalo?" he asked. "Why not Timbuctoo?" Broodie said people liked these interpolations. "Then why not interpolate the Toreador song for the Beauty?" asked my master ironically. He also objected to the suggestion that the fairies should walk about in the auditorium, collecting in little boxes for the Kedgwith Sociological Association. "People expect fairies to fly," he said, "and you can't have fairies hanging from the ends of bits of wire and asking for sixpence. It destroys the illusion."

XV

The suggestion, made as a mere matter of courtesy by our vicar, that Lady Shortcake should play the Queen of the Fairies in the pantomime, was taken quite seriously by my master. He was under no illusion as to her size and weight, even remarking to Mr. Broodie that she would need a wand like a barge-pole. And the way he fussed about the wire that was to be fixed to her, asking anxiously if it would "take the strain", caused a good deal of silent mirth among the company. When she made a trial flight, my master had a net spread to break a possible fall, and he watched her so anxiously that, as she herself remarked, she might have been a crate of perishable goods being unloaded at the Surrey Docks. However, she made a happy landing, apart from the pushing over of a castle wall, and a slight collision with Mic and Mac, the baron's butlers, which those gentlemen ever after referred to as worse than the fall of a wardrobe.

XVI

Lady Shortcake, during rehearsals for the pantomime, did not take kindly to the part. My mistress was a large, stern lady, who frowned whenever she spoke, owing to an affection of the eyes, so that when she addressed her attendant sprites she looked more like a sergeant-major than a fairy. Also, there was an altercation when my master wanted her to sing "My heart's a-chime in elfin time". Lady Shortcake had, in her youth, sung drawing-room ballads in a rich and powerful voice, but she refused to oblige him now, and the song was given to the Sleeping Beauty, a very beautiful but rather backward young lady, who squirmed upon her couch of flowers whenever the Prince stooped to deliver the kiss that was to awaken her. My mistress also persuaded Mr. Broodie to delete the line "We tiny folk assembled here". "I don't *look* tiny, and I don't *feel* tiny," she said gruffly.

XVII

The villagers were allowed in to watch the dress rehearsal of the pantomime, but their criticisms and comments were a little too unrestrained, and that was the last year they were admitted. When the fairies entered, there were cries of "Six to four on the field", and one impudent youngster greeted the entry of the Fairy Queen (my mistress) with shouts of "Threepence a ton freightage," and "Whoa! Big Bertha!" and "Down comes the balloon." What with these comments, and the noise made by my master who was acting as prompter, there was considerable confusion on the stage. And when the witch, with a hideous cackle, departed on her broom, a voice yelled "Bring us back a vacuum cleaner, Mrs."

XVIII

The pantomime of which I have been writing was certainly the most troublesome production I ever remember. Everything went wrong. Even at the dress rehearsal the Fairy Queen (Lady Short-cake) got her wire entangled with the orchestra. In her powerful voice, at the end of a very beautiful scene, she uttered the words:

"Now, having summoned all the elfin band,
Behold, I take my flight to fairyland."

And off she went with a violin hanging from her wand and a harp trailing from her feet. My master, in the wings, shouted, "My love, you've summoned the wrong band," and laughed uproariously.

XIX

No second pantomime was ever produced at Boulton Wynfevers. When the curtain rose on "The Baron's Kitchen", Lord Shortcake was caught on the stage, and the opening words of the performance were heard in amazement. For my master cried, "By George! I oughtn't to be here, eh?" Amazement was followed by wild laughter. In Act II Lady Shortcake's wire went wrong, and she fell into the orchestra, slap into the lap of the trombonist, while "My baby is some baby" was being sung. The trombone tore her wings, and my master could be heard shouting, "Put her down, man!" In Act III the real horse came on too soon, ate a fairy lantern, and was sick. Mr. Broodie never came to the Manor again.

194

MRS. McGURGLE CHRONICLES OF MARINE HOUSE

Atta la belle McGurgle!

A SMALL contretemps might have marred the almost ceremonial reopening of Marine House yesterday. A man in what Mrs. McGurgle described as "an ostentatious felt hat" booked a room, and described himself on the form as a bee - keeper. Mrs. McGurgle pounced. "I take it," she said, "that you do not propose to keep any bees here." The stranger removed his hat with an angry sweep, and said, "Is there anything derogatory in bee-keeping, mum?" "There is a time and place for everything," retorted the stalwart landlady. "Well, I don't carry my bees about with me," said the stranger sarcastically. Mrs. McGurgle softened somewhat, and the stranger added, "As far as I am concerned, my lady, you are the only honey in this dump." Despite herself, the landlady smiled, and a mulberry tint spread over her damask cheeks. "Go on, there!" she replied, with a massive simper.

At the evening meal a lugubrious young man with a fair moustache said out of the blue, "I hear a boiled egg calling to its young." A deathly silence greeted this sally, which was not of the kind appreciated at Marine House. The young man has not spoken since, and is expected to be frozen out of the house within a week.

Mr. Powder is put in his Place

Mrs. McGurgle was personally dealing out one tea-spoonful of marmalade to each boarder at breakfast, when a commercial gentleman named Powder said, "Why not use a salt spoon?" "What," retorted the McGurgle, "are you hinting? Pray speak out, Mr. Powder. If you desire to suggest that I am a fifth columnist of the black market, I here and now inform you that marmalade does not grow on trees in these days. If one attempts to conserve supplies, that does not mean that one is a quiserling, not by a long chalk, Mr. Powder. Your sarcasms fall flat to the ground in my ears, and a little more of your sauce and you will forfeit the extra spoonful per Saturdays which is the traditional reward at this establishment for keeping a civil tongue in your head."

Poor Mr. Powder grew red and hung his head. The boarders sniggered.

There was an ugly scene recently when Mr. Fetlock sent back his slice of mutton, on the plea that he couldn't cut it. "I cannot exchange this bit," said the McGurgle, "you've bent it." "Then put it on the salvage dump with the other iron bedsteads," said the ironical Fetlock.

Mrs. McGurgle writes to me from Marine House as follows: ". . . And the lifting of the seaside banns has now brought an influx of clientele. I am trying to establish contact with some of my old boarders. I would be glad if you could help me, but not by sending any disreputable characters like that Captain Foulenough. He came with a recommendation from you, and in 24 hours he had cleared the gas meter and telephone box, proposed to a res- pectable married boarder whose husband was in steam carpet beating, played what Mr. Stulloe called 'questionable poker' with more aces than were thought strictly possible, and tried to dance a tango with me in my own kitchen. While I live, the standard of Marine House shall not be lowered. . . ."

Mrs. McGurgle gets an Egg

The latest arrival at Marine House brought a hen with him, and craved permission to put it in the back-yard. Mrs. McGurgle reluctantly consented on being promised the first egg. But the bird turned out to be broody, and the owner became the butt of the

boarders. "Shall we have that egg poached or fried?" asked Fred Parsley maliciously. "I prefer an omelette," said the Bulstidge girl. After two days the bird became normal again, entered the house in search of warmth, and laid an egg on the second-floor landing. There it was found by old Mrs. Pasham, who, never having seen an egg on a landing, went into hysterics and swore it was a little bomb, which would explode at a touch. Having calmed her, Mrs. Mc- Gurgle bore the egg away in triumph to the kitchen, boiled it and ate it. Next day the bird died, and the owner departed. Upon the McGurgle's face was a self-satisfied smile.

The Egg on the Landing

Mrs. McGurgle writes: ". . . I fear that your description of this odd event may lead perspective clientele to imagine that the laying of eggs on landings is a normal occurrence at Marine House. This is not so, and the eccentric gentleman to whom the bird belonged made adequate apology before leaving. The late Mr. McGurgle would never have an animal in the House, with the exception of our cat Malcolm and a parrot which said, 'Oh, what a dirty trick.' The parrot bit a gas-inspector, and we had it destroyed. As for Malcolm, he went off one August day and was found dead in a dustbin in Fawgus Road, and he was much missed. Since my husband's decease no animal has crossed my threshold until this hen arrived—if I except the frog which got in at a ground-floor window in damp weather and made Miss Brinker scream so loudly that the fire brigade came and 'smashed the window and carried her off in her neglijay. . . ."

DEAR SIR,—How opportune was that egg laid on the landing! What a publicity stunt! No other landlady would have thought of such a thing. But let Mrs. McGurgle remember this. Such tricks may increase her clientele temporarily, but the kind of boarder who books a room merely because an egg has been laid on a landing is not the steady type which returns in fair weather or foul. In the long run it is those houses which are run without sensationalism that retain their customers, and all this egg-laying fuss is but a short-term, catch-penny policy. Mrs. McGurgle is clever, I admit, but unless she can reveal an egg on the landing every morning, lack of custom will stale her impudent variety.—Yrs. truly, M. P. GARSTANG.

DEAR SIR,—Mr. Garstang's wicked assumption that I arranged for the hen to lay on the landing is as unpremeditated as it is insulting. I had hoped the incident closed, but since idle tongues are still a-wagging, as wag they will, I must repeat that nobody was more surprised than myself by the discovery of the egg, and he who imputes vulgar motives only shows the depths of his own mind. Though it is easy to make fun of a widow, it is not what I would call the act of a gentleman. If the cap fits, let Mr Garstang put it in his pipe and smoke it.—Yrs. in indignation, FLORENCE McGURGLE.

DEAR SIR,—What on earth does it matter where a hen lays an egg in these days? Is Mrs. McGurgle's first floor landing sacred? That lady should have been only too glad to be the indirect means of increasing Britain's breakfast-table delicacies, instead of adopting an attitude of disapproval, as though egg-laying on inhabited premises were a disgrace. If every landing could show one egg per day there would be fewer disgruntled faces at boarding-house tables, and I, for my part, as proprietress of an old established house, would gladly welcome a rain of eggs in every room. If you will put me in touch with the gentleman who owned the hen, I will let him a room cheap, with the use of the landing for that sporting bird.—Yrs. truly, PHOEBE BASKETT.

Lunch at Marine House

It did not escape the notice of the boarders at Marine House that the gentleman who had called Mrs. McGurgle "honey" got the only potato without a flaw at lunch. This gentleman's name was Twivens, and every time he looked at his hostess he smacked his lips and said, "My word!" The result was that Mrs. McGurgle became nervous, lost her grip, and poured cold gravy over the tapioca. This elicited a cry of "Yoicks!" from Mr. Fred Parsley, and the Bulstidge girl laughed so hysterically that a hearty old warrior, thinking she was choking, caught her a whack in the small of the back which sent her crashing forward on to a chipped cabbage-dish. With greens clinging to her contorted features, she shrieked an unprintable word and left the room. Mrs. McGurgle then begged to remind the assembled company that they were not at a circus.

An Old Tradition

The hanging of the mistletoe at Marine House is always an embarrassing business. This year, more than ever. There is only one pretty girl in the establishment, the telephone operator in No. 4. It is obvious that every male would like to be the first to salute her beneath the bough. But every lodger knows that the first kiss belongs by mere courtesy, to the portly châtelaine.

Every year Mrs. McGurgle enacts the same little comedy, and the lodgers join in. "Take care, Mrs. McGurgle! You are in danger!" "Danger? How? What do you mean, Mr. Snackett?" "Er—why, you are standing right under the mistletoe." "Oh, My goodness. So I am! What a silly I am! Oh—Mr. Snackett, please! You wicked man! . . . Mr. Grape, how could you!. Why Mr. Burple, you're as bad as the rest of them!"

But this year their hearts are not in the business, and as each man brushes the brow of the McGurgle one eye is on the pretty girl who laughs near by. And well the McGurgle knows it. For as the last in the queue, Mr. Trowney, tries to side-step, she cries, "Why, surely you are not going to take advantage of my position, Mr. Trowney?" And, of course, poor Trowney has to fall into line, and go through the dismal routine. "Mr. Trowney, I'm surprised at you, and you such a quiet one: but they say still waters run deep."

The front door bangs. The pretty girl has gone out. The lodgers gape at each other in disappointment. And the fair McGurgle withdraws, well contented.

A cascade of melody from the old larch—in many a ferny dell the shy lesser celandine—A flash of wings announces the arrival of the tiny beercrest—By tilth and loam spring's message, etc.—feathered songsters of this fronded isle, and/or jovial chanticleers of highway and hedge—bits about age-old plough turning up the benignant soil—greystern nesting in old blow-pipe there to lay her mottled eggs—quack-quack from the slime-strewn pond—willow-catkins, etc. Sticky chestnut buds lambs gambolling on many a lea call in at Campbell's about the smell in the attic snakes sloughing winter skins on sunny uplands.

PRODNOSE: It seems to me your rough notes have got mixed up with your copy.

MYSELF: 'Tis no matter. The public likes a glimpse of a writer's workshop.

Poetry

Somebody has sent me one of those old-fashioned magazines which brighten a dark hour. Opening it at random I find this under the heading of poetry:

> "I shall bind green branches to my forearms
> Walking between dead trees
> While the sun stares
> At my white face
> A carved altar
> To a smile."

I hope it keeps fine for you, sir.

'Oh, Godfrey! I'm afraid it's beer again.'

THE ADVENTURES OF CAPTAIN FOULENOUGH

The bar-parlour of the Garibaldi seemed to be gunwale under, and taking it green. The faces before Captain Foulenough revolved in a mist as he stood leaning against the bar, with his right elbow in someone else's pint-mug. He had reached the garrulous stage.

"We were north of North Cape," he said, "and in those parts the long summer hours of darkness have little daylight. Icy spray swept our decks. Suddenly, in the Arctic dawn, I heard the Captain shout, 'Ship ahoy on the port beam, making three points south of southeast at thirty knots.' Using my telescope, I could just make out the name on her bows: *Scharnhorst.* Suddenly the ship rocked as our fifteen sixteen-inch guns fired a broadside. The noise was deafening, and when the smoke cleared away, the *Scharnhorst* was no longer there."

"But no, gentlemen," continued the Captain, "we had not sunk her. That was left to our colleagues of the Royal Navy on a subsequent occasion. She had turned and run for it, before a following wind. So we of the convoy steamed on with our cargo."

"What were you, an Army man, doing aboard?" asked one man.

"Liaison work," said Foulenough, "aboard the sweetest bit of timber in Lloyd's."

"And what *was* your ship?"

Foulenough laid his finger along his nose. "No names," he said, "no pack-drill. Defence of the Realmegulations, gentlemen. Jolly old defence. Jolly old realm. Careless talk costs wives, as the whelkstall man said when the old sailor told him his wife was out on the ragamadolio with a traveller in linoleum."

★   ★   ★

"For some time in the Boer War," Foulenough was saying, "I was buying horses for the Army."

"I thought you were a good judge of horseflesh," said the barmaid of the "Marquis of Granby."

"Yes," said Foulenough, "one has to be."

"And who rode your horses?" asked the silly girl. "Was it the cavalry?"

"Nobody rode them," said Foulenough. "I was buying them for the Army to eat, my dear."

★   ★   ★

"I was standing amidships with the Admiral," said Foulenough, "when I heard the threshing of propellers behind us. 'Don't look round,' I said to him, 'but I think we're being followed'".

"The Admiral listened intently. 'It's a U-boat,' he said. We then searched our wake, but nothing was visible. 'She must be under the water,' said the Admiral gravely. He then gave orders to drop a depth-charge. 'Stay!' I cried, 'she's too near us. We shall only blow ourselves up. Why not, instead, stop dead and pretend to abandon ship? She'll then surface, and we can despatch her to Davy Jones's locker.' He liked the idea, and gave the necessary orders to the officers. Several men shouted 'Away-ho! Heave-to! Oh! Oh! We are sinking fast! Admiral, Admiral, she's careening fast.'"

"After a while," continued the Captain, "up bobbed the U-boat, her conning tower crammed with excited German sailors. That was our moment. We gave her a broadside at point blank range, and the concussion blew the Admiral's cocked hat into the crow's nest, where it killed our mascot, the broody hen Alicia. When the smoke cleared nothing was left on the sea-top but a patch of oil and a few splinters."

"Did you get any medals?" asked Edna, the barmaid.

The Captain was understood to reply that he nearly got three or four, but a steward surprised him as he was opening a drawer in the gunnery officer's cabin.

*　　*　　*

In the bar of the "Spread Eagle" Captain Foulenough was explaining the naval strategy of the war in the Pacific to an enthralled audience.

The counter was a mass of ashtrays (islands), beer-pools (coral reefs), bottles (battleships), mugs (aircraft), match-sticks (assault barges), cigarette ends (pincer movements), pocket-knives, buttons, tintacks (three-prong drives). The Captain worked in silence, shifting his material with a total disregard for the customers, and it was only when an angry man shouted, "Where's Rabaul?" that the Captain became flustered. He gave a vague answer, but the man persisted. "Where's Rabaul?" he shouted every thirty seconds. Finally Foulenough lost his patience. "Here," he cried, seizing a full pint-pot and emptying it over the customer.

*　　*　　*

The crowd in the saloon-bar of the "Horse and Mermaid" was as tense as an egg in midwinter, while Captain Foulenough, in the Kipling vein, spoke on in an even monotone.

"Her stringers and her larboard lockers were shuddering as the combers pooped her. A loose thrust-block, jamming the bulk-head plates, left the butt-staps cagged against the bucket-staves of the screw-shaft-hammer. At last we raced into harbour before a nor-nor-easter that froze the teeth in your mouth. That night we celebrated and I went to bed with a rather bad head. I was awakened by a bang. Rushing on deck I saw that there were lights all round us, the riding lights of ships. They seemed to be red and green and yellow and even other colours. I roused the Admiral and his staff.

" 'What is it?' asked the Admiral.

" 'I think we've run into something, sir,' said I.

" 'Into what?' riposted the old salt.

" 'It looks like a chemist's shop, sir,' said I.

" 'Unlikely, nay impossible,' vouchsafed the deep-sea mariner. 'We are at sea.'

" 'All at sea, sir,' said I, 'speaking for myself.'

" 'Tut, tut, tut,' averred the experienced tar, sweeping the harbour with his telescope and cursing the darkness. 'They are only ships. Go back to bed, you ass.' "

An incredulous gasp ran through the bar like fire through stubble.

"What had you hit?" asked the barmaid, Primrose.

"Nothing," said Foulenough. "The bang I heard was my head hitting the wall when I awoke."

*　　*　　*

"We were sitting over our port in the senior wardroom," said Foulenough, "when suddenly the ship lurched and jarred, as though she'd run into a building. We were all thrown to the floor, and the Captain cried, 'Torpedoed!' 'Not at all,' said the officer of the watch, looking in at the door. 'We have fouled an iceberg.'

"We all ran on deck, and were in time to see a large polar bear jump from the top of the berg on to the main deck. It slipped, broke two legs and rolled over. I shot it with my revolver, and we had bear-steak for the next month. The head of that bear is now over the mantelpiece in my lodgings."

"Where was this?" asked the proprietor of the "Lord Nelson", himself an old sailor.

"In the Western Mediterranean, longitude 43, latitude 81," replied Foulenough.

"That must have been the only polar bear ever seen in those parts," said the proprietor, suspiciously.

"It was," said Foulenough. "It had escaped from the Venice Zoo."

"And the iceberg?" continued the proprietor. "I suppose it brought it with it."

"No," said Foulenough, "the iceberg, we found out later, had been dragged from the Arctic on the keel of a destroyer, and had finally broken loose."

"Didn't it melt?" asked the proprietor.

"Partly," said Foulenough. "If we'd been a bit later there wouldn't have been much of it left."

"Oh," said the proprietor.

*　　*　　*

Amazed that an Army Captain should have had so many naval adventures, a pretty widow who frequents the "Lord Nelson" asked him if he liked liaison work. The captain turned slowly to look at her, rubbed his forefinger along each wing of his moustache, flicked an imaginary crumb off his shoulder, cleared his throat, rolled his eyes, and answered in a low voice, "I adore it." There were roars of laughter, and the widow got as red as a blood-orange. "I meant war-work," she said. "*I* didn't," said Foulenough with a prodigious wink.

*　　*　　*

Captain Foulenough appeared in a West-End club yesterday without a single medal on his tunic. General surprise was expressed. The Captain said, "One does not want to be ostentatious at this time. One's service is one's own affair, one hopes. One does what one can. One needn't boast about it, need one? One hopes one's efforts are appreciated, without one's chest becoming a kind of public hoarding." This new mood was so startling that an old member said, "My dear sir, you're entitled to wear medals honestly earned, surely." "Yes," said Foulenough, "even the Guildford Regatta medal of 1934." "I don't follow you," said the member. "You're about the only person in plain clothes who doesn't," replied Foulenough ruefully.

*　　*　　*

". . . And so," said Foulenough, addressing the hushed bar, "And so I set off from the West

End with those despatches for a certain admiral. When I got out of the train at a certain port it was a foggy evening, and I saw that I had not much time to spare before a certain destroyer sailed. I could not find a conveyance, so I ran through the town, and when I came to the quays, I could make out the faint shadow of a destroyer. It was gliding slowly in the fog! I had missed it! With a superhuman effort I covered the last few yards to the quayside, and then, gathering myself like a horse at a hedge, I shut my eyes and jumped. The ship must have been a good twenty feet from the quayside, but I had been a good jumper in my time. Anyhow, I landed on the deck, all asprawl.''

"And then?'' gasped Daisy, the barmaid.

"Willing hands helped me to my feet,'' continued the Captain, "and the kindly old Admiral asked me who I was and what I wanted. I said, 'I have despatches, sir, but I fear I nearly missed the boat, as it were. Another minute and you'd have been at sea.'

" 'Don't be a fool,' said the Admiral. 'We're coming in, not going out.'

"And sure enough,'' concluded the Captain, "a moment later the destroyer berthed, and I was put ashore.''

★ ★ ★

In the bar of the "Marquis of Granby'' you could have heard a bottle drop, so tense was the silence while Foulenough was speaking.

"It was about three or three and a half bells,'' he said, "when we sighted her. She had laid a smoke screen, but the wind backed eight points nor-nor-east, and blew the smoke to leeward. I was standing by the Admiral's side in his crow's nest. 'Can you see her name?' he asked me. Tirpitz,' I replied with awe. The admiral shouted down his telephone, 'Hullo, Hullo! Get me Guns. No! No! Guns. G for guttersnipe, u for unbeknownst, n for nickelplated, s for sausage-meat. . . . . Hullo! Is that Guns? Give her all you've got. Who? Why, the ship, you dolt. Can't you see her? Yes. Well, fire at her, you booby.' Then we all waited tense'y.''

"A flash,'' continued the Captain, "a sudden roar as of a volcano. And when the iron voices had belched their fire, the *Tirpitz* had disappeared.

"Did you sink her?'' asked Trixie, the barmaid.

"Well, she's never been seen since, and nobody knows where she is,'' replied the Captain. "She couldn't have submerged, as she's not a U-boat. And there was black smoke pouring from her funnel when we last saw her.''

"Didn't she fire back?'' asked Trixie.

'She hadn't time,'' said Foulenough. 'She never knew what hit her.''

And then the entry of a boy with four empties from Mrs. Mockpudding interrupted the comments.

★ ★ ★

"Were you never in any land adventures during your military career?'' asked Edith, the barmaid at the "Leg of Mutton''.

Captain Foulenough smiled quietly. "Did I never tell you,'' he asked, "how they dropped me on the Balkans?''

"Whatever for?'' asked Edith.

"To co-ordinate resistance,'' said Foulenough. "I was dropped by parachute, and landed on the top of a mountain. I didn't know where I was, but there was a small village nearby, and I could quite safely talk about resistance, as I didn't know whose side the villagers were on. Nor did they. In fact, they had not heard about the war, and so my job was very difficult. And when they did hear about it, they said I was a Rumanian, and drove me out."

"Is that what this medal-ribbon was for?" asked Edith, fingering a gaudy strip of ribbon.

"No, my dear," said Foulenough. "That's the Bourne End Regatta ribbon for 1928."

"How did you get away?" asked Edith.

"I wandered across the Balkans," said Foulenough, "until I was captured by a German General. I knocked him down, and took his uniform. Whenever anyone spoke to me, I said 'Heil, Hitler!' and often added, 'Gesistchliche Ausgeskumpfen!' "

"What does that mean?" asked Edith.

"I don't know, my dear. I made it up. It sounds the sort of thing to say. Anyhow, I got to the coast, and stole a speedboat. Arriving in Lisbon——"

"Lisbon?"

"Well, Zurich, anyway."

"You are not telling the truth," said Edith.

"Fiction is stranger than truth," said Foulenough, "and who cares about a lot of damned details?"

DR. STRABISMUS IS BUSY

Dr. Strabismus (Whom God Preserve) of Utrecht, is working hard on about fourteen thousand and fifty more inventions. These include a collapsible salt-bag, a bottle with its neck in the middle, a rice-sifter, a stanchion to prop up other stanchions, a suet-container, a foghorn key, a leater grape, a new method of stencilling on ivory, basalt cubes for roofing swimming baths, a fox-trap, a dummy jellyfish, waterproof onions, false teeth for swordfish, a method of freezing meat-skewers, a hand-woven esparto grass egg cosy which plays "Thora" when released from the egg, a glass stilt, a revolving wheel-barrow, an iron thumb for postmen, a hash-pricker, a beer-swivel with blunt flanges and a red go-by, a fish-detector, a screw for screwing screws into other screws, hot pliers, a plush sausage-sharpener, a rope-soled skate for using in mountain quarries, an oiled cork for holes in rabbit-hutches, a cheese-anchor and a chivet for screaming radishes.

MR. JUSTICE COCKLECARROT

HOME LIFE

COCKLECARROT always refers to his retiring and very silent wife as Mrs. Justice Cocklecarrot. For the first eight years this raised a wan smile on her face, but the joke has now worn thin, and he gets no encouragement when he trots out the phrase. Since, however, it is his only jest, some of his friends still greet it with a short and insincere burst of laughter. One or more mutter, "Jolly good!" Others sigh heavily and turn away. And she, the source of the phrase, sits as impassible as a lump of earth, listening, always listening, but taking no part in any conversation. Which explains why the servants were recently staggered to hear her say suddenly, in a loud, clear voice, to her lord and master: "Wivens fell down a manhole on Christmas Eve." Cocklecarrot was in the hall, about to set out for his club. He turned in astonishment, gazed at his wife, said "Thank you, my love," and went out dreamily into the street.

Ten minutes later he returned, with a puzzled frown on his face, and sought his wife in her boudoir. "What Wivens was it that you were speaking of?" he asked. "E. D. Wivens," said his wife. "I see," said Cocklecarrot, who had never heard of the man. Silence fell. After a quarter of an hour, Cocklecarrot, happy in this new talkativeness of his wife, said pleasantly: "Did you know him, my dear?" "No," said his wife. So Cocklecarrot again set out for his club.

*　　*　　*

Many times in the next few days Cocklecarrot endeavoured to recapture the first fine careless rapture of that conversation. He would say, "Now, this Wivens you mentioned, my dear . . ." But the fish always refused the bait. Sometimes he would try a different opening gambit. "Wivens was the name, was it not, my love?" But all he got was a solemn nod of assent. Whatever volcanic eruption, deep in that massive frame, had thrown up the glittering lava of small-talk was now quiescent. Somewhere in her secretive brain the Wivens incident died of inanition. Quiet reigned in the house once more.

*　　*　　*

Mr. Justice Cocklecarrot was convinced, after the incident described above, that Wivens was the magic word which might one day again open the floodgates of Mrs. Justice Cocklecarrot's eloquence.

There was something a little pathetic in the way he would watch her large, empty face as he uttered the word Wivens, now coaxingly, now indifferently, now with vigour and decision. But it was of no avail.

Who, he asked himself, was this Wivens, whose fall through a manhole had made so profound an impression on his wife? The name began to haunt him. He awoke in the night, from dreams of vast landscapes pitted with manholes, and heard himself cry "Wivens!"

Sometimes he would try a new tactic, and say, "Talking of man-holes, my love. . . ." But stony silence met him. It seemed that nothing would ever again make so strong an impression on

Mrs. Justice Cocklecarrot as the misadventure of this unknown man. One day he entered the breakfast room breezily, and began at once, "My love, I do wish you would tell me about this man Wivens," hoping to surprise her into speech. But her only reply was to point to his chair and hand him a cup of tea. "Damnation!" he roared, as his nerves snapped. Mrs. Justice Cocklecarrot laid her finger to her lips. Half an hour later, as he was going out, she said, "Every swearword goes through me like a spear," turned, and went upstairs.

Wivens. Wivens. Wivens. The name rang in Cocklecarrot's head. He became obsessed by it. He even began to ask his friends if they knew anybody of that name, but it was all to no purpose.

Then one day a hideous suspicion reared its head, and grimaced at him. He realised that his wife was still very handsome and in the flower of middle age. What if her silence hid some secret passion? What if Wivens were an admirer, whose name had escaped her lips in an unguarded moment? Should he set detectives to work? Perish the thought! But he began to watch that serene and inexpressive face furtively, hoping to surprise it off its guard. He might as well have watched three yards of blank wall.

* * *

Once when he returned home at night he heard a man's voice in the drawing-room. Cold beads of perspiration bedewed his massive brow. Quietly he advanced across the hall, rehearsing denunciations, and clutching his umbrella like a sword. Flinging open the door, he entered. The voice was saying, "The kitchen sink in these new houses is one inch wider than that in any other prefabricated house." And there sat his wife listening to the radio, while she knitted. He was so relieved that he cried, "Top of the evening to you, Mrs. Justice Cocklecarrot," and kissed her cheek. "It's a talk on sinks," said the lady, and relapsed into silence.

* * *

Cocklecarrot began to scrutinise the envelopes of his wife's letters, a thing he had never done before. One morning she sat with a flushed cheek, reading and re-reading a letter. "Any news?"

asked Cocklecarrot airily. There was no answer, so he said: "You seem to be deeply interested, my love." Slowly Mrs. Justice Cocklecarrot raised her beautiful blue eyes. "Tony's son is ill," she said. "But in one place it says measles, and further on chicken-pox." "Perhaps," said Cocklecarrot, with a light heart, "it is both."

* * *

Cocklecarrot was well aware that the silent Dame Cocklecarrot had to be humoured when she was in one of her talking moods. He had hoped that the phrase about Wivens might be the precursor of a spate of perhaps a dozen other phrases, making, possibly, one complete and intelligible sentence. But the task of persuading her to reveal the meaning of her cryptic fragments of speech was always like coaxing dew from a stone. He therefore waited patiently, but, losing his nerve after four days, said pettishly, "Talking of Wivens, my love, . . ." This was far too clumsy, and his reward was a look sour enough to re-curdle the reconstituted milk essence on his processed herb-porridge. After breakfast, taking the cook, Mrs. Rampound, aside, he asked her had she ever heard her mistress mention Wivens. Mrs. Rampound, smelling a cross-examination, barked, "Certainly not, sir. Never heard of the gentleman."

* * *

Next day the learned judge called on a psychologist of his acquaintance and asked him, "In your opinion, Lancelot, is there any significance in the sudden utterance of the word Wivens?" Professor Lancelot Jiver removed his spectacles, cleared his throat, and replied, "Every word spoken by a waking adult is an echo of a thought unexpressed and lying dormant in the dream-consciousness. A subliminal thought-germ may be revealed unconsciously. This is known as the Delmonico complex, and is refractory in its function, being subconscious, and an extension of Flauber's dream-state. Was she dropped when she was an infant?" Having been lulled into a doze by the preceding balderdash, Cocklecarrot was startled by the direct question which ended the disquisition. "I expect so," said Cocklecarrot. "Then it's undoubtedly sex," said the Professor triumphantly.

* * *

As time passed, Cocklecarrot began to forget his suspicions, and the customary silence settled over the house. Then one day, as he was going out, and his wife had come into the hall to speed him on his way, he heard words which froze him in his tracks. The voice of Mrs. Justice Cocklecarrot said languidly, "Wivens fell down that manhole again yesterday." Cocklecarrot, after recovering from his first shock, turned to his wife and said, "Pray repeat that, my love." She did so. Then, speaking very gently but firmly, Cocklecarrot said, "Is this Wivens—E. D. Wivens, I think you told me before—a great friend of yours?" Mrs. Justice Cocklecarrot smiled happily. "He's adorable," she said. Cocklecarrot winced. "You should see him lap up his milk," she said. Cocklecarrot started as though stung by a hornet. "Who—what is this Wivens?" he said. "A cat, dear. The Marshams' cat." "But cats don't have initials." "This one does." The relief was so great that Cocklecarrot thought he was going to faint.

* * *

The *dénouement* of the Wivens affair led Cocklecarrot to try again to draw out his silent wife. Very briskly he said to her at breakfast, "Well, has E. D. Wivens fallen down that manhole again?" "Yes," said his wife. "They ought to keep it covered," said Cocklecarrot. Exactly twenty-three minutes later Mrs. Justice Cocklecarrot replied "They do." "Then how does the accident happen?" he asked. But this time there was no reply. A heavy silence pressed on the room, and the judge had to leave home with the slender hope of the question being answered that night.

This "delayed-action" form of conversation often results in Cocklecarrot receiving answers to questions long forgotten. His wife will say, out of the blue, "Not necessarily", or "They didn't, though", or "If you really think so." To all of which he usually answers, "Of course, my dear." And then silence falls again.

*　　*　　*

One day a cat made its way into the Cocklecarrot mansion. Believing it might be E. D. Wivens and therefore an agent for the restoration of speech to Mrs. Justice Cocklecarrot, the judge began to call softly, "E. D. Wivensy-Pivensy, then! Diddums! Come up, now, there, Wivy-Pivy, did he, then!" The cat ignored these puerile advances, and the judge shouted louder endearments, hoping to bring his wife downstairs. When she arrived, he said, "My love, we have a visitor! Look! Wivens, I take it, eh?" His wife, drawing her skirt aside with disapproval, went on into the dining-room. Cocklecarrot remained to play with the cat, though he was much disheartened. Two hours later his wife said, "That was not Wivens. It was Scrounger." And once more silence reigned supreme.

*　　*　　*

Thirsting for conversation the other day, Cocklecarrot sought to kindle his wife's imagination and awaken her enthusiasm by saying at breakfast, "My love, hasn't E. D. Wivens fallen down that manhole again yet?" He awaited the answer anxiously, uncertain whether he hoped for a yes or a no, and tempted, as the silence remained unbroken, to admit that it really didn't matter much, either way. Presently his wife looked up and spoke. "He has tried to," she said, "but the manhole was shut." "Did he always do it on purpose, then?" pursued the judge, intoxicated with this unaccustomed babbling. But there was no reply, and he returned with a sigh to his unexciting porridge-powder. Twenty minutes later she startled him by saying, "Why else would a cat fall down a manhole?" Having no reply ready, he grinned happily.

CITY NOTES

The Brazilian plan for settling the foreign debt means, bluntly, that with fundings at £66 10s., readjustments must be made in the Grade 5 bonds. Otherwise there will be no sinking fund at the usual contractual rate. There will be a sharp rise in the current interest rates, under option, of the 1931 bonds, and existing securities will have to be pooled, to avoid cash payment on a single unconsolidated loan. That, briefly, is the position.

WORDSWORTH AND THE DRUID

As Wordsworth sang:

I met a Druid on the wolds,
*   He was ninety-eight, he said.*
His nightshirt hung in graceful folds,
*   His hat was on his head.*
"Tell me," said I, "Why are you here?
*   What do you in this place?"*
And while I spoke, a little tear
*   Meandered down his face.*

ROUND THE ART GALLERIES

The Burnwade Gallery is well worth a visit for the water-colours of Tyangrog. They are remarkable for their use of paint and for a certain dissolving fluency of rhythm which recalls Nitouche in his Soissons period. Tyangrog's angular approach to his subjects has the merit of, as it were, stabilising his backgrounds, so that in such pictures as "The Veiled Laundress" one seems to be looking at the central figure backwards, as though the planes were reversed. His smooth, confident treatment of nostrils is reminiscent of Manholt—the Manholt of "Gospudden Beach"—and in his more serious subjects there is more than a hint of Tavani. But, in spite of this, or because of it, Tyangrog is essentially independent in his approach. My only complaint is that his landscapes are, if anything, too hard and rounded.

DR. RHUBARB'S CORNER

Isabel : For two days now my rabbit Barlow has lain quite still and motionless. What can be wrong?
    Dead, my dear.
Tom : My hat keeps on slipping down over my eyes, as though it were miles too big for me. What should I do?
    What do you mean by "as though it were too big for you" ? Get a smaller one, you fool.
Rhoda : A niece of mine has such long arms that in crowded places her elbows rub against her knees and make them sore. What do you advise?
    Kneecaps.

TO SOOTHE THE SAVAGE BEAST

The orchestra was playing a dreamy Edwardian walruz.

(Morning paper.)

One after the other the violinists drew their bows across its shaggy back. But when the drummer petted with his little sticks, the beast awoke with a cry and lolloped out of the ballroom.

THE FIRST ATTEMPT TO REACH THE MOON

Dr. Strabismus (Whom God Preserve) of Utrecht has announced his intention of making an attempt to reach the moon in a stratosphatic rocket-ship, to be named Utopia.

Preparations have been made in great secrecy at Waggling Parva, where the enormous rocket is already in position, clamped between two helionic struts, and built into a concrete base. The rocket works on the pressure principle, and is propelled by its own energy, generated in a forward nozzle made of plutonium. The backward drive of the radio-active force encased in the central chamber is sufficient to expel the gases which set up continuous explosions in the tail, thus reversing the force of the earth's surface, and enabling the two dynamos in the steel cylinders to replenish the nucles as fast as they are used up. There the matter rests at present.

* * *

An electrical engineer writes to tell me that in my diagram of the automatic reversing drum for the electric boring mill, the circuit-clamps were upside down. He is wrong. The star-wheel device for face-plate starters is so close to the Ilguer gear hoist that the radial drillers on the platen are only partly whelved. Hence the upside-down look of the circuit-clamps, each of which is connected with a screw-plunger by a potentiometer, with Grayson single-phase wrought brass shafting followers, decked on pull-level slotters of pedestal design, each eye-bolt being dependent on a bearing brush, as in the Ward-Leonard system of weir-type dippers on a fixed blow-out.

* * *

According to a statement published some moments ago, the Strabismus expedition to the moon will include, besides the Doctor himself, Professor Gneiss, the eminent lunologist, Rinanka Bam, a Siamese student, and Mimsic Slopcorner, representing the Society for Cultural Relations with the Moon.

When Mimsie's mother was told of the honour conferred on her daughter she said: "In my young days nobody would have let me go to the moon without a female companion, not even for cultural relations, but what I say is times are changed." The proud father said: "If our girl is the first girl to land on the moon, I for one won't blame her. We've always tried to give her the best."

The Doctor is working out a table of tides and weather, so as to fix a final date for the great attempt. The launching of the rocket into space will be broadcast with a running commentary, and the machine will be named "Utopia" by a film actress yet to be chosen. The trip is expected to take five days, counting the return journey.

At Waggling Parva scenes of the utmost activity are taking place, in spite of Rinanka Bam, who understands nothing of what is going on, and keeps peering into the rocket and crying "Usopsa chash verang!" a phrase without meaning for the workmen. The Doctor sits at his desk in a small bungalow, calculating the exact point in the stratosphere where the pull of the earth will give place to the pull of the moon, and testing with a small gilt hammer the welding plates and screw-screens which will protect the delicate zinc ratchets and lug-drives.

* * *

Distinguished scientists, I note, are expressing doubts as to whether a rocket constructed on the principles outlined here would be capable of reaching the moon.

Strabismus himself answers their doubts. He said yesterday: "Never before has the method of hydraulic pressure, used in compressed cylinders, been applied on such a scale to jet-propulsion. By this means the weight of the nozzle is taken off by the curve of the pin-protectors under the leading-edge of each percussion-piston."

When shown this an expert said: "Science does not even recognise the strange terms used, apparently haphazard, by this extraordinary man. Strabismus is either a genius far ahead of his age, or else a deluded visionary. It is utterly impossible to understand his pronouncements."

Meanwhile, a rumour that the rocket may be launched within the next six days is bringing thousands of people to the district. A shilling is being charged for a visit to the rocket, and the money goes to a fund to supply ballot-boxes and educational literature for the inhabitants of the moon, if any. An attempt to find out what, exactly, will be the functions of Mimsie Slopcorner, representative of the Society for Cultural Relations with the Moon, has failed dismally. Mimsie confined herself to the statement that she did so think that the people in the moon needed to know what was happening in our world, and, she added with a grin, "Vice versa, of course."

* * *

Professor Gneiss, the lunologist attached to the Strabismus Expedition, said to reporters yesterday: "Landing will be our greatest difficulty, owing to gaseous rock strata. The lunar air is filled with particles of throbodium, a powerful reagent. At night the mist that rises from the canals and craters is knee-deep, and as our machine has a horse-power of 3,798,421,931, we may find, if we land in darkness, that the atmospheric pressure is one in six, corresponding to the permeation of the ether by globules of radio-disseminative harpelion, which being emblative to changes of temperature tends to nullify any conglomeration of artificial protective devices, such as may be supplied by spoll-generators, attached to little nacket-tanks under the nozzle of the rocket."

Enquiries about the best place to see "Utopia" from are pouring in from all over the British Isles. I can only answer that it will travel so fast that the chances of seeing it are very slight. Watchers in the Peak district may possibly see a tiny object about the size of the pimple on a lawyer's nose, but not for more than a quarter of a second. And who wants to see that sort of object for longer than he need? Eh? Well, then.

* * *

Tomorrow, in the presence of the members of the Strabismus Expedition and a vast crowd of officials, Miss Topsy Turvey, star of "Swing It, Sailor!" will break a champagne bottle containing tinned apricot juice over the stern of the stratosphatic rocket, and christen it Utopia.

The rocket is ready to start, and the Doctor is waiting for the latest reports of interstellar and interplanetary weather. Asked whether the experiment, if successful, would benefit the housewife, the Doctor said: "We have reason to believe that the vegetation on the moon could be adapted for human food; if this is so, as soon as transport between earth and moon has been nationalised, we should be able to bring strange herbs to the British breakfast-table."

* * *

(*From my Special Correspondent* Waggling Parva, Friday.)

A deep-throated roar from 10,000,000 throats greeted mink-clad, smiling Topsy Turvey, as she advanced towards the huge rocket, its nozzle pointing skywards.

" 'Ow pathetically small she looks beside it," vouchsafed a spectator. And she looked still smaller when Dr. Strabismus (Whom God Preserve) of Utrecht handed her an enormous bouquet which blotted her out from the sight of the surging crowds. A second bouquet, proffered by Mimsie Slopcorner, tittering happily, seemed to

209

embarrass the star, who got caught in the fragrant mass, and emerged with her hat over one ear and a mouthful of greenery. Laughing officials disentangled her, and the Doctor led her towards the rocket, and handed her the champagne bottle, attached by a broad green ribbon to the stern of the expectant projectile.

Strabismus, stop-watch in hand, stood beside her. Almost lovingly she held the bottle, as a tense hush fell on the countryside. Then, at an almost imperceptible sign from the Doctor, the colourful sweetheart of two continents bent her head, took careful aim, and swung the bottle vivaciously on its way. It went off at a tangent, and caught a Cabinet Minister on the chin. A howl of horror went up from the crowd, but the gallant politician, jumping up, seized the microphone and cried, "That's the first time for 20 years I've had a bottle thrown at me by an actress." Under cover of the laughter and applause, the Doctor returned the bottle to Topsy Turvey. This time a broad space was left clear, and with unerring aim the public's darling crashed home the luxury missile. A dirty trickle of tinned apricot juice appeared on the stern. "Ai naime thees rawcut uteaupyah," shouted Topsy. The crowd went mad with delight.

Immediately after the christening of the Rocket, lunch was served in a large marquee, and the Minister of Bubbleblowing made a speech.

He said: I am sensible (laughter) I am—er—very sensible (applause) that the (applause) name given (laughter) to this rocket, Utopia (applause) by our charming guest (laughter) Miss Topsy Turvey (applause) is especially (laughter) gratifying to a Socialist (laughter) Government (laughter). I hope this rocket may (applause) appear in the moon (applause) as the (laughter) symbol (applause) of that free (applause) democratic (applause) State which we are attempting (applause) to build (laughter). The name of Waggling (applause) Parva (laughter). . . .

The rest of the speech was drowned by the noise of the guests, who were struggling for Topsy's autograph.

* * *

No sooner was lunch over than Food Ministry narks, disguised as mechanics, gave notice that Regulation No. 74,986,412, supported by Order in Council No. 8,463,841, had been infringed, in that the half of a potted shrimp served on top of the reconstituted egg-dust pudding should have counted as an extra course, seeing that corned gravy had been served with the processed halibut, in lieu of sauce or sauces, and that fish-sausage, served alone, constituted both meat and fish, within the meaning of the accursed foolery.

* * *

Reporters at Waggling Parva yesterday asked Mimsie Slopcorner whether she was looking forward to travelling faster than sound.

Mimsie replied: "I do so think that everybody is most kind. It isn't every girl who is lucky enough to go faster than sound, much less to the moon. I do so think it's the dawn of a new era, I always say."

Asked when he expected to start, Dr. Strabismus (Whom God Preserve), of Utrecht, replied: "It depends on the currents in the upper air. A high wind at an altitude of, say, 19 miles, will not counteract the pull of gravity. I have therefore fitted Utopia with self-rotatory gauges to enable us to sideslip the accumulated pockets of stationary air in the wind's wake. Transverse cloud-formations will be artificially dispersed by blasts of heat from an exhaust-pipe groined into the forward galbules."

The Doctor spends most of his time among his delicate scientific instruments. These include a kind of tuning-fork with curved ends, which is so sensitive to zinc that small bubbles appear on its surface at a distance of 40 feet from a zinc slab. As each bubble dries, it leaves a dirty blob of froth-like substance on the tuning-fork. Transferred to the zinc slab these blobs slowly melt and are absorbed. Asked what bearing this had on the expedition the Doctor said that with this tuning-fork he would be able to detect the presence of zinc on the moon.

* * *

Utopia is almost ready for the great attempt: Mechanics are at work on her, cranking up her shelf-ventilators and testing her chutes: Rinanka Bam, the puzzled Siamese student, says repeatedly "Sango ma nakok." Mimsie Slopcorner is stacking copies of War and Peace in Turkish, for distribution in the moon. Professor Gneiss is studying tables of lunar drifts. The Doctor himself is shut up in a refrigerator, testing the effect of low temperatures on his Batgol binoculars. The rocket, pointing skywards at an angle of 46°, looks almost fragile, yet when she is launched, the concrete base will melt in the heat of her backwash. Inside the rocket, nothing is to be seen but gadgets, each one a delicate but powerful instrument. The tiny windows are strutted with bdellium, to resist the forward wall of air projected by the uprush of the projectile itself. At an approximate height of 34,000 miles above Shrewsbury the inmates will lash themselves to the floor with ropes, to counteract the pull of the moon.

How will Utopia make a landing? The Doctor tells me that the rocket will slow down to a speed of three miles a second on getting within 143,791 miles of the moon. The nozzle is banked up with rubber mattresses to take the initial shock, and the whole under-part is fitted with a strong web of woven stilicon. The impact will be terrific, but these shock-absorbing methods have been tried on mice dropped from a great height in an iron basket by men dressed in asbestos suits, with helmets of fortified tin. The mice survived, but were restive for 12 hours, and their cheese made them sick—partly because it was beastly stuff, a job lot kept in the window of the Waggling Parva grocer's shop.

Tomorrow the final preparations will be completed! The rocket will be launched at 8.34 a.m. on Saturday morning. A report will be telephoned to me, and will appear in Saturday's paper.

PRODNOSE: Surely a great feat of journalism to get a story telephoned at 8.34 into every edition of the paper on that very morning.

MYSELF (modestly): Yes. Not bad. It's never been done before.

PRODNOSE: But how will it be done? What's the secret?

MYSELF: Efficient organisation, team spirit, and extraordinary energy and enterprise. (Less modestly.) You may quote me as saying so.

* * *

Saturday, November 30, wind and weather in the stratosphere permitting, is the DAY.

PRODNOSE: How could wind and weather affect such a mighty machine?

MYSELF: Mighty, I grant, but extraordinarily delicately put together.

"On Saturday," writes my correspondent, "a new era of world history will open as the rocket Utopia soars far faster than sound out into the dim, untrodden wastes of the upper stratosphere; out into the mysterious hinterland of Lunar space which no eye has beheld."

Stores are being loaded, and the special galvanised ropes which will tie the passengers to the floor of the machine, until they are beyond the pull of gravity, are being coated with mychrose to make them retroversative to air-pressure.

* * *

When Mr. Zazer asked the Minister of Bubbleblowing whether he could say why the tax-payer's money should be used to pay for Miss Slopcorner's trip to the moon, the reply was: "The Society of Cultural Relations with the Moon is paying for the trip." Mrs. Vobbe: Do not their funds come from the government? And therefore out of taxes?

The Minister: I am glad of this opportunity to explain why. Mr. Teffler: Why what? Mr. Fluff: Which question is the Minister answering? The Minister: Neither. I am endeavouring—(cries of "What about the grant?")—to state why this is so. I am surprised that this young lady should be attacked in this manner. What we have to do is to find a way of—or rather to state what the position is with regard to these things being done. This cannot be done until the recommendations of the committee are published in a yellow paper (cries of chagrin and rage).

* * *

WAGGLING PARVA,
Saturday.

(By telephone 8.34 a.m.)

So deep was the hush of expectation that the clock in Waggling Parva market place, striking 8.30, was heard for miles around. There stood the great rocket. Already Mimsie Slopcorner had been helped in by the Mayor, wearing his chain of office and his dog-snatcher boots. Rinanka Bam, jabbering unintelligible Siamese words, had joined her. Then came Professor Gneiss, carrying charts and geological hammers in a pig-skin reticule of vast proportions. 8.32. Dr. Strabismus (Whom God Preserve) of Utrecht appears with the crew, six sturdy fellows. The crew gets into the rocket. The Doctor, dressed in an atmosphere-proof suit of plastic serge, and wearing a small felt hat, slowly climbs into the great machine.

The hush grows deeper. You can hear a lady spitting out apple-pips. Somewhere a dog barks. Then sudden cries of "Contact!" ring out. We all lean forward. 8.34. A new era is about to begin, fraught with who knows what for mankind. The sky is cloudless. Every second now we expect to hear a terrible sound as the monster breaks from its concrete moorings and cleaves its ruthless passage into the mysterious beyond. Not a muscle moves in all that agonised crowd of watchers. 8.35. We rub our eyes. No. Utopia is still there. The Doctor leans out and taps the side with a felt-topped swivelguard. Then silence, deep and impenetrable. Then murmurs "What's going on? What's happened?" The new era is more than a minute late.

8.39—Utopia is still there. The crowd is beginning to grow hysterical. The suspense has been too great a strain. The Doctor's head appears at a window. He is giving instructions. The crew dismount. Swift as fire in an Eastern bazaar a rumour spreads. Something is wrong.

Utopia will not budge. "A technical error," say the knowing ones. Presently the Doctor dismounts, goes to the rear of the rocket, and pushes; doubtless endeavouring to ascertain whether it is caught in anything. He scratches his little hat, absentmindedly. Then he issues his statement. "There is a flaw somewhere," he says. "Probably one of the ratchet-spans has become detached from its coliber. A small matter which can be rectified in 12 hours. A slight postponement, that is all." The disappointed crowd disperses, while mechanics work on the land-bound monster.

Meanwhile, the women will want to know what Mimsie Slopcorner was wearing. She was dressed in grey damask overalls, with starched leggings of rectified organdi, and a kind of diver's helmet with ear-holes and eye-pieces. Nothing very feminine, but all designed to suit the vagaries of stratospheric weather. Interviewed later, she said, "At first I thought we were moving so fast that we didn't seem to move. Then I noticed that we were still at the launching-place. It has been a wonderful experience."

"We should be ready for another attempt on Monday," said the Doctor.

* * *

Monday. Once more a hush fell on the countryside. Crew and passengers were already in the rocket Utopia and the moment of launching drew nearer.

So great was the suspense that several women fainted, and even men held their breath. Then the tiny hat of Strabismus appeared out of the fore-window. He was about to give the signal for a new era to begin, an era of peace, satellite towns, prosperity, nationalised haulage, democracy, etc., etc., etc. (*See Hansard, passim*). Then, as the moment approached, the crowd raised its eyes to the sky, for all had been warned that if they looked at the rocket they would see nothing, so swift would be its passage into the empyrean. A minute passed, and then a boy who had cheated, and kept his eye on the rocket, shouted, "Ow! Look!"

Twenty million eyes switched from the sky to the ground, and there, 15 feet in the air, was Utopia, sailing slowly upwards, far more slowly than sound, like a gigantic kite. Exclamations of incredulity broke out. In a leisurely fashion the rocket drifted higher and higher. After ten minutes she was about 500 feet up, and still climbing. The crowd prepared to spend the day watching her when suddenly she gathered speed, and, leaving a trail of filthy smoke behind her, dashed upwards and in four seconds was a mere speck. A cheer rose from a myriad throats. The mayor, howling like a wolf through a megaphone, was heard to say: "A new era has begun. Space is conquered." The speck in the sky disappeared.

* * *

No word came from the rocket Utopia today, but no anxiety is felt by unofficial spokesmen out of touch with authoritative quarters.

The only report worth mentioning comes from the Buluwayo Observatory. This report says that at 7.43 (Stockholm time) yesterday evening, a series of flashes was observed in the western sky, at an estimated altitude of 1,437,981 statute miles. These flashes were of a colour which suggested friction in the super-stratosphere of a kind likely to be produced by the cleavage of the air by a large foreign body travelling under rocket-impetus.

It is felt that the rocket would have reached the moon by now, had it not been driven (as reported) so far out of its course by tremendous sideslips and down-falls.

* * *

No word has reached the earth

from the rocket Utopia, so presumably it is still soaring towards the moon. One may discount those strange rumours which any scientific experiment always attracts to itself today.

A Dauphinois herdsman in the Graisivaudan valley reports a "ball of flame upside down" high over the Doigt de Dieu. From Nicaragua comes word of a sausage-shaped meteor plunging into space. Watchers on Corfu saw a series of sparks blown across the sky. A shepherd in the Caucasus heard a whirring sound in the night, but saw nothing.

LATER: A radio message from the Utopia says that the rocket is 1,126,000 miles above Upsala, and going sideways.

*   *   *

Little is to be learned from a rambling and disconnected radio message received at Waggling Parva early this morning. Pieced together it reads like this:

Sideways flight ended 10.46 upwards again. . . . Slopcorner sick... Darkness. . . . Pull of gravity and bumps. . . . Instruments behaving queerly owing to pressure . . . sideways again and down, then up . . . 10,462,129. . . . Are we nearing the moon?

That is not for me to say. Natives of Uruguay report that an empty can, labelled, Tinned Egg Dust Powder (Reconstituted) fell on the little town of Quevedo del Obispo yesterday. It is thought that it may have been dropped from the rocket Utopia.

A later message says: *Utopia out of hand, darting to and fro in every direction . . . now slowing down. . . .*

*   *   *

No further word from the rocket Utopia, but more strange flashes in the sky . . . At this moment I have news from Waggling Parva. A radio message received at 11.26 a.m., says:

All well. Pressure terrific. Speed increasing. We think we must be approaching the moon. All instruments out of order. Darkness all round us, but far ahead a faint haze of light. Gneiss says he can detect water—doubtless a lunar canal. Hydraulic (unreadable) ready for landing. Everybody standing by. We are now slowing down somewhat. . . . The haze of light is growing. . . . Wild excitement in the rocket. . . . Are we to be the first people to visit the moon? A new era in human affairs, fraught with (*the rest of the message was indecipherable*).

*   *   *

The night was moonless, and there was a thick white mist. At about 2 a.m. Colonel Cruddock-Mildew started to walk home from an evening of bridge.

He was feeling his way slowly along the promenade when he heard voices on the beach to his right. Someone said, "Here is dry land. We must have landed on the very edge of a canal." "Or," said someone else, "an ancient crater filled with water."

Puzzled, the Colonel stopped and peered into the darkness and mist. Presently a dim figure was visible, which at once hailed him. The Colonel made no reply. The figure grew more distinct. An old man in a tiny felt hat, and with a sweeping beard, approached cautiously. The Colonel grew equally cautious. "I know not," said the old man, "in what tongue to address you." "Damn it, sir!" said the Colonel, "isn't English good enough?"

"Good heavens!" said the old man. "Do the moon-folk speak English?"

"The *what* folk?" thundered the Colonel.

"This is incredible," said the old man. "Surely nobody has anticipated us. Surely we are the first."

"I don't know what you are talking about," said the Colonel, "and I doubt whether *you* do. May I ask what you are up to?"

"We have come from the earth," said the old man, in a voice quivering with emotion. "We have but now landed on the moon. This is the moon, I presume, and not some other planet. It *is* the moon, isn't it?"

"No," said the Colonel gently, as though humouring a child or a lunatic. "No. Worthing."

*   *   *

Interviewed yesterday, Colonel Cruddock-Mildew said: "I am afraid I did not appreciate the fact that the old gentleman who addressed me was the leader of the expedition to the moon, about which I had, or course, read in the papers.

"It was only when the rest of the expedition emerged from the mist that I realised what had happened. There was another gentleman named Gneiss, who fainted on hearing that he was in Worthing; a dark student who muttered unintelligibly—a Siamese I understand; and a foolish young person who kept on saying that she must say she did so think it was all wonderful. When I asked how they could have mistaken Worthing for the moon, Strabismus said that Miss Slopcorner had meddled with the delicate space-compass, and put it out of order."

Dr. Strabismus (Whom God Preserve) of Utrecht said that moon-rockets were in their infancy, and that the Utopia, before reaching Worthing, had without doubt gone higher and further than any other projectile to date, and that he had acquired some invaluable information during the trip. He added that he was not sure it had been wise to include Miss Slopcorner, whose foolish behaviour had spoiled the experiment, and whose idiotic conversation had got on the nerves of her companions from the very start.

Mimsie Slopcorner said, "I do so think it was a marvellous experience, and it isn't every girl who gets a chance of going to the moon, or even to Worthing these days, I do so think." Mr. Slopcorner, interviewed in his home, said: "It's all right by me." The proud mother said: "We do so think our Mimsie ought to do her best for the world." Rinanka Bam swore softly in Siamese. Professor Gneiss sulked.

Anthology of Huntingdonshire Cabmen

It can hardly be claimed for the newly published *Anthology of Huntingdonshire Cabmen* that it is, in the words of an over-enthusiastic critic, "a masterpiece of imaginative literature." The Anthology consists of the more striking names (with initials) from each of the three volumes. It is a factual and unemphatic work, and the compiler has skinned the cream from the lists. Here are such old favourites as Whackfast, E. W. Fodge, S., and Nurthers, P. L. The index is accurate, and the introduction by Cabman Skinner is brief and workmanlike.

*　　*　　*

Long-eared spokesmen in touch with abominable circles characterised as "The height of folly" a suggestion that Vol. III of the *Huntingdonshire Cabmen* should be translated into French, and issued in France.

It was pointed out that the French cannot be expected to show much interest in a list of English cabmen, without even biographical details, and an expert with a wide knowledge of France and her people said: "There is nothing to translate. Moppett, E. F., can only be translated Moppett, E. F. The same is true of Owle, P., and Oxhall, D. N. B. There is no nuance of translation by which the names could be changed. It would be just as sensible, and just as idiotic, to 'translate' into English a list of the tram-drivers of Bordeaux. As for the suggestion that 'Monsieur' should be put in front of each name in the French edition of the work, it is too puerile to discuss. To call Nugstraw, T. R., Monsieur Nugstraw, T. R., will not improve Franco-British relations."

Meanwhile there are carping critics who suggest that even the publication of the list in English is an egregious folly while *War and Peace* is so hard to obtain. "The foreigner," writes the Dalrymple Professor of English Literature at Swindon University, "may get some idea of our culture by reading this and similar lists, but we in England take such things for granted. The compilation of lists of names is too much akin to that regimentation which no Briton will stand for a moment. Nor is this list literature, in the best sense of the word."

More favourable opinions

This list of Huntingdonshire cabmen is sure to be the standard work on the subject. Beautifully written. . . . Suave integrity.

Full of quotable bits. . . . Satisfying, vital, human, dynamic.

A humble litany that clutches the heart.

We read on eagerly from name to name, knowing that this is life passing before us. . . .

A triumph of concealed art. . . . Irresistible appeal.

Written in simple, easily understandable English, yet giving an authentic thrill.

At times touches the heights of poetry. . . . All who have a feeling for the music of words will be haunted by the "Hubbleborough, T.K.," which ends Section IV.

—Wugwell comes for Mrs. Wretch—

The annual attempt to induce Mrs. Wretch to return to her first love, and do a short Christmas season with Wugwell's circus, is in full swing.

Wugwell called in person at Wretch Manor, and put his proposition to Colonel Wretch. "These are democratic days," he said. "Not democratic enough," replied the Colonel, "for any wife of mine to go round the ring with her feet on two horses' backs." "Colonel," said Wugwell, "would it surprise you to know that the lady who balances the glass of port on the seal's nose is the cousin of a baronet?" "Nothing surprises me nowadays," said the Colonel, "it merely disgusts me."

"All I want her to do," persisted Wugwell, "is to jump through the burning hoop, and then get sprayed with ink by the clown Anselmo." "Is that all?" retorted Colonel Wretch, sarcastically. Disliking this tone of superiority, Wugwell said, "Let me remind you, old sporty-guts, that your lady wife began life by handing our ape the bell to ring for its dinner." The Colonel winced as though he had received, smack in the face, an enormous lump of decayed bloater.

★   ★   ★

Some days later all was calm at Wretch Manor. The Colonel was dozing in his study, with a copy of *Horse, Gun, and Rod* in his lap. Mrs. Wretch was cutting out of a newspaper a recipe for making a turnip omelette.

Suddenly, from the front of the house, there came a murmur like the low growl of a mob in movement. Mrs. Wretch pricked up her long ears and ran to a window. A strange sight met her eyes. She saw Wugwell and his clown Anselmo, the Filthistan Trio and the Twelve Red-Bearded Dwarfs. They were all gesticulating and talking loudly and happily. Then the bell rang, and a scared maid announced that nearly twenty visitors requested the honour of a word with her.

A misunderstanding

The visitors were shown into a large drawing-room, and as Mrs. Wretch came in, the yammering died down, and Wugwell stepped forward. "To what do I owe the pleasure——?" Mrs. Wretch began. Whereat the twelve dwarfs cheered lustily, waving their nondescript hats in the air. The Trio joined in, and Anselmo produced a Union Jack from a clock. The cheering brought the Colonel hot-foot to the drawing-room. Thinking his wife was presenting a cup to some local football team, he added his voice to the uproar, which sent the visitors wild with delight. In vain did Mrs. Wretch try to interpose. The good-natured Colonel then led the singing of "For they are jolly good fellows." Then his eye lighted on Wugwell, and the words of the song stuck in his throat.

★   ★   ★

Colonel Wretch stared angrily at Wugwell. Then, unluckily, he used the very words which had started the uproar—"To what do I owe the pleasure——?"

He got no further. At the word pleasure the cheering broke out again. Never was there a happier little group. Moreover, the festive sounds induced other members of Wugwell's circus, who had been lurking in the grounds, to slip in through side doors or open windows, and so mingle with the throng in the drawing-room. There were Battista the Snake-Woman, and Lo Fung the Human Wheelbarrow, and Fifinella, Empress of the Tightrope. And soon the dwarfs had begun to tumble and leap, and the Persians were using a loose book-shelf to improvise a see-saw.

In a corner of the room the Colonel was roaring at his wife, demanding an explanation of this strange incursion. But Mrs. Wretch could not make herself heard. By now the dwarfs had begun to be impudent. Churm Rincewind was shouting: "Send up tea for forty!" and Scorpion de Roof-trouser, Edeledel Edel and Molonay Tubilderborst were playing trains round and round Amaninter

Axling and Listeris Youghaupt. Frams Gillygottle was half way up the chimney and Guttergorm Guttergormton was barking at him. Anselmo was producing the flags of all the nations from his mouth. Never had the rafters of Wretch Manor rung with such whole-hearted merriment.

* * *

"Christmas seems to have come a little early this year," was the comment in the village, as the noise at Wretch Manor increased.

Every time the Colonel tried to speak he was cheered to the echo. Every time Mrs. Wretch opened her mouth the dwarfs jumped up and down in their glee, crying out, "Oh, very bravo! Oh, well done, lady!" The improvised see-saw was crowded with people, and Soboldigo the Demon Cyclist had found an old bicycle, and was threading his way round the room backwards, waving the detached handle-bars above his head. Farjole Merrybody was imitating a lion-voiced cuckoo, while Badly Oronparser and Barkayo-Tong danced the Kickadillo on the table. Bitato, the trapeze-king, was testing the strength of a chandelier.

It was only when the Colonel had fetched an old megaphone, which he used when coaching the Wych Green Rowing Club, that he was able to shout loudly enough to make his meaning clear. The revelry died down, and all crowded round eagerly, like children who expect cake after games. "Mrs. Wretch and I," he said, "are at a loss to explain this—er—all this—er—business. Perhaps Mr. Wugwell would like to say a word." Perhaps Mr. Wugwell would have liked to say a word. We shall never know. For at that moment the local fire-engine passed through the village, with its bell clanging, and, with a cry of "Muffins!" the whole rag, tag and bobtail pelted out of the house, and rushed down the drive and into the village.

FOULENOUGH AND VITA BREVIS

Psychologists have often said that the apparent dislike of Captain Foulenough shown by Miss Vita Brevis masks a kind of involuntary admiration.

He is certainly a persistent wooer, and on his return to England he has once more begun to lay siege to her. He said yesterday: "If I don't marry her, I won't marry anyone—at least, hardly anyone." Miss Brevis said yesterday: "It's his practical jokes I can't stand. He called the other day while my brother the Dean was with me. The maid announced 'Mr. Claude Thirst,' and he bounded in, seized a decanter of sherry, shouting, 'Thirst come, Thirst served,' drained it, and handed it to my brother, saying: 'Give me twopence on this empty.' My brother was nonplussed."

* * *

It appears that the Dean, in order not to appear priggish, handed the Captain twopence and took the decanter. "Fill it up," said Foulenough, "and here's another twopence for you." And he handed the Dean one of his own pennies. "Are you on the stage, Mr. Thirst?" inquired the Dean courteously. "Didn't you see my Macbeth at Ashby-de-la-Zouch?" asked the Captain. "I did not have that pleasure," replied the Dean. "The pleasure," said Foulenough, "according to the audience, was all mine. My next appearance, old boy, is as Romeo." "Indeed, and where?" asked the astonished cleric. "In this very room, when|dusk falls," said the Captain, ogling Vita Brevis. The Dean coughed, and took his leave with a puzzled expression.

* * *

From the Dean to his wife

. . . I don't know what Vita is up to. The other day I was at her house, to discuss the bazaar, when a man called Thirst bounded in, drank all the sherry, and gave me a penny change out of twopence I had handed him as a jest. I thought he was a music-hall comedian, but he apparently plays Shakespeare on tour. I suppose Vita knows what she's up to, but I must say he was a queer customer. . . .

From the Dean's wife to her husband

. . . I think you should have withdrawn before being dragged into all that monkey business. Surely, as a high dignitary of the Established Church, you can find some better employment for your time than giving pennies to mountebanks at rowdy sherry parties. You had better come home before worse happens. . . .

Financial notes

Should the Government underwrite unconverted stock? When there is a balance needed for redemption, this question often arises. The answer depends on our attitude to the $2\frac{1}{4}$ per cent paid for a 30-year bond. Any conversion offer under these conditions will presumably ignore the option to redeem. Otherwise the stock-holders will be left with an undisclosed margin of loss. This in turn, leads to sudden demands for a release of old stock, which cannot be readily redeemed. Government action is then needed to restore the balance.

Among the Christmas books

How to Feed Ferrets, by Constance Blood: In a modest foreword Miss Blood says that she has done nothing but feed ferrets for thirty-one years. If this is true, her book should become a standard work on ferret-feeding.

Whither Formosa? by Marcus Drain, M.P.: Those who prefer the hurly-burly of politics to the more domestic annals of the lowly ferret will be deeply interested in this account of a six months' tour of Formosa. The author was one of the party of six M.P.'s whose mission of good will ended so abruptly.

Unfermented Fish, by Timothy Tallboyes: These poems, by the author of *Burnt Grocer,* show a mastery of form and language equalled only by an almost physical integrity of subject.

For your anthology

> *Take back your tricycle. The moon's a bird,*
> *A silver osprey flying along the clouds,*
> *A traveller who will bring us back no word*
> *To solace the mad, the unregenerate crowds.*
> *Yet where the darkening waters swirl, his light*
> *Flashes a moment and is for ever gone.*
> *As on the borderland of quiet night*
> *Flickers the wing of an unsleeping swan.*

(Andrew Molsan: Crystal Fear.)

An old custom

Since Saxon days the people of Cheopham Bivney have brought in the snedge on August 26. Today at dawn the snedgebringers will assemble in the old tithe-barn. Then, led by the Master-Snedger, they will walk on stilts to the Gold Cross in the Market Place, singing the eighth-century huck-song, and wearing their gilt cardboard hats.

The oldest woman in Cheopham Bivney, Mrs. Brass (104), will then read out the scrin-list, after which four young men will haul the snedge from Cow Down to the crossroads. It is a picturesque ceremony, and Professor Towell states in his *East Mercian Folk Ceremonies* that it probably goes back to the days of Eggfrith the Bald.

PRODNOSE: But what is the snedge?

MYSELF: That has never been disclosed.

THE FILTHISTAN TRIO

Our old friends Kazbulah, Ashura and Rizamughan, known as the Filthistan Trio from Thurralibad, were demonstrating their folk-game of see-saw in the lounge of a West End hotel yesterday, when an accident occurred which was to have far-reaching effects.

The plank was laid across the belly of Ashura, but as the other two climbed into position the plank split in two. The three men decided to apply for a permit to get a new plank, on the grounds that see-saw is not only entertaining but also of intellectual value in encouraging international friendship and dissipating Russian suspicions. It is said that the British Council is sending the trio to Korea to demonstrate the similarity between British and Persian see-saw.

After waiting for nine weeks, they received a large number of forms which they dealt with as best they could.

* * *

How the Filthistan Trio filled in form 719046/JL/274619 b.n./42: 19/646/F.K.:

1. *Have you made any previous application?*—Ho yes, if we do not get it.
2. *How long is the required plank?*—Till it breaketh.
3. *Can you guarantee it will not be used for building?*—We are too much honoured, please.
4. *Where is the plank to be set up?*—On the belly, sir, of Ashura, ho yes.
5. *Have you changed your address in the last year?*—Please, Kazbulah hath changed his cloth trousers for Sundays. Ashura and Rizamughan remain clothed in see-saw overall.
6. *Give rough estimate of current upkeep expenses.*—No, but we eat no currents and keep none up, O official.

Part II.

1. *Is the plank, when in use, polished or unpolished?*—Sir, what is in use, polished or unpolished, please?

2. *Where is the plank to be delivered?*—To Ashura's belly, we have said.
3. *How long does your act last?*—Nine years, please, since we hath begun in Thurralibad market place.
4. *Do you guarantee not to lend the plank to any unlicensed person or persons?*—We are toteetalers, ho yes.
5. *Do you belong to a union? If so, which?*—If so not, sir, what?
6. *State maiden name of Mother.*—O, sir, there be no State names for ladies in Persia. Private name of Mother Jiviaumaleeshara.

And here is how they filled up the supplement to form 8796/GH/27419 OH/71.

1. *What was your acreage of wurzels in 1934?* . . . We want one plank, sir.
2. *State condition of same when reaped?* . . . Oh, see above.
3. *Average width of your wurzels in 1929?* . . . Never have used wurzels, ho yes.
4. *Description of soil.* . . . We want one plank, sir.
5. *Average yield per acre in 1937.* . . . Same dittoo of above.
6. *Average height per ton per acre.* . . . Per, per, per, what good is this, please, Minister?

* * *

Owing to the mess they made of their forms, the three Persians were asked to go to the Ministry of Bubbleblowing, where the following conversation took place.

Official: I'm afraid, gentlemen, these forms are no good.

Kazbulah: Thus did we say, sir, when of reading them. No good, I said to Ashura. No good, quoth Rizamughan, no good. Bad forms, we said, sir, ho yes. Then did Kazbulah——

Official: Excuse me——

Ashura: We excuse, sir. It is——

Official: One moment, please, these forms——

All three: Ha, ha, please, no good! We all say it, ho yes, you and us Persians. Forms no good.

Official: What exactly do you want? These forms——

Rizamughan: We asked no forms, please. What, sir, do you want?

Official: Let's get this straight. I will give you some more forms.

All three (loudly): Please, no good! We all say forms bad, you and us Persians. We give you no forms, why, therefore, give you them to us? Forms no good, you say, ho yes, then why forms please?

Official (grinding his teeth): Your forms are all wrong.

All three: Hear and hear! Ho yes, forms all wrong. Tear oop, say we to you, please.

(*Conference adjourned.*)

* * *

The Filthistan Trio were passed to a higher official, who asked them to state what it was they wanted as shortly as possible.

They replied reasonably enough that they wanted a plank in order to play see-saw in hotel vestibules and other places. The official then asked them if they had anything to do with the Friends of Asia League or the Society for Cultural Friendship with the New Mongolia. Of this they understood not one solitary word. The official then said he didn't see why they needed a plank to play leapfrog. This flummoxed the three gentlemen, who shouted, "But what is lipfroog?" "Who?" said the official. "Lipfroog," said the Persians. "Is it your English word for seesaw?" "What's seesaw got to do with it?" asked the official. So another deadlock set in.

A still higher official then took over, a breezy fool. "Now," said he, "what's all this about leapfrog? What's the trouble?" Patiently the three Persians explained what they wanted. "Ah, yes," said the official, "but in England, you know, leapfrog and see-saw are quite different things. Adults don't play see-saw." "We are not Adults, we are Persians," said Kazbulah, "and we never hear of lipfroog, ho yes." "That's good," said the official, "but I doubt if we can allot any wood for a game like that. Can't you do without a plank?" "O sir," said Ashura, "none but a mighty magician can play see-saw without a plank, for there is naught for the players to go see and to go was upon but the empty air." "Very sorry," said the official, "but leap-frog isn't see-saw, you know." And the disconsolate Persians were shown out.

* * *

The Filthistan Trio were next sent to an even more important fool in the Ministry of Bubbleblowing. He was one of those sly ruffians who try to ingratiate themselves by hinting that everybody is as unprincipled as themselves.

The moment the Persians came into his room, he winked broadly, as much as to say, "We understand each other." The Persians, being devils for etiquette, and thinking it the right thing to do, winked back. Believing this to be an admission of villainy, the official leered at them. They leered back. Then the official said: "So you want to play leapfrog in public, eh? Well, why not?" But his eyes said, "Make it worth my while, and the new plank is yours." "See-saw," said Ashura sulkily.

"What?" said the official. "See-saw," repeated Rizamughan. "How do you mean?" asked the official. "See-saw," said Kazbulah. "Why do you all keep on saying see-saw?" asked the official. The three Persians glowered and remained silent. The official consulted the papers in front of him. "It says nothing here about leapfrog," he said. "See-saw," shouted the three Persians. "Oh," said the official. "See-saw. That explains the plank. Why didn't you say so?" "O Minister," replied Riza-mughan, "we say nothing else day and night, ho yes." "Who sent you to me?" asked the official, hoping it was some friend, with whom he could go fifty-fifty on whatever he could get out of the trio as a bribe. "Your undermate, please," said Ash-ura. "Oh," said the official dis-appointedly.

By a happy chance the Filthistan file found its way to the office of C. Suet, Esq., the man whose grasp of inessentials has made him revered wherever bureaucracy reigns.

In his friendly way, Suet opened the interview with the three Persians by saying how much he would like to visit Persia. Kazbulah, thinking they had been sent for to give Suet some information about their coun-try, and to facilitate his journey, at once began to describe the beauties of Filthistan, and of their own town, the capital of that province, Thurra-libad. "Pray call to see my aged mother," said Ashura. "And my three aunts," said Rizamughan. "And bring us back a janeui," added Kazbulah. "Happy journey!" they cried in chorus, as they prepared to leave the room.

* * *

DEAR BEACHCOMBER,

We are shaken with delight, ho yes, at our publoocity by you, but no use is of our publoocity if no-body is given us a fresh new plank. Why sir will you not poot at our services the great oroganizations of your news-pooper to ittack the Government for wothholding from we three the wooden we need for our entertainance of a vawst poobloic? We would enjoy to see a large topline across the front page of all iditions saying, "Where Please Is Plank For Persians?" and also saying Govern-ment must go away if see-saw inter-fered with. Respectably, ho yes, we are

ASHURA, KAZBULAH, AND
RIZAMUGHAN.

* * *

O MINISTER,

We will be given, please, licences for a stout plank which to replace that which was broke on the belly of Ashura in the vostibool of the Hotel Majestic during see-saw, oh yes. Shall we also say that with the festival season so at hand, it is for us to make mirth for the pipulace to forget their troublesomeness and a feemous Hartlepool-street phosoocian hath written in the paper that see-saw open the paws and thus promoteth pospir-ation for health. O, Minister, pray give us a piece of plank wood now at once that we may resuim our great Persian sport in your fine demo-cracy. We vote Labaw, ho yes.

KAZBULAH, ASHURA, AND
RIZAMUGHAN.

* * *

Charlie Suet met the difficulty in the approved bureaucratic fashion with form S.N/26/4.b/290/aN/h.36. 926489.W.L./636 94/1.214. The Per-sians filled it in thus:

1. *Have you made any previous return of uncontrolled waste products under section 631 of form N.S.6348?* . . . One plank we desire for see-saw, ho yes.

2. *Was your previous application for a permit to return the gross waste products counter-signed by a food officer?* . . . Same answer to as quaestion one.

3. *Have you a licence from the Board of Disposals?* . . . We say plank, sir, you say board. Send us plank of disposals if such be lan-garidge of Government.

4. *What percentage of waste is covered by your surplus waste permit, per unit of personnel?* . . . One plank we desire for see-saw, ho yes, for personnel use.

5. *State nature of waste products* . . One plank for see-saw, please.

6. *State purpose of application.* . . . See-saw, O Minister.

On reading all this bilge, C. Suet Esq., laid his forefinger along his upper lip and breathed noisily down his nose. At that moment Miss Clutter came slinking in, flicked her cigarette ash into Suet's glass of water, and said, in a shrill drawl, "Sorry and all that, but you've given Mr. Armitage's form about his stinking old factory to these people, actually." And out she walked with the form. For want of something to say, Suet said, "That was Miss Clutter." "How greatly we care, ho yes!" said Ashura sarcastically.

* * *

Dismay at the Ministry of Bubble-blowing. Form F.7649138/64/BN 42/ 8ch/6981 R9. D.S.K./73 P.1081/49. es. B./917249/W.V. 68765491 N., dealing with engine-turned pot-nails, has been sent to the Filthistan Trio in error. A high official said, "It may be all right. They don't under-stand forms, and what they fill in doesn't even make sense, anyhow."

The three Persians, despairing of ever getting a new plank, set to work and mended their old one. An inspector called while it was being mended, and accused them of being about to erect a cowshed. They pointed out that they had no cow, whereat the official said that it made it worse to erect a cowshed which was not going to be occupied by a cow. They said they had not thought of erecting a cowshed; the wood was for a see-saw. They were then given three forms to fill, dealing with the Use of Wood for Inessential Activities. They filled them in all wrong and received a call from a Freightage Rate Adjuster, who said they were constructing a portable maisonette. He also confiscated their little pot of glue, saying that glue without a licence was illegal. A telephone call from Whitehall ordered them to sow clover. They said they had nowhere to sow it. It was then found that the call was intended for a farmer in Leicestershire.

* * *

The Filthistan pioneers decided to use the old plank for mending which they had got into so much trouble. There was much sympathetic applause when they marched into the vestibule of the Magnificent and took up their positions. The plank was laid, gingerly, across the capacious belly of Ashura, and Rizamughan and Kazbulah settled themselves at either end. The hotel guests watched with admiration and delight the rhythmic motion of the plank and the cool efficiency of the three virtuosicles. Æsthetic pleasure was writ large on every face, and one ass was heard to say: "One ought to have this sort of thing in ballet." Suddenly there was a crack. Ashura shouted a Persian oath. Kazbulah and Rizamughan alighted gracefully. The plank had again split in two.

* * *

Alas! The day after the second breaking of the plank, the Persians received a permit to "Mend or otherwise restore a plank, provided that it is not to be used for erecting a cowshed, goose-house, hen-house, duck-house, pig-pen, turkey-hut, garage, tool-shed, potting-shed, bicycle-shed, tricycle-shed, motor-bicycle-shed, greenhouse, conservatory, larder, kitchen, coal-shed, coke-shed, wood-shed, turf-shed, outhouse, bus-shelter, sun-room, garden-room, boiler-house, belfry, attic, barn, garret, box-room, sheepfold, beehive, dovecote, dog-kennel, cat-kennel, aviary, ape-house, or rocking-horse." But the plank is now beyond mending, as glue is forbidden by the food-police. It is all needed to stick the heads on the new synthetic fish.

* * *

At a hastily convened meeting held in the Boeotian Hall, delegates of nine branches of the see-saw Union decided to send a deputation to the Minister of Bubbleblowing to protest against the employment in England of Persian See-sawists, who are not members of the union. The Society for Cultural Relations with Persia at once protested. They claim that see-saw, as played by the Filthistan Trio, is the ancient Arvanian dance called zeezawa, described by Strabo, and shown in the Turanian tapestries at Mahallat. Mr. Colin Velvette, the great choreographile, goes as far as to see in this ceremonial dance the origin of the ballet.

Mr. Vormul Spoot, the eminent balletophobe, says that see-saw was never an integral part of ballet, but was a divertissement introduced by Mossbock into "The Three-Cornered Wheelbarrow" by the Hong Kong Saltimbanques for the Melbourne Festival of 1938.

By the way, let us never forget what the father of that illustrious leaper, Vestris, said of his son. "It seems to me that Auguste would be in the air all the time, if he were not afraid of humiliating his fellow-dancers."

Mrs. Rumpus, the Socialist Member for Bibney, asked the Minister of Bubbleblowing at question-time whether his attention had been drawn to reports that three Persian entertainers were trying to obtain a permit for a plank on which to play see-saw; whether, in view of the crisis in the affairs of the country, he thought this a favourable moment to encourage aliens to play see-saw in hotel vestibules; whether it was true that the version of see-saw played by these aliens was not the English version; and what steps he proposed to take to direct these Persian gentlemen into some activity connected with the export drive. The Minister was understood to say that his departmental experts were dealing with the matter.

Meanwhile:
"O Minister, we three get no further, please. We now have more forms, but since they all make large mention of lipfroog, of which we know nought, we cannot be of filling them, ho yes. Pardon, but of this delaying of our plank we lose gold, so how can we do an engagement for a hostel without our plank? Ho, hurry, Minister, by goodness sake, can you? Honourable Minister, we are true to you, ho yes.

Filthistan Trio."

* * *

Mr. Colin Velvette, producer of such ballets as "The Tub of Lard," "L'Oiseau sur le Chapeau de Nelly," "Adieu, Beau Fromage!" and "Sea Moonlight," is seriously considering the possibility of engaging the Filthistan Trio for his new production, "Iphigenia in Tauris."

Mr. Velvette said yesterday: "One definitely does so want rhythm in ballet, and these Persians are definitely rhythmic in their *soulèvements*, actually, if you know what I mean. One cares most frightfully about getting these things utterly right." Mr. Velvette is married to Konsatina Putimov (Agnes Griffith?) of the Peabody Opera Company, who did the famous double *glissade* on her elbows in "The Melancholy Brewers."

Mr. Velvette rang up the Trio yesterday.

MR. V.: Hullo.

KAZBULAH: Ho yes, please.

MR. V.: Is that the-er-Mr.-the Persian Trio?

KAZBULAH: It is but one of us. Mr. Minister, have you our plank?

MR. V.: Actually, I'm Velvette.

KAZBULAH: Is plank coming, O official?

MR. V.: I'm afraid there's a mistake. I have no planks. I——

KAZBULAH: Ring down! We want no other talk, ho yes.

* * *

Mr. Colin Velvette interviewed the three Persians yesterday in his office. But the moment he said "actually" (which he pronounced "ekchulah"), they broke into ribald laughter. "What's so funny?" he asked touchily. "Ekchulah," said Kazbulah. "Oh, very good, ho yes, where you have learned to speak Persian?" "Persian?" asked the astonished choreomane. "Ekchulah," replied Rizamughan, "is indeed very good Persian for manure. We laugh because you say 'manure'. Ho-ha, very funny." "I really had no intention of saying manure, actua——," began the perturbed montagiste. But the rest was drowned in peal after peal of happy laughter, as the dusky visitors held their sides and rolled their eyes.

* * *

The dark eyes of the three Persians were round with wonder as they listened to Mr. Colin Velvette telling them about the ballet in which he hoped they would appear.

He began, "Ekchu——," and just checked himself in time. "The scene," he said, "is a forest glade. The queen of the butterflies lies asleep. Enter a hunter——." "Tillyho!" cried Ashura. "Tintavy!" cried Kazbulah. "Foxy, foxy!" cried Rizamughan. They were all anxious to show that they understood. "The hunter," proceeded Velvette, "sees the sleeping queen, and adjusts his bow and arrow." The Persians exchanged incredulous grins. "It is fun," said Ashura, "lot of fun! This hunter is stalking booterflies and mooths with his bowanarrow, ho yes, bravo him!"

"Just as he is about to shoot," continued the choreographomane, "the Flower Chorus enters." The Persians gaped. "They surround the queen, protecting her, and the hunter cannot shoot." "Hath he no dogs?" asked Kazbulah, "wherewith to hunt this booterfly?" "No, no dogs," said Velvette patiently. "The Flower Valse is played—you know, Tchaikovsky." "We not know Choopovsky," said Rizamughan sulkily. "The Flower Valse is played," persisted Velvette, "and here I thought you three could form a colourful background of see-saw, ekchulah." The fatal word. How the three cheered, and shouted "Manure, ho yes!" until a high

executive official poked his head in and asked if there were a Farmers' Convention in progress.

* * *

Discouraged but pertinacious, Mr. Colin Velvette continued to explain his ballet to the gentlemen from Filthistan.

"The hunter," he said, "does not actua——" (a gleam in Kazbulah's eyes warned him just in time)— "does not really kill the Queen of the Butterflies." "Honly a wownd?" asked Ashura. "No," said Velvette. "It is symbolical, if you like." "Ho, we don't like it," said Rizamughan, "thank you, but if it is sombilical, wherefore the bowanarrow?" "It's mime," said Velvette. "Yours, ho yes?" asked Ashura. "Mime," repeated Velvette, "M-i-m-e." "Who's he?" cried all three. "Listen," said Velvette. "It is a like a fairy story, you see. The bow and arrow business is mime." "Ho yes, yours, and you give it to the hunter to slaughter the queen mooth," said Kazbulah.

"I think" said Velvette "that you might understand better if you saw a rehearsal in progress actually." Then came a great cry of delight, volleying and thundering, as the three Persians chanted, like some Eastern college cry, "Ekchulah! Ekchulah! Ekchulah! Long live manure, ho yes!" At that point a hairy stage manager, in a hairy brown suit, with a yellow tie covered with a pattern of red dogs, and a green shirt, poked his head in at the door. He said in a cold drawl, "One wonders why people have to keep on shouting manure. It's definitely worrying, Colin. We can hear it all over the building." The three Persians gazed at the intruder, and Rizamughan said, "He moost be sombilical. Cannot he have a haircutting?"

During the remainder of his conversation with the Persians Mr. Colin Velvette was considerably handicapped by constant attempts to avoid the word "actually," which, pronounced in his odd fashion, reminded the Trio of that homely word of their own. Mr. Velvette's task was made more difficult by the fact that this word constitutes a large proportion of his vocabulary. There were no

more accidents until Ashura said, "What is this daycor, please?" "Ekchulah," began the eminent calisthenictician, but the rest was lost in a tumult of laughter. The rhythmicologist winced. The Persians repeated the word to each other with increasing delight. When Velvette said, "Todays' conference is over," a concerted howl of "Ekchulah!" completed the sentence.

* * *

Mr. Colin Velvette led the three Persians to a corner of the stage, where a rehearsal was in progress. The hairy man in the hairy suit was shouting wearily. A shivering girl was standing on her toes with one hand in the air and the other on her hip, while a man in a leopard skin knelt at her feet, both arms stretched imploringly towards her. "He hath come for the rent, ho yes," said Ashura in a loud voice. "She reacheth for his hat," said Kazbulah. "It is sombilical once more," said Rizamughan. "They is neether of them there at all, except her." At that moment the girl began to pirouette on her toes, and the man rose and leaped in the air. The Persians roared with laughter.

A gloomy man stood up in the front row of the stalls. "Ekchulah," he said, "it isn't meant to be funneh, you know." "Manure!" cried the three, gleefully. "What?" said the astonished manager. "Manure, ho yes," repeated the three. "I don't get it," said the manager. "He doesn't get any," said Ashura. At that point, the hairy man intervened. "They always say manure," he explained. "But why, man?" replied the manager irritably. "It's a sort of habit, I suppose." "But what are they doing here? Who are they?" "They're here for that see-saw bit I thought of adding." "Well, we'll come to that later. You really must keep them quiet." "O.K.," said the hairy man.

* * *

Mr. Colin Velevette finally decided that the best place in which to introduce the see-saw was during the very beautiful scene in which Iphigenia, having been saved by Artemis from being sacrificed by her father, Agamemnon, dreams that her brother Orestes is dead.

(See Thumen: *Die Iphigeniensage in Antikem und Modernem Gewande*. Also Bothe and Kirchoff on Madvig's theory of the Tauric moon-goddess in *Kirchwasser Gehart von Diesen Euripidismus*, quoted in Borntraeger's *Analecta Euripidea*, Wicklein's edition of 1887; also Monk and Porson's commentary on the Nauck-Heimsoeth defence of the Stasimon and the Epeisodion.)

Said Mr. Velvette: "The butterfly episode and the Dance of the Flowers was merely a divertissement, and the appearance of a see-saw might set the wrong tone for what follows." The Persians bowed, and Kazbulah said: "When we play, sir, please not to promit your dauncers to ontifere us with all that kicking and jomping about. No dauncing hon our plonk ho yes." "They won't bother you," said Velvette. "Hart for hart's sake," said Ashura somewhat insconsequently. "Precisely," replied Velvette, merely to aid the conversation. "Who?" asked Rizamughan. "Precisely," repeated Velvette. "Very well," said Ashura, smiling amicably. "Procizely, too, if you pleace."

* * *

"The right thing for this see-saw interlude," said the hairy man, "is definitely the Barcarolle from Hoffman." "Who is Hoofman, please?" asked Ashura. "Oh, just Hoffman. Surely you've heard——" "There will be not room for Hoofman upon our plank, ho yes," said Rizamughan firmly, glancing at his companions. "Honly places for we three," said Kazbulah. "Command Hoofman to use his own plank, why not," said Ashura. "Listen," said the hairy man patiently. "Nobody is going to butt in on your plank. I'm talking about music. It's a piece of music." "What is?" inquired Kazbulah suspiciously. "Tales of Hoffman," shouted the hairy man. "Sir," said Rizamughan, "if Mr. Hoofman settles foot upon our plank, we walk forth. Is he belonging to the onion? We belong to no onion, ho yes." "We'd better leave it for a bit," said the hairy man.

One of the dancers was in a towering rage. "Do you think," she asked a flinching impresario, "that I come all the way from Moscow to get mixed up in see-saw? I am a dancer, not an acrobat"—(She lied. She was an acrobat or nothing)—"I am Tumbleova, I would have you know"—(She lied. She was Daisy Criggs of Dalston.) "And I know my job here," said the impresario—(He lied. He was merely a lump of money.) "I am Raoul de Galoche"—(He lied. He was Sidney Falconi, *alias* Fred Wivenhoe.) "It is an insult to my art," cried Daisy. (She lied. She had about as much art in her as a gasworks.) "And you are insulting me by questioning my authority to run my show as I please," retorted Fred. (He lied. He was far too vile for anything to be an insult to him.) So there we will leave them, while we take you over to Jixo Mockanugga's Swingaroo Six in a refined rendition of Moments with Beethoven.

* * *

The soft notes of the famous Barcarolle rent the air gently. On the stage the three Persians played see-saw. They ignored the music completely, and laughed and chattered loudly. "It's no good," said Velvette gloomily, "See-saw and ballet won't mix. No, no, NO!" he shouted from the stalls. "Yes, yes, ho YES!" shouted back the Trio. "We now do ballet," roared Kazbulah, striking an attitude. "Hoonting mooths," yelled Rizamughan, shading his eyes and searching the horizon. "Where are Hoofliganiera?" grunted Ashura, as he shifted the plank on his belly. "Poolerdees and Huristes," they cried in chorus, "O manager, send hon they dauncers, we like to be having a hordiunce." "Stop, stop!" called Velvette. The music ceased, but the see-saw went on.

* * *

The next rehearsal seemed to be going well. The dancers were doing their silly business, which was not unlike an exhibition of all-in wrestling by the executive officials of a Liberal Summer School. The see-saw was in full swing. But Mr. Velvette had not been warned of the weird chant that accompanies the game in Persia. Loud cries of "Bwa kijala! Bwa kijala bwa!" began to distract the dancers. Orestes, making a graceful dive for Iphigenia's waist, missed it, as she turned round towards the Persians, and the wretched fool measured his length on the floor. Pylades, who was to have caught Iphigenia when Orestes threw her at him, waited for the catch like an alert slip at Lords. Velvette rose in the stalls and shouted something which was drowned by the increasing noise of the chant. The Persians, unconscious of everything but their own fun, continued their see-sawing, while scene-shifters, carpenters, electricians, and dressers crowded on to the stage. Undoubtedly our dusky friends had stolen the show.

* * *

In the foreground Orestes and Pylades, with Iphigenia, and the Chorus grouped round them. In the background, Ashura, with the plank, painted crimson, laid across his belly. At either end, waiting to mount, Kazbulah and Rizamughan. All three are dressed in Greek costume, with fillets of ivy-leaves round their heads. At a word from Mr. Velvette the orchestra strikes up. The dance begins. Ashura is laughing so much that the plank shifts sideways, and catches one of the chorus a gentle tap on the hip. She stumbles forward into Orestes, who overbalances, dragging with him Pylades, whose legs trip Iphigenia and send her hurtling into the well of the orchestra. Rizamughan, springing to the rescue, gets a slap in the face. He steps back, knocking Kazbulah sideways into Iphigenia, who again falls into the orchestra pit. Velvette stops the rehearsal.

* * *

"Definitely," said Mr. Velvette, "you three must control that plank." "Pardon, please," replied Ashura, "it is they dancers which to be controlled. See how what occurred. We do not move. We await signals to begun, when, lo, a lady with small breeches and a gontleman in a nightdress begun to leaping up and down so near to my belly, ho yes, so I laugh, so plonk is shifted and catch a person bang on a leg, so she falls down." "I know, I know," replied Mr. Velvette. "But one does so feel that this plank must not interfere with the dances." "Sir manager, please," said Kazbulah angrily, "when hoondereds of persons in mad clothings honterfere with hus, we honterfere back, for how can see-saw be playing with a long crowd pushing amongst our plonk, ho yes?"

Tempers were rising. Rizamughan began to mutter. "You three," said Mr. Velvette, "seem to forget that it is the ballet that we must think of. The dancers are the important people, actually." At the sound of the well-known word the frowns became smiles. The three Persians beamed. "Ekchulah!" they cried. "Ho-ha, very good, manure!" shouted Ashura. "Most certainly pleese, Ekchulah!" shouted Rizamughan. "Long live manure! Three cheerings for manure!" shouted Kazbulah. And they cavorted and pranced round the embarrassed Mr. Velvette. "I think," said Pylades to Orestes, "Velvette is going mad." For answer came a ringing cry of "Ekchulah!"

Having decided to give the three Persians another chance, Mr. Colin Velvette devised a kind of interlude which would leave them the stage to themselves. "You represent," he said, "the incalculability of things." "Do we?" replied Ashura sulkily. "The ups and downs. The motion of the see-saw is symbolical of life with its changes and chances." The three exchanged glances. "O Manager," said Kazbulah, "last time we was of being sombilical they hath banged uggainst our plonk. We play a simple game, ho yes, and what is this oncolcability, please?" "Never mind," said Velvette. "Just play it as a game, with music, of course." "Not music, thanks," said Ashura. "My dear fellows," said Velvette, "you can't expect a ballet audience to watch a silent see-saw." "We was not caring," said Rizamughan, "if they watch." "Hall of them may go home," added Ashura grandly. "One feels you've got the wrong idea, actu-er-definitely," said Velvette.

* * *

Dear Sirs,

After consultation with Mr. Pemmico, I have reluctantly come to the conclusion that your see-saw turn, while admirable in itself is definitely not suited to serious ballet, actually. I hope that, when we bring into our repertory, later on, one or two lighter works, it may be possible to offer you a part in one of them. I regret this decision, but I am sure we can part in friendship.

Yours sincerely,
Colin Velvette.

* * *

O Mr. Velvette,

We think, we three, we was being a lot far more happier on the good old days which we was preforming in vostibules of luxuriant hostels, ho yes. What does not ogree with hus was all them crowd of dauncers honterfering about us, leaping up and twoddling above their toes like mad things, and making faces in the air, and kicking. We have never before saw such wonders, and they was rude to us. But we have replied mony a wicked Persian woard what they was not oonderstonding, ho yes, berneath hour breathing hov course for perliteness. O sir, thank you from hus three for oncerluding in youz goodbye document manure, but you spell wrong ekchulah. Whenhever we see that woard for the futcher we think hov you, ho yes. Hour love to Hofroginiera, ekchulah.

The Filthistan Trio, sir.

TIBETAN MOONFLOWER

Down the yak-track that winds from Shamatse-Bu to the sun-baked town of Dung rode Colonel Egham and Mr. D. J. Mince. The former was busy with bitter-sweet memories. The latter, with trade figures. For Mr. Mince, one of those dull men whose silence is mistaken for profound meditation, had no idea of what was before him. Egham had not dared to let him know that he was to meet, not the politicians and business men to whom he was so accustomed, but the toast of Asia, the dazzling, the incomparable Dingi-Poos. As they drew near Dung, Mince broke his silence. "Can we see our hotel from here?" he asked. "That large lump of mud on the left is the inn," replied Egham, "The Eight Monastery Bells." "Doesn't look up to much," said Mince. "It isn't up to much," replied Egham. And once more silence fell as they reached the first mud-walls of the town—not unobserved by the loveliest eyes in Tibet. For Dingi-Poos had received word from her retainers that the trade delegation was approaching. With an enigmatic smile she flung a sweet-meat to a pet marmot.

Note on Mr. Mince

Born 1902. Served on General Purposes Committee, and contributed to Report on Schedule Routine. Chairman of Bouncing Committee. Helped to prepare interim report on personnel. Member of Trade Delegation to Lofoten Islands. Secretary of Society for Cultural Integration. Member of Fish Inquiry Board. Sat on Zonal Committees in Bedfordshire, Monmouthshire, and Kent. Contributed to Overall Regional Plan. Served on Boskin Committee. Took part in flatiron talks with Argentine delegation. Sat on Tilfick Committee. Sat on Nubhurst Committee. Sat on Caltenach Committee. Gave evidence at fishball and eel products inquiry. Unmarried. Hobby: Statistics. Club: Junior Smoke-Abatement.

*   *   *

Mr. Mince was awakened by a large hairy animal, which had knocked down the thin wall of the cubicle where he and Egham were sleeping. The animal was blowing on his face, as though to cool it. "You've seen your first yak," said Egham sleepily. "Good," said Mince testily. After a breakfast of rancid butter and brick-tea, served by an old man covered with fluff, Mr. Mince began to put his papers together. He had little doubt that they would soon be summoned to the first meeting, and he wanted to have all the facts about the nuji-fields at his finger-tips. He was therefore somewhat surprised when an enormous woman shouted, "Chani-yud!" in the doorway, and delivered to Egham a note so highly perfumed that the beetles dropped senseless from the broken ceiling. Egham seemed to be the prey of some violent emotion as he read the note. "She wants us to start business this evening," he said. Mr. Mince's idea of the woman he was about to meet had been based on his recollections of Mrs. Scadder of the Crockery Board, and he was a little disconcerted by the perfume, and by his companion's heightened colour and foolish manner. With a shrug, he concentrated his attention on his work.

*   *   *

Across the forecourt of the summer residence of Dingi-Poos walked Colonel Egham and Mr. D. J. Mince, each carrying a neat black attaché case. "To get this deal settled," said Mince, "a lot will depend on her figure." Egham, whose mind was not on the negotiations, replied dreamily: "You won't find anything to complain of in her figure!" "I hope you're right," said Mince, "but we've had no hint yet. It was a good nuji-harvest, I believe. That may make her tough with us." "A dark, wild rose," said Egham softly. "*What?*" snapped Mince, wondering if the sun had affected his chief. "Sorry," said Egham, "I was thinking of something else." Presently they came through a great marble entrance into a vast hall, and Mince began to picture the usual austere conference room, the big table, the pens, ink and paper, the chairs. And at the table the usual delegates and secretaries. And this woman Dingi-Poos—a fussy little business woman, he supposed. A girl in what looked like a golden night-gown conducted them across the hall to a large door. The door opened wide—and Mr. D. J. Mince gasped.

*   *   *

It seemed to Mr. Mince that he had walked not into a Conference room, but into some stage representation of the Arabian Nights. He saw a vast room, dimly lit by aromatic torches in golden sconces. The walls were covered with richly glowing Persian tapestries, and on the floor were spread costly carpets of ancient design. A low divan, bejewelled, and with casters of pure chrysoprase, was placed near a bronze Moorish lamp, so that the light fell mysteriously on the occupant. A beautiful young woman, dressed in some shimmering silver material, slashed with scarlet, reclined on the divan, one hand under her perfectly moulded chin. If she had arranged herself to create an impression, she could not have done it more cunningly. Her eyes, which were on Egham, were mocking, and the smile which played about her parted lips drew an involuntary cry from her old suitor. Mr. D. J. Mince felt as though he had been caught looking at questionable pictures on a South Coast pier. He dropped his eyes and shifted his feet. And then he heard Egham introducing him.

*   *   *

Dingi-poos languidly extended her exquisitely manicured hand to Mr. D. J. Mince. Mr. Mince was about to grasp it, English fashion. But Egham whispered "Kiss it." As he brushed the fingers clumsily with his lips he noticed, as he said afterwards, that "she seemed to be wearing a remarkably scanty evening dress, although it was only 10.30 in the morning." Egham and Dingi-Poos then talked together, and Mr. Mince sat himself down awkwardly on a pile of large cushions and consulted his papers. Presently he heard the lady say: "Your friend is the strong, silent type of Englishman, is he not?" He felt himself blushing, and when she said: "Come and talk to me," he approached the divan with the air of a schoolboy who is going to be birched. "You are shy," she said in a low voice. "Tell me about yourself." And then the clever woman talked to him about herself so interestingly that he thought he was being brilliant every time he uttered a monosyllable. Egham, watching the scene, began to grow angry. "What about a conference?" he asked. But there was no reply. Mr. D. J. Mince had become human. Dingi-Poos was at her old tricks.

* * *

"Do you think," said Mince, "that I ought to see her alone, to put the figures before her?" "No," replied Egham. "I think I'd better see her first, to give her a general idea of the thing." "I promised her I'd look in this afternoon," said Mince. "She asked me, too," said Egham. "Are you going?" "Are you?" asked Mince. "Well, n-no. I rather think not. Are you?" "I might," said Mince. "Oh, I might look in," said Egham. "We haven't got very far yet," said Mince. "How do you mean?" said Egham sharply. "I mean with the negotiations," replied Mince. "What else could I have meant?" "Nothing else, of course," said Egham peevishly. Both men's nerves seemed to be on edge. They darted glances at each other, and neither of them said a word about the lady—until Egham asked casually, "What do you think of her?" "Who?" asked Mince. "Dingi-Poos." "Oh, I haven't had time to think about her. This draft of the proposed agreement, you know——." "You hideous liar," said Egham under his breath.

* * *

Dingi-Poos cared about as much for the British waterproof typewriter covers, which Egham succeeded in mentioning at the eighth interview, as she cared for the snouts of rocking-horses. In fact, she said irritably: "Didn't your Government tell you that we don't use typewriters?" "Then what are we here for?" cried the exasperated Mr. D. J. Mince. Dingi-Poos tilted her head sideways and regarded him with languid amusement. "That's not for me to say," she answered with mock schoolgirl modesty. "Even if we wanted the covers," she continued, "you wouldn't want the nuji-beans. They're inedible. We use them as fuel." "Couldn't *we* use them as fuel?" asked Egham. "This," said Dingi-Poos, picking a speck of dust off his ear, "is a food conference, not a fuel conference." She spoke so softly that Egham leaned involuntarily towards her. "Tck, tck, tck," went Mr. Mince.

*　　*　　*

Egham was beside himself with delight when he was handed a little note asking him to look in on Dingi-Poos for a quiet chat—"Just the two of us, like old times." He did not know that Mr. Mince had also received an invitation, for an earlier hour—("I thought you might care to relax from business worries. I would show you the gardens"). As Egham arrived, he thought he saw someone going out by a back door—someone rather like Mr. Mince. "Impossible," he said to himself, "she hardly knows him." What would Egham have said if he had known that Mr. Mince had cried "Call me Duncan!" but a few minutes before, and that Dingi-Poos had replied, "Duncan! What a beautiful name!" Egham found her reclining on the usual divan, but as he stooped to smother her hand in burning kisses, he noted, peeping from under a cushion, a small wallet marked D.J.M.

With elaborate sarcasm Egham said, pocketing the wallet: "I wonder who D.J.M. can be?" "Duncan must have left it behind," said Dingi-Poos with maddening serenity. "Duncan!" shouted Egham. "So he's Duncan to you already, is he? You're a fast worker." "You ought to know," replied the recumbent siren. "He's not the marrying kind, I may tell you," said the infuriated warrior. "I should worry!" riposted the nonchalant beauty. Egham pouted. "Are you here," inquired the impudent charmer, "to talk of nuji-beans, or to interfere in my private affairs?" "Neither," said the sulky colonel. "I thought we were to have a pleasant tête-à-tête." "And who spoiled it? Is it my fault if men find me attractive?" Something deep down in Egham whispered: "Of course it is." But a wave of emotion surged over him, and falling on his knees beside the divan, he poured out a torrent of wild endearments which flowed off her back like water.

*   *   *

Mr. D. J. Mince appeared to Egham to be strutting about with all the insolent complacency of a successful suitor. "I think she'll do a deal with us over the beans," he said. "But they're inedible," said Egham. "What isn't today?" countered Mr. Mince. "They could be called powdered meat or something." "And what makes you think she'll change her mind?" Mr. Mince smiled. "I think she and I understood each other," he replied pompously. "Yes," said Egham savagely. "Everyone who meets her goes through that stage." Mr. Mince frowned. "Are you hinting that she is frivolous in affairs of the heart?" he asked. "Or are you merely annoyed that she should like me?" Egham assumed a dignified air. "I think this is all rather childish and unworthy of trade delegates," he said. "Maybe," said Mr. Mince, "but I will lay my cards on the table. I hope to make her Mrs. Mince." "You will live and learn," replied Egham sadly.

*   *   *

Dingi-Poos, swathed in a one-sided smock of green snakeskin, reclined on a large scarlet cushion. Her old nurse, Moompi, stood beside her. "Are you serious about this Mr. Mince?" asked the nurse. "My dear nanny!" cried the toast of Asia, "he's a bigger ass than Egg." "Then what is your game?" Dingi-Poos disclosed the whitest teeth north of latitude 64 in a dazzling smile. "I want to get them both into such a state," she said, "that they won't inquire too closely into what they are signing. I could get rid of any amount of their waterproof typewriter cases at a good price, but they'll only get a couple of yak-farms or something like that in exchange—and not the nuji fields they are expecting." "My baby, my clever little girl," said the old nurse with revolting sentimentality.

*   *   *

The fatuous old nurse, Moompi, was very busy these days, letting in Egham at one door, letting out Mince at another, and seeing that the two visitors never crashed into each other. For the Witch of Dung was playing her cards cleverly. She had Egham on his knees at least once a day, and even permitted him to fondle her left ear. Mince, on the other hand, was allowed to kiss her cheek ("Don't spoil our friendship, Duncan," as the infatuated Mince aimed a frenzied salutation at her inviting lips). Each man began to think he was the favoured suitor and therefore each became more complacently insolent to the other. And then, came a complication. An old flame from the Altai Mountains arrived—a wealthy merchant. Poor old Moompi, who began to feel like a juggler who is keeping three plates in the air, had to fit this newcomer into the general scheme of back doors and private staircases. Only once did the time-table go wrong, when a native landowner had to be hidden in Moompi's linen-cupboard until the merchant had gone.

*   *   *

It was Egham's hour. Never had he seen her in more yielding mood. He held her hand in his, and he was so accustomed to having it snatched away that he couldn't think what to do with it. So he pressed it meaningly. Slowly she met his gaze, her large eyes, still as forest pools, seeming to encourage him to hope once more. "My Tibetan moonflower," he murmured, drawing her towards him. "Can it be that you love me at last?" Dingi-Poos, who was listening for Moompi's signal on the wall to say that time was up, did not answer. Egham became more daring. His arms were round her. He was about to rain kisses on her upturned face when she heard the two low taps on the wall, which meant that Mr. D. J. Mince had arrived. Gently she repulsed the warrior. "You are so impetuous," she said. "It grows late. I must feed my canaries. Return tomorrow, dear Egg." "For my answer?" "Who knows?" she replied tauntingly. And she pushed him gently out of a side-door. Moompi immediately opened a secret panel in the wall, and in stepped Mr. D. J. Mince.

*　　　*　　　*

It was Mr. Mince's hour. Never had he seen her in more yielding mood. "Duncan," she breathed. "My prairie rose," responded the spellbound bureaucrat. And as she nestled in his arms, listening for the signal on the wall that would announce the merchant (or the landowner), he began to picture their life together in Carshalton. "It will be different from this," he said. "But we shall be together," murmured the entrancing beauty. "My bit of almond blossom," said Mince. Knock, knock went Moompi on the wall. "It grows late, and I must consider my reputation," said Dingi-Poos. Sliding back a panel, she pushed him through. But Moompi was gesticulating frantically. It was Egham back again, and on his heels the merchant. The footling old nurse had just time to push Mince into a linen-cupboard and put Egham in a larder. She then showed the merchant in to Dingi-Poos— and the landowner arrived. She transferred Egham to the linen-cupboard. "You!" shouted Mince. "You!" roared Egham.

In the hot linen-cupboard, with sheets, pillow-slips, and towels tangled in their legs and arms, the two men cursed each other. "I'd only come to persuade her to sign," said Egham. "Why, so had I," said Mince. At that moment the landowner was pushed in by Moompi, who had begged him to share the cupboard with two English noblemen until her mistress was disengaged. "You are pardoon," said the landowner. "Big you are pardoon, how do, no?" "Who are you?" growled Egham with a towel sagging over his head. "Sumatse Swo," said the landowner, flattening himself against the shelves. "What's he gabbling about?" asked Mince, dragging his foot out of a pillowslip. Then silence fell, and after half an hour Moompi released the three sweating and exhausted suitors. The landowner was shown in to Dingi-Poos, and as Egham and Mince left by a side door, they saw the merchant lowering himself from a scullery window. "This place is full of people," said Egham discontentedly. "Business men," said Mince. "I hope so," said Egham.

*　　　*　　　*

Egham and Mince, summoned to conclude the business concerned with the nuji fields, found their hostess in a sentimental mood. Each thought he was the favoured suitor, and each was winking at her behind the other's back. Dingi-Poos, who had sold the nuji fields to the landowner, and been offered a good price for the waterproof typewriter covers by the merchant (acting for a Chinese firm), was thoroughly enjoying herself. To make sure of swindling the infatuated pair, she had brought up from her cellars an 80-year-old bottle or two of Clos de Lhasa, queen of Tibetan Burgundies. There was also a bottle of fiery josh-brandy, made of fermented yaks' milk, josh berries steeped in coasu, rancid butter, marata, and vengi-juice. "Is this stuff very strong?" asked Egham. "It has a kick like a moth," replied Dingi-Poos disarmingly, "you can swill it down by the bucket-full." Then she added, in more lady-like manner, "There's not a headache in a barrel of it."

*　　　*　　　*

Dingi-Poos had determined to make quite sure of getting the water-proof typewriter covers for nothing. Hence the display of drink. She had also attempted to introduce an atmosphere of business into the luxurious apartment in which she had received the two gowks. For instance, a bejewelled fountain pen lay invitingly on a 12th century macaw-inlaid Annamese table. Dingi-Poos herself was dressed in a simple one-piece redingote which left her back, sides, arms, shoulders, and legs bare. She had given orders to that asinine old nurse Moompi that not even the merchant or the landowner was to be admitted. Furthermore, she now began to hum an old Tibetan love-song, her snake-like hands rippling across the keys of a golden pianoforte from Chocho. And as she played, she glanced provokingly over her shoulder at the two delegates. Mince, thinking of home, wondered how she would go down with his Aunt Charlotte at Weston-super-Mare.

As a matter of historical curiosity, here is the song Dingi-Poos was singing:

Lhata-mul Tsari
Thakpo yuli, bo.

This is repeated as often as you please—or, rather, as often as the singer pleases. It means: "If you come to Tsari, bring your own rice, beloved."

*   *   *

Dingi-Poos clapped her hands. An old footman in a pointed straw hat brought in another bottle of josh-brandy. Mince's speech was growing thick. Egham's eyes were looking seven ways to Sunday. Their heartless hostess watched them as a starving boa watches a brace of rabbits. Presently she pointed to a table at her side. "Shall we get the tiresome signing over?" she asked. "Jolly old sign-igning," said Mince, jerking his head forward violently. "Signature tune," said Egham, with a foolish giggle. Dingi-Poos held out the pen. "Wa-one little kiss first, eh?" said Mince. "Business before pleasure," replied Dingi-Poos. "Pleasuresallmine," said Egham, trying to catch hold of the pen. "Better see what it says," he added. Dingi-Poos frowned, and withdrew the document. "You don't trust me," she said. "Kisses before pleasure," said Mince, ogling the lady. "Oh, let's sign all this rubbish," said Egham and took the pen.

*   *   *

Dingi-Poos, in sentimental mood, was singing an old Tibetan air, accompanying herself on the duz, a kind of five stringed zlopa. Behind her, bending over her and breathing down her neck like a couple of horses, stood Mince and Egham. The josh-brandy had gone further to their heads, and they nodded foolishly out of time to the music. Egham wagged his fore-finger, as though he were conducting. Mince shut his eyes and hummed, and nearly fell over backwards. When the song ended, Dingi-Poos rose, and as each man grabbed at her, she sidestepped, leaving them with bleeding noses. Her low, mocking laughter came to them from the bamboo-inlaid escritoire at the other side of the room. They slithered to the floor and fell into a profound sleep. Dingi-Poos blew a high note on a long trumpet, and her attendants bore away the bodies of our two heroes to the Chigwe airfield, where a plane awaited them.

The plane, piloted by a sulky Himalayan, was slightly west of Cape Shagarola (lat. 64, long. 326), 934 miles from Tibet, when Colonel Egham and Mr. D. J. Mince struggled out of their drunken sleep. "We took a drop too much of that brandy stuff," said Egham. "Drop is a mild word," said Mince ruefully, "and to think that she called me Duncan!" "If it comes to that," said Egham, "she's been calling me Egg for years. Where has it got me?" "Well, anyhow," replied Mince, "we've pulled off our deal. The last thing I remember is the signatures." "That's true," said Egham, "though I'm rather vague about clauses and things. I don't seem to remember much discussion about the delivery of the nuji beans. Let's take a look at the document." The Colonel pulled out his despatch case, opened it, and drew out an official-looking sheet of paper. Then he turned pale and uttered a low moan. "Look at this!" he groaned.

The sheet of paper bore these words:
Give my love to each other.

Dingi-Poos.

NOTHING TO DO WITH ME

Dear Sir,

Your Correspondent, Mrs. Marsham, is very sarcastic about elephants. May one ask how she would like to have a Maharajah and his suite sitting on her back under a canopy in the jungle, with their guns cluttered all over her, and their luncheon wine trickling into her ears, and curry dropping all over the place, and native beaters gabbling Indian and swinging from her nose and courtiers, statesmen, distinguished foreign visitors and Indian villagers wiping their turbans on her legs? Eh?

Yours faithfully,
(Mrs.) Daisy Mockpudding.

Dear Sir,

Mrs. Mockpudding's ludicrous travesty of Indian life is no answer to my complaint about elephants, and merely reveals her innate ignorance of what goes on in the entourage of a Maharajah. No beater would swing from an elephant's trunk in the presence of the Ruler of his State. If Mrs. Mockpudding had lived in India, as I have, she would not be so fond of elephants. Perhaps their size appeals to her. And if a recent photograph of Mrs. Mockpudding judging the cake-weighing at a village hall does her anything like justice, size is one thing she has in common with elephants; that, and a tendency to trumpet stupidly.

Yours truly,
(Mrs.) Elspeth Marsham.

Dear Sir,

Mrs. Mockpudding has started a mare's—or an elephant's—nest. Her idea of this beast, and I use the word in no derogatory sense, is a Westerner's idea of all things Oriental. There is no proof that an elephant dislikes having a Maharajah on its back. Sentimentalists forget that the elephant is pretty big, and capable of supporting a burden which to, say, Mrs. Mockpudding would be a great strain. Anyhow, Indian education has more pressing problems to solve than this matter of age-old routine, and I trust that the India Office will not be deflected from its constructive task by such red herrings (in the form of elephants) as Mrs. Mockpudding drags across the long, long trail of our Imperial destiny.

Yours truly,
Carrie Ravensfoot.

Dear Sir,

Several of your correspondents seem to have the old Victorian idea of India as a place full of Maharajahs on elephants covered with spilt curry and rare luncheon wines. For 48 years I lived in Butteragong, and I can safely say that I never saw a Maharajah having lunch on an elephant. I never even saw an elephant, until I came home on leave and took my nephew to the Zoo. Wine I never saw, either. Curry, yes, but not what we mean by curry. No good is done by misrepresenting Mother India to the ignorant public.

Yours truly,
Ronald D. Lashforth.

Dear Sir,

How would Mrs. Mockpudding cure an elephant's hiccoughs? My uncle, when up country, used to make the beast drink backwards from a tilted bucket with a rusty axe in it. But this never had any effect. When down country, he tried the same cure, with the same negative result.

Yours truly,
Ernestine Falcon.

Dear Sir,

Whatever Miss Falcon saw with the hiccoughs, it was not an elephant. They don't have them. If they did they would blow the Maharajahs clean off their backs, and the native beaters would think that India had been invaded by gigantic cuckoos.

Another point, for Mrs. Mockpudding. Comparatively speaking the weight of a Maharajah on an elephant's back is no more than the weight of a bluebottle on Mrs. Mockpudding's nose—no offence.

Yours truly,
Gertrude la Force.

Dear Sir,

Miss la Force's letter is merely vulgar. A bluebottle is not a Maharajah, and my nose is not an elephant. I can flip the bluebottle off my nose when I please, but the elephant can't flip the Maharajah off its back, because the native beaters are armed to the teeth. The parallel would be more striking if, which is not the case, of course, armed men shot me every time I tried to dislodge the bluebottle. But even so the comparison is far-fetched.

Yours truly,
Daisy Mockpudding.

Dear Sir,

It seems to me very silly that Miss Falcon should contribute to a question of curing elephants' hiccoughs by giving a prescription which she admits did not work in any part of India. Anybody can suggest things that would not cure hiccoughs. Miss Falcon belongs to that tiresome type which, unable to be constructive, is always ready with expedients which achieve nothing but the opposite.

Yours truly,
Gwendolen Babbling.

Dear Sir,

Mrs. Marsham and Mrs. Mockpudding are vainly beating the air. The question is not what either of them would do if she were an elephant, but whether elephants are maltreated in India. The suggestion that it is cruel of a Maharajah to sit on an elephant's back is a childish one, and the talk of wine and curry splashing over its hide is mere music-hall vulgarity. There are far smaller animals worse treated—e.g., the Indian beetle—without any voice being raised in their defence.

Yours truly,
Ada Rockett.

Dear Sir,

Miss Rockett, in her reference to the ill-treatment of Indian beetles, seems to hint that in other countries beetles are well treated. This is not so. I have before me the figures for beetle-mortality in twenty-six countries. They are, owing to the difficulties caused by the war, incomplete, but they show that the numbe for beetles which die a natural death is very small. Unless there is a very different attitude adopted to beetles after this war, all our fine words about planning and reconstruction will be proved to be humbug and hypocrisy. The beetle cannot speak for itself. This is the hour, for those who care, to speak for it.

Your faithfully,
Raymond Bickering.

Dear Sir,

I was much interested in the letters you published about elephants in India. We of Swindon have an Elephant Protection Society. We circularise Maharajahs and others, and we endeavour to get questions asked in Parliament. Mrs. McQuacking, our chairman, is known in Anglo-Indian circles as the Elephant's Friend, and if Mrs. Mockpudding can give us actual facts, with dates and photographs of natives swinging from the trunks of elephants and Princes dropping wine and curry over the beasts, we will forward the documents to the India Office, and send copies to the newspapers.

Yrs. truly,
Mabel Blood.
(*This correspondence is now closed.*)

TWENTY YEARS OF UPROAR

Italian baritone Mariano Stabile puts on his 21-year-old wicker-work stomach to play Falstaff. He and his wife made it in Cairo in 1927, when his old one burst.

This is not the fumes of my imagination, wreathing like smoke among the stars.

It is copied, word for word, from a newspaper cutting sent to me, with the obvious comment that the only hat to go with such a stomach is a little round wickerwork one. Would that I had been in my stall when the old stomach burst. Probably the conductor thought the drum had come in in the wrong place.

I wonder if the lady who was singing with Signor Stabile had time to murmur, in between the singing, "I say! Your stomach's burst." "I know, but it's not real." See-ee how the dawn *hold it up with your hands* comes o'er the mountain crest *I can't, the tape's broken* Aaand when my heart *chuck it into the wings* beats to hear thy footfaaaal *my breeches would come away with it*—Soft-ly the gentle spring *another time don't fasten your stomach to your breeches* . . .

———

At a concert in the *Conservative Royal de Musique* in Brussels, Sprautz had just begun to conduct Dvorak's New World Symphony when a kindly thought occurred to him. Turning to the audience, while still waving his baton, he shouted: "Stop me if you've heard this one!"

———

A critic who complained that a man went to sleep and snored all through a tenor's song at the Opera, does not realise how much worse the situation might have been. Some years ago a prolonged yell from the tenor awoke a sleeper. "This must be my station," he muttered, and pushed his way out, shouting, "Porter! Por—ter!"

———

While singing the part of Lombata in Sporco's *La Verruca* Rustiguzzi had to faint and be carried by Broccoli into a nearby castle. But it was discovered at rehearsals that the most Broccoli could do with his burden was to unclamp, as it were, one massive leg from the ground. So it was arranged that a platoon of the Duke's footmen should take over from him, and Sporco was persuaded to write a special bit of music, based on an old folk-melody of the log-haulers of Pistoia. But one night the footmen were laughing so much that they dropped her. She had to be dragged into the wings, while a ribald audience roared the Volga Boatmen's Song—Aa-ha-haa-haaa, aa-ha-haa-haaa!

CHARLIE SUET

The admirable C. Suet, Esq., speaking at Nuneaton on the Huge Four Year Investment Programme, astonished his audience by his command of tumble-cum-trivy.

Some said that he had got all his facts wrong, but had put them in the right place. Others said that by transposing his facts he made the whole affair clearer than it was before.

Suet began by saying that if invisible imports were adjusted to invisible exports, the mechanisation of home production would mean a higher rate of investment abroad, particularly if non-dollar resources were used to decrease foreign consumption. At this point the chairman leaned over and spoke to Suet, who glanced quickly at his notes, laid his right fore-finger along his upper lip and breathed down his nose.

Suet went on to say that to close the gap in the balance of payments sterling should be devalued. There was a gasp from the audience. "Revalued," said Suet with a grin. He then continued: "There is no harm in an adverse trade balance if it is due to the import of goods which we do not require, or to the export of goods which other countries do not require. By redeployment of man-power industrial output can be lowered to such an extent that it becomes an invisible asset, to set against distribution."

When C. Suet, Esq., sat down there were a few lukewarm cheers, "but many people were puzzled," says the *Economist*.

Questions followed. Asked what he meant by invisible exports, Suet said: "Speaking widely and in general, invisible exports are those which we do not see." "Ghosts?" suggested an intellectual. Suet nodded. Asked what he meant by industrial output, Suet said: "Taken by and large, I should say it means the output of any given industry or group of industries in relation to the goods which they are putting out." He added quickly: "It is basically a fiscal matter." Asked what was the "flattening out" in the graph of industrial productivity, Suet paused a moment and then said: "Broadly speaking it is a levelling process, not unconnected with economic factors."

I am often asked, "What is this man Suet really like?" One word would describe him—if I didn't get paid more for several hundred—"Dynamic".

If you go into his office, you see, seated behind an enormous desk, kept absolutely empty, a ferocious, tall, thin, pale man of forty-two, with untidy dull brown hair, small reddish eyes and a lumpy nose. On a second desk, at which Charlie's uncle sits, are 31 telephones, two dictaphones, 12 bell-pushes, a wireless-set, a gramophone and a photograph (in a large silver frame) of Charlie and his uncle playing halma in Boulogne in 1937. The telephones are always in use, and as Charlie never stops talking, his uncle finds difficulty in answering the calls.

Charlie deals with everything at once, and nobody at the other end of any of the telephones ever knows whose question is being answered. When he is not telling his uncle what to say, or talking to himself or to a visitor, Charlie is sticking coloured pins and pegs in all the maps which cover the walls. On these maps England is divided into 4,037 districts and sub-districts. Charlie's desk has no papers on it. Everything is done by telephone and when there is a rush Charlie's uncle calls in several girls from the secretarial room and tells them what to say. The great difficulty is to get Charlie himself to stop talking while poor uncle, like a man playing the zither, darts up and down the desk from one telephone to another, bumping into irritated secretaries who are trying to help.

BIOGRAPHY

OUR HERO, Charlie Suet, was born in the tiny Cornish village of Polwaddle-in-Tretoothpic. His father, Henry Suet, was a humble fisherman who lived in a gem of Victorian architecture justly famed as the smallest house in England.

It was the house in which Henry had been born, and to it he brought his very large bride, Amanda Coopstake, of Balmoral, Chesney-St-Vitus, Bedfordshire. In attempting to carry her over the miniature threshold, Henry Suet cracked her head against the coping, and laughed heartily at the omen. She bore the mark to the day of her death.

When Charlie was born she pleaded with her husband to build on to their home, but he replied that there wasn't enough to build on from.

A chance encounter at Weymouth with an aged mariner who kept a model ship in a bottle turned Charlie Suet's thoughts to this humble occupation. He made a dainty ship, but every time he tried to push it into the bottle he smashed the yards and tore the sails.

Finally he overcame the difficulty by inserting into the bottle a very small canoe made of match-ends glued together. He gave the whole thing an original turn by leaving on the bottle the label, which said 'Rampounde's Pale Foamy Ale'. He exhibited his work on the promenade, but nobody took much notice of it—chiefly because the canoe was too small to see, and they thought he was some eccentric, advertising beer.

Encouraged by this experience, C. Suet, Esq., obtained work with a clockmaker. At the end of three days the clockmaker, a Mr Towelbird, said, 'I have never met anyone like him for pulling clocks to bits. He is the best man I ever had for that branch of work. But he doesn't ever seem to put them together again. That side of the work apparently doesn't interest him. When I said to him. "Where is that grandfather clock you took to pieces for Sir Stephen Blood?" he said, "Ah, I know all about it now", and made no further reference to the matter. When I was forced to get rid of him he said ruefully, "I didn't just want to mend clocks. I wanted to get behind the inner workings." So we parted rather coldly.'

An eccentric peer, hearing of Charlie Suet's passion for knowledge, said, 'His energies must be curbed. He will never keep any job. He should devote himself to the study of abstract knowledge, and to do this he must withdraw from the world.'

So he sent for C. Suet, Esq., and informed him that he would place at his disposal a three-roomed cottage in a lonely part of the Cheviots, where he could pursue knowledge without financial worries or mundane contacts. Suet accepted, not knowing what the peer was talking about. On a bitter winter's night he arrived at the cottage with his carpet bag. He had no idea what he was supposed to study, and he nearly froze to death. On the second night he took the roof off to see what it was made of. Next day, with a bad chill, he decamped.

We next hear of the incomparable Suet in a public library on the outskirts of London. He said to the head librarian, 'I don't just want to know what people write. I want to see how the books are put together and bound.' With this purpose in view Charlie began to ignore those who asked for books, and spent all his time in pulling volumes to pieces and examining the fragments under his microscope (the gift of a foolish aunt). There were naturally complaints, and the whole affair came to a climax when an old gentleman who had asked for the Victoria *History of Surrey* found one hundred and seventy-nine pages torn out of Volume II.

C. Suet, Esq., was given his marching orders.

As an attendant at the Stockport Municipal Baths Charlie Suet was a resounding failure. To find out where the water came from he scraped a large hole in the side of the bath, carried it through the outer wall, and flooded the street outside. When dismissed he said, 'I didn't just want to see how municipal baths are run, and how people swim about. I wanted to know how the water got there.'

Influence secured for the man Suet a post in a well-known picture gallery. 'This,' said his friends, 'will give him a chance to study art—or, as he would put it, to find out what is behind art.' And indeed Suet's first words, on being presented with his uniform, were, 'I don't just want to look at pictures. I want to find out what—'

'I know, I know,' interrupted the proprietor petulantly.

On his first day Charlie stayed late. The proprietor admired his zeal and devotion to duty, and left him to lock up. Charlie at once got to work to discover what was behind art. Daylight found him amid a pile of canvases which had been taken out of their frames, scratched with a penknife, and thoroughly investigated. By ten o'clock he had handed in his uniform and keys.

Charlie Suet's passion for acquiring knowledge, writes Miss Dredger, led him along strange paths. He once took a job as a nightwatchman at a large factory where water-tube steam-generating boilers were made.

On his second night he yielded to his old temptation and began to meddle. He had the whole place to himself, and it was not long before he had pressed a small button. Then things began to happen. A horizontal electric steam churn-belt slid rapidly along towards a super super-heater. This started a 250,000-horse-power pressure-boiler, and almost at once a hydraulic riveting machine burst its multi-drum geared rollers. There was a bright flash.

Next day Charlie Suet was sacked.

Charlie Suet was very fond of an evening at the theatre. He was not in the least interested in plays or in acting, but he had a theory that the seats could be made more comfortable. So, whenever he had the money, he would purchase a stall for an evening performance.

He always brought with him his bag of tools, and as soon as the lights were lowered, he would set to work on his stall, humming and whistling happily as he sawed and filed and planed and hammered. The management usually protested, in response to the complaints of his neighbours, during the first interval. And after Charlie had been asked to leave, a man had to come and clear up the bits of wood and nails and screws.

In the case of the noisier and more rowdy operas he was often able to work even through the intervals, thanks to the din in the stalls. His record was three stalls sawn in half and painted bright yellow on a Wagner night.

Suet's next job was as a toast-master. He had a resonant voice and a good appearance. But at his first banquet he got to work on the back of the chairman's tail-coat. When the chairman rose to propose a toast his coat came in two, the seam down the back having been picked open. His braces had been severed, and down fell his breeches with a surprising swish. Furthermore, Suet had done something to his collar, which came off the shirt. There were titters all over the room, but Charlie kept on shouting, 'Pray silence for your chairman', and finally the toast was proposed by the rubicund, indignant gentleman, who grasped his breeches in both hands in a manful effort to preserve his dignity.

Charlie Suet was once employed at a telephone exchange, but his interest in the mechanical side of the business exceeded his interest in the needs of the subscribers. At the end of his first spell of duty nine Kensington subscribers, all of whom had asked for London numbers, were amazed to find themselves talking to a dye works in Scotland. Flashes of blue light terrified his fellow-workers, as he pulled things to bits. 'No man,' he said, 'can do his job thoroughly until he has mastered what lies behind the machinery of it.' By tea-time he had melted down his earphones on a small stove. But it was only when he began to take the switchboards to pieces that the controller asked him to go. 'Any fool,' said Charlie, 'can get a telephone number, but it takes brains to find out the why and the wherefore.'

A report in the files of a certain railway company says: 'The idea of entrusting such an individual with the delicate operation of testing the wheels of train-coaches was little short of madness.' This sentence refers to Charlie Suet's short-lived career as a wheel-tapper in the west of England. On his first day he knocked seven wheels to pieces, thus disorganizing traffic on the line and doing considerable damage. It was only when he smashed the hammer that he reported his misadventures to the station-master.

He wrote recently to the Ministry of Supply offering as waste paper 43,726 perforation holes which he had cut out of tear-off calendars. An official said, 'But if they are perforation holes, they are just holes, and not paper at all.' Charlie replied that when cutting the holes out he was compelled to leave little bits of the paper round them, otherwise there would be nothing left. When he said that if there was not enough paper he could paste small circular bits over the holes, the official screamed twice and fell to the floor with a sickening thud.

'There the matter rests at present,' commented an unimpeachable neutral spokesman in touch with authoritative circles.

At a theatre the other night Charlie Suet decided to salvage a good deal of metal. He stealthily cut off thousands of trouser buttons, thus rendering the braces useless. At the final curtain, the hoosh of falling trousers was mistaken by the leading lady for hissing. She left the stage in hysterics and the male members of the audience did their best to hold up their breeches while making for the exit. Many a man was forced to wear his shirt outside his waistcoat, while using his braces as a belt.

THE CASE OF THE FALSE BEARD

The present position in the Beard Case, which is the talk of the town, is that the Hotel Gorgeous is suing Beards Ltd., who are suing the L.C.C. The man who borrowed the beard is suing the Despard Glue Quarries, who supplied the glue for the false beard. Mrs. Tuft-Calvally, who was in the swing-door when the beard caught in it, and gave her a stinging flip on the mazzard, is suing the Hotel Gorgeous, and Miss Varge, who laughed at her and tugged the beard clear of the door. A clergyman named Umbold has decided to intervene, and the L.C.C. is suing him for intervention. Mr. Justice Cocklecarrot said yesterday, "All these cases must be heard concurrently."

The Case of the False Beard suddenly took on a profound significance yesterday. A dreadful hush fell on the court-room as the barristers wrestled with truth, and the judge leaned forward as though he were at a Cup Final, encouraging now one litigant and now another with that suave impartiality which is the hallmark of British justice, and has done so much to etc., etc., etc.

For the first time since the opening of this remarkable case, several of those taking part stuck to the main point at issue, and refused to be sidetracked by intruders with other and more ridiculous irons in the so-called fire. It was Beard first and the rest nowhere, as Macaulay said when he was introduced to Mme La Sepinoletta at the Ramsgate Fair.

Mr. Gooseboote: It has been established that this Beard was pulled off the lessee's chin by the action of a swing-door. It must therefore be asked whether a false beard is a fixture or a fitting.

Mr. Snapdriver: The Housing Act of 1927 makes no mention of false beards.

Mr. Gooseboote: Yet I venture to state that it is a fixture, like a gas-oven.

Mr. Snapdriver: To be connected or disconnected by an official? I maintain that it is a fitting, like a towel-rail.

An official of the Gas Light and Coke Company was then called.

He said that the Company had never regarded false beards in the light of gas-ovens.

Cocklecarrot: Anybody could have told us that. Mr. Gooseboote's illustration was a fanciful one. You might as well say that a real beard is like a water-system, because it can't be detached at will.

Mr. Gooseboote: But it can be, by switching off at the main. Nobody can switch false beards off at the main.

(*Laughter and fruit throwing.*)

The tall gentleman whose false beard was caught in the swing-door of the Hotel Gorgeous was cross-examined yesterday by Mr. Emery Paper, K.C., under the mistaken impression that he was the carpenter who was being sued by Gospudden Steam Dredger Services Ltd. and Connie Cabbidge. Mr. Honeyweather Gooseboote objected. So did Mr. Tinklebury Snapdriver. Mr. Justice Cocklecarrot, who thought the tall gentleman was the solicitor for the Nandeville Brickworks, addressed the stupefied jury for eighty minutes on the lack of evidence of anything. Mr. Paper withdrew his attack on the tall gentleman, whose name turned out to be Stanley Mulberreigh, and a Miss Cutler was carried out yelling.

Mr. Cowblossom, K.C.: M'lud, am I in order in asking for, pursuant to the testimony of the defendant's mother, a warrant of *quomodo?*

Cocklecarrot: Meaning what?

Mr. Dendergast, K.C.: M'lud, retainder having been non-proven, I submit that the prosecution should demand an injunction, in default.

Cocklecarrot: Are you referring to anything within the knowledge of this court? *What* are you referring to, either of you?

Mrs. Lussock: They are getting at me, m'lud.

Cocklecarrot: And who may you be, if I might make so bold?

Mrs. Lussock: Am I bound to answer, m'lud?

Cocklecarrot: No. It is immaterial. Nobody here knows or cares who anybody is, really. For you to give your name would only confuse matters further.

In the midst of a brisk exchange about the law of patents between Mr. Cowblossom and Mr. Telfife, Mr. Purdnop intervening, a tall man said with weary patience, "May I venture to suggest——"

"Who are you?" Cocklecarrot asked. "I", said the stranger, "am Stanley Mulberreigh, the cause of all the trouble about this beard." A gasp of astonishment greeted these words. The plaintiff had been forgotten in the hurly-burly of court life, and even Mr. Snapdriver, for the prosecution, muttered, "Impossible!" "What do you want?" asked Cocklecarrot. The position was explained in whispers to the judge, who grew very flustered. Mr. Gooseboote, for the defence, was arguing with a laundress when the news was brought across the court to him by a hideous usher. Messrs. Flobb, Desigger, Flobb, Desigger and Flobb, solicitors for the Hotel Gorgeous, were hastily extricated from the bar and the case looked like starting at last.

Mr. Gooseboote: Mr. Mulberreigh, where were you on Thursday, January 18, 1926?

Cocklecarrot: Does that matter?

Mr. Gooseboote: M'lud, I hope to show that this is not the first time this gentleman has had his false beard caught in a swing-door.

Cocklecarrot: Answer yes or no, Mr. Mulberreigh.

Mulberreigh: The question, as I understand it——

Cocklecarrot: You are not here to understand questions, but to answer them. Even we do not always understand the questions, so how can you hope to? I confess I do not know what Mr. Gooseboote is talking about, but you must reply to him.

Mr. Gooseboote: I will put it another way. On Thursday, January 18, 1926, where were you?

Cocklecarrot: That's better.

Mulberreigh: Taunton.

Cocklecarrot: What do you mean? "Taunton". You can't just say "Taunton". It doesn't make sense.

Mr. Stanley Mulberreigh, the tall gentleman whose false beard is the cause of more than fourteen cases now being heard in Mr. Justice Cocklecarrot's court, caused consternation yesterday by saying that he was willing to settle out of court. "Settle what out of court?" asked the judge courteously. "Surely there is nothing, as yet, to settle. Nothing has transpired. We have no evidence of anything, either for or against. In fact the preliminaries of all these cases have merely accentuated the confusion. Surely you would be well advised to wait a day or two, so that we can find out what all this is about?" Mr. Mulberreigh was then understood to say that he would wait a few days, to find out what was happening. The judge at once made an order of restraint of capacities.

Mr. Caulme-Frozett, K.C.: On the night of the 14th Mrs. Webfoot——

Cocklecarrot: One moment, Mr. Caulme-Frozett. Which case is this?

Mr. C.-F.: M'lud—er—(*consults document*)—it is Moulting *versus* Carke.

Cocklecarrot (consulting papers): Is that the Tacknold case?

Mr. C.-F. (consulting papers): Er—no, m'lud. (*Whispers to solicitors.*)

Cocklecarrot (after whispering to Mr. Gooseboote): I have no trace of this case.

Mr. Boundaway: M'lud, Mr. Carke is the man who took the false beard out of the swing-door.

Cocklecarrot: Ah! And who is Mrs. Webfoot?

Angry voice: I am!

Yesterday the Beard Case had a regrettable relapse. Interventions by Mrs. Stocking, Pompo Ltd., the Upshott Dye-works, Canon Narrable and Mouse, Escallop and Fremling-

ham so bewitched, bemused and befuddled the gleaming cohorts of barristers that the court was like an ice-hockey rink during a match between the Terrible Tigers and the Frightful Fellows. I hesitate to make a verbatim report of the proceedings, as my readers would accuse me of talking rubbish — an accusation which cuts me to the marrow for a moment, and then runs off me like liquid egg-powder off a chef's hat.

What, for instance, is one to make of this?

Mr. Tumbler: Is your name Enid Stocking?

Miss Taverner: No. Why should it be?

Mr. Hirst: M'lud, is this in order?

Cocklecarrot: Is what in order? Nothing I have heard to-day is particularly in order. Who are these people?

Mr. Tumbler: What people, m'lud? Here is Miss Taverner who——

Cocklecarrot: The people whose names I keep hearing! Mr. Gooseboote, pray continue.

Mr. Gooseboote: That is not Miss Taverner, m'lud.

Cocklecarrot: Who isn't? Do you mean Mrs. Stocking isn't?

Mr. Pelpe: M'lud, he means Miss Taverner isn't.

Cocklecarrot: Well, as they both aren't, make a note of it, to avoid future mistakes.

One of those clashes between Mr. Tinklebury Snapdriver, K.C., and Mr. Honeyweather Gooseboote, K.C., to which the Law is now inured, held up the Beard case or cases yesterday.

Mr. Snapdriver: The Hotel Gorgeous cannot be expected to employ a man to disengage false beards from swing-doors.

Mr. Gooseboote: Why not?

Mr. Snapdriver: My learned colleague surely cannot imagine that false beards are the rule at this establishment?

Mr. Gooseboote: My learned colleague is not entitled to assume that a false beard is an exceptional ornament. Also, a real beard may get caught in a door.

Mr. Snapdriver: A real beard would not come off. Unless shaved off.

Mr. Gooseboote: It might. You are not entitled to assume that it would not.

Cocklecarrot: Gentlemen, gentle-

men! Please! What is the use of arguing about a real beard? It is a false one we have to deal with.

Mr. Gooseboote: I hope to show that it *was* a real beard.

Cocklecarrot: But people do not send for glue to stick on real beards.

Mr. Gooseboote: They do, when they wish to appear to be wearing a false beard.

Mr. Snapdriver (sarcastically): I see. The plaintiff grew a real beard and smeared it with glue. And it came off in the door! Very plausible, ve-ry plausible, I'm sure.

Mr. Gooseboote: It was the false beard that came off. It was glued to the real beard.

Cocklecarrot: Might one ask why?

Mr. Gooseboote: That, m'lud, is what I hope to discover.

Mrs. Greddie, whoever she may be, got going to-day in fine style. She said, apparently addressing Mr. Honeyweather Gooseboote: "When my niece discovered where Tom was, she went round to Rawlins and asked him about the address. But Mrs. Baines was there, and she said that Fred and Mabel had left their place on the Monday, so Archer—"

Mr. Gooseboote: I think there is some mist——

Mrs. Greddie: So Archer, who hadn't heard about it, left some sandwiches for the boys, and went back to see if Nellie had got hold of Ted.

Cocklecarrot: (*with heavy sarcasm*) And had Nellie got hold of Ted?

At that point Mrs. Greddie burst into tears and said she wouldn't be bullied, and an usher led her out. Cocklecarrot asked Gooseboote: "What was all that about?" Gooseboote shrugged and said, "M'lud, I am as much in the dark as you."

(*Roars of laughter and more fruit throwing.*)

After lunch the case returned to normal.

Mr. Gooseboote: If a false beard is a fitting rather than a fixture, what is a false beard attached to a real beard?

Cocklecarrot: To whom are you addressing this idiotic question?

Mr. Gooseboote: I can answer it myself, m'lud. It is still more a fitting than the other.

Mr. Snapdriver: I don't see why. It will come off just as easily.

Mr. Gooseboote: That is exactly why. If it didn't, it would be. And vice versa.

Cocklecarrot: No. Come, come. Not vice versa. You can't attach a real beard to a false one.

Mr. Transom: Surely you have all misunderstood the question. There are two beards in question, one real, the other false.

All: Well?

Mr. Transom: I leave it at that.

Cocklecarrot: Thank you.

A curious incident occurred yesterday in the Beard case. The representative of a firm of beard-makers was called to give evidence. Before he was sworn, an argument broke out between Mr. Snapdriver and Mr. Gooseboote, on the question of fees. Various other barristers joined in, and as the noise increased, the judge began to shout orders. The public laughed heartily. The clerks cried out in bewilderment, the solicitors banged their desks with heavy books, the ushers stamped their feet, the Puisne Sergeaunt-at-Arraigns rang his bell, the robing atten-dants, wig-bearers, wardrobe-women, cleaners, sweepers, dusters, scrubbers, scrapers and washerwomen bawled derisive remarks, the police drew their luncheons and began to eat. And when the uproar was at its height, the unheeded witness left the witness-box and went away by a side door. By the time calm had been restored there was no witness.

"Who on earth are all these people?"

This question was asked by Mr. Justice Cocklecarrot again to-day as he contemplated the swarming courtroom. "So far," he continued, "we have seen remarkably little of the man who started the trouble with his false beard. Is he—I forget his name—in court?" Answer came there none. But a woman's voice was heard to say, "I think I can explain." "Explain what?" queried the judge courteously. "The theft of the jars," said the woman. "Ah," said Cocklecarrot, "the jars. Of course. You will pardon me, madam, if I ask you what you are talking about."

"My uncle," said the woman, "had sent my little boy to fetch the jars. But Mr. Craven said they had been stolen by the girl who had applied the week before." Cocklecarrot gazed hopelessly at a little knot of barristers. "Does anybody know anything about this?" he asked. "This must be Mrs. Kenmole," said Mr. Transom. "No," said the woman. "My name is Tulse."

Silence fell, broken only by the low cursing of the judge and the giggling of the barristers and solicitors.

When the Beard Case was resumed to-day Messrs. Niddo and Bollgrease, glue factors, were asked by Mr. Constant Tangent, K.C., whether the accident to the beard might not have been caused by inferior glue of a not very adhesive quality.

Cocklecarrot: Surely, false beards are not glued to the chin?

Mr. Emery Paper: In this case, yes, m'lud.

Cocklecarrot: Then does the owner soak it off every night?

Mr. Walpurgis: No, m'lud. He sleeps in it; that is, in the beard.

Cocklecarrot: Does the beard fall inside or outside the bed-clothes?

Mr. Smallwaters: Is that material to this case, m'lud?

Cocklecarrot: No. Oh, no. A mere private inquiry. You must allow me a little latitude in a case of this description.

Sir Charles Niddo, cross-examined, said that on May 4 the firm received an order from a Mr. Curlew for a penny pot of beard-glue. Sir Henry Bollgrease answered the telephone, and gave the necessary instructions to the packers and loaders.

Mr. Walpurgis: Did you examine the glue yourself?

Sir Charles: Certainly not. The Managing Director of a firm of this size does not concern himself with penny pots of glue.

Mr. Walpurgis: But your colleague answered the telephone?

Sir Charles: Yes. He thought it was a very large order from Lady Possett.

Cocklecarrot: A lady with a very large beard, I take it? (*Laughter and cat-calls.*)

Sir Charles: M'lud, it would injure our firm greatly if the public were to be given an idea that we were always supplying glue for beards. It is a very small item of our trade.

Cocklecarrot: Perhaps Lady Possett collects false beards.

An attempt to reconstruct the accident to the Beard was held up when Mr. Snapdriver said that if the beard came off too easily, Messrs. Niddo and Bollgrease would claim that this was a bad advertisement for their glue.

Cocklecarrot: We are not here, Mr. Snapdriver, to advertise glue—though one might think we were from the way we go on.

Mr. Gooseboote: M'lud, if my client had grown a real beard, we might have been saved a lot of trouble, and expense.

Cocklecarrot: What are you whining about? You'll be well in pocket at the end of the case, if I know you. This is the way you make your money, isn't it? And as for you solicitors, pullulating like ants, everybody knows how you make *your* money. £36 8s. 4d. to endorsing endorsement of stamp, eh? And the ushers and clerks taking tips. Upon my word, this court is a sink of iniquity.

The legal world can talk of nothing but Mr. Justice Cocklecarrot's daring experiment of hearing several cases at once, in order to clear off arrears of business. "The Law," he said yesterday, "has too long been taunted with being slow." Yesterday some doubts existed among the various barristers and solicitors and their hangers-on as to which of the cases was actually being dealt with at any given moment. But since the whole ragamadolio centres round the False Beard, the subsidiary cases arising out of counter-actions, interventions, and so forth will tend to be swamped in the general hurly-burly and brou-haha of the proceedings. Leading for the Hotel Gorgeous, Mr. Tinklebury Snapdriver, K.C., cross-examined the wrong witness so heartily that Mr. Honeyweather Gooseboote, K.C., for Mrs. Stocking, demanded a stay of replevin—but in vain.

Mr. Snapdriver: Your name is Jean Graham?

Witness: No. It's Agnes Buck-wheat.

Mr. Snapdriver (shuffling papers): Oh. Were you in the Hotel Gorgeous when the defendant caught his beard in the swing-door?

Witness: No. I was in Wales.

Mr. Snapdriver (angrily): Oh.

Cocklecarrot: Mr. Snapdriver, which case is this?

Mr. Snapdriver: M'lud, I will endeavour to find out. Miss Buckwheat, what is it—er—why are you here?

Witness: I took delivery of the wheelbarrow.

Cocklecarrot: What wheelbarrow would that be? We have heard of no wheelbarrow so far.

Mr. Gooseboote: M'lud. I thought this was Mrs. Stocking. Miss Buck-wheat is my witness.

(*Sensation in court.*)

Cocklecarrot was heard to ask who was this Mrs. Stocking.

Mr. Gooseboote: M'lud, she is suing the Ormesby Lodge Filter Company.

Cocklecarrot: What has this to do with the beard incident?

Mr. Transom: I can explain, m'lud. The beard was sent to a laundry three days before it was caught in the swing-door. It was brought by mistake to Commander Pembroke's house in a wheelbarrow, as there was a shortage of vans. The Commander is in the Persian Gulf.

Cocklecarrot: But where is the man who hired the beard?

Mr. Cluckhard: M'lud, I propose to call him later.

The Beard case ended yester-day with dramatic suddenness. The S.O.W.S. (Shirts outside Waistcoats Society) intervened, information having been lodged by a common informer, who maintained that under an Act of Edward the Confessor a false beard was the responsibility of its wearer, who could seek no redress at law for an accident to it. This appeal was allowed, and before Mr. Justice Cocklecarrot could sum up, the jury, barristers, solicitors, clerks, ushers and other officials had rushed from the court. Nothing remained but to apply for a writ of cestui qui veult, which was done by the Deputy Puisne Sergeaunt-at-Arraigns in no uncertain manner.

THE SAGA OF THE
SAUCY MRS. FLOBSTER

Those who hoped that the *Saucy Mrs. Flobster*, Headquarters and Flag Ship of Admiral Sir Ewart Hodgson, Governor of Lots Road Power House, would be towed to her resting-place, to be broken up, are likely to be disappointed. She is to be sold to Afghanistan for £341 12s. 8d.

There was a scene in the House when a Liberal member protested that this was no moment to sell our ships. A Ministerial reply revealed that the famous craft could hardly be called a ship any longer, being neither seaworthy nor river-worthy. Not even stagnant pool-worthy. Boys on the embankment have removed her stern bit by bit. There is no port-side to the after-deck. The Captain's bridge is a yawning cavity. The anchor has no chain, and lies in the mud, independent of the ship. When the Afghans see her it is doubtful whether we shall get the 114 tins of onions promised in exchange, much less the £341 12s. 8d.

*   *   *

In answer to a suggestion that the *Saucy Mrs. Flobster* should be broken up, the Minister of Bubbleblowing said: "I understand that this ship is already as much broken up as possible." Asked why we did not sell her to some foreign Government, the Minister said: "We were offered sevenpence for her by the principality of Lichtenstein, but on seeing a photograph of her, the intending purchasers called off the deal." Asked why she was not used for fuel, the Minister replied: "I understand she's too wet."

*   *   *

Mrs. Withersedge, caretaker on board the *Saucy Mrs. Flobster*, has received orders to make all shipshape and Bristol fashion in readiness for the visit of inspection of Captain Gharikhar Girishkand of the Afghan Navy. She will begin by driving the hens off the poop, and nailing bits of felt over the holes in the deck. A new chain has been bought for the anchor, but it does not fit. Four steps are missing from the main companion-way, and the stump of the only remaining funnel is stuffed with rotten wood. Admiral Sir Ewart Hodgson, attempting to adjust the ceiling of his cabin, fell over a dead cat into a bucket full of mouse-traps, tins, sacking, and fish-scales. But today the Lots Road burgee flutters from an old piece of stove-pipe tied to the smashed roof of the chart-house.

*   *   *

A knock on the side of the *Saucy Mrs. Flobster* brought Mrs. Withersedge on deck. It was Professor Hugetrouser, who had arrived to examine the old hulk for signs of erosion. The Professor said grumbingly, "This is more like a heap of rubbish than a ship." He then attempted to take soundings, and found that "while the front part of the ship is stuck fast in mud, what remains of the back part peters out into slime. She can hardly be said to be afloat, unless there is some water under her middle portion. The railing at the blunt end is missing, but this is not due to erosion." Mrs. Withersedge obligingly pointed out the nest of a bearded tit, but the Professor snapped, "Even that doesn't make the thing seaworthy."

*   *   *

Before leaving the *Saucy Mrs. Flobster* Professor Hugetrouser asked to see the log. "We don't burn wood," said Mrs. Withersedge. "Of course not," said the Professor. "But I want to see the reel and line with which you record the ship's speed." Mrs. Withersedge laughed. "We 'aven't 'ad any speed, as you might say," she replied, "since we was blown a mile down the river in a storm and fetched up crack against the embankment near Chelsea Bridge. Since then we're an 'ome-lovin' craft, as you can see." "I wonder she has not sunk long ago," said the Professor. "She couldn't sink much more," said Mrs. Withersedge, "an' the rats seem to think she's safe enough." The Professor blew his nose in embarrassment.

*   *   *

An unexpected message from Admiral Sir Ewart Hodgson to his ship, the *Saucy Mrs. Flobster*, anchored off the Embankment, near Lots-road Power Station, threw the caretaker into a state of frenzy yesterday.

The boy who brought the message said, "You're to put to sea, Mrs. Withersedge." "Put to *what?*" shouted the lady. The boy surveyed the miserable hulk. "There's an 'ole in the deck, ma," he observed maliciously.

"There's 'oles everywherest," replied the caretaker. "Why, you couldn't float this muck'eap in a public bathin' 'ouse. Not at the shaller end, neither. What does 'e think we are, 'im and 'is puttin' to sea? Hadmiral my foot!"

*   *   *

Mrs. Withersedge, caretaker of the *Saucy Mrs. Flobster*, was confronted by what looked like the remains of a sailor—a scraggy, whiskered scarecrow in a jersey marked "Blackburn Rovers." "I bin sent," said the seedy mariner, "to get 'er ready to sail."

"Sail?" thundered Mrs. Withersedge. "An' what d'yer think she's goin' ter sail with? The last sail we 'ad aboard was used to plug 'oles in 'er stem when she rammed 'erself against the embankment. Why, I'll bet even 'er keel's bin et by fishes."

"Any rope?" asked the gloomy salt, with the air of having a hanging in mind. "Only a bit what's used to tie a lot o' loose planks to 'er sides where she rammed 'erself against an old dray the boys pushed into the water on Guy Fawkes night, when they burnt 'er mast." The sailor scratched his head meditatively.

*   *   *

"D'you reckon," asked Mrs. Withersedge, "As 'e *reely* means to put to sea in this old skow?" "No knowin'," replied the disconsolate sailor. "Maybe 'e'll get 'er towed down river." "Towed my foot!" said Mrs. Withersedge, "Why, the 'ole thing'd come apart. This mornin' one o' them 'ens pecked a hole in a smoke-stack. Soft as blottin' paper everythin' is 'ere." "Ow's the engyne-room, Ma?" "Like a scrap 'eap. You could run 'er with a couple o' type-writin' machines as easy as with all that worm-eaten junk." "Steerin' gear O.K.?" asked the sailor. "There's a bit of a wheel with no spokes, but it don't connect with nothin'." "Leaky?" "Leaky! Why down below there's a reg'lar swimmin' pool for all 'Ollywood." The sailor sat down gloomily on a stanchion, which broke, and the pieces rolled noisily across the so-called deck.

*   *   *

Admiral Sir Ewart Hodgson had rung up from Lots-road Power Station to say that he would come aboard at 11 a.m. Mrs. Withersedge and the disconsolate sailor received him, and helped him to clamber over a heap of broken crockery and torn rigging to an almost roofless chart-house, where two hens were kept. "Where's the wind?" inquired the Admiral, wetting his finger and holding it up. "You'll need a 'urricane to dislodge this lot," said Mrs. Withersedge.

The Admiral then studied an inventory of ships' fittings, which included a cat's basket, three old cycle tyres, a roller-skate confiscated from a boy who fell through a hole in the deck, a stuffed raven given to Mrs. Withersedge by her son-in-law, a painter's ladder with eight rungs missing, a Brazilian oil-stove without any inside, and a fireman's helmet won in a raffle by the late Mr. Withersedge. The Admiral then went back to Lots-road.

*　　*　　*

Captain Garikhar Girishkand of the Afghan Navy was surprised when, expecting to be taken out in a launch to look over the *Saucy Mrs. Flobster*, he was shown into Admiral Sir Ewart Hodgson's office near Lots-road Power House.

"Here she is, as she was in her prime," said the Admiral, pointing to a photograph on the wall, "You'll find her changed." An hour later the Captain, having put his foot through the deck twice. considered this a gross understatement. "Does she float at all at high tide?" he asked. "As much as she ever floats," replied the Admiral. "And where," inquired the visitor, sarcastically, "might her stern be?" "It *might* be in its usual place," said the Admiral, "but it isn't." The Afghan cursed softly under his breath.

*　　*　　*

"Do you go with the ship?" asked the courteous Afghan mariner.

"Go?" repeated Mrs. Withersedge, mystified.

"Yes," continued the dusky seafarer. "I mean, when one acquires the ship and she sails for her new berth, do you sail with her?"

"Don't make me laugh!" retorted the caretaker. "This 'ere ship stopped goin' years ago. As for sailin', St. Paul's is just as likely ter sail."

"Put it this way," said the sunburned foreigner. "Are you a member of her crew?"

"I'm all the ruddy crew I ever seed," replied Mrs. Withersedge vigorously. "But now she's crumblin', I'm gettin' ready to go back to 'Oxton."

The Afghan surveyed the preposterous craft in gloomy silence.

*　　*　　*

The following significant passage from a leading article in the *Jamrad Jokhta* (the journal of the Afghan Navy) speaks for itself, but not for me: *Ghazi bustan shutargi vemul "Zaucy Misses Vlobster" wana han Kandahar, kala bist landi diaram.* As I haven't the faintest idea what this means, as Seymour Hicks used to say when he recited a "Czech poem," we will turn to matters more easily dealt with, smiling through our tears as we do so, for we are jolly good fellows, and so say all of us.

*　　*　　*

"Come in," cried Mrs. Withersedge, forgetting that she was on board the *Saucy Mrs. Flobster*. The knocking was repeated. The caretaker went on deck and craned over the side. There she saw the errant anchor knocking against the ship. Moreover, mud had given place to water under the so-called bow, and the good ship was as nearly afloat as possible. Mrs. Withersedge had a sudden vision of being washed out to sea and round the Cape before she could say sausage. She ran forward, nay forrard, and pulled on the rope which hoisted the flag, so that the Admiral, from his room in Lots Road, might see the signal. But it was not a flag, but a blue flannel nightdress which fluttered from halfway up what was left of the mainmast. The Afghan Captain, arriving for a second tour of inspection, clicked his heels and saluted the ensign. "These English are mad," he muttered.

★   ★   ★

"Mrs. Withersedge speakin', hadmiral . . . yes . . . I thought you'd like ter know about the hanchor . . . we was pullin' at it, me and that sailor, like you said, to see if it would come up, an' all that 'appened was the ole chain come up by itself, like, and there wasn't no hanchor at the end, so we think, as you might say that the hanchor's got lost in the mud, and there ain't nothin' to 'old the old tub firm but that bit o' rope the policeman tied to the seat on the embankment, an' the sailor says that if there's a storm an' a bit of a off-shore wind the 'ole caboodle's goin' ter get dragged out from 'er moorin's, so I and 'e got a bargeman ter twist some wire off of the 'en coop amidships round a lump o' stone, and there she rides as easy as you never saw. . . . Hi! You've cut me orf! . . ."

★   ★   ★

As the *Saucy Mrs. Flobster* lay, or rather mouldered, at her so-called moorings, there came alongside a little boat rowed by a fat old man in a peaked hat. From the stern floated the flag of Lots-road Power Station. The fat man heard the voice of Mrs. Withersedge and approached an open porthole. "*It hadder be you*," sang Mrs. Withersedge as she emptied a pail of fish-scales and dirty water over the fat man, who was standing up in his boat. "Yus, it had to be me," retorted the visitor, wiping the muck from his head and clothes. He then delivered a letter from the Admiral. "Sealed orders, I suppose," said Mrs. Withersedge. "to be hopened at sea."

★   ★   ★

"The front part of the *Saucy Mrs. Flobster* is now afloat," said an official spokesman in touch with tomfoolery yesterday. The back part has got wedged under the embankment wall, and is loaded with garbage and rubble and refuse well above the plimsoll line. Ignorant workmen have glued the rudder on to the front part, but as there are only two temporary spokes (made from saucepan handles) of the steering wheel left, this will not affect life on board, particularly as the wheel itself has come off.

★   ★   ★

Last night's theft of the anchor chain from the *Saucy Mrs. Flobster* is regarded in naval circles as a comparatively trivial event, owing to the droll fact that there was no anchor attached to it.

Mrs. Withersedge, the caretaker who sleeps aboard, heard noises which she attributed to roving vermin, or to the usual disintegration of the bounding barque. The proximity of what is left of the stern to the embankment makes it easy for marauders to scramble aboard. "She's still anchored securely," said Mrs. Withersedge in an interview. "Leastaways, what I mean is the anchor's stuck in the mud orf of what the Admiral calls 'er starboard beam. For all the good it does us it might as well be 'angin' from the roof o' the National Gallery. Them Afghans won't 'ave to 'aul it up when they sail away for the Spice Islands, an' yo ho ho an' a bottle o' rum served ice-cold in the crow's nest."

* * *

Rumours that the *Saucy Mrs. Flobster*, crack and only craft of the Lots-road squadron, was about to waddle to sea, reached the public houses both north and south of the river.

The local wits taunted the gloomy sailor with requests that he would bring them back a bag of groundnuts or a giant baboon. Mrs. Withersedge coming ashore for a breath of fresh air, was heard to admit that another bit of the stern had dropped off at high tide. "Dessay as 'ow that won't matter much," she added. When asked if it was true that sea-faring folk got to love their ship like a home, she said, "Not me! I'd rather go to sea in a disused railway kerridge." "Steam or sail this trip, Ma?" asked a jaunty young landlubber. "It'll 'ave to be oars," replied Mrs. Withersedge, "an' the only one left 'asn't got any blade."

Yet, at that very moment, welders and blowers and plate-rifters and cordwainers and caulkers and baulkers and keel-haulers were swarming over the ship, and getting her ready for the great moment, when her snout would once more sniff the tempestuous brine. Mrs. Withersedge came out on deck and stared incredulously at all this activity. Approaching Admiral Sir Ewart Hodgson, who was leaning nonchalantly against a forward bunnion, she said: "Then we hare reely outerd bound, hadmiral?" The Admiral slapped his thigh breezily with his telescope, and replied, with nautical bonhomie, "Shipshape and Bristol fashion, my dear."

* * *

At 11.23 ship's time a wisp of dirty smoke stole gingerly from the worm-eaten funnel of the *Saucy Mrs. Flobster*. A moment later a thudding and a shuddering and a rattling announced that the engines had started. The siren emitted a hoarse note, like an old crow with laryngitis. The Admiral, on the bridge, was thrown to the ground. The gloomy sailor, standing by the wheel, put his elbow through the spokes and got it stuck there. Mrs. Withersedge, who should have shouted to a pavement artist on the Embankment to cast her off, remarked instead, "She's blowin' up! All 'ands to the boats, if there was any 'ands, if there was any boats." Before the pavement artist could do anything, the ship had swung round, the cable had parted, and there was that queen of the inland seas more or less headed for distant landfalls, notably the Surrey shore.

Orders and counter-orders poured like water on to a duck's back from the lips of Admiral Hodgson. And like the same water off the same duck's back, they poured unheeded by that gloomy sailor at the wheel.

Having banged into the Surrey shore, the *Saucy Mrs. Flobster* suddenly lurched sideways, swung round and lumbered back to the muddy spot she had left. Still trailing the parted rope, the damnable craft sank to rest with an almost audible sign of contentment. The engines spluttered and died. The sailor spun the wheel derisively and mopped his forehead. "The old place 'asn't changed," said Mrs. Withersedge with a broad smile.

"She is no longer seaworthy," said the Admiral breezily to the Press, "or even riverworthy." "Mudworthy's the word," added Mrs. Withersedge. As the sunset gun boomed from Lots-road Power Station, Admiral Hodgson saluted. Mrs. Withersedge approached with an egg. "One o' them 'ens laid during the voyage," she said. The Admiral shook his head reflectively. Nothing was heard but bits off the ship slithering into the dirty water, and the sailor whistling "Rolling down to Rio" as he clambered on to the Embankment for shore leave.

★　　★　　★

An unfavourable report on the *Saucy Mrs. Flobster* having been made to the Afghan Government, the deal has fallen through. The part of her which was afloat at high tide came to bits at low tide, and Captain Girishkar Garishkand said sardonically: "If my country is ever to have a navy, we must make a better start than this." The whole question as to whether Lots-road Power House really needs a ship at all is to be thrashed out in Parliament soon.

Sonnet

That which perfection's self imperfect makes,
　By reason's own unreason is betrayed,
Since he who loyalty for treason takes,
　In this same act is reason's traitor made.
Yet reason, in perfection's sure despite,
　By traitorous faith unreason doth conceal,
While faithless loyalty, in treason's right,
　Shall loyal treachery to herself reveal.
So one who still pursues a falling star,
　Shall at the last make full acknowledgment
That they who by themselves abandoned are,
　May, lacking reason for their true content,
Hold fast to truth, not seeking to descry
This loyalty in reason's treachery.

Obvious

A man who habitually dined in a certain restaurant noticed, at a near-by table, a tall fellow with a bit of lettuce sticking out of his ear. He was alone, and was eating his dinner without any sign of embarrassment.

On the next three nights he was there, and always with the lettuce sticking out of his ear. On the fourth night the man who had observed this strange sight, and was puzzling over it, ventured, on passing the stranger's table, to address him. "Pray excuse me, sir, if I appear impertinent," he said, "but why do you have lettuce sticking out of your ear?"

"Because I can't get celery," replied the stranger angrily.

Odd Occurrence

"I—er—I'm so sorry. I didn't catch your name."

"Filth."

"I—beg your pardon. I don't quite——"

"Filth. My name is Filth."

"Oh—but it can't be. I mean. *Filth?*"

"Yes, Filth."

"Lorna—this is Mr. Filth."

"Don't be silly, Muriel."

"There, you see, Mr. Filth? Nobody will believe that's your name. What do your friends call you?"

"Filth."

"Oh, well, let's just leave it."

Graphic Moments on the Radio

(Wheelbarrow report)

... That was a woman sneezing—now here comes a wheelbarrow—yes, it's a wheelbarrow, I can see it from where I am standing—a man is—yes, a man is wheeling it along—you can hear the sound of it—it's—yes, it's coming along now towards the place where I am recording this message—that was another sneeze—the woman has a cold—you can just hear the wheelbarrow going down the road. It's getting fainter as it gets farther away, and now—yes, now it's gone—you can't hear it any more.

Alone With Nature

From a tulse-fringed grot among the tansy a weed-warbler pops his tousled head to snap at a bobfly for breakfast. His nest, hidden from prying eyes by the tall snodgrass and thick-growing chickflower, is but a short flight from the wood where he finds the succulent parsley-fly. Here is a glory of tinkersfoot, dwarf umbrella, sharksfin bugloss, sweet chumbril, duckspur, St. Anselm's-wort and mopsy-under-the-wall.

Odd occurrence

DEAR SIR,

Yesterday morning I noticed that a blue-tit had pecked the cap off my milk-bottle. The milk inside was frozen, and the little bird had tiny skates on its feet and was skating round and round on the milk.

Yrs. faithfully,

Mrs. Emily Gifthorse.

Just for a change

I have been entrusted with the task of writing the *Life of Henry Pouch*. I should be most grateful if all those who have any letters of his would send them to me. They will, of course, not be copied or returned. They will not even be read. As a matter of fact, they will be torn up and thrown away.

Music of the week

Three graceful little songs from the *List of Huntingdonshire Cabmen* were sung at the Æolian Hall on Tuesday by Mme Orlona Travella. She made the mistake of singing them too sentimentally, and her pronunciation of some of the more difficult names was at fault.

The settings, by Mr. A. L. Reeves, were adequate, but too solemn, and in the third song one was conscious of a certain monotony of effect, when Gackwind, E. P. H., was repeated twice in a very slow passage. Possibly recitative is the best setting for such material.

The Answer? Snibbo

No rhinoceros ever has a shiny nose. . . . Why should a pretty girl yield first place to a rhinoceros? . . . SNIBBO will do for women what Nature has done for the rhinoceros. *It will dull those gleaming noses*. If the rhinoceros had a shiny nose his presence at the water-hole would be betrayed to the hunter. So girls who go down to cocktail holes to drink are betrayed by shiny noses, and become the prey of unscrupulous hunters. The answer —always, everywhere, is SNIBBO.

MIMSIE SLOPCORNER AT THE PAGEANT

THE Mayor of Pibney St. Vitus is to be congratulated on securing Mimsie Slopcorner for this summer's Carnival and Pageant, "Pibney St. Vitus Through The Ages."

On the opening day she will stand on a hay-cart in the procession, attired as Boadicea. The Pageant Master, Mr. Vincent Boltyle, has had the assistance of the noted antiquarian Professor O. K. McTootzie, author of "Some Bronze Age Middens," "Pre-Saxon Churns," "Neanderthal Place-Names," etc.; and externe lecturer in Palaeontology at Renfrew University. The refreshment tent will be organised by Dame Ruby Knowes, President of the local Folk-Dance Circle, and chairman of the Pibney St. Vitus branch of the Society for World Betterment.

Mimsie Slopcorner arrived at Pibney by train last night, and was welcomed by the mayor and several councillors—or would have been so welcomed had she not climbed back into the train before the mayor could get at her with his "few word of welcome," in search of her handbag. While the mayor was saying ". . . I and my colleagues, therefore . . ." she disappeared, and was carried on to Lunty-on-the-Hill, two miles down the line. "I hope I have not said anything to offend her, commented the mayor with a fatuous grin.

* * *

The great difficulty is to make Mimsie Slopcorner realise that she is an ancient Queen of the Britons, not a silly little oaf standing on a hay-cart. When told to look regal, she simpers. When told to advance one foot and tilt her head haughtily, she drops her spear, and shakes her helmet awry, so that she looks like an intoxicated "extra" in an opera crowd. With infinite patience she had been coached to hold her shield defiantly, but she still holds it as a timid sandwich-man might hold an advertisement for a tea-shop. Yesterday her queenly robe got caught in the prongs of Father Neptune's trident, and the red-faced deity, lowering the implement to disentangle it, had the air of a man trying to toast something on an enormous fork. Pibney is enjoying all this so much that everyone hopes it will be all wrong on the day.

* * *

At the first full-scale rehearsal of the procession which will open the Pibney St. Vitus Carnival, Mimsie, as Boadicea, got on to the wrong cart, and found herself in the middle of "King Edward III granting a charter to Pibney Monachorum." Edward III pushed her into a baron, and her spear-point ripped up his doublet. In trying to disengage the spear two other barons rolled off the cart and tripped up two serfs carrying a dead deer slung upside-down on a pole. The deer, which was a plastic one, broke in two with a loud spink. The Master of Ceremonies, dashing to the scene, fell over a crusader who had fainted, and his megaphone cut the cheek of a Seneschal, rebounded and caught Dame Edith Umbrage (the Spirit of the Renaissance) a hefty swipe on the left hip. The procession then halted.

* * *

I am great Boadicea,
Of stout old British stock,
Who stood up to the Romans
As firm as any rock.

These lines, to be spoken in a tableau vivant, are the subject of debate. Mr. Nudgett thought that the name of some local rock or hill should be mentioned. He suggested that the last line should run: *As firm as Bobbleworth Rock.* Mrs. Bird objected that this ruined the scansion, and that Bobbleworth was an unpoetical word. That wag Charlie Trott said, "Why not Worthing rock?" a suggestion which was received coldly. A further difficulty is that Mimsie Slopcorner finds Boadicea hard to pronounce, and keeps on saying B*eodo*cea.

The Pibney St. Vitus band was called yesterday for a rehearsal of the Carnival music. It was agreed that they should meet in the Eagle's Head, before proceeding to the Assembly Rooms. All were present (in the inn) a full hour before the arranged time. All were still present (in the inn) a full hour after the arranged time. All were still present (in the inn) when the indignant Councillor Cringe came to fetch them.

* * *

To avoid accidents when the second rehearsal for the Pibney St. Vitus band was called, the instruments and music were brought to the Assembly Rooms in Mr. Wopshay's grocery van. But the band did not turn up. Noises borne on the breeze from the Eagle's Head suggested the reason for their absence. They arrived in high spirits, and before the conductor, Mr. Harry Elkin, had smoothed out his copy of Rigoni's "Dixie Quick-Step March"' they were well into the valse "Heartsease," which they played with inappropriate vigour. They were called to order, and half of them switched to the march, while the other half stuck to the valse. Later, a compromise was struck with the "Bird of Dawn" two-step. Mr. Charlie Geldon and his trombone finished three bars ahead of the rest.

* * *

The tableau "Pibney St. Vitus in the Days of the Druids" was rehearsed yesterday. Owing to a high wind the magnificent beards of the Druids blew about so wildly that no Druid could be sure which was his own beard and which his neighbour's. This caused many a ribald jest from the onlookers and the excitement became a frenzy of mirth when one Druid's beard got hitched round the waist of a baker's daughter. The simple maid, finding herself lassoed by a beard, screamed with delight. Her mother cut the offending tentacle loose with a pair of scissors, and the Druid, suddenly thrown off his balance, fell over backwards. Order was partially restored by the Rev. Edgar Farragut, but for his pains he received a whiplash in the face from an errant beard belonging to Archdruid Gravepound, who was having trouble with the sacrificial goat. "Will all Druids kindly tuck their beards under their nightshirts," cried the voice of authority.

* * *

Mimsie Slopcorner was taken yesterday to the shop of Pibney's leading costumier, to be fitted for the helmet and robes of Boadicea. By the error of a young assistant she was handed a dressing-gown made for Mrs. Tumult, the wife of the Vicar. As the foolish girl preened herself in dressing-gown and helmet, who should come thundering in but the burly Mrs. Tumult herself. "And who," she roared, "is this minx? Claxton, what is the meaning of this?' Apologies fell as thick as autumn leaves in Vallombrosa. "This lady," said Claxton, "is Boadicea. I really apol——" "I don't care if she's Cleopatra," shouted the Tumult. "Why we should wear a tomfool helmet with *my* dressing-gown is a matter that needs a deal of explanation." With ludicrous dignity Mimsie removed helmet and dressing-gown, and swept out of the shop like a Marquise side-stepping the guillotine.

* * *

Yesterday Mimsie Slopcorner mounted the hay-cart on which she will make her triumphal journey through Pibney as Boadicea. Mr. Camphor assisted her to mount. She slipped, and knocked his hat off. Her helmet rolled under the cart, her shield fell into the road, her spear got stuck in a wheel, the horse took fright, and the driver, Fred Ambley, was helpless with laughter. From an upper window of the Eagle's Head the landlord's ne'er-do-well son blew repeated kisses to Boadicea, who was trying to twist her spear clear of the wheel. The band, which should have been playing Sossinger's "March of the Vikings," petered out with a few discordant notes, and a railway porter, off duty, trod on Miss Faggot's poodle Raymond. "All this," remarks the Pibney St. Vitus and Fosbett Evening Echo, "looked more like a night at the Victoria Palace than a rehearsal for the Great Day."

* * *

I quote from a recent outspoken leading article in the Pibney St. Vitus Weekly Messenger:

. . . Once again we ask who is responsible for importing a stranger to portray Boadicea. Has Pibney no young girl capable of essaying the role? This stranger, who, we understand, was once the Nuneaton Plastic Dustbin Queen, holds her spear as though it were a hockey stick, and she herself a nervous junior girl at St. Ethelfrida's. Her royal robe looks like a clown's overcoat, and without being offensive we may point out that her face has as much ancient queenliness about it as a stale suet pudding. If this is the best that Pibney can do, no wonder foreign tourists prefer Paris, and no wonder the Mayor himself is reported to have referred to Miss Slopcorner, in a

statement not for publication, as "This idiotic little dolt."

* * *

The Pibney St. Vitus and Fobsett Evening Echo, in a leading article, says:

. . . Who is ultimately responsible for making Pibney a laughing-stock all over Europe by importing Miss Slopcorner to play Boadicea? Her ludicrous antics on the hay-cart are the ribald jest of every ale-house, and things have come to a pretty pass when our band, which won the Halford Cup at the King's Knucklefurther Band Festival in 1949, spends more time in laughing at Boadicea than in playing the spirited march specially composed for it by Mrs. Huxtable. Either the Boadicea incident should be struck off the programme ruthlessly, or some more fitting exponent should be found before it is too late. We intend no discourtesy to Miss Slopcorner when we say, in the racy and homely phrase of Councillor Townsend, "She is enough to make a cat sick."

* * *

Trouble has arisen over the Battle of Flowers, which is to wind up the Pibney Carnival and Pageant. In a powerful speech Mrs. Sylvester Gladde characterised the idea as not only un-British but Continental. "Young louts," she said, "will make flower-throwing an excuse for scraping acquaintance with girls.

Already the publicans are clamouring for an extension of the drinking-hours. The question is, do we of Pibney St. Vitus wish to see intoxicated youths reeling about our town with their arms full of floral missiles? To throw a rose gently to a girl of one's acquaintance may look charming, but it can degenerate into the violent throwing of heaps of variegated blooms at perfect strangers. It can become a noisy chaos, and when I tell you that a niece of mine was kissed at Nice on the Promenade des Anglais by a foreigner who reeked of wine, need I say more?" "No!" thundered her audience.

* * *

Lady Dashett of Dashett Hall known to the local wits as Lady Damnit of Damnit 'All) having received from Sweden a remarkable mechanical fish, wished to have it included in the Mechanical Progress tableau at the pageant. She pointed out that, when wound up, it could walk on and. The Mayor, anxious not to appear unreasonable, said "Doubtless," under his breath. Councillor Pargetter, anxious to offend the lady, asked truculently, "What good does that do?" Mrs. Pouncer pointed out that in a village so far from the sea a mechanical fish would not arouse much interest. "What about a fresh-water fish?" asked Councillor Dubbe. "Have you ever caught a mechanical fish in

our river?" queried the Mayor. Lady Dashett then said quietly, "The interesting thing is that here is a fish that can walk on land." "Would it drown if it fell into the water?" asked a wag. There was no reply.

* * *

Wearing an anthracite-grey strapless reefer cocktail jacket, with a facecloth skirt of camel-ochre organza braided with chic blue *ravigotte*, Mimsie Slopcorner attended a Carnival lunch given by the Mayor of Pibney St. Vitus. The ribbons of her diamanté surcoat got into the soup, and were wrung dry by a J.P. who quoted a passage of Homer about a banquet. "Is that Homer Khayyam?" asked Mimsie. The table went into roars of laughter. Mimsie, disconcerted bit heartily on a lobster-claw and fractured a tooth. As had been anticipated, a Mr. Wallgrove drank too deeply of the heady wine of France and began to sing "Oh, girls, I'm a devil for fruit, what, what, what!" during the Mayor's speech. Mimsie glanced at her neighbour, Major Scoundrell, and said primly: "Tck, tck, tck.'

* * *

The traditional roasting of the ox during the Pibney St. Vitus Carnival will be continued this year, with a slight modification. Instead of roasting an ox, the villagers will open a tin of Russian crab.

The Filthistan Trio

MANY managers of big hotels suspect that it may take more than constant iced water to retain American visitors on their way to Paris. One of them is planning what he calls a super-cabaret, and has approached the Filthistan Trio.

These three rascals have hitherto wrecked every show in which they have taken part, the truth being that their seesaw turn cannot be incorporated into any programme, owing to their natural ebullience and impudence. This manager has suggested that the seesaw should be crowded with beautiful girls before the Persians get to work on it, and that the girls should dismount, and sing and dance a seesaw number, while the plank is occupied by the Trio. The difficulty is that the Persians have always preferred to indulge in their pastime, as the whim moves them, in the foyers of hotels. The hotel industry awaits with interest the reply of these sturdy individualists.

*   *   *

Ho, maniger, flottered we be to your hoffer, but we are of saying that seesaw is of men and not of sexypeal and barthing buties. Moareover, kindest of sirs, we orl have wifes at hoame what know inuf uv uman natua to cry to the Persian goships, "Yow, yow! So hour usbans wish hus to berleeve that they ave to kuddel hondreds uv glomerus bells and platternum blons hin there perfeshunal tasks, ho, yes." Mixed seesaw, honared manigement, is uneard uv hin Persia. I, Ashura, wood not erlow Misses Ashura to go nere a seesaw worked by marskulins, hand the sayme goeth for Mrs. Kazbulah and Mrs. Rizamughan. We be ever reddy to perform hin vestybools and furoyas, but we fermly reffuse of getting a mixtup with dancing girls what know nort uv hour hart, ho, yes.

Yores rispickfully,
Ashura, Kazbulah and Rizamughan.

Ho, manigers, we three wifes of seesaw men will be of conculting hour solikiters and loiryers for stopping that orful talk of there seesaw getting crowded with what the paypers korl blon bomshles and plutinum bells and sairuns. We are not wishing to have hour osbans bowancing abart hon this plonk with advenchesses which is arfter there welth. Thus we now rite to hour nobul osbans to be shaking the dirt of the motripilis out of there foot and to come back to hoame, rarther than of hixchanging oombraces with all of yores shaymerless uzzes. For we say wot a ottbed of ennikity moost be this western hend hif three peasfull sottizens of hour land does not be able to sit hon that seesaw befour opp come dredfull hactrisses bloing kisses and germaces and sperorling orl over that plonk to make hart impozzibul.

Mrs. Kazbulah and those
huther wifes.

*   *   *

A committee of restaurant and hotel proprietors yesterday asked whether, in view of their refusal to take part in a spectacular floor-show, the Filthistan Trio would consider allowing girls to dance to the rhythm of the seesaw at the back of the stage, as far from the three performers as possible.

"Ho, gintelfoke," replied the Trio, "we hare but yuman beans so if we see buties too cloose to hus, we hare trubbled and sossoptibul with sooch charms. But if we see these blon bonshles further hoff, we hare wurse, for as then hour inagiminations start to wurking, and we long to himbrace them hall evan moare than if they was hon the plonk of seesaw. So why temt hus with vompyers at hall? As for rithum, we once hall lost hour bilance joost bekors a gawjous widder smoled hat us from a dorway. Hour motter is buties in life, but not in hart. Thus on the seesaw we are of shutting hour eyes to vozions of delite, ho yes, hand we hare rospictobull osbans of hevvingly wifes with phaces more better than orl yore folm-stars. P. Ess. That kissing we gave a vompyer just now was hartistric hopprusiasheon, ho yes."

*   *   *

Is the arrival in Edinburgh of the Filthistan Trio connected with the Festival? Their offer to perform was refused, but the civic authorities are nervous. Hotel lounges and other places suitable (or unsuitable) for seesaw are being watched. It has not been forgotten that the three Persians arrived last year at one of the biggest hotels, dressed as workmen, and carrying their plank. Before the management could interfere, they were in full swing in the entrance lounge.

Among the recent arrivals is an enormous dancer named Pequeña, who is to gambol in the Spanish ballet, "La Botonera," with décor, montage, choreographics, and lighting by Pubcan. The three Persians are staying at her hotel.

Pequeña, the dancer from Caceres (she was born near the bull-ring on the Trujillo road), had a public row with the choreographer Pubcan in the hotel yesterday. The Filthistan Trio had asked her to launch their seesaw by breaking a bottle of beer over it. Pubcan argued that this would not be good publicity for a dancer. Whereupon the great-hearted lady embraced the three Persians, who cried, "Oh, us! Pot luck for we three! Yum-yum, we say, more kisses, if you please, mum! Ho, yes!" Pubcan shouted angrily, and Ashura stooped and tore out his bootlaces. Then the three did a fantastic dance with Pequeña, ending in a tumble. When they all got up they found they had been sitting on the hotel manager. The Macaroon of Macaroon was a disgusted witness of the incident.

*   *   *

The Management of the hotel at which the three Persians are staying in Edinburgh is determined not to allow seesaw in the lounge, although most of the guests would welcome it as a prelude to the Festival.

Every time the little gentlemen cross the lounge carrying their plank to practise in a neighbouring yard, the staff waits anxiously, to interfere if necessary, and the guests hold their breath. Yesterday they came down from their rooms wearing turbans of the Cameron tartan, and Kazbulah cried, "Hoch, aye, ho yes, the noo!"

* * *

The suggestion that their seesaw should be surrounded by massed beauties has made the Filthistan Trio very nervous. Last week, while performing in a big hotel, they noticed a pretty girl approaching. Kazbulah yelled: "No blon bomshles ermitted to plonk!" Ashura roared: "Vompyers is death to hart!" Rizamughan shouted: "No hinfilteration of glammer waunted, ho, yes!" The girl only wanted their autographs, and the Persians were so relieved that Ashura said "We give hortogiraffes and halso kisses for chority." "What charity?" asked the girl. "Hus," said Ashura. "Plenty kisses of blon bomshles holp to keep hup hour morals, ho, yes." "We pleeze like your toliphoon nomber. We give you termendious suppa with shrompine," said Ashura. The girl laughed. "What would your wives say?" she asked. Kazbulah replied. "The Persian profferb sayeth, a wife out of sight his but the buzz of a gnat hin sumerone helse's ear."

* * *

It is being said pretty freely in Edinburgh that Mimsie Slopcorner refused, with almost overwhelming dignity, a request from the Filthistan Trio that she would "hact as hour moscott and pinnup lady, to point hat the plank with a pharey wand as a signal to start the seesaw."

Mimsie left Edinburgh in tears having expected a much more spectacular role in the Festival. To make matters worse, the Macaroon of Macaroon made an ill-natured comment on a Press photograph of himself and Mimsie, under which was written "The Gathering of the Clams." "Apart from the foolish misprint," he wrote, "one has not heard of any Clan Slopcorner in Scottish history."

* * *

A cry of "Stop thief!" outside the Edinburgh hotel entrance soon emptied the lounge. By the time the guests returned, a moment or two later, the plank was laid across Ashura's belly, and the game of see-

saw had begun. The manager's expostulations were drowned by weird Persian cries and by the applause and chatter of the spectators. The Macaroon of Macaroon, who had written another long letter to the Press about the abuse of the Cameron tartan by the Persians, witnessed the display with distaste. The Persians' reply to his letter still rankled. . . . "It mought supperize you, Sir Macaroon, to know that Kazbulah's grandmither were a McCapercailzie from Muckie, whom fought at the battle of Floddum, ho yes. . . . We wish you Ould Long Sign, as the song saith."

* * *

Dear Sir,

Who on earth is paying for these Persians? Is some Persian counterpart of the British Council trying to reveal Persian culture to the Scots? Or is the Arts Council at work? Or the Friends of Anglo-Persian Solidarity, Co-operation, and Co-ordination? Upon the answer to these questions depends the attitude of many to this unconventional form of seesaw.

Yrs. truly,
The Macaroon of Macaroon, Kilcockrobbin, The Minch, Jean Doantavenniemore of Doantavevnniemore, McNocher of Dornoch, Rummie, The Bannoch of Rannoch, Airlie Bird, Dame Whetwhistle, Auld Ben Buttoch fra Drumsnaddie.

* * *

Someone wants to know what an obvious commoner like Ben Buttoch was doing among the signatories of the anti-seesaw manifesto. Buttoch, though untitled, belongs to one of the oldest highland families. There were Buttochs at Drumsnaddie before there were Bannochs at Rannoch or McAwphulls at Glenpiffle. His grandfather was Laird of Lochstoch and Barrell, and his mother was descended from the Lobster of Kintyre. The Buttochs were out in the '15, in the '45, and half in and half out in '74, when the last Earl of Eigg and Rum made a foray. The family coat of arms is four ptarmigan tierced or, on a field argent, with cinquefoil gules guardant and pas-

sant, barbed proper, and a caber vulning on a bordure sable eight estoiles or; in chief a demi-annulet of the fourth, all counterchanged. The motto is: "Sic wha' we ha' we hae."

* * *

Seeing the fuss made of the Filthistan Trio, a father of four asked Ashura for his autograph for the eldest son. Said Ashura, "We are having no hautocar, we coom up by railway train." "No, no," said the father, "I mean your name." "Ashura my name," was the reply. "I know," said the father, "but I want you to write it down on this bit of paper for me." "Write down of what?" asked Ashura. "Your signature," said the father. "Have got no snignita," said Ashura. "What is snignita, please?" "Look," said the father, "I mean this." And he wrote his name on a slip of paper. "You hare my fanmail," said Ashura delightedly. "Mony thanks." And he went off with the father's autograph.

* * *

A bevy of girls with pencils and autograph books, rushed the seesaw last night. "Ho, what is this?" said Kazbulah. "Wummin repoarters? Ho, we think youre porleezwummin is mervalus." "Ush, brother," said Ashura. "These ones is of wanting to skitch hus for the Okkidimy." Said Rizamughan, "Perhaps they be a kew for rarshuns. No sossigies today, purls of delite, nor no fishanships." The girls giggled and held out the autograph books. "They be pooblishers' laydies," said Kazbulah. "Hit is some buks of the munth." Said Ashura, "It is contraks for hartikkuls erbout pollertiks." Said Rizamughan, "Stay! They wish hus to wrote letters to thim." A manager explained what was wanted. "Orkografs?" said Ashura. "Boot can these not rite down there hoan names? What yuze is hours? We do not sine *there* names, so what wawnt they of hours? We think it is so we shull buy knovuls or growseries. We go karefool, maniger, ho yes." So the girls retreated, and Rizamughan said, "A eep of blon bomshles is as a zworm of blewbottuls. Orkografs leeds to orkomowbells. We give no prezints, ho yes."

* * *

The Macaroon of Macaroon came face to face with the three Persians in the lounge of the hotel. He was about to pass by when Kazbulah plucked his arm and said, "What about hintranatural friendship, ho yes?" The Macaroon released his arm. "You vetto hour plonk," said Ashura. "Scotchland a free cowntry," said Rizamughan. "We hillow you to play crocket and foodball hin Persia." The Macaroon side-stepped as though confronted by a puddle, and went on his way. "Oop the prollyterias and warking men, hif you hare of being a igh-born village esquire," shouted Ashura. "The Roman blood uv the hasitocrasy," cried Rizamughan. "Ate your porridge with a gilded spaown," yelled Kazbulah.

* * *

The three Persians beheld a black-haired, sallow-skinned man in the lounge of their hotel. They thought he looked like a fellow-country-man.

Ashura asked the reception clerk where the man was from. "Pershore," said the clerk. Highly delighted, the three approached the guest, bowed low, and Kazbulah said, "Ardabil bam pahvi fahan, jasoran seis?" "What's that?" asked the guest. Much surprised Rizamughan said "You from Persia?" "That's right," said the man. Ashura's eyes narrowed. "What part of Persia?" he asked. "Evesham-road," was the reply. "Evisham sounds like Persia," said Kazbulah, "but what is Rode? What name, you?" "Barrington," said the man.

"Barrington not Persian name," said Kazbulah severely. "Persian my foot," said the man. "It's English. Pershore's in Worcester." "Ho, yes," shouted Ashura. "So Persia now in Woosta. We think you a spy." Whereupon the three of them shouted, "We catch a spy! Send for the Perproetor!" And they seized the astonished man. "Send for Persian consool and embressader," cried Ashura. "Poolees! Poolees!" yelled Kazbulah. "Zibertage and

Fofth Kollum!" roared Rizamughan. Then the manager intervened and explained, and quiet was restored. The Macaroon of Macaroon said to the Laird o' Kilcockrobbin, "This is not *my* idea of a cultural festival."

To please the manager of their hotel the three Persians penned a note of apology to Mr. Barrington:

Mr. Barrington, joggraphy maps is so much changed today we was of thinking the Nations Union bosses was of pooting Persia hour country in Woosta in account of merjorities hor mernorities hor some sort of things. Not being wishing to hinsult a fine nativ uv Woosta we hippolerjize, halso we are of being happy that your country of Woosta hath called a place Persia in onour of hour country. We say such jestchers hare of simmenting intranational coolture and frendships, ho yes. Why not you call your capertal place of Woosta Teheran?

* * *

A Meeting of protest against Persian seesaw was called today by the Macaroon of Macaroon. It was attended by the Laird o' Kilcockrobbin, Lord Rummie, the Kyle of the Kyles, Mrs. Doantavenniemore of Doantavenniemore, the Bannoch of Rannoch, the McNocher of Dornoch, Mr. Airlie Bird, Dame Whetwhistle, the Minch, and Auld Ben Buttoch fra Drumsnaddie. It was decided to issue a second statement to the Press deploring the presence of the Filthistan Trio at the Edinburgh Festival.

* * *

An absurd leaflet, widely distributed, has further annoyed the Macaroon of Macaroon. The leaflet says: "Oyez! Oyez! Hoyes! Onder the potronage of that cellibrated and famoose Highlands Chieftain the Macaroon of Macaroon, three Persian Scottofills will render a seesaw preformance of galla and yamburee at the —— Hotel. Hall welcum. Come and see the orld Laird o'McAshura, the McRizamughan of McRizamughan, and the Mackazbulah of Mackazbulah Castle and Dear Forest and Loch Mackazbulah. Rally round the clans, ho yes!"

We live in democratic days, and many of the old landmarks are dis-

appearing. But the suggestion that the representative of one of the oldest Scottish families should referee a game of seesaw played by three Persians in an hotel lounge is democracy run mad. Our sympathy is with the Macaroon, who, through no fault of his own, has become involved in this fantastic nonsense. Too much publicity has been given to the antics of these Persian mountebanks. The Home Office should act with decision before other countries seize on this disgraceful incident as further proof of British weakness and folly.

(From a leading article.)

The Home Secretary is to be asked in the House: (I.) Whether it is conducive to English prestige abroad to allow two Persians to play seesaw on a plank laid across the belly of a third in the vestibules of hotels which may be used by foreign tourists. (II.) In the event of such performances proving necessary for the earning of dollars, whether an English team could not be substituted. (III.) Whether such performances are legal on Sundays, having regard to the wearing, by the Persian performers, of clothes which seem to bring these performances into the category of stage performances.

* * *

A certain section of opinion in Edinburgh has protested against the distribution of another seesaw leaflet. The leaflet says: Edinborg is of wanting glamma, we have it. The haces uv the seesaw world is of sweeping Scotland hoff its foot. "This," said a igh-born counsellor uffishall, "is of being hart hat hits most collarfull, the ighlite uv the Foostivle, sumthing classicle about thes verthuozos uv the plank, the old spirrit uv the clans, ho yes, with a moddrern tooch, so welcum Persia to the Hathinns uv the Nawth, onder the potronage uv that brore cheeftun and sompathitic laird, the Macaroon of Macaroon."

The Macaroon of Macaroon has retired, in high dudgeon, to Macaroon Castle, Macaroon; the Laird of Kilcockrobbin, in even higher dudgeon, to Kilcockrobbin Castle, Kilcockrobbin, Kilcockrobbinshire. The three Persians are left in possession of the field. On his first night at home the Macaroon was rung up from Edinburgh. A dread voice said: "Ho, yes, hillo, Mr. Macaroon, we of coming hup to your castle for seesaw if it is hinconvenience." The Laird recived a similar message.

* * *

On the floor lay a couple of swords, crosswise. The Macaroon of Macaroon was practising the old Dinwhiddie Glide, while the Laird o' Kilcockrobbin (Och! sic a sonsie gaufer!) supplied that mournful air "Clachans Awa'" on a brace of nickel-plated bagpipes. Suddenly into the room burst those three Persians. The Scotsmen stopped their play, and glowered. Ashura stepped forward. "We was of thinking," he said, "that onebody was hill of diseezes, so much of moan and crying." "It was the bagpipes," said the Laird haughtily. "Poor people," said Kazbulah, "was all of the fambly ill, littel Bagpipes as well, and Mr. and Mrs. Bagpipe?" The Scotsmen exchanged a look of profound annoyance, as Rizamughan picked up a telephone and shouted, "Doctors, please! Mr. Bagpipe and fambly dying!"

* * *

Sir, ho yes, if Mr. Macaroon the Macaroon has thinking that hour hact be not Scottish enuff, we will in onour of this here Fostival play our see-saw to the hair of "Bony Bunks off Locklomun," or "Hi love Alassi," and we shall wearing spurrans too, and of shouting we drappy parritch hon hour plank. Wood this Macaroon enjoy to place plank in pozittian hon Ashura's belly and of being rifereer? Kazbulah's grandmither not truly Scottish, she being a maiden Kuhbana from Nishapur, just a joak of us, her father too from Bashasaadin, noothing Scottish ebout that, ho yes, no hoffinse, Mr. the Macaroon, for as you inhibit a castle us three most glad to preform seesaw hon your drahbridge or hin feestinghall.

* * *

Yesterday an American film actress, who had come by air, arrived at the hotel where the Persians were performing in the foyer. As she crossed to the reception desk, Kazbulah and Rizamughan dismounted and Ashura lifted the plank from his belly. The actress turned to see three small dusky gentlemen bowing courteously. "You like hour aukograph?" asked Ashura. "Not particularly," replied the actress. "Ho, do not be shy," said Kazbulah. "Say," said the actress, "is this a loony-bin? What goes on? If you guys want *my* audo ——" "Ho, fi!" shouted Rizamughan. "What uses are your aukograph to hus? We arsk you first. Give hus paper with pensul, O maiden of ten thousand charms." A publicity man intervened to say that the actress was tired. "We halso is tired," said Ashura. "But she doosent have to be doing anything but harsk us sivilly for hour aukographs." "Look," said the man, "she doesn't *want* them." "Then why she of coming to here?" shouted Kazbulah, "warsting hour time like this?" And they turned and went back to their plank, muttering in low tones.

* * *

Mr. Beachcomber, hour blud is thikker and wrathfuller than warter, and we are uv such contemtusness uv them Scottish baroons and chiefs that we will be of furbidding heven hour dog to lick the phaces uv them. Hinsulted, we shull go from the seens uv hour troumphs to nivermore sat feet in Scotland soil. Pish for the soakalled Fostivool and hits hart! And pish for the pooritunicle spoalspoorts which is halarmed at hour pipulority! Alsoo a thurd pish for them hotel jests and vusiters which got no more eye to jodge hart with than a ded yackass of a donky hin a awfull durty yarde. The Macaroon can kepe is cursid carstel, bottlements, drorbrige, harmor hand hall. We darkin not his throsheld, ho yes. Farewell, bony Scotland, land uv vindels, pholisteens, hand hilloturate scavergers. We hare, ho yes,

The Filthistan Trio.

THE QUEEN OF MINIKOI

by J*hn B*ch*n

WE WERE TALKING OF COINCIDENCES. IT HAD BEEN A HARD DAY. FOR eleven hours we had stalked a shootable sixteen-pointer over the Runnoch screes and up and down the corries of Sgurr Beoch, until old Mac, who had been with me in the Bourlon Wood show, groaned: "Yon beastie's a deil." Finally Lord Trasker had flung himself down and fired up-wind into the eddies of mist; a chance shot, the outcome of overwrought nerves. But as he fired, the stag came loping from behind a knoll, and took the shot full in the mazzard. "Deid," cried old Mac, "a straucht shot for a braw cantlin. I wull no' ha' seen mony better shots at all." "It was a fluke, you know," said Trasker, "I just had an instinct . . ." We dragged our quarry down Glenlivet and across Ruiseach Side to the Tollig, and arrived back at Sir Robert Manningham's shooting lodge, weary but well pleased with ourselves. And then, after an admirable dinner, prepared by Marston, who had been with Sir Robert in the Festubert show, somebody had remarked that Lord Trasker's shot had been a coincidence. And General the Hon. Derrick McQuantock had said, in that voice which always brought Eton back to me: "Yes, but what is coincidence? There are forces outside the world of which we know next to nothing. Why did I meet Eric————" he pointed his pipe-stem at Sir Eric Chalmers Troope— "Why did I meet Eric in Zerka when we were both supposed to be in Bigadich? Or what made Philip" (indicating Admiral Sir Philip Delmode) "suspect our Dutch friend Joos Vuyterswaelt?" We all laughed at the memory of the neat way in which the Admiral had outwitted the Roumanian Secret Service. And while we were still laughing, the squat little figure of Sandy Argyll, that astounding baker from Forfar, who had become a merchant adventurer and had helped to save the Queen of Holland from the Red Hand Society—that squat figure moved in a chair by the fire. "Coincidence," he said. "Hm! Ask Graham to tell you about the hat that didn't fit."

We all turned to the Earl of Moorswater, and in a silence deeper than that of the night-shrouded Whang Scaur outside the windows, he told this story.

"Any of you fellows ever hear of Minikoi? No, it's not the name of a girl. It's an island in the Arabian Sea, and I myself had only heard of it vaguely, when, on a certain spring day after the war, I came out of the Premier, and turned down Pall Mall. I had dined well, and old Fossett, who was with me in the St. Quentin show, had brought up a bottle of the club port—'58. I was feeling pretty pleased with life. As I passed through the door into the street I noticed that Carson, the head hall-porter——"

"Sorry to butt in," said the General, "but wasn't he given the D.C.M. after the Cambrai stunt? I thought so. A white man."

"—Old Carson," continued the Earl, "stared at me curiously. At the same time I felt a pressure on my head. Now as you all know, I get my hats from Challoner, and no man in town makes a better hat. And yet my hat was too tight. I took it off, and to my amazement found a thick piece of paper stuffed inside the lining. There was writing on it, and I stood under a lamp-post to read it. Now, I'm considered pretty good at languages, as you all know, but I must confess this screed puzzled me. It was written in faded red ink, and it seemed to be no modern tongue. Well—it wasn't any modern tongue. After puzzling over it for some minutes, I noticed a certain syllable which recurred very frequently, and at once I knew what the writing was. It was the language of the old Icelandic sagas of Snorre Sturlason—the Heimskringla—stories of the Norsemen just before they were Christianised by the Anglo-Saxons. I recognised it thanks to a job of work I had done for the Foreign Office towards the end of the war. I took the paper home with me, intending to get to work on it, but my man Truslove—you remember him, Derrick, at Le Cateau"—the General nodded—"Truslove informed me that there was a gentleman waiting for me in the library. It turned out to be Sir Ronald Waukinshaw, my old chief at the F.O. You should have seen his face when I said: 'Ronnie, ever hear of Minikoi?' The old boy glanced round nervously. Then he said: 'In heaven's name, Graham, what on earth do you know about it?' I produced the bit of paper, and he whistled softly. 'This is a pretty big thing,' he said. 'It's old Icelandic, of course. But how did you come by it?' I told him that I had found it in my hat. 'Then somebody,' said he, 'must have mistaken your hat for someone else's.' 'But what does it mean?' I asked. 'Read it yourself,' he replied dryly. I read slowly: 'The sword of the giant-queen of the rock and snow, the ring-bearer, shall be dyed in the gore of Geysa's sons on May 4th at Minikoi.' 'Isn't it clear?' asked Ronnie. 'Not particularly,' I said. 'We must go back to your club at once,' he rejoined. And in the taxi he told me the most incredible story I have ever listened to.

"It appeared that for some time past the Foreign Office had been worried by signs of unrest in the Laccadive and Maldive islands. There was talk of an ancient Arabian Queen who had returned to earth to lead the islanders against the English in India, and to re-establish a vast heathen Empire from the Malabar coast to the Himalayas. As a sign that she was the expected monarch she was to show a heavy ring of beaten gold to her followers, chief among whom was a certain Afghan, at present in England to raise money for the rising, which, it was hoped, would quickly spread to the islands in the Bay of Bengal and the South China Sea. 'This message,' he said, 'must have been intended for that Afghan's hat, for it gives the date of the rising.' 'But what has the Icelandic business to do with it?' 'They thought they'd be safe if they used that language. As it is, you and I are probably about the only people who understand it.' 'And why are we going back to the club?' 'To hunt for that Afghan—unless——' We met each other's eyes, as men do at such moments, and I read his purpose. 'You want me to be that Afghan, and put a stopper on the whole affair.' 'It's almost certain death,' he said. 'That's one's job,' I answered. 'Good man,' he said. 'To-day's May 1st. Not much time.'

"Ronnie came back to my flat and watched while my man made me up as an Afghan. Then we rang up Donald Ritchie, who had been with my mob in the first Somme push. To my delight he was just starting off on one of his mad flights round the world, for though he had left an ear at Loos and a thumb at Suvla, he was the same old Donald who had trekked across Greenland to cure his insomnia. He said he could have his 'plane ready in an hour. At that moment Truslove informed me that a message had come from the garage to the effect that my car was out of action. 'It was all right this morning,' I said. 'That Afghan works quickly,' said Ronnie. 'Luckily there is still mine.'

"So under cover of darkness he drove me down to Donald's private aerodrome, and a fine shock the dear old fellow got when he saw me in my outlandish togs, and with my face stained and my hair darkened. That flight was a perfect nightmare. We took charge in turn, and lived on coffee and sandwiches. And we were actually flying over the Arabian Sea, and almost in sight of the island of Minikoi, when the trouble began. Throughout the journey I had kept my eyes open for signs of pursuit. I was just congratulating myself that we had won the race, and the first battle in the campaign, when the engine began to flutter and spit and jerk. 'Damn,' said Donald. As we dropped like a plummet seawards I had just time to note a blob on the horizon which I knew must be Minikoi. The impact with which we struck the water temporarily stunned us. Then, disentangling ourselves from the wreckage, we struck out in the direction of the island. Now I'm considered a fairly strong swimmer, but the long flight and the crash had knocked it out of me a bit. And as night fell, and the sea roughened, I began to wish I had not left my comfortable flat. However, after perhaps three hours, Donald, who had not turned a hair, said: 'There's your comic island, old man.' Exhausted, we plugged away, and were soon stumbling over the wet rocks of a small creek. And there, still intact on a little spit of sand, was an aeroplane. 'Dilcott monoplane,' said Donald. 'That landing was a miracle, whoever made it.' I had my own ideas about that, and my blood boiled when I remembered that this was May 3rd and that within twelve hours the British Empire would be tottering. Ronnie had trusted me, and I had let him down. Despair lent me new strength. I half-crawled, half-stumbled over rocks and through swamps, now hauling myself up crumbling cliffs by slimy ·tree-branches that threatened to snap at any moment, now staggering into bottomless ravines, where, in the impenetrable darkness, swollen torrents roared over stony beds. Once a huge bird slashed my cheek with its wing and buffeted me sideways into a quagmire, and once some swiftly moving animal snapped at my legs, and was kicked back into its cavern by Donald. The poisonous roots of nauseating plants twined round our feet and tripped us, and moment by moment boulders, loosened by the damp, tumbled into the abysses all about us. Cascades of wet earth blinded us, and blood poured from a square cut over Donald's left eye. And all the while a pulse in my brain kept on beating out: 'You may be in time yet. You *must* be in time.' And then, just as my heart seemed to be bursting through my chest, and a moment after Donald had said: 'This is probably the wrong island,' I heard voices. We crept nearer. Somebody said, in the Laccadive dialect: 'If thou art the Great Queen who is to lead us to victory, show us the ring.' A roar as of a thousand voices cried: 'Yes. The ring. The ring.' The first voice went on: 'How can we know that thine order to start the rising tomorrow at dawn is not a device of the enemy?' Then a very beautiful voice—the voice of a young girl, answered: 'I am indeed the Great Queen, and at the appointed time I will show the ring.' Menacing shouts replied to her, and in a flash I forgot that the Empire was in danger, and thought only of a girl in deadly peril. Followed by Donald I dashed forward and found myself on an uneven plateau of light coral sand covered with pulse and coarse grain. We were only just in time to pull ourselves up on the brink of a precipice of sand and rock. Flinging ourselves down we gazed at a kind of rugged amphitheatre, fringed by banana trees, fifty feet beneath us. And then we saw the strangest sight that white men ever looked upon—a sight that froze our blood. I saw Donald clutch his revolver, but I checked him. One doesn't shoot sitting birds in the back, and the crowd below us was unaware of our presence.

"The amphitheatre, lit by a hundred banana-root torches, was packed with Moplas, wild, half-Arabian Malabars and lithe Hindus. The light shone on their dusky bodies and the steel of their long hunting-spears. They crouched pell-mell, with their backs to us, and in their forefront was a big fellow in a scarlet sari. He was evidently their leader. Facing them, and not a hundred yards from us, was the most beautiful girl I have ever seen. She was tall and slim, and the carriage of her head as she confronted the mob made me want to cheer. She was dressed in a long white robe, which was fastened at the waist with a golden girdle. Her long auburn hair flowed loose to her waist. She looked every inch a queen. As we watched, the leader took a menacing step forward. 'Where is the ring?' he demanded, 'and where is Humbullah?' 'That's you,' whispered Donald. The leader's question was answered by a roar from all those savages. But the girl did not flinch. She was staring up at us, and I put my finger to my lips. She nodded imperceptibly. Before she could speak again to the leader, a drum began to beat, one of the devil-drums of the Yalabalim, and immediately the mob was on it feet. Spears were brandished and a weird death-dance began. The leader held up his hand, and the noise died down. 'For the third and last time,' he said, 'where is the ring, and where is Humbullah? Answer, or you die at dawn.' And even as he spoke the sky seemed to brighten in the east. 'She's forgotten the ring,' said Donald. And upon my soul, I could not follow her game. But I had seen enough. The blood-intoxicated horde was slowly closing in on her. By good fortune I always wear a heavy gold ring which a minor Balkan royalty had given me for a job of work I had done in Cettinje. 'Come on,' I said to Donald, and we skirted the amphitheatre very stealthily, keeping on the lip of the precipice, until we were behind the girl. As we leapt, two men were moving forward to secure her with ropes. While Donald placed himself before her, I knelt at her side and kissed her hand, taking care to slip the ring into it. She seemed amazed, but she held the ring up, and said: 'It is here.' 'And here,' I shouted, 'is Humbullah.' The effect was magical. The leader prostrated himself, and the mob, frantic with joy, followed suit. 'We strike at dawn,' said the Queen. 'And now I must withdraw to consult with Humbullah.' She then took my hand, and led me behind a little screen of coco-nut trees, and I nearly jumped out of my skin when she said, in perfect English: 'That was a near thing.' 'Who on earth are you?' I asked. 'Sylvia Farquharson,' she answered. 'Perhaps you've heard of General Farquharson?' I should say I had. Every man who was in the Thiepval show had cause to bless 'Tiger'

Farquharson. 'Please explain,' I said. And there, behind the coco-nut trees, she told me how Sir Ronald Waukinshaw had let her into the secret of his plan to scotch the rising, and had asked her to take the place of the expected queen; how she had arrived by 'plane, made a difficult landing, and announced her 'return' to the natives; how they were to be made to rise at dawn on this very day, so that troops landed from a cruiser could deal with them, and put an end to the business before it had time to spread. I was about to congratulate her when a low-caste Hindu approached us, and said to me in a dialect of the Dushkandhila hill-country: 'If you are Humbullah, how is it that your skin is white?' I had forgotten that my long hours in the water had washed the stain off my face and body and hair! But I had to bluff it out. I replied in Afghan: 'Alas, my brother, it is my shame. A white trader dishonoured my mother, and that is why I have sworn vengeance.' This appeared to satisfy him, and I was about to ask Miss Farquharson what I was to do next when we heard three blasts of a syren. 'The signal!' she said. A moment later there was the whistle of a shell, and an explosion in the very middle of the amphitheatre. I caught her arm and ran with her towards the shore. Behind us came the maddened natives, aware at last that they had been betrayed. Sylvia was as lithe as a young deer, and I am considered a pretty good long-distance runner. Never had we greater need of speed and endurance. Once a well-aimed spear struck a tree four feet ahead of us, and hung quivering there, and once a serpent sprang at us, and missed by a hair's-breadth. 'All right?' I breathed. 'You bet,' she panted back, and I swore to get her to safety. Our most dangerous man was the big leader, and I saw that he was gaining on us. I could have done with that fellow, I told myself, as my second-string in the three miles at Queen's in 1913. He had the long stride and the natural poise of the born runner, and even as I cursed him, I admired the confounded chap. Sylvia, I could see, knew that he was gaining. I kept on wondering why he didn't chuck his spear at us. He got to within twenty feet of us . . . fifteen, ten, five feet. I turned and prepared to dot him one, for big as he was, I'm considered a fairly useful man with the gloves on. To my amazement he grinned, and said: 'This is my revenge for the beating you gave me in '12.' And there I was, looking into the artificially darkened eyes of dear old Leamington-Furze, my opposite number in the 'Varsity sports before the war. 'Keep on going,' he said, 'and I'll follow. Don't give the game away.' 'Wonders never cease,' said Sylvia, as we plunged through a swamp, and came in sight of the shore. And there, ahead of us, were English infantrymen disembarking from several boats, and preparing to scatter across the island, and to round up the rebels. We sat down on a rock, and Leamington-Furze explained that Sir Ronald Waukinshaw had sent him out to work up the mob, but had kept the idea secret, so that Sylvia would act her part better. 'You knew who I was, then?' asked Sylvia. 'Oh, yes. Ronnie told me.to expect you. I knew your father. We were in the Dickebusch affair together.'

"Well, to cut a long story short, we were put on board the cruiser, where Sylvia's father took one look at me, and said: 'Who's this wallah?' Donald was on board, too. Not liking the look of things when the mob closed in on Sylvia, he had rushed for her monoplane, but couldn't start it. So he had swum out to sea for help, had bumped into the cruiser, and had told them to hurry up and do something about it.

"That night, as we walked about the deck, Sylvia said to me: 'By the way, remind me to give you back your ring. It's in my cabin.' 'Is our engagement broken off, then?' I whispered. Down came her lovely lashes over her eyes. 'I couldn't possibly wear a great hulking thing like that,' she said . . .

"Now it seems to me," concluded the Earl, "that the long arm of chance played a pretty big part in that little adventure. Not many men have met their wives under such conditions."

"But why Icelandic?' asked Trasker.

"Oh, Ronnie saw to that," said the Earl. "He knew I'd fall for it."

"One more question," asked the General, "who put the paper in your hat?"

"That," said the Earl, "I never discovered. One of Ronnie's men, I suppose."

"Did you not notice any queer people in the club that night?" asked Sandy Argyll.

"Why, no. I don't think so."

"The man that gave you your hat, for instance?"

"Now I come to think of it, I didn't recognise him. He was a new fellow—bright red hair, I remember. Looked like a wig."

"It was a wig," said Sandy. "And it was me."

BIBLIOGRAPHY

Arthur Wayneeflte : Vie du Connétable de Bourbon.

Birdhouse (Professor I. H. O.) : A Statement Relating to the New Science of Aquatherapy.

Bradshaw : Railway Guide of 1912.

Carr (F. J.) : The Persian Gulf in Song and Story.

Cocia : Port Talbot and its Environs in the Late Seventeenth Century.

Coswell (Miss Agnes G.) : Adrift in Portugal with the Ex-Crown Princess Hedwig of Saxe-Rothenburg.

Document No. 78 from Documentos Relativos a la Historia del Conde Pedro de Leon (Coleccion de Documentos Ineditos, Vol. CXIX.).

Fennimore (H.) : A History of the Girl Guides of Leicestershire, Compiled from Documents in Possession of the Author's Grandmother, and from the Caldicott Collection of Letters and Telegrams.

Flavius Vegetius : De Re Militari.

Lostgarden (A.) and Pargetter (Ralph) : Primitive Football.

Nannton (Mrs. B.) : Caspian Days and Caspian Ways.

Nardi : Istorie della Citta di Firenze.

Niggler (B. W.) : How You Get Your Electric Light.

Parker (J. M.) : Thibetan in Ten Lessons.

Sapling (M.) : Letters of Charles XIV. to John of Orange.

Stinkl : Geschichte.

Vaurien (Gaston de) : La Vie Tumultueuse de Mme. Humphrey Ward.

MODEST GENIUS REFUSES GREAT OFFER

BEACHCOMBER NOT TO EDIT TIMES

'I love my Public'

NEW 7/6 FICTION

SWIFT AS THE SWALLOW: By Marion Forbes.

The story of Elsa; how she fought and conquered the man of her desires. This is a forceful and repulsive story of passions unguarded. Miss Forbes ought to be watched.

A SOCK ON THE JAW: By Brass Williams.

An unalloyed narrative of stark frenzy in the Southern Seas. Tells of a Hawaian maid and her gypsy lover; how love came to them amid island enchantments, and how Desmond, disillusioned, threw her to the cuttle-fish, with a careless laugh.

BILL—THAT'S ALL: By Pomona Knott.

A first novel of terrifying power and precision. Gives the reader the whole world in a few rapid and bold strokes. The drawing of Stuff, the diseased bartender, is as good as anything in modern balderdash.

PLUCKY PAM: By Norah Buttress.

A rattling story of life in lodgings—and the temptations and trials that go therewith. Pam Pettigrew was young and ugly. To her came Sir Harry, slim, six feet nine, and Oxford! But he went bald! This book was awarded the Golden Bun for Good Literature; also the Prix Hampstead.

MUCKADUCK: By Jim Horsecroft.

Should an average-adjuster tell? To Cosmo Tuck, an average-adjuster, comes love, in the shape of Felicity Sproll, a fat old harridan of fifty-four. What is he to do?

SEWAGE SUE: By Badcock Sevenhouse.

Mr. Booster confessed that nothing since "Twopenny Tom" had so moved him. "It is a world in little," said "Cuspidor" of the *Evening Beast*.

THE SMELL OF FISH: By Lucy Taplow.

A poignant chronicle of low life as it is lived. Fanny is a masterful creation, reeking of the docks. The scene in which she forges her aunt's name to a postal order is unequalled since Balzac.

WHOMSOEVER: By Brenda Cayle.

An unusual novel with a strong religious flavour. Bob was a Baptist, but he fell in love with Nita, a Seventh Monarchy Woman. Neither would give way. Out of this struggle is woven a forceful tale of strong wills opposed. Canon Ravenscourt has called this "The Iliad of Humble Hearts."

BID ME TO LOVE: By Rex Carstairs.

A scathing indictment of modern ideals. Thracia was a girl like you and I. She loved, even as you and me. Yet the cup was dashed from her lips by a bounder. How she won through, after refusing herself to a soap-king, makes enthralling reading.

WITH WYCLIF TO WESTMINSTER: By Mrs. E. D. Gudgeon.

Mrs. Gudgeon has been called the English Sienkiewicz. Her grasp of historical detail sustains the comparison. Her study of our Morning Star of the Reformation brings an ache to the eyes, and makes the fastidious reader sick in no time.

NEW 7/6 FICTION

NOUGHT BUT THE DUSK: By Lolita Cox.

Do women like men? This typically modern question is answered by Miss Cox in language that sears the intellect and scalds the heart. There has been nothing so emancipated in modern letters since Miss Box's "Withal."

BLOOMSBURY BELLE: By Norma Stensch.

She was only a servant, but into her area stepped Prince Charming, in the guise of a High Holborn undertaker. How love struggled to fulfilment, maugre the opposition of Mrs. Mason, fills 973 pages of resonant prose, Dickensian in its allure. This book was awarded the 1930 prize for fiction by *Art and Graft*. It has already been translated into Danish, Swedish and Norwegian.

LOVE AT THE BYRE: By Hedwig Johnson.

A racy story of peasant passion, which shows an intimate knowledge of farm-folk. The character of Thomas, the brooding plough-boy, is a masterly creation. Miss Johnson has never done better.

ASLEEP IN THE DEEP: A ROUSING NAUTICAL YARN: By Robert Howes.

Jim Bolsover, shipping before the mast on a piano-laden clipper, is seized with sleeping sickness. The subsequent story of how he is awakened by the kiss of a dancing-girl holds the reader enthralled.

OLD NEBUCHADNEZZAR: THE LOVE STORY OF A VEGETARIAN: By Paul Entwistle.

He brought her carrots and onions instead of flowers. But she was a great singer, and the management objected. The miracle by which a vegetable diet turned her from a soprano to a mezzo is told with fire and economy.